VISION, DOCTRINE, WAR

MENNONITE EXPERIENCE IN AMERICA SERIES

The Mennonite Experience in America series attempts to tell with disciplined integrity the history of the first three centuries of Mennonite and Amish in America. The first three volumes are:

1. *Land, Piety, Peoplehood: The Establishment of Mennonite Communities in America, 1683-1790*
    by Richard K. MacMaster, 1985.
2. *Peace, Faith, Nation: Mennonites and Amish in Nineteenth-Century America*
    by Theron F. Schlabach, 1989.
3. *Vision, Doctrine, War: Mennonite Identity and Organization in America, 1890-1930*
    by James C. Juhnke, 1989.

VISION, DOCTRINE, WAR

MENNONITE IDENTITY AND ORGANIZATION IN AMERICA 1890-1930

James C. Juhnke

HERALD PRESS
Scottdale, Pennsylvania
Waterloo, Ontario

Library of Congress Cataloging-in-Publication Data
  Vision, doctrine, war : Mennonite identity and organization
in America, 1890-1930 / James C. Juhnke.
    p. cm.—(Mennonite experience in America ; v. 3)
  Bibliography: p.
  Includes index.
  ISBN 0-8361-3104-5 (alk. paper)
  1. Mennonites—United States—History. 2. Amish—United
States—History. I. Title. II. Series.
BX8116.M46 1985 vol. 3
289.7'73 s—dc20
[289.7'73'09034]   89-34243

The paper used in this publication meets the minimum requirements of American National Standard for Information Sciences—Permanence of Paper for Printed Library Materials, ANSI
Z39.48-1984.

About the cover: Baptism by immersion. Probably a Mennonite
Brethren congregation in the early twentieth century. Note the
four candidates awaiting their turn and the man playing a port-
able box organ. Photo courtesy of Center for Mennonite
Brethren Studies, Hillsboro, Kansas.

VISION, DOCTRINE, WAR
Copyright © 1989 by Herald Press, Scottdale, Pa. 15683
  Published simultaneously in Canada by Herald Press,
  Waterloo, Ont. N2L 6H7. All rights reserved.
Library of Congress Catalog Card Number: 89-34243
International Standard Book Number: 0-8361-3104-5
Printed in the United States of America
Design by David Hiebert

1 2 3 4 5 6 7 8 9 10 96 95 94 93 92 91 90 89

For Bill and Meta

CONTENTS

Series Introduction by Robert S. Kreider
9

Editor's Foreword by Theron F. Schlabach
11

Author's Preface
14

1
Patterns of Mennonite Peoplehood Around 1890
21

2
The Old Order Way of Yieldedness
56

3
The Dutch-Russian Congregation Christendom
80

4
Swiss-American Mennonitism
106

5
Denominational Advance: Missions
136

6
Denominational Advance: Colleges and Hospitals
162

7
Mennonite Mobility—Geographic, Economic, Social
189

8
The Great War
208

9
The 1920s: Moving Forward and Holding Back
243

10
Leaders, Women, Peace
275

11
Ironies of Acculturation
and Achievements of an Emerging Denomination
300

Key to Abbreviations
318

Notes
319

Select Bibliography
354

Index
377

The Author
394

SERIES INTRODUCTION

In 1683, when the Mennonite experience in America began, there was no U.S. nation. Thereafter, Mennonites and Amish, like their fellow Americans, came to the New World at different times and for different reasons, with different background, languages, and dialects. Along with other immigrant groups they eventually began to ask who they were as a people. Like others, they searched for identity and mission. And provincially, in fragments, they began to tell their stories. Now they see more and more that their separate Mennonite and Amish stories weave into one story which in turn is intertwined with national and world history.

Mennonites have always understood history as a statement of faith, a tracing of God's ways with God's people. The Mennonite Experience in America books are also to be history with disciplined integrity. They are to portray both failure and faithfulness, both shadow and light.

In four volumes the series savors the meaning of the Mennonites' three hundred years in the New World. That meaning tells also of America. In America Mennonites and Amish have found both paradox and promise. The MEA books invite us all to come, read, learn tales never before told, and reflect on how Mennonites fared during three centuries of growing nationhood. As the story entered the twentieth century Mennonite windows were beginning to open also to a world beyond the nation, an international world.

James Juhnke's volume finds that as the twentieth century opened, Mennonite and Amish were struggling to cope with an open, pluralistic, and rapidly changing society. The challenge was as formidable as others their forebears had faced in times of persecution, migration, and flight. In twentieth-century America they began to see themselves less as separate and sectarian and more as a respectable part of the American denominational mosaic. Belatedly they were learning the creative arts of denomination-building. But then came the great patriotic war. For these pacifists the war brought shock and alienation. Once again Mennonites in America faced the fact that they were a people apart.

This book describes how Mennonites became one of "the late bloomers of American Protestantism." From it we gain an alternative perspective on the American experience. Mennonites were a people who wanted to be true to the pacifist faith which they had kept through four difficult centuries but who also wanted to be accepted as good American neighbors and citizens. On the turbulent flood of a young, virile, confident American society, their story bobs and moves like a small, sturdy craft.

> Robert S. Kreider
> Chairperson, Editorial Committee
> The Mennonite Experience in America project
> North Newton, Kansas
> November, 1988

EDITOR'S FOREWORD

The four decades of which James C. Juhnke writes throbbed with activity. As they moved from the nineteenth into the twentieth century, the people of the United States were struggling with industrialism, with burgeoning and all-too-wretched cities, and with a new peak of immigration. In 1898 they fought the Spanish-American War and took over the Philippine Islands in the Far East. Closer home, they established their power in the Caribbean. Meanwhile science and modernity were challenging many older ideas, including religious ones. What was passing, it seemed, was not only a century but also an era.

The problems, the expansion, and the challenges made Americans uneasy. For a time they remained optimistic, still believing they could purge their nation of modernity's evils and keep it headed up a ladder of progress. Then from about 1915 to 1920 the optimism began to sour. Americans entered World War I with hopeful slogans, but when the war did not make the world safe for democracy after all, they took to quarreling among themselves. Too often official wartime propaganda had turned public opinion against minorities and dissenters. Inside the churches also, feelings grew bitter. Fundamentalists wanted to meet modernity's challenges one way, while others had different ideas. Conversation among Christians took a nasty turn.

James Juhnke tells how, in that kind of America, Mennonites and Amish hunted for their niche. In wartime, these conscientious objectors were one of the mistrusted minorities. Although they had long since taken the nation as their own, all too many of their neighbors judged them to be hostile.

They were caught religiously as well. The Fundamentalist-Modernist quarrel was not really their affair, yet its whirlwinds tore at them. Even earlier, before the sour times, Mennonites and Amish were not sure about that ladder of worldly progress. Some among them were progressives, having become so either by the route of American revivalism or more by way of American education and its acculturation. Others rejected progressivism, seeing human pretensions more as pride than as progress. In the late nineteenth century some of the rejectors had tried to renew their churches by clarifying the boundaries separating Christian practice from that of the world. Those who did so with great rigor became the "Old Order" Amish and the "Old Order" Mennonites.

Most Mennonites and Amish remained neither fully progressive nor Old Order. They simply operated cautiously, keeping their own sense of peoplehood. That caution and that peoplehood run throughout James Juhnke's story. The story is not only about Mennonites and Amish, it also is about the United States of America. More, it is about America's way of both engulfing and rejecting one of its more humble minorities.

Juhnke did not pursue that story by himself. Behind him was the MEA Editorial Committee: Robert Kreider as chairman, Cornelius J. Dyck, Leonard Gross, Peter J. Klassen, John A. Lapp, Wesley Prieb, Willard Swartley, and Carolyn C. Wenger. These persons gave the MEA project its shape, worked through policy questions, in some cases read manuscripts, and, not least, found money. The money came from many, many generous contributors. Even if doing so is unfair to others not on my list, as MEA editor I wish to convey the project's thanks to some of the principal ones—Paul Detweiler, C. J. and Wilma Dyck, John E. Fretz, Horace Longacre, Merle and Phyllis Good, David and Mary Groh, Walton Hackman, Gerald and Gwen Hartzel, Dwight and Ellen Hartman, Albert and Leanna Keim, Robert and Lois Kreider, Michael Loss, Richard and Betty Pellman, Herbert and Louise Regier, John and Rebecca Rutt, Willard and Verna Smith, Edward C. Snyder, Will Stoltz, Carolyn C. Wenger, Lloyd Zeager.

Numerous others have contributed through organizations. We in the project greatly appreciate sizable grants from the Commission on Education of the General Conference Mennonite Church, the Schowalter Foundation, the Mennonite Central Committee, Mennonite Mutual Aid, the Goodville Mutual Insurance Company, the Franconia Conference of the Mennonite Church, the Associated Mennonite Biblical Seminaries, the Mennonite Historical Society, Eastern Mennonite Associated Libraries and Archives, the two Centers for Mennonite Brethren Studies at Pacific and Tabor colleges, Lancaster Mennonite Historical Society, Illinois Mennonite Historical and Genealogical Society, Virginia Mennonite Conference, Iowa Mennonite Historical Society, the Indiana-Michigan Mennonite Conference, the Mennonite Historians of Eastern Pennsylvania, and Jayco, Inc.

Some of these and other institutions have contributed further by maintaining archives for Mennonite study and research. For this we especially thank Bethel College in Kansas, Goshen College, Tabor College, Fresno Pacific College, Eastern Mennonite College, the Archives of the Mennonite Church, the Mennonite Historians of Eastern Pennsylvania, and the Lancaster Mennonite Historical Society. Bethel and Goshen colleges also contributed significantly by providing the author and the editor with leaves of absence, office space, secretarial assistance, and other help.

Finally, our gratitude goes also to the Institute of Mennonite Studies at the Associated Mennonite Biblical Seminaries for handling the project's finances. Willard Swartley and Richard Kauffman, the Institute's directors, especially deserve such thanks. To all contributors, thank you.

Theron F. Schlabach
Goshen College
November, 1988

AUTHOR'S PREFACE

This book was born in community. I am a child of the tradition of Mennonite peoplehood which has long been sustained by mutual support and admonition in the fellowship of believers. My life and spirit finds strength especially in small groups who seek God's guidance in Scripture, prayer, and sharing with others of like commitments.

I am also a product of an American educational community which provides a professional set of procedures and standards for historical work. As scholars we seek guidance in professional journals, association meetings, and the Chicago-Turabian *Manual of Style*. The challenge of this *Mennonite Experience in America* (MEA) project has been to embody the best values of both Mennonite peoplehood and professional scholarship without compromising the integrity of either. To meet this challenge I owe much to a community of scholars who have joined to chart the territory between Anabaptist-Mennonite tradition and American modernity.

In July 1975, in a Chicago hotel room, the core group of Mennonite historians in the MEA project began generating ideas. How might we synthesize the historical experience of the various Mennonite groups in America? As we divided the work and undertook our research we met in six MEA conferences held from 1976 to 1987. There, in Mennonite centers in Indiana, Kansas, Pennsylvania, California, and Ohio, we celebrated special events and honored accomplished senior scholars such as Guy F. Hershberger and Cornelius Krahn. We heard from different kinds of Mennonites— traditionalist and progressive, Dutch and Swiss, conservative and liberal. We presented our findings and evaluated each other's work. Mennonite scholarly journals, especially *The Mennonite Quarterly Review* and *Mennonite Life*, published many of these MEA papers so that a wider circle of thinkers had opportunity to offer comments and suggestions. The activity became a process through which we discovered new insights and made adjustments.

We learned much of the relationship of Mennonite groups to each other. Perhaps even more, we learned how Mennonites have related to the North American nations, especially the USA. Our volumes are not only about Mennonites. They speak also of the American nation, by showing how one religious group, loyal but often dissenting, has fared within it.

An MEA Editorial Committee guided the project under the rubric of the Institute of Mennonite Studies, Elkhart, Indiana. For me, its chairman, Robert S. Kreider, is an especially important mentor. Since we are both at Bethel College in Kansas we have consulted often on matters of content, interpretation, and style. As I wrote the various sections and chapters of the book, I shared drafts also with others who had special expertise and concerns in given areas.

I cannot give adequate credit to all who thus advised me, but I should mention some. Amos Hoover helped me on Old Order Mennonites; Guy F. Hershberger on World War I and other topics; Allan Teichroew on World War I; Elizabeth Horsch Bender on John Horsch and Harold Bender; Paul Toews on Mennonite Brethren; Lois Barrett on Native Americans; Wilbert Shenk on Fundamentalism; Donald Durnbaugh on the ecumenical peace witness; and Anna Juhnke on Mennonite women. Editorial committee members who supplied me with helpful written comments on a completed draft of the manuscript included Kreider plus Cornelius J. Dyck, Willard Swartley, and John A. Lapp. Rodney Sawatsky and Beulah Hostetler also criticized it in helpful ways. I look forward to further conversations with these generous persons about why I incorporated some of their suggestions but not others.

The directors and staffs of various Mennonite library and archival centers were unfailingly generous with space, time, and energy. I especially wish to thank Grace Showalter and James O. Lehman at the Menno Simons Historical Library of Eastern Mennonite College (Harrisonburg, Virginia); Carolyn Charles Wenger of Lancaster Mennonite Historical Society (Lancaster, Pennsylvania); Joseph Miller of Eastern Pennsylvania Mennonite Historical Library (Christopher Dock High School near Lansdale, Pennsylvania); Leonard Gross of the Archives of the Mennonite Church (Goshen, Indiana); John Oyer and Lena Lehman of Mennonite Historical Library (Goshen College, Goshen,

Indiana); Robert Kreider and David Haury of Mennonite Library and Archives (Bethel College, North Newton, Kansas); Wesley Prieb of the Center for Mennonite Brethren Studies (Tabor College, Hillsboro, Kansas); Paul Toews of the Center for Mennonite Brethren Studies (Pacific College, Fresno, California); and Delbert Gratz of the Mennonite Historical Library (Bluffton College, Bluffton, Ohio).

A number of history students and former students at Bethel College assisted in special tasks: Barbara Thieszen, David Harder, Kurt Harder, Mary Sprunger, and Rachel Waltner Goossen. Tim Schmucker and D. J. Greaser of Goshen College helped me during my sojourn there. My daughter, Joanne Juhnke, served as an editorial and research assistant in the later stages of the project. I owe a special word of thanks to Theron Schlabach, MEA project editor. Schlabach has had a central role in defining the issues and clarifying the categories which give shape to the MEA volumes. He was unselfish in sharing his own voluminous research notes. The endnotes do not adequately reflect Schlabach's influence on matters of fact, interpretation, and style. His high standards of scholarship in research, writing, and editorial critique have been a model for me as a college teacher and a historian.

In the twenty-five years since I began graduate study, the field of American church and religious history has gained new vitality. While this book was being researched and written I learned much at meetings sponsored by the Conference on Faith and History, the American Society of Church History, and the Christian College Coalition. Sprinkled throughout the endnotes are the names of the scholars whose works helped me to put the Mennonite story into perspective.

The pious rituals of American professionalism require the scholar to take personal and individual responsibility for the failings of his work and to absolve all others for any errors or infelicities. I accept such responsibility. From experience I well know that before the ink is dry, new and additional items will appear for revising and correcting the text. But I should also confess my Mennonite unease with the individualism of such disclaimers. This book is not simply my own. Its insights and its limitations are partly mine and partly my people's. The book reflects the ways some Mennonite scholars in America see the story of their people at this point in their history. We have been especially insistent that American Mennonitism be seen as a whole of interrelated parts, and as a movement shaped by its social and political environment. Not far beneath the surface of these chapters is a yearning, shared with previous generations of Mennonite historians, for the revitalization of the people-hood and for the wider fulfillment of God's shalom on earth. I am grateful for the opportunity to take part in this task.

James C. Juhnke

VISION, DOCTRINE, WAR

CHAPTER

1

PATTERNS OF MENNONITE
PEOPLEHOOD AROUND 1890

"The great World's fair at Chicago was opened today noon—
Columbian Exposition," wrote John S. Coffman of Elkhart, Indiana, in his diary for Monday, May 1, 1893. Coffman along
with many other rural and small-town Mennonites seemed fas-
cinated by the city. He made the comment even though he was a
busy evangelist, editor, writer, and correspondent who normally
kept his diary entries personal and hasty. Seldom did he mention world events. But Chicago World's Fair caught his attention. He considered it a "grand affair no doubt."[1]

"REALLY AND EXCLUSIVELY THE WORLD'S FAIR"

Coffman's words breathed a certain wistfulness. Mennonites—at least his kind of Mennonites—were a separate and
nonconformed people who were not supposed to attend such
worldly events. The Indiana-Michigan Mennonite conference of
1893 resolved that fair attenders would "fall under Church
censure."[2] Coffman's employer and mentor, the "old" Mennonites' pioneer editor, John F. Funk at Elkhart, Indiana, wrote in
his *Herald of Truth* that "the great Exposition at Chicago is
really and exclusively the '*World's*' Fair. It is not for the Christian, but for the world."[3] Writing in his diary on July 7,
Coffman noted that only a "few of our people have gone there. I
am truly thankful for that."[4]

Within the next six weeks, however, Coffman journeyed to
Chicago twice, editor Funk once. There, selectively, they tasted
some fruits of the exposition. Funk, carrying credentials as an
official delegate of the Philadelphia-based Christian Arbitration
and Peace Society, went to the Art Palace at Michigan Avenue

and Adams Street to attend the World's Peace Congress.[5] Coffman, finding the Peace Congress "rather tame," went to hear sermons by nationally famous preachers—including the foremost revivalist of the day, Dwight L. Moody, and the notable dispensationalist, Cyrus I. Scofield. To the Mennonite evangelist, Scofield's explanation of the book of Revelation offered "a better line of thought than I ever had of that book."[6]

Meanwhile the two Mennonite leaders avoided the more frivolous enticements. For them the Midway, with its spectacular "Ferris Wheel," and the Great White City, with its 150 acres of exhibitions in praise of human progress, were off limits. So had they *really* attended the event they officially opposed? Yes and no.

Coffman and Funk had acted with typical Mennonite ambivalence. They had gotten in touch with the latest in modern ideas and techniques of American Christendom (pacifism, evangelism, dispensationalism); but they had hedged and limited their city contacts to protect themselves from that which they recognized as worldly and dangerous. "I can make practical use of many things I have heard today," Coffman wrote in his diary on July 26. He returned from Chicago to northern Indiana as an agent of change among a people who were cautious about change. Mennonites did not want the world to press them into its own mold.

The Columbian Exposition celebrated the four hundredth anniversary of the discovery of America. As it did, it symbolized both change and progress. In Chicago, Henry Adams, descendant of two American presidents, stood before a whirring dynamo and discovered his symbol for the incredible acceleration of forces that marked an emerging modern industrial civilization. Historian Frederick Jackson Turner delivered a landmark essay about how free land had fashioned distinctive American character traits: democracy, individualism, and nationality. Dwight L. Moody lit a spark for national and international Christian revival. Suffragists Susan B. Anthony, Julia Ward Howe, and Lucy Stone addressed the Women's Congress, which proposed to transform outmoded conceptions of women's role in modern society. The World's Fair was a monumental cultural event, a "clearing house of civilization." It marked the watershed between a simpler, agrarian-commercial past and a complex, urban-industrial future. As Americans of all kinds responded to the event in Chicago, they revealed who they were and were becoming.[7]

(*World's Columbian Exposition Illustrated*. Vol. II. 1893. p. 172)

Manufacturers Building at the Chicago World's Fair, 1893.

Ada May Landes, a nineteen-year-old high school student from a "new" Mennonite family in Bucks County, Pennsylvania, spent eight euphoric days at the Exposition. Her "new" Mennonites were a group in eastern Pennsylvania who had begun their own conference in 1847 partly because they were more open to American "progress." Landes wrote to her sister back home that the Fair's main building covered forty acres. "Just think of it," she exclaimed, "as large as your farm!" Her detailed account revealed how the exhibits drew people into reverent appreciation of the military symbols of American nationhood: "We also saw the saddle on which General Grant rode from the beginning to the end of the war, the Bible used by John Brown up to a few days before his execution . . . a sword presented to Commodore Perry, and thousands of similar relics." She found a French-fashion display so overwhelmingly lavish that her almost-forgotten Mennonite scruples touched surface: "I tell you if you didn't have a pretty sensible head you'd most go off [lose control]." Unlike Funk and Coffman, Ada May Landes was not very ambivalent or indiscriminate about what she saw. Like many another Mennonite youth, she was rushing into Americanization. But at least she returned home to Pennsylvania.

Franklin Zimmerman of Blue Ball, Pennsylvania, did not. He left for the Fair and was never found again, not even to receive money willed him from two estates![8]

John A. Sprunger, a successful Mennonite businessman and religious entrepreneur from Berne, Indiana, took advantage of the World's Fair in his own way. On the southwest corner of Harrison and May streets in Chicago stood a home which Sprunger intended to turn into a center for deaconess training, hospital work, and rescue mission. In the summer of 1893 this new center was only getting started, so Sprunger set it up as a Christian lodging place for Fair guests. Living in Chicago were a few scattered Mennonites, but they had no organized congregation. An earlier meetinghouse had been destroyed in the great Chicago fire of 1871. In 1893 Mennonites and others who stayed at the Sprunger center found a safe and friendly place in the city. They also could learn details of Sprunger's expansive dreams for an interdenominational "Light and Hope Missionary Society." The ambitious free-lancer wanted to establish a network of benevolent institutions in the Midwest—orphanages, hospitals, nurses training schools, retirement homes, and foreign missions projects—staffed by idealistic young Mennonite volunteers. Although he remained on the margins of Mennonite denominational-institutional developments, Sprunger set patterns that more denomination-minded Mennonites would soon follow. He, too, was an agent of Americanization. In 1893 he reported an income of $1,487.24 from World's Fair guests.[9]

Christian Krehbiel of Halstead, Kansas, lodged at the Sprunger center and traveled in the city with one of the new deaconesses as a guide.[10] A south-German immigrant of 1851, Krehbiel was a leader in the General Conference (GC) Mennonite Church. GC leaders encouraged their members to purchase round-trip railroad tickets to the Fair, with a side trip to Bluffton, Ohio. At Bluffton, in October, the GC body was holding its triennial general conference.[11] Three years earlier that body had addressed the World's Fair issue which most agitated American Protestants: whether the Fair should remain open on Sunday. The conference said no.[12] In December of 1893, back in Kansas after attending the Fair and the Bluffton conference, Krehbiel preached a sermon summarizing his impressions. He neglected the Sunday-closing issue but spoke of hearing a glorious sermon by Reuben Torrey, superintendent of Moody Bible Institute. In Krehbiel's view the Fair offered magnificent opportunities for preaching the gospel of Jesus Christ. To him its exhibitions of human invention were "a great work of the Lord, who created nature, and who placed the powers of nature under the human spirit, that man might rule over them." But almost as an afterthought Krehbiel also injected a Mennonite warning against pride. When man once seeks to displace God as Creator, he admonished, "at this point his proud waves will break."[13]

On Chicago's 22d Street several idealistic and educated young Mennonites—William B. Page, DeWitt Good, and Solomon D. Ebersole—set up a restaurant where they received visitors and discussed grand plans for a Mennonite witness in the city.[14] In November their friend Menno Simon (M.S.) Steiner, of Beaverdam, Ohio, rented a former saloon at 145 West 18th Street and inaugurated a Mennonite city mission. Steiner's mission, officially mandated by a two-year-old institution known as the Sunday School Conference, seemed more closely tied to official Mennonite structures than was Sprunger's establishment. Nevertheless, institutional ties would have to be clarified. Especially troublesome was the relationship of Steiner's mission to a "Mennonite Evangelizing Board of America" based at Elkhart, Indiana. It was a time of beginnings. Mennonites were coming off the farm with fresh energy to take up new relationships. They were venturing into what Steiner called "our modern Ninevehs," into the shadow of the World's Fair, on a path lit by Moody.[15]

One progressive Mennonite contributed substantively to the Fair's displays. Heinrich R. Voth, GC missionary to the Arapaho and Hopi Indians in the American West, had collected Native American artifacts for the Smithsonian Institution, and the Fair exhibited them. Voth himself was a curious mixture of missionary and ethnographer, religious tradition and modernity. He wanted to rescue the natives from heathen darkness, but his greater success was to document, photograph, and chronicle Hopi life in the style of modern social science. Eventually he offended his mission board by personally profiting from the sale of Indian artifacts, and offended the Hopi by having made their ritual secrets public. He had to give up his mission career. There was more than one way for a Mennonite to be burned by the modern values which the Fair advertised.[16]

Regarding the Fair, Mennonite newspapers reflected both the variety and the ambivalence in Mennonite attitudes. The

Herald of Truth and *Herold der Wahrheit*—since 1864 the English- and German-language products of John F. Funk's press at Elkhart—took rather different editorial paths. The German edition apparently was influenced by an immigrant assistant editor named John Horsch. In any case, it condemned the Fair for using the mantle of art and technology to cover manifold evils of infidelity, paganism, and nudity. The English edition, whose assistant editor was Coffman, was more moderate.[17] Editorials, articles, and letters to the editor in Mennonite papers expressed varying degrees of concern about the Sunday-closing issue, expressions of militarism, and reports of rampant prostitution. They also worried about the tendency of the World Parliament of Religions to put Christianity on the same level with other faiths.[18]

Far from Chicago, in the old Mennonite heartland of Lancaster County, Pennsylvania, the winds of change in 1893 produced a historic church schism. Bishop Jonas H. Martin of the Weaverland congregation opposed innovations which were relentlessly invading the brotherhood: English-language worship, Sunday schools, revival meetings, fire insurance, singing schools, modern pulpits, and much more. On October 6, 1893, at the Mellinger meetinghouse, Martin faced seven fellow church leaders—one of whom pulled out his watch and gave Martin ten minutes to recant from his stubborn resistance. Martin held to what he considered to be the "old ground," the tradition of the fathers. In so doing he became a founding father in his own right. His new group, the Old Order Mennonites (distinguished from the "old" Mennonites, "new" Mennonites, and others) forged an alliance with like-minded folks in Indiana, Ohio, Ontario, and Virginia. Among such Mennonites, attending world's fairs and starting rescue missions in the city were out of the question. Nevertheless, the city beckoned. Some years later Bishop Martin himself passed through Chicago on a preaching tour to Canada and stopped to visit the city's stockyards. For this lapse into worldliness he had to make public confession before his old-order congregation. The confession was an act of submission in a community where humility and yieldedness to God and to the church were prized above all virtues.[19]

And so Chicago stood as a symbol for the manifold hopes and dreams and fears of Mennonites facing the changing world of the 1890s and the new century. Mennonites were deeply divided on what it meant to be faithful disciples of Christ in a modernizing world. In relating to American society they chose various levels of participation and separation. Within the Mennonite mosaic each group was aware that other groups were drawing lines at different places. So the groups carefully avoided contamination from each other as well as from American society. The meanings and the consequences of their choices depended both upon the newly forming character of American society and upon the tensions inside rural Mennonite communities themselves.

THE DENOMINATIONAL IMPULSE

In 1893 Joseph S. Taylor, the first Mennonite in America to hold a doctor's degree (a Pd.D.—Doctor of Pedagogy), optimistically assessed Mennonite prospects. "The Mennonite Church," he wrote, "proves its vitality by the fact that it is adapting itself to the requirements of a new civilization."[20] Taylor knew something about adaptation. Reared in the small Springfield Mennonite congregation in Bucks County in eastern Pennsylvania, with a family name anglicized from "Schneider," he became a successful educator in New York City. From his position of urban sophistication Taylor often spoke at GC Mennonite conferences and wrote for the GC paper, *The Mennonite*. Often he called for more aggressive borrowing from American Protestantism's finer ways. "I want the church carpeted. I want the smokers and chewers to leave their tobacco at the door. . . . I want an organ that is in tune, and a player who can play. I want a pleasant Sunday school room and pleasant people in it. . . ."[21] In subsequent decades Mennonites borrowed a great deal indeed from American Protestants: forms of piety, organization, music, architecture, and much more. Impatient progressives such as Taylor were seldom satisfied with the slow pace of adaptation.

Mennonite experience in America from 1890 onward showed that Taylor's thesis about church vitality was partly right. Mennonites and Amish Mennonites experienced renewal and revitalization through adaptation—sometimes selective and sometimes inadvertent—to a new American civilization.

The reverse of Taylor's argument had equal merit. Mennonites and Amish Mennonites found renewal and revitalization also by looking back to their tradition. Even in Taylor's more liberal branch of the church—the GCs' Eastern District—there were those who sought renewal through appeal to *heritage* rather than through borrowing. Allen Fretz, pastor of the Deep Run Mennonite church (GC) in Bucks County, called for looking "back upon our own fore-fathers, the church of the Apostles, martyrs, and reformers, studying God's work in her and asking Him to revive the spiritual life in her again."[22]

Nothing was more characteristic of Mennonites than to ground an agenda for change—or to justify resistance to change—in an appeal to history. For them the high points of history were the apostolic church and the sixteenth-century Reformation. Fretz argued that the new mission work, Bible studies, Sunday schools, and other changes were not to be seen as borrowings from Protestant America. They recovered a rich and beloved heritage.

Many changes in Mennonite and Amish Mennonite churches from 1890 to 1930 and beyond constituted a broad and belated response to American *denominationalism*—the distinctively American form of church life which resulted from separation of church and state. American Protestant denominations first took shape in the early nineteenth century in response to a disestablishment which denied favored status to would-be state churches and enabled former sects to gain respectability. To the degree that they were Protestant, Mennonites were among the "late bloomers" of American Protestantism.[23] After decades and centuries of defensive self-protection, most Mennonites gradually adopted forms of religious organization and self-consciousness which let them take their place in the mosaic of American Protestant pluralism. Some individuals and groups strongly resisted the denominationalizing process. Yet even for those who resisted change, that process provided the model for change and determined the issues.[24]

Before 1890, with a sectarian mentality and lack of central church organization, most Mennonites had held off the forces of American denominationalism. To be sure, long before 1890 there had been many borrowings from the religious styles of American neighbors. Denominational-related issues had brought many arguments and even church splits. The First and Second Great Awakenings in American Protestantism and the developments of American revivalism had influenced different Mennonites differently. Some Mennonites and Amish resisted defensively and lost membership to revivalist groups. Some attempted to become more revivalistic themselves. Even the strictly separatist Mennonites did not want to be known as a sect. In 1844, in a context of Protestant denominational pluralism, a few Pennsylvania Mennonites who wrote for a general *History of Religious Denominations* had attempted to overcome the "sect" label and its stigma.[25]

In 1860 a "General Conference Mennonite church" was founded with ambitious dreams for nationwide denominational activity. Vigorous efforts in the 1870s and 1880s at publication and creating Sunday schools also paved the way. But the period of rapid mainstream Mennonite denomination-building did not come until the 1890s. Part of becoming a denomination was a process of intentionally *organizing*. Between 1890 and 1930 the Mennonites and Amish Mennonites established a series of denominational institutions—schools, colleges, missions agencies, relief and benevolence committees, publishing houses, hospitals, retirement centers—which set patterns for still further denominational organizing in coming decades.

The protracted organizational revolution had wide consequences. More than ever before, Mennonites found themselves busy in a great variety of purposive activities. Earlier they had been oriented to the primary associations of family, farm, and congregation. Now they increasingly took cues from institutional centers removed from the local community. The denominationalizing process tended to concentrate power and information in organizational centers. Mennonite leadership flowed not only to those who had shown spiritual gifts in addressing local situations but also to those with skills to manage bureaucracies on a regional or a national scale. As time passed, structured organization empowered Mennonites as a group to do much they could not have done otherwise. They set new goals and acted to achieve them. But in their rational, goal-directed organizing, Mennonites and Amish Mennonites became more like American Protestant denominations. They became so even when they wanted their organizations to serve the cause of separatism.

Becoming a denomination also brought a gradual change in the *consciousness* of Mennonites as a people. America's tolerant denominational pluralism was quite a challenge to the Mennonite separation and nonconformity. During the Reformation in sixteenth-century Europe, Mennonites had been marked as sectarians—small, isolated, marginal groups over against the dominant and established Catholic, Lutheran, Reformed, and

Orthodox churches. Gradually the Mennonites had made a virtue of separation and subordination. But America had no official church establishment. Its environment gradually transformed the meaning of religious separatism. Sects might become denominations. As denominations they would be socially acceptable among other groups—groups equally proud of their distinctive beliefs and practices but ready to accept each other's legitimacy. For Mennonites, even in the late twentieth century, the decline of sectarian self-consciousness and the gaining of a sense of denominational legitimacy remains a complex, controversial, and unfinished process. But American toleration and variety were powerful solvents. With notable exceptions, most Mennonites thought and behaved more and more like Americans. They did so even in the ways they tried to maintain a distinctive identity. Gradually, in America, Mennonites found a legitimate and acceptable home.

Among Mennonites there was never a consensus on whether the denominationalizing process was a case of awakening or of apostasy. From the perspectives of American Protestantism and of progressive Mennonites such as Joseph Taylor the new institutions for education and mission signaled renewal—a belated blooming of long-hidden potential. But more traditional Mennonites and Amish opposed American denominational methods and mentality, with ample reason. Since the sixteenth century, Anabaptist-Mennonite teachings and the Mennonite reading of the Bible had defined a charter of community values which were genuinely in tension with the ways of American individualism, materialism, and upward mobility. Intentionally limiting themselves to primary school education, the traditionalists were not as articulate as the progressive denomination-builders. But in their holding to the ways of humility, simplicity, and obedience, they pressed an important question: whether the acclaimed denominational blooming was not in fact a loss of an original and authentic Mennonite vision. The Old Order Mennonites and Old Order Amish, as well as many conservatives more in the Mennonite mainstream, managed to survive and to hold their own as well as did the progressives.

Thus, patterns of Mennonite social change were far more complex than suggested by sociological theories of straight-line acculturation to American ways.[26] Not all Mennonite change moved toward conformity to the outside world. Some groups fostered renewal, revitalization, and long-range growth precisely in *resistance* to modernization. Meanwhile others found new vitality through selective adaptation—by choosing to borrow elements from the American scene which would both renew Mennonite peoplehood and extend a Christian witness to the world. Finally, in all groups there were individuals—and sometimes there were whole groups—who let themselves be swept along uncritically to accept American modernity and its affluent ways.

The story of American Mennonites is not simply one of how Mennonites in general became Americanized or modernized. Instead, it is a complex account of how groups related to each other and to the outside world as they made widely differing choices, or similar choices but at different times. The choices were about where to draw the lines of accepting and rejecting change. Often they were painful and controversial. Some cases represented stagnation and attrition. But for most Mennonites the encounter with American society did not destroy communal religious vitality. Instead, it brought a diverse renewal of the Mennonite heritage in response to changing American conditions.

Through the nineteenth and twentieth centuries Mennonites and Amish looked both backward and forward. They organized and they resisted organization. They adopted revivalism and they resisted revivalist excesses. They used American ways in order to oppose Americanization. From 1890 to 1930 the process of becoming a denomination, broadly defined to include matters of both organization and identity, gave some unity to their varied responses.

PATTERNS OF PEOPLEHOOD

The new denominational institutions worked a gradual transformation in the patterns of Mennonite peoplehood. Colleges, church boards, and publications developed their own constituencies of supporters and critics. Institutions helped bring growth to the small towns where they were located. Individuals and congregations developed new loyalties as they became contributors to conference-organized benevolence, readers of denominational publications, and alumni of schools and colleges. The new loyalties redirected, reshaped, and sometimes reinforced historic group identities—identities which varied according to geographical origin in Europe, time of immigration, and different development in America.

The common core of Mennonite life had its roots back in European origins. These origins remained important to a people so deeply rooted in history.[27] Mennonites all shared a label derived from an early Dutch leader named Menno Simons. Nearly all of them either spoke some dialect of German or were part of a bilingual culture gradually changing to English. They shared an orthodox Christian set of beliefs articulated in the widely used Dordrecht Confession of Faith of 1632 and an Elbing Catechism of 1778. They all remembered a history of persecution and migration which resulted from their Radical Reformation rejection of the state church and from their distinctive practice of adult baptism upon confession of faith. Despite differences in discipline they all agreed that the church was a body of believers who were accountable to each other. They shared a strong perception that the Christian life involved a costly discipleship which ran against any separation of ethics and salvation.

By and large all Mennonite groups (if not all individuals) rejected military service—an issue which, in an age of increasing nationalism and militarism, more and more replaced rebaptism as the point of greatest tension with worldly authorities. They all sustained their faith in a traditional framework of religious ritual and nonverbal behavior which governed the ways in which children were reared, members were won and accepted into congregations, special events were celebrated, leaders were recruited, suffering ones were comforted, and the dead were buried. Ritual forms varied widely from group to group. But all Mennonites took their religion seriously in day-to-day life.

Beyond the commonalities of name, history, belief, and practice, many Mennonites were scattered into a mosaic of quite small groups. The pattern has bewildered outsiders and has not fit standard academic categories of church and sect, assimilation and acculturation, and ethnicity. Mennonite variety reflected three overlapping kinds of divisions: (1) Swiss and south-German versus Dutch and north-German origin in Europe; (2) differences between the earlier established settlers in the East and those who arrived later or migrated from the East and settled in the frontier Midwest or West; and (3) differences due to separate group or conference affiliation in America.

TWOFOLD EUROPEAN ORIGIN

The most fundamental distinction of Mennonite historical development as transmitted to America grew out of two regions of origin in the sixteenth century. One was Switzerland and south Germany. Another was Holland and north Germany. Harold S. Bender, leading Mennonite historian in the mid-twentieth century, went so far as to write that "the Swiss-south German and the Dutch-north German-Russian types of Mennonites are two historical families of Mennonites who have had practically no historical affiliation with each other." He may have exaggerated for effect. Moreover, recent historians of sixteenth-century Anabaptism tend to find multiplicity and complexity rather than a simple duality. There were numerous points of Anabaptist origin, multiple proliferations of Anabaptist groups as they spread in various directions, and many cases of mutual aid and mutual influence among Mennonite groups of different areas. Overarching the complexity, however, was the dual pattern. Mennonites with Swiss or south-German roots were discernibly different from those whose origins were Dutch or north-German.[28]

The shaping events of the Swiss and south-German Anabaptists included: their origins on the radical wing of Ulrich Zwingli's reform in Zurich; an early definition in the Schleitheim Confession of 1527; the role of the free city of Strassburg as an Anabaptist refuge and conference center; a general pattern of government persecution and repression which extended well into the eighteenth century; and a major schism between Mennonites and Amish in about 1693.[29] Government opposition, which at various times brought imprisonment, exile, taxation, and restrictions on church activity, prevented full development of economic, church, and literary life. For their devotional literature, confessions of faith, catechisms, and histories, Swiss and south-German Mennonites came to depend on their Dutch coreligionists and on European Pietists. Their worship services and the architecture of their meetinghouses were markedly simple. They allowed no musical instruments in worship—a legacy of the Zwinglian Reformation which continued on the American frontier. Subordination and subservience led them to special emphasis on certain themes present in Anabaptism from the beginning: a decisive dualism of church and world, reluctance or refusal to become involved in public life, and a rejection of worldly pride accompanied by a premium upon humility.[30]

From 1776 to 1783 Mennonite experience in the American Revolution vindicated and enhanced the doctrine of separation from the world. Once again Mennonites and Amish suffered for their refusal to bear arms and pay war taxes.[31] Although they were part of a regional language and culture group known as "Pennsylvania Dutch," they remained politically and socially marginal to American public power. In time they developed regulated patterns of dress which helped ensure distinctiveness in the American context. Within the Anabaptist family, Amish and Mennonites remained keenly aware of how they differed from each other. Swiss-Americans of Amish or Mennonite background inherited and developed a religious tradition which made a virtue of their marginality.

The Dutch Mennonite tradition was rather different.[32] In the early years after the Reformation, under Spanish Catholic rule, Dutch Anabaptists suffered a persecution as vicious as that in Switzerland. But as early as the 1570s Mennonites in the Netherlands began to be tolerated. Few of them migrated directly to America.[33] In the seventeenth century Dutch Mennonites enjoyed growth and cultural renaissance. Thieleman Jansz van Braght's *Martyrs Mirror* of 1660, Jan Philip Schabalje's *Wandering Soul* of 1635ff., Menno Simons' writings, and other Dutch Mennonite literature helped bring consolidation and focus.

Meanwhile early Dutch Mennonite refugees fled eastward toward Prussia. There, on the Vistula River Delta (near Danzig), they settled and gained a foothold. Then, responding to an invitation from Catherine the Great for German settlers to occupy and develop the farmlands in the Ukraine, many moved southeastward into the Russian Empire. Along the way they adopted German as their official language for church and school and developed a Low German dialect for house and farm. They adopted a more varied church architecture than the Swiss and accepted musical instruments more readily for worship and home.

Until World War I and the Communist Revolution, the Mennonites under Russian rule were able to develop community life in a framework of political and cultural autonomy. Nowhere else had Mennonites experienced such autonomy.[34] Russia's Mennonites chose their own local public officials, controlled their own quasi-public schools, and created a vigorous agricultural economy whose leaders (especially one Johann

Cornies, 1789-1848) were respected figures in Russia's empire. In education and economy the "Russian" Mennonite villages outstripped those of the Ukrainian peasants around them. This experience of well-developed, relatively autonomous communities created a modified, Mennonite sort of "Christendom" whose inhabitants gradually gained in worldly self-confidence. Russia's Mennonites learned to accept responsibility for public affairs and to wrestle with the contradictions of an Anabaptist remnant which had achieved a measure of worldly power. In their German-language enclaves they took separation from the non-Mennonite outside world for granted. In that, they were different from Swiss-background Mennonites and Amish in America. Faced with the freer social environment of tolerant democracy which undermined group autonomy, the Swiss and south-German Mennonites in America had to devise more intentional mechanisms of separation.

Shortly before a substantial segment of them migrated to the North American plains in the 1870s, Mennonites of the Russian Empire suffered a deep religious schism. The rift separated the main-body *"Kirchliche"* ("churchly," or "establishment") Mennonites and a reforming, Pietist-influenced *Mennonitische Brüdergemeinde* (Mennonite Brethren). This division plus several earlier, smaller ones became definitive in the consciousness of Dutch-Russian Mennonites—much as an Amish-Mennonite division had long since been definitive for Swiss-American Mennonites. A Mennonite child in the 1890s growing up in Lancaster County, Pennsylvania, learned clearly that he or she was *not* Amish, and vice versa for an Amish child. And a *Kirchliche* Mennonite child growing up in Marion County, Kansas, learned clearly that he or she was *not* Mennonite Brethren, and vice versa. Other smaller groups which splintered from the major bodies defined themselves in the same way, over against the larger groups.

SWISS AND SOUTH-GERMAN
HUMILITY, NONRESISTANCE, AND SEPARATION

Despite various splintering and distinctions within each of the two broad Anabaptist-Mennonite streams, in general each stream had given its Mennonites in America a corresponding community ethos which shaped habits, attitudes, and folkways. In 1890 people of Swiss and south-German background were by far the majority of Mennonites in America; and their ethos was characterized by *humility, nonresistance*, and *separation*. The ethos had begun in scattered, intimidated Mennonite settlements in Switzerland, Alsace, the Palatinate, and other regions. From such places Mennonites and Amish had fled persecution and become the "quiet in the land." Two centuries of Mennonite settlement and development in America had defined and refined the ethos further.

Politically, at first the Swiss and south-German Mennonites had cooperated with colonial Pennsylvania's Quaker party. Eventually, however, their refusal to cooperate in the Revolutionary War and in many developments of the new nation had pushed them to the political periphery. Religiously, leaders named Heinrich Funck (d. 1760), Christian Burkholder (1746-1809), John M. Brenneman (1816-1895), and others wrote books to help their people resist the lures of Pietism and revivalism. Such major Mennonite writings revealed a shift in theme. Suffering, no longer as appropriate as in the Anabaptist days of persecution, gave way to a new paradigm of humility or yieldedness.[35] The Mennonite ethos of humility (*Demut*) involved submission both to God and to the Christian community. Failure to submit was a mark of the opposite sin, pride (*Hochmut*).

The ethos of humility found expression in nonverbal behavior as well as verbally. If it were possible to recover the patterns of gesture and voice from the 1890s, one would likely find the Swiss-background Mennonites typically holding their heads somewhat lower, modestly diverting their eyes, and speaking more softly than did their brothers and sisters of Dutch-Russian background. They expressed the humble lifestyle of separation from the world also in church regulations against participation in politics and against various kinds of association with worldly people. It was common to say that individuals and groups who left the main body had "gone high." Despite varieties of Mennonite behavior produced by schisms and by manifold accommodation to American ways, the strong ethos of humility, nonresistance, and separation generally persisted as a strong characteristic of Swiss and south-German Mennonites.

DUTCH-RUSSIAN MENNONITE COMMUNITY CHRISTENDOM

The community ethos of Dutch-Russian Mennonites may be designated a *Mennonite community Christendom*. Cornelius H. Wedel, leader from the Alexanderwohl congregation in Kansas, was the first to use the term *Christendom* to describe the Mennonite tradition.[36] By *Christendom* Wedel did not mean the state-church pattern of Western Christianity since Emperor Constantine. Instead, the Mennonite Christendom was a counterculture, an alternative community, and a way of life which rejected coercion from the state. Nevertheless, more than the Swiss, the Dutch-Russian Mennonites were ready to accept some responsibility for the civic community's welfare. The Mennonite Christendom consisted of the congregation-oriented culture of Mennonite communities.

Even while they saw the politics of nations and empires as alien and worldly, Dutch-Russian immigrants from the semi-autonomous Mennonite villages of the Ukraine assumed that they as Christians could be involved positively in local public institutions. They were active in the social, economic, religious, and to some extent political tasks of building a Mennonite place in the world. The goal was a congregation-centered order, a congregation Christendom. That Christendom saw itself as separate from worldly Christendoms; yet its people participated more affirmatively in the life of local institutions than did their coreligionists of Swiss and south-German origin.

A Low German (*plautdietsch*) dialect helped preserve this folk culture. In 1919, after several years among the Dutch-Russians in Kansas, a Swiss-background college teacher named Samuel Burkhard observed that language was "the gateway to the social psychology of the group." "I never got into the gossip nor did I get the drift of the public mind except second hand."[37] In addition to its affirmation of language the Dutch-Russian ethos fostered a positive sense of place and an appreciation of material culture—eventually expressed in the establishment of the first Mennonite museums in America. As Anabaptists these Dutch-Russian Mennonites knew they were a people of Christ's kingdom as well as of worldly kingdoms. But their own life in community included more dimensions of worldly involvement than did that of their brothers and sisters of the Swiss and south-German stream.

The forces of American denominationalism which gathered momentum among Mennonites after 1890 represented a challenge both to the Swiss and south-German ethos of humility and to a Dutch-Russian ethos of *Gemeinde* Christendom. The new organizers of institutions marched to a progressive drumbeat of aggressive activism which contradicted the more hum-

ble and modest ways of their parents and grandparents.[38] New
institutional centers for Mennonite education, publication, and
mission deflected attention from the local congregation as the
main arena of Mennonite life. As decades passed in the twentieth century, the differences between Mennonites of these two
types would gradually erode. The deterioration would prepare
the way for a new ecumenical-denominational alignment including the main bodies of both the Dutch and the Swiss
streams. However, throughout the period of this volume (1890-
1930) the Mennonite polarity between Swiss-south German and
Dutch-Russian remained strong.

EAST AND WEST

A second distinction important for the Mennonite experience in America corresponded to geography and to time of immigration and settlement—the difference between East and
West. Heartlands of the Mennonite "East" were the large communities of the Lancaster and the Franconia conferences, the
one centered in Lancaster County, the other in Bucks and
Montgomery counties, in southeastern Pennsylvania. Usually
the East also included communities growing from early extension beyond the original settlements: those of the Washington
County (Maryland) and Franklin County (Pennsylvania) and the
Ontario and the Virginia conferences. In most respects the East
became a stronghold of conservatism compared to settlements
in the Midwest and West—western Pennsylvania, Ohio, Indiana,
Illinois, Iowa, Missouri, and beyond. Indeed, the settlements on
the western frontier were crucibles of creative unsettlement.
Living nearer the frontier often involved more contacts with
non-Mennonite settlers and more mixing with newly arriving
Mennonite immigrants from Europe with rather different folkways and ideas. The more open and pluralistic environment of
the West stimulated people to experiment with new ideas and
institutions. Most of the significant innovations in Mennonite
faith and practice in the late nineteenth and early twentieth
centuries came from the West and were resisted by the East.

The early Amish Mennonite settlement of Wayne County,
Ohio, illustrated the variety on the frontier.[39] While most early
settlers were from Mifflin and Somerset counties in Pennsylvania, early ministers in the 1820s through 1840s included not
only men born in America but also one ordained in Switzerland
(Christian Brandt), one born in Prussia (Peter Naftzger), and one

from Alsace (Christian Rupp). In those years, contrary to normal Amish practice, the Wayne County congregations chose their leaders by vote rather than by the lot. Because they had a somewhat more tolerant and progressive spirit the Wayne County leaders came to be denied fellowship back in Mifflin County. Tensions between the more liberal West and the more conservative East complicated inter-Mennonite relationships through the nineteenth and twentieth centuries. The Oak Grove congregation of Wayne County proved to be one of the most volatile and innovative of all Amish and Mennonite congregations.

"The West is more American than the East," reported John Horsch, an 1887 immigrant from south Germany, after a visit from Indiana to eastern Pennsylvania in 1893. "In the East the children are not as wild and as ill-mannered. In the East people take more interest in each other, have more concern for each other, are more guided by fixed customs and rules. As a result they do not feel as free and as independent as in the West."[40] Horsch's comments agreed with an interpretation which American historian Frederick Jackson Turner expressed in the same year. Turner found the essence of American character in the frontier's dynamic encounter of man and nature.[41] The frontier was a safety valve for the discontents of Eastern civilization. The newly formed and reformed American frontier culture—more fluid, democratic, and individualistic—fed its influences back into the more settled East.

There was paradox in the fact that more recent immigrants would be more Americanized than were Mennonites whose families had been in America for two centuries. Horsch reached back to New Testament history and said that the East was like Jerusalem and the West like Antioch. Eastern congregations resembled the Jewish-Christian congregations—legalistic, conservative, and suspicious of developments on the Gentile-Christian frontier. Western congregations were in the vanguard of change, like the apostle Paul who moved out of Antioch with an ambitious program for preaching the gospel and spreading the kingdom of God. Horsch recommended that American Mennonites from the West follow Paul's example and "go to Jerusalem" to keep congregations in touch with each other.

The bridges between East and West remained in reasonably good repair, maintained by vigorous interchange of correspondence and personal visits. There were no major Mennonite schisms along East-West lines. For example, despite their geographical separation, the "old" and Amish Mennonites of Pennsylvania and Indiana found it easier to overlook differences and work together than did the Swiss- and the Dutch-background Mennonites who lived right next to each other in Kansas and Nebraska. Culture separated more than did distance.

CONFERENCE AFFILIATION AND ORGANIZATION

A third set of differences among Mennonites in America was the product of their clustering into several dozen conferences or groups which often differed widely in how much they united, expected uniformity of belief and practice, and perpetuated themselves. From the 1890s onward a major tendency in nearly all these groups was to shore up their structures of organization. At times this was a defensive act, a strengthening of discipline in order to stand against outside influences. At times it was an aggressive development, a fashioning of corporate institutions to make possible a larger witness to the world. The Mennonites were entering an age of organization. Their district conferences and institutional affiliations would increasingly shape their identity and behavior.

Mennonite conferences in about 1890 could be grouped into three broad categories: those of Swiss and south-German background, those of Dutch-Prussian-Russian background, and those who combined both Swiss and Dutch.

I. SWISS

A. Mennonite

1. *"Old" Mennonites.* The largest group of Mennonites, known in 1890 as the "old" Mennonites (later "MC" or "Mennonite Church" Mennonites), were organized into eleven separate and autonomous district conferences.[42] The conferences extended westward in a broad belt from the easternmost Franconia body to the westernmost Kansas-Nebraska one. A northern extension reached into Ontario and a southern extension into Virginia. The nickname "old" distinguished them from various "new" Mennonites who had separated from the Lancaster conference in 1812 (Reformed Mennonite), from the Franconia in 1847 (East Pennsylvania Mennonite conference), and from the Indiana and Ontario conferences in 1874-1875 (Mennonite Brethren in Christ). The 1890 census reported that the "old" Mennonites had 17,078 members.

Early district conference organization had emerged gradually out of informal meetings of ministers. As decades passed, the agendas of these meetings expanded and the powers of the leaders grew. Something of an episcopal form of church governance emerged in the adoption of the term *bishop* to refer to the highest office of authority. The change accompanied language transition from German to English, as the office known in German as *Älteste* was translated as "bishop." (By contrast, among the more congregationalist Dutch-Russians the German-language *Älteste* was translated as *elder*.) "Old" Mennonite bishops oversaw a number of congregations in a "bishop district." Yet a bishop's power was kept in check by the prevailing Swiss and south-German ethos of humility and by the use of the lot. With the lot as the way to select new ministers, deacons, and bishops, established bishops could hardly control the choices.

The district conferences, with approximate dates of organization, were:

Franconia, 1725	Lancaster, 1725
Ontario, 1810	Virginia, 1820s
Washington-Franklin,	Ohio, 1834
by 1830	Illinois, 1872
Indiana, 1854	Southwestern Pennsylvania,
Missouri-Iowa, 1873	1876
Kansas-Nebraska, 1876[43]	

Prior to 1898, when most of these conferences (not including the three oldest ones in eastern Pennsylvania) organized a general conference, the "old" Mennonites did not have formal churchwide structures. Yet there were a number of bases for common identity. For the most part the "old" Mennonites were ethnically unified, since nearly all members came from Swiss and south-German Anabaptism. Their differences of lifestyle, faith, and religious practice were great enough for considerable tension and separation, yet were less marked than the differences any of them might have felt regarding Low-German-speaking Mennonites of Dutch-Russian origin. Through family and communal ties also, the "old" Mennonites of all districts were linked to the early settlements in eastern Pennsylvania, out of which many had gone westward. The bishops tried to keep themselves informed of proceedings and decisions of other district conferences. Often they attended each other's conferences as guests.

A major force for "old" Mennonite unity were the publications of John F. Funk, a denominational entrepreneur in Elkhart, Indiana. Funk, born in 1835, was a child of the Franconia conference, converted at age 23 in a Presbyterian revival meeting in Chicago, where he had gone to work in a family lumber business. After conversion he did Sunday school work in the same circles as Dwight L. Moody, before Moody was famous. Then in 1867 Funk turned his back on a promising urban career and established a publishing company in the small town of Elkhart, Indiana. From that base he invested his time and his life's resources in Mennonite denominational renewal. His mouthpiece was the periodical *Herald of Truth*, published simultaneously in a German edition called *Herold der Wahrheit*. Through his paper Funk promoted his renewal agenda: a grounding in Anabaptist-Mennonite historical literature and doctrine; introduction of Sunday schools, evangelism, Bible conferences, and higher education; support for an "old" Mennonite general conference; and assistance for Mennonite immigrants from Russia in the 1870s. In the pages of his *Herald*, Mennonites could read minutes and reports of district conference and other church meetings, travel accounts of Mennonites who visited other states or countries, letters from widely scattered communities, and selected items from the American Protestant press.

Both Funk's aggressive style and his programs for change were controversial among Mennonites oriented to humility and tradition. Well before 1890, however, Funk succeeded in getting most "old" and Amish Mennonites to consider the *Herald of Truth* to be their own paper. His New Year's editorial of that year showed how Funk equated his own work with the work of the church:

> Brethren and sisters, come up to the work like the men in rebuilding the walls of Jerusalem, in the days of Nehemiah. . . . Let the Mennonite Church be our church; let Mennonite doctrines be our doctrines; let Mennonite principles and practices be our principles and practices; let the Mennonite people be our people; let the *Herald of Truth* be our paper; let the Mennonite Bookstore and the Mennonite Printing Office be our Bookstore and Printing

Office; let us help to support and sustain it, and therewith
support and sustain the church.[44]

John F. Funk and the "old" Mennonites generally assumed
that theirs was the Mennonite mainstream. This seemed to be
the middle course between "new" Mennonites on the left and
Old Order Mennonites on the right. The Franconia conference
schism of 1847 cast an especially long shadow, as "old" Mennonites tended to see the entire General Conference Mennonite
church in terms of that division. (Dutch-Russian Mennonites on
the plains, quite unaware of the 1847 schism which preceded
their immigration, considered themselves to be the center of
their *own* mainstream.) In the "old" Mennonite view the GCs
were guilty of indiscriminate accommodation to the ways of the
world. Progressive "old" Mennonites such as Funk had to deal
with the appearance that their proposed changes for education,
publication, and general conference, and their borrowings from
Protestant evangelicalism, were simply replays of the Franconia
innovations a generation earlier. Meanwhile, to the right of the
"old" Mennonite mainstream were the old order groups, both
Amish and Mennonite. The Mennonite Old Order had its beginnings in 1845 with a conservative group led by Jacob Stauffer
in Lancaster County, Pennsylvania.

In a different metaphor, "old" Mennonites seemed to stand
at the center of a well-defined "ladder of acculturation," with
different levels of outside contacts and influences. Individuals
who wanted more change and openness could move up the ladder to a more acculturated Mennonite group. But throughout
the process the "old" Mennonites continued to hold a majority
in their own camp. Leaders such as John F. Funk and later
Daniel Kauffman wielded major influence in defining and holding the center.

Each separate "old" Mennonite conference had its own
characteristics. The Lancaster body, somehow avoiding the 1847
Franconia schism, grew in numbers and expanded outward
more than did the Franconia. But in 1893 it experienced a
schism on its right wing. Virginia Mennonites mixed more with
their Protestant neighbors than did those in Pennsylvania. They
developed a particularly strong choral music tradition around
music teacher and publisher Joseph Funk (1778-1862) of
Singers Glen; an early mission outreach among mountain folk
of West Virginia; and, in 1917, the only Mennonite school of

higher education in the East. The Ontario conference developed in Canada's somewhat different environment. Nevertheless, that conference's primary identification was southward across the border to "old" Mennonites in the United States rather than westward to Dutch-background Mennonites in the prairie provinces.

The Ohio conference was shaped by the presence of nineteenth-century immigrants from Switzerland and Alsace, whose understandings of Mennonitism were not the same as those of fellow settlers from the American Mennonite East. The Indiana conference led in midwestern institutional developments for publication, education, and missions. In 1872 and 1874 the Yellow Creek congregation west of Goshen, Indiana, underwent far-reaching schisms led by Daniel Brenneman, a revivalist progressive, and by Jacob Wisler, a traditionalist. The Illinois conference, located on a later frontier and close to influences from Chicago, was more progressive. By the 1930s it was "regularly under surveillance as to whether or not it should be excluded from the body, or at least shunned."[45]

The ebb and flow of westward settlement resulted in the extinction of many informal and formal Mennonite congregations in Ohio, Indiana, Illinois, and in other midwestern and western states. The same ebb and flow created new and thriving congregations. Amish Mennonites showed similar variety.

2. *Reformed Mennonites.* In 1890 the Reformed Mennonite Church, founded by John Herr in Lancaster County in 1812, was a conservative and exclusive group. Its people vigorously exercised the ban (excommunication) and avoidance (social shunning of banned members). Such strict enforcement of group conformity seemed to inhibit long-range growth. In 1890, according to the U.S. Census, they had 1,655 members in 34 congregations, more than half of them in Pennsylvania. During the twentieth century the group suffered a gradual decline of membership.[46]

3. *Mennonite Brethren in Christ.* This group was an amalgamation of a number of smaller ones, including two from Ontario, who had left more traditional Mennonites to take up a warmer piety and evangelistic zeal.[47] Gradually they had abandoned the stricter separatist rules of the old ways and taken on the organizational patterns of Methodism and the doctrines of the holiness movement. The first Mennonite women ministers (Janet Douglass, Mary Ann Hallman, Katie Hygema—1885), as

well as the first Mennonite overseas missionary (Eusebius Hershey to Liberia in 1890), came from this group. In 1878 their strongest leader, Daniel Brenneman (1834-1919), founded a conference periodical, *Gospel Banner*. In 1890 the Mennonite Brethren in Christ had three conferences (Pennsylvania, Ontario, and Indiana-Ohio) with a total membership of about 2,390. More than other Mennonites they succeeded in winning converts of non-Mennonite background, but at the price of losing Mennonite identity. In 1947 they changed their name to the United Missionary Church.

4. *Old Order Mennonites*. Between 1872 and 1900 the conservative resisters of change among the "old" Mennonites withdrew to form separate groups in Indiana and Ohio (1872), Ontario (1889), Pennsylvania (1893), and Virginia (1900).[48] Originally they were labeled "Wisler" Mennonites after Bishop Jacob Wisler of the Yellow Creek congregation in Elkhart, Indiana. Holding onto the German language and rejecting revivalism, Sunday schools, and missions, they constituted the right wing on the continuum of Swiss Mennonite attitude toward the world. In 1890, before the addition of a "Jonas Martin" group in Lancaster County, there were about 1,110 Old Order Mennonites in Indiana, Ohio, and Ontario. Another Old Order Mennonite fragment was the Stauffer Mennonite church, begun in 1845. In 1890 Stauffer Mennonites were located mainly in Lancaster and Snyder counties in Pennsylvania and in a small communitarian group in Osceola County, Iowa.

B. Amish

In the latter half of the nineteenth century, Amish congregations in America underwent a major realignment. Differences of religious practice had appeared among Amish congregations separated by geography, time of immigration, and environment. A series of general conferences from 1862 to 1878 endeavored to reconcile the differences, but in the end the Amish separated into four groups plus additional fragments.

1. *Old Order Amish*. The Old Order Amish formed some of the most highly regulated communities in the Mennonite family.[49] When others accepted the popular and handier buttons, they held to the hook-and-eye fasteners which had been a point of distinction since 1693. When others erected church buildings for worship, the Old Order Amish continued to build homes and organize communities in ways to keep worship in

their houses. When shaving became common, Old Order Amishmen continued to grow beards. When some others grew lax in discipline, the Old Order Amish continued to shun the errant. When others organized regional and national institutions for their churches, the Old Order Amish continued to forego centralized administration, publications, and boards for mission and education. Extreme decentralization, and especially an absence of centralized conferences to make policy, produced remarkable variation in the prescribed rules from one community or region to another.

Nonetheless, the Old Order Amish experienced substantial vitality and growth in twentieth-century America. In doing so they defied the predictions of progressive critics who looked down on their allegedly "fossilized" ways. Their religious communities remained close-knit and met their members' basic human needs. So they were able to attract and hold their own large families in numbers sufficient to ensure a long-range future. In 1890 the U.S. Census reported a total of 2,038 members in 22 congregations. There were another six congregations in Ontario.

2. *Amish Mennonites.* Between 1889 and 1893 most of the more progressive Amish—those more ready to accept language change, meetinghouses, and some relaxation of dress rules—organized themselves into three district conferences: the Indiana-Michigan Amish Mennonite conference (1889), the Western Amish Mennonite conference (Kansas-Nebraska, 1890), and Eastern Eastern Amish Mennonite conference (Ohio-Pennsylvania, 1893). All three became part of the constituency of John F. Funk's *Herald of Truth* and began a path toward affiliation with the "old" Mennonites. Although the Amish Mennonites were of the more conservative Amish stream of Mennonite history, one barrier to "old" Mennonite and Amish Mennonite union was that often in fact the Amish Mennonites were the less prescriptive in their enforcement of rules. Polity of the Amish Mennonites was more congregational, and therefore would need adjustment before there could be affiliation with the more episcopal "old" Mennonites. The U.S. Census of 1890 listed 10,101 Amish Mennonite members in 97 congregations. The states with the largest numbers of Amish Mennonites were (in order) Ohio, Illinois, Indiana, Pennsylvania, and Iowa, each with more than 1,000 members.[50]

3. *Stuckey Amish.* Joseph Stuckey (1825-1902), bishop of

the Rock Creek congregation in McLean County, Illinois, became the leader of a group of progressive Amish congregations in Illinois and formed alliances with others on the liberal Amish fringes in Iowa, Nebraska, and Indiana. Held together by their powerful leader, the Stuckey congregations did not formally organize a conference until 1899. They first took the name "Illinois Conference of Mennonites" and then "Central Conference of Mennonites." After 1912 they cooperated with the Egly, or Defenseless, Mennonites in the Congo Inland Mission. Leaders of the General Conference Mennonite church courted them, but not until 1946 did they join that branch. In the U.S. Census of 1890 the Stuckey Amish were included with the Amish Mennonite conferences even though they were on the road to a separate history.[51]

4. *Defenseless Mennonites.* Henry Egly (1824-1890) was a strong Amish bishop from Adams County, Indiana, with an emphasis on a definite personal experience of regeneration. Gradually he gathered under his leadership a group of Amish congregations. The "Egly Amish" took the name of "Defenseless Mennonites" and over the decades made a number of shifts in the direction of American evangelicalism. They began regular yearly conferences in 1895, established their own paper (*Heils-Bote*) in 1897, and incorporated in 1908. In 1948 they took the name "Evangelical Mennonite Church." In 1890, according to the U.S. Census, they had 856 members in 9 congregations, nearly half of them in Adams and Allen counties, Indiana.[52]

5. *New Amish (Apostolic Christian Church).* The Apostolic Christian Church was founded by Samuel Froelich, a dissenting Reformed minister in Switzerland in the 1830s, and their first congregation in America was organized in 1852. By 1890 some twenty-four congregations had been organized, mainly in Illinois and Ohio. Because the group was influenced by Mennonite teachings and succeeded in winning some Amish and Mennonite members, it was popularly identified as Amish or Mennonite. Actually it had a separate history. Both its beginning and its eventual development were outside the Amish-Mennonite stream.[53]

II. DUTCH

In 1890 there were a number of ethnically homogeneous Dutch-Russian Mennonite groups who, after arriving in America in the 1870s, had organized among themselves rather than merging with Swiss-background American Mennonites. The largest of these exclusively Dutch-Russian groups was the *Mennonite Brethren* (MB) which had grown out of a religious renewal movement and socioeconomic changes in the Ukraine in 1860.[54]

The Mennonite Brethren were influenced by European Pietism as well as by an effort to return to the vitality and the teachings of Menno Simons and Anabaptism. In 1879 under the leadership of elder Abraham Schellenberg in Kansas, the MBs organized a general conference with yearly meetings. By 1888 their conference periodical, *Zionsbote*, appeared and they were moving vigorously in evangelism and home and foreign missions. In 1909-1912 they reorganized into three district conferences--Southern, Central, and Pacific. The general conference continued to meet, triennially. Its people shared a common cultural orientation with other Dutch-Russian immigrants of the 1870s. Yet a special emphasis upon experiential conversion and baptism by immersion set them apart, especially from the *Kirchliche* Mennonites who came at the same time. In 1890 there were 1,388 MB members in the United States, located mostly in Kansas and Nebraska. Smaller numbers settled in Minnesota, South Dakota, Manitoba, and Saskatchewan.

The *Krimmer (Crimean) Mennonite Brethren (KMB)* were a smaller body that had originated in an evangelical renewal in the Crimea in 1869 and emigrated as an intact congregation to Kansas in 1874 under the leadership of elder Jacob A. Wiebe. Having been influenced in Russia by a group known as the *Kleine Gemeinde*, the KMBs were somewhat more strict than most other Dutch-Russian Mennonites in nonconformity to the world and in literal observance of scriptural commands such as the holy kiss. By 1890 the KMBs had three congregations in Kansas, one in Nebraska, and two whose members were ethnically different (people of Hutterite background) in South Dakota. Combining traditionalism with a strong missionary thrust, the KMBs in 1886 began "foreign" mission work among blacks in Elk Park, North Carolina. The proximity of KMBs to the MBs in geography, ethnicity, faith, and practice led to the merger of the two groups in 1960.[55]

In 1889 several Dutch-Russian congregations in Nebraska and Minnesota, which had separated from *Kirchliche* congregations in an emphasis upon spiritual rebirth and stronger church discipline, combined to form a *Conference of United*

Mennonite Brethren of North America.[56] This group underwent a number of name changes. In 1937 the group became "Evangelical Mennonite Brethren" and in 1987 the "Fellowship of Evangelical Bible Churches." It also formed temporary alliances with other groups, including the "old" Mennonites and the Evangelical Mennonite Church. Different modes of baptism inhibited cooperation with MBs, with whom it had much in common. The MBs baptized by immersion, the EMBs by pouring. Language and culture inhibited cooperation with Swiss-background "old" Mennonites. The Evangelical Mennonite Brethren grew slowly. In the twentieth century, influences from American evangelicalism led to a weakening of their historic Anabaptist-Mennonite identity.

Dutch-Russian Mennonites in America often had ties with groups in Canada of similar ethnic and family background, especially with migrants of the 1870s in Manitoba. Even for many Dutch-Russians in the General Conference Mennonite church, these north-south cultural ties were more decisive than organizational affiliation with Swiss-background Mennonites farther east. The Mennonites on the Canadian plains also were separated into a variety of subgroups, but in general they were more conservative and less inclined to become involved in missions, higher education, and the ways of organized denominationalism. Major migrations of Dutch-Russian Mennonites to Canada in the 1920s and 1940s contributed to a substantial increase of this broad stream of Mennonite people in North America.[57]

III. SWISS AND DUTCH COMBINED

The Swiss and Dutch associated together in the General Conference Mennonite church, which in 1890 was an association of 44 congregations with 5,231 members.[58] It was the largest Mennonite church conference in America to be successful in embracing an ethnic pluralism which included both the Swiss and Dutch streams of Mennonitism. Jacob H. Langenwalter of Halstead, Kansas, a young GC representative of south-German background, expressed amazement at the "marked differences in the customs" of Mennonites who hosted subsequent GC conferences. In 1902 it was the Jura Swiss at Berne, Indiana; in 1905 Dutch-Russians at Mountain Lake, Minnesota; and in 1908, Dutch-Prussians at Beatrice, Nebraska. "One begins to realize the social problems before the General Conference," Langenwalter wrote.[59]

In its slogan—"unity in essentials, liberty in nonessentials, and love in all things"—the GC body signaled its progressive and ecumenical intentions. Regulations of dress, so important for some groups, were among the nonessentials (although the 1890 conference meeting adopted a resolution "against all vanity and slavery to fashion"). Members of the conference sought unity in a broad statement of orthodox faith and in vigorous organizing for educational and missionary activity. The conference hoped to join with European Mennonites in cooperative missionary endeavors. At the 1890 conference in South Dakota eight congregations in Switzerland were represented with official (proxy) votes. In 1867 the GC branch organized a short-lived seminary (*Bildungs-Anstalt* or educational institute) in Wadsworth, Ohio; in 1880 it sent out its first missionary to Indian territory; and in 1890 it authorized legal incorporation of the conference.

In 1890 the GC body consisted of three districts—Eastern, Middle, and Western. The Eastern was the most cohesive, consisting primarily of congregations which had broken away from the Franconia conference in that progressive split of 1847.[60]

The Eastern District published an English-language monthly paper it called *The Mennonite*, edited by the dynamic Nathaniel B. Grubb, formerly a student at the Wadsworth school. Grubb was pastor of the First Mennonite Church of Philadelphia, in 1890 the only successful urban Mennonite church in the United States. Congregations of the Middle District were more scattered. After the Wadsworth Institute closed in 1878, initiative in the Middle District shifted to the First Mennonite Church of Berne, Indiana. There progressive Mennonites were actively involved in the public life of a small midwestern town.

The Western District, organized from 1877 to 1892 as the Kansas Conference, consisted mainly of congregations founded by immigrants of the 1870s to the American plains. Several Dutch-background congregations, such as the Alexanderwohl congregation in Marion County, Kansas, took leading roles in missions and education. But the Western District as a whole was an inter-Mennonite polyglot which included south Germans from the Palatinate and Bavaria, Prussians, Prussians via the Ukraine, Swiss via Volhynia, Prussians via Volhynia, Galicians, and Swiss.[61]

However, nearly every individual congregation was ethnically homogeneous. The cultural variety among the various congregations dictated a *congregational* polity for the Western District and for the General Conference branch as a whole. Delegates to national conferences represented congregations, not districts. Conference resolutions on faith and practice were advisory, not binding upon individual congregations.

Between 1890 and 1929 the GC fellowship grew from 44 to 159 congregations. The goal of the conference from its founding in 1860 was eventually to attract *all* other Mennonite congregations and districts to join under one denominational and organizational umbrella. From the progressive GC viewpoint this could happen as the forces of change detached traditionalist Mennonites from their cultural backwardness and taught the benefits of cooperative denominational action for education and mission. This stance meant that other groups perceived GC Mennonites as an ongoing threat—a magnet which might seduce individuals and congregations with alluring promises of respectability and upward mobility. In fact, most GC growth did come at the expense of other groups. Yet the GCs never realized their dream of ecumenical Mennonite hegemony. Other groups who accepted education and missions developed parallel organizations of their own.

Church of God in Christ, Mennonite (Holdeman). A second organized body of Mennonites with members of both Swiss and Dutch origin was founded by John Holdeman (1832-1900), a conservative visionary and reformer who broke with his "old" Mennonite church in Wayne County, Ohio, in 1859.[62] Holdeman was of Swiss ancestry, through families who had migrated to Ohio from Bucks and Montgomery counties in Pennsylvania. Holdeman's program consisted of stricter enforcement of the rules of church discipline, combined with evangelistic emphasis upon personal conversion. Among his own people he met little success; in the 1890s there were only about two hundred scattered Swiss-background (plus a few Lutheran-background) followers of Holdeman. The descendants of the Swiss were scattered in Ohio, Missouri, Michigan, West Virginia, Illinois, and Indiana. But Holdeman found a more substantial following—among two groups of Dutch-Russian Mennonites whose Low German household language he did not speak.

One group was the "Ostrogers," a poverty-stricken and leaderless cluster who had migrated from Antonofka village in Polish Russia to Kansas in 1874-1875. The other was the Kleine

Gemeinde, a small but more educated and well-established group which had originated in a schism in Russia in 1812 and migrated to Manitoba in the 1870s. There were, then, three main origins of the small (perhaps 500 to 600 members in 1890) Church of God in Christ, Mennonite. The two Low German groups in Kansas and Manitoba referred to those of Swiss background as "American Mennonites." The Dutch provided most of the members (70 to 80 percent), but the "Americans" provided the main leaders, partly because Kansas-Manitoba tensions made it necessary to find a leader from outside. Frederick C. Fricke (1867-1947), converted from Lutheranism in 1882, became leader after Holdeman's death.

The Church of God in Christ, Mennonite, remained a fascinating laboratory of intercultural Mennonite development. It was far more prescriptive and unitary in its formulation and administration of rules for doctrine and life than was the General Conference Mennonite church. All Holdeman men had to wear beards, and all women a special kind of dress and headgear. Under Fricke, who spoke English more comfortably than High German (and Low German not at all), this body gradually accepted English. Its basis of nonconformity, then, was quite different from that of Old Order Amish and Old Order Mennonite groups, who continued to use language as a badge and a guarantee of separation.

IV. OTHER GROUPS

The *Hutterian Brethren* (Hutterites), a branch of sixteenth-century Anabaptism which practiced community of goods, originated in Moravia. By the latter third of the sixteenth century the group had from 20,000 to 30,000 members in a hundred *Bruderhofs*, or farm colonies.[63] Early Hutterites, named after Jacob Hutter (d. 1536), had had ties with the Anabaptist Swiss Brethren. But an eastward movement combined with official persecution led to more associations with Mennonites in the Russian Empire. In the 1870s three Hutterite groups established settlements near Yankton, South Dakota. In 1890 they had only 352 members, but were beginning to enjoy substantial economic success and numerical growth. During the persecution of German-speaking Americans in World War I there was a major Hutterite migration to Canada. Members who left their communitarian society tended to join Mennonite groups who had arrived from the Russian Empire in the 1870s, especially (in South Dakota and California) the Krimmer Mennonite Brethren.[64]

Two additional groups with historic Mennonite affinities were the *Dunkers* (Church of the Brethren) and the *River Brethren* (Brethren in Christ). The Church of the Brethren was of combined Anabaptist and German Pietist background (beginning 1708), but was similar to the Mennonites in a number of doctrines and practices—nonresistance, nonconformity, foot washing, and the holy kiss. Their more aggressive evangelism and warmer piety attracted many Mennonite members in the colonial and early national periods. In the twentieth century the Church of the Brethren together with Quakers and Mennonites have cooperated as the "historic peace churches."[65]

The *Brethren in Christ* emerged from a revival in western Lancaster County about 1770 and attracted quite a few Mennonites who reacted against formalism in their own tradition.[66] This group also combined influences from both Pietism and Anabaptism. Moreover, in the late nineteenth and early twentieth centuries they were especially influenced by the Wesleyan holiness movement. In 1883 one fragment found its way into the Mennonite Brethren in Christ. After 1940 the Brethren in Christ expressed their kinship with the Mennonite churches by participating in the Mennonite Central Committee.

A SCATTERED AND SMALL-SCALE PLURALISM

Thus Mennonites and Amish had overlapping identities. The layers were European Swiss and Dutch ethnicity, regional East-West American differences, and a complex of organizational affiliations. So in 1890 they were a pluralistic collection of religious groups rather than one social or religious unity. There was no single normative Mennonite body of doctrine or social practice. Although leaders of several Mennonite bodies were more than willing to set forth norms for all true Mennonites to follow, no central Mennonite agent or institution had authority to establish such uniformity of teaching or behavior. The groups disagreed among themselves and divided from each other on practical issues ranging from how to choose leaders to what clothes to wear. Faced with this bewildering pluralism, one historian who endeavored to write a history of all Mennonites in a single state (Illinois) lamented, "I have become disillusioned with regard to the unity of my subject."[67]

Yet Mennonite pluralism flowered among a relatively small

population group. In 1890, according to the U.S. census, there was a total of only 41,541 Mennonite and Amish members in the United States.[68] These official figures were probably too low, for many Mennonite groups did not keep or report reliable statistics. But at most the Mennonites were a tiny religious minority, fewer than one-tenth of one percent of the 1890 American population (63,056,000).[69]

Nonetheless, Mennonite fragmentation did not cause a decline of membership even relative to the burgeoning American population. In four decades—1890 to 1930—with a high birth rate and substantial immigration, the American population nearly doubled. The Mennonite population grew correspondingly. In 1929 the census office reported a total of 100,505 Mennonites and Amish.[70] Whether or not this represented a doubling of membership (poor statistics make it impossible to be sure), it is clear that Mennonite pluralism and fragmentation did *not* prevent growth. Mennonites throughout this period were a tiny, fragmented minority, yet they were surviving and growing.

Mennonites and Amish were more keenly aware of membership losses than of gains. Nearly every family could count sons and daughters or nieces and nephews who had departed from the fold. When they compared themselves with some rapidly growing American denominations, their record seemed almost a failure. Around 1930 Mennonite leaders said that if they had held all of their own offspring or if they had done as well as the Methodists, they should have had five million members instead of a scant hundred thousand. Amos D. Wenger, evangelist and college president, listed thirty-one weaknesses that rendered Mennonites an "easy prey" to other groups. Mennonites, he wrote, were too resistant to revivalism and to the English language but too eager for politics and worldly amusements. They slid too easily into similar denominations or succumbed to "raids by heretical sects" such as Zionism, Russelism, Christian Science, and Seventh-Day Adventism.[71]

The Mennonites and Amish most vulnerable to loss of religious-ethnic identity were those who moved out to urban or agricultural frontiers which separated them from their groups. For a church whose major population center and ancestral heartland was in rural eastern Pennsylvania, westward scattering presented a great challenge. In 1890 Pennsylvania was home for 37 percent of the Mennonites in the country. Pennsylvania, Ohio, and Indiana—the main corridor of Mennonite westward settlement—accounted for 60 percent. Kansas, which in the 1870s had received an influx from the Russian Empire and Eastern Europe, had the third largest number of Mennonites in 1890, a total of 4,620. The drama of group decay and renewal had to do with the vitality of the established and populous settlements, and with the ability of newer and more isolated families and congregations to construct strong community life.

In coming to America to enjoy the benefits of religious freedom, material well-being, and strong communities, Mennonites necessarily subjected themselves to an open and pluralistic environment. The openness and pluralism challenged their faith and life as surely as had persecution and migration in Europe. In Europe Mennonites had been trapped as minority sectarians in societies dominated by established churches—Swiss Reformed, German Lutheran, Russian Orthodox. But in America Mennonites could hope to be accepted as equals among other nonestablished denominations. The denominational pattern in America allowed Mennonites to gain legitimacy and yet maintain a distinctive and separate identity. The Mennonite experience in America is a complex story of finding fulfillment and disappointment in many ways—even as they met, and sometimes failed to meet, the challenge of adjusting to a denominational society.

The traditionalists who resisted the transition were the starting point for popular images of Mennonitism. The Old Order Mennonites and Old Order Amish were picturesque people who attracted worldly attention. Ironically, they did so through their very efforts to be separate from the world.

CHAPTER

2

THE OLD ORDER
WAY OF YIELDEDNESS

Under cover of darkness on Thursday night, September 26, 1889, members of the Martin W. and Anna Martin Zimmerman family made their way about ten miles from their home to the newly built Lichty Mennonite meetinghouse in the Conestoga Valley of eastern Lancaster County in Pennsylvania. The brand-new meetinghouse, built of native Turkey Hill red sandstone, was to be used for the first time on the following Sunday. Standing on the western edge of Caernervon Township, near the Zimmerman graveyard and the Zimmerman lime kilns, it was to serve an "old" Mennonite congregation of the Lancaster conference, Weaverland district. Nearby to the south the Conestoga Creek wound westward past sawmills, gristmills, and cigar factories toward Lancaster city. Native sons and daughters thought the Conestoga Valley was "an American earthly paradise." The nighttime mission of the Zimmerman family showed that even in paradise, all was not well.[1]

THE PULPIT AND THE PREACHERS' TABLE

As they expected, the family found the meetinghouse locked. So they forced their way in by entering through a transom and unlocked the building from the inside. Quietly they attacked their enemy—a new pulpit and the raised platform on which it stood, midway along the northern wall of the meetinghouse. After loosening the pulpit from the platform, they deposited it in the cellar. In its place they put a traditional preachers' table which father Zimmerman had recently built. Then they stole home, undetected.

The pulpit vandalism became a local sensation. The Lichty

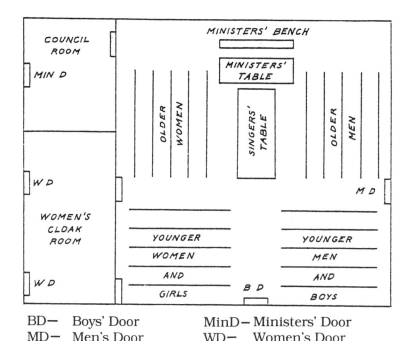

BD— Boys' Door   MinD— Ministers' Door
MD— Men's Door   WD— Women's Door

(Sondra Cronk, "Gelassenheit." p. 136, based on a sketch by Amos B. Hoover)

Weaverland Old Order Mennonite meetinghouse, 1894-1969.

church building committee had introduced the pulpit without permission from the congregation, bishop, or conference. No other Mennonite meetinghouse in the area had a Protestant-style pulpit. However, one minister in the district, John M. Zimmerman, had only one arm, and the committee reasoned that he needed a pulpit on which to lay his Bible. That reasoning prevailed despite opposition from Jonas Martin, the Weaverland district's tradition-minded bishop and overseer. The congregation did not have a Protestant-style dedication service for the new meetinghouse; such a ceremony might imply that a building wrought by human hands could be rendered holy. But some 1,200 persons attended the Sunday "first day of church," or (in the Pennsylvania Dutch dialect) *erst mohl g'meh*. No doubt they wanted to know what would be done about the absent pulpit. But neither bishop Martin nor any other speaker mentioned it.

Troubled months and years followed. One official committee after another investigated but failed to discover the vandals. At one point Martin excommunicated eleven people for discussing the matter irresponsibly. The pulpit incident was one event (not necessarily the most critical one) in an extended, stressful series of controversies which finally divided the Lancaster conference. In 1893 some conservatives withdrew and founded a Pennsylvania branch of Old Order Mennonites.

The old order option was not entirely new in Lancaster County. John Herr in 1812 and Jacob Stauffer in 1845 had led conservative secessions and had published extended defenses of their views. In the decades after the U.S. Civil War the Mennonites' coinheritors of Anabaptism, the Amish, had divided across the nation into the Old Order Amish and the Amish Mennonites. However, the clearest model for the 1893 schism in Lancaster County was a movement led by Jacob Wisler of Elkhart County, Indiana, in the 1870s.

In 1908, nineteen years after the pulpit incident and ten years after her husband had died, Anna Zimmerman decided to yield before the judgment of God and the church and confess her family's secret. The Zimmermans had suffered problems which she traced to their transgression. One daughter, Martha, who by some (not all) accounts had been along on the expedition, had joined the Jehovah's Witnesses. In any case, in 1908 Anna took the family's story to Lancaster conference bishop Benjamin Weaver (1853-1928). Astonished by the revelation, bishop Weaver quickly went to beg forgiveness of a younger man who for many years had been denied church fellowship on the mistaken charge that he had been the culprit. In a community of only a few family names (Lichty, Zimmerman, Weaver, Martin, Newswanger, Horst, Sauder, and Shirk), his name also was Martin Zimmerman.

PATTERNS OF OLD ORDER MENNONITE SCHISM

For all its drama in conservative, heartland Mennonite country, the pulpit incident was more symptom than substance. Old order schism had now come to bishop Jonas Martin's home congregation, Weaverland. The central issue was whether to introduce Sunday school. Martin did not want to. After all, by awarding stars to the winners of Bible memory contests, Sunday school teachers induced children to learn through competition rather than cooperation. Women taught classes, violat-

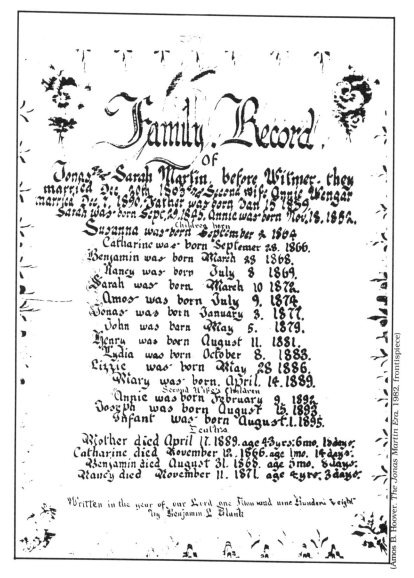

Record of births and deaths in the Jonas and Sarah Witmer Martin family (and second wife, Annie Wingar).

ing the scriptural injunction to remain silent in church. Men
rose to leadership through personal initiative and eloquence rather than by submitting to the community. The English
language displaced the German, and everyone sang new lyrics,
rhythms, and harmonies which stirred emotions rather than
convictions. There were other issues. Should ministers perform
marriage ceremonies for young people who were not yet church
members? Should the church allow members to vote in political
elections? What about lightning rods and property insurance?
On these issues and more, traditionalists and progressives
polarized. The 1893 schism was painful, but afterward there
was a time of restabilization. Both groups gained in membership. As decades passed, the split between "old" and Old Order
Mennonites became fixed. Both groups claimed to be faithful to
the ways of the ancestors.[2]

The "old" versus Old Order Mennonite schism had regional
patterns. Troubles that started in the West recurred in the East
about two decades later. "It grieves me that I have ever seen the
West," lamented bishop George Weaver (1818-1883), a Pennsyl-
vanian who had tried without success to conciliate during the
schism in Indiana.[3] In 1872 in Indiana and Ohio the "old" Mennonites separated from the "Old Order" who had supported Wisler, and vice versa. Many families who chose the old order path
were Martins, Weavers, and Hoovers who had cousins back in
the Conestoga Valley. Family visits and correspondence kept
Mennonites of Pennsylvania, Ohio, and Indiana in touch with
each other. Although many of the issues were the same as earlier in the 1845 Stauffer schism, in 1893 the fellowship and the
model of the West provided new inspiration for the old-order-
minded such as Jonas Martin and his friends. Also, in 1889, old
order congregations had emerged in Ontario. In 1901, partly
with the counsel of bishop Martin, others would emerge in Virginia.[4]

In the new century, in 1907, another series of schisms began among the Wisler group itself (with a similar twenty-year
lag from West to East). Once more, an old order bishop complained, "I hold that the whole disturbance comes out of the
West."[5] In Elkhart County, Indiana, John W. Martin (1852-1940),
a traditionalist bishop and son of a Lancaster County deacon,
led ten preachers and four deacons out of the semiannual Ohio
and Indiana (Wisler) conference. The issue was whether to allow
telephones. In the East, also in 1907, Old Order Mennonites un-

der the more diplomatic leadership of Jonas Martin avoided a "telephone split" by a compromise—forbidding telephones for ministers and deacons but allowing them for members who were willing to "bear the guilt" themselves.[6] But in 1927, two years after bishop Martin's death, his congregations divided over a similar issue, automobiles. The conservatives, soon known as the Groffdale conference or Wenger or "team" Mennonites, rejected the new device. Automobiles would allow members to travel to meeting while living farther from their own people. That pattern would loosen the bonds of community. By a different logic the Weaverland, or "Horning," branch of Old Order Mennonites, allowed automobiles so long as they were painted a solid black, bumpers and all. Black bumpers became a major mark of humility and separation from the world.

Another pattern in old order schism was that in general the traditionalist leaders were younger than the progressives. For example, in the Weaverland division of 1893 the average age of leaders in Jonas Martin's group was forty-six, while that of the more progressive leaders was sixty-four. The pattern was the same, although less marked, in the Wisler schism of 1907 and the Weaverland-Groffdale schism of 1927. A social scientist who gathered and analyzed these age patterns has confessed bewilderment. He had expected to find support for the conventional hypothesis that young people are innovative and progressive. Apparently something at the core of Old Order Mennonite values and lifestyle attracted the idealism of youth.[7]

Conventional sociological wisdom would predict also that traditional ideals are eroded by wealth.[8] Yet the statistics of Old Order Mennonite origins reveal no such pattern. The evidence is unclear. Sometimes progressive innovators were a bit wealthier, and sometimes the reverse. In 1927 Weaverland leaders who were ready to accept automobiles were less wealthy than were those who insisted upon horses and buggies.[9]

In individual cases some Old Order Mennonites became relatively prosperous. When they did, their wealth may have fostered more liberal attitudes. John S. Kurtz (1859-1927), who lived near Martindale in Lancaster County, was a successful Old Order minister, farmer, inventor, and business entrepreneur. He pioneered in the artificial incubation of chicken eggs, produced flour in his Keystone Mills, and manufactured the Keystone tongue support for horse-drawn binder shafts—an invention which found a national market. Although he was committed to old order ways, Kurtz was an agent of change. Because he found it awkward to use horse and wagon to transport industrial parts four miles from the rail line at New Holland, he was open to using trucks, automobiles, and telephones. He favored more use of English, particularly for funerals at which some people might not know German. He was married to Maria Horning, sister of Moses G. Horning, another relatively progressive man, who was ordained bishop in 1914 in a dramatic and controversial lot.[10] Although entrepreneurs such as John S. Kurtz undoubtedly brought some measured change, to most Americans the pace of old order change would have seemed very slow.[11]

In any case, in times of actual schism wealth was not a statistically significant matter. Lancaster County may have been full of prosperous ex-Mennonites who sought upward mobility outside the Mennonite churches. But the central dynamic of old order life itself was rooted in religious belief and tradition, not in sociological patterns such as age and wealth.

THE PATTERN OF YIELDEDNESS AND HUMILITY

Progressives in the "old" Mennonite and the General Conference Mennonite churches—persons who sought renewal through denominational organization and activity—understood old order traditionalists by what the old order groups rejected. What was more obvious than that the old order people *rejected* modernity and progress? Old order groups sometimes suffered new schisms; but otherwise, having apparently set their faces like flint against change, they seemed to progressives to have no eventful history. They founded no colleges, sent no missionaries, and started no homes for the aged. In short, they stood apart from the very movements and events which seemed to give shape and meaning to progressive Mennonites' denominational development. The progressives wrote the histories. So in popular understandings, Old Order Mennonites and Old Order Amish came up short.

However, for old order people themselves, life in community flowed from a set of positive values whose roots were in the Bible, the apostolic church, and the Anabaptist Reformation. From its outset old order life enjoyed vitality and growth which bespoke affirmative answers to the most fundamental questions in the human search for meaning. Old order people had their own ways of meeting needs—needs which others tried to meet through denominational institutions of higher education, publication, and mission. Elderly members did not need old people's homes; they lived with or near their families. Ministers did not need higher education; they had the Scriptures and a community-guided tradition of interpretation. For old order folks, social and religious life flowed more from what they affirmed than from what they rejected.[12]

The Zimmerman pulpit versus preachers' table showdown was only one clue to old order values of humility and yieldedness. The secret vandalism was an act of desperation in a time of impending schism. But even such an act pointed to the positive values which shaped old order life in more placid times. The raised pulpit and the ministers' table symbolized different understandings of Mennonite leaders' authority and how to exercise authority. A pulpit platform raised the minister above the level of the people of whom he was a part. A tall pulpit suggested "proud" leadership and an educated, professional, Protestant clergy.

Like Christ, Mennonite leaders were supposed to be servants. Ministers had no professional training nor were they paid. Young Mennonite men with genuine leadership potential were expected to have the virtues of humility and self-effacement rather than to claim a personal "call" or a gift for aggressive leadership. No aspiring minister would openly seek the burden of leading the church. Congregations chose ministers by "lot," a process which protected them against the consolidation of power which comes when leaders choose their own successors. For the lot, the congregation nominated candidates democratically: each member was allowed to submit one name. The nominees were examined for their willingness to obey God and the church, a promise implicit in their baptism. New ministers, deacons, and bishops were finally selected and ordained to office in a single solemn ceremony in which the candidates (as many as a dozen in a single lot) each chose a book from a set of songbooks on the singers' table. One book contained a slip with a certain Bible verse indicating that the holder had been chosen: "The lot is cast into the lap; but the whole disposing thereof is of the Lord" (Proverbs 16:33).

The lot conferred divine authority. Yet it was an authority of submission and humility, as Jesus had submitted in humility to the will of God and to the cross. Upon ordination new ministers and their families often made changes in their style of life, moving to conform more completely to the prescribed "order" of the church—the *Ordnung*. More than ever, they tried to avoid any appearance of testing the boundaries of acceptable behavior. In every Sunday sermon the minister included a ritual statement of his own unworthiness and of his openness to correction by the congregation. A minister who became arbitrary, arrogant, or personally willful was subject to discipline by fellow ministers and the congregation. Bishop Jonas Martin once confessed having visited the Chicago stockyards. Paradoxically, to have influence and a kind of power, ministers and bishops had to master the rituals of powerlessness, nonresistance, and humility.

Although from the outside the old order tradition has seemed static, it is rich in stories of momentous ordinations. In the spring of 1914 the Weaverland group chose an assistant bishop to work with Jonas Martin. Nominated were five candidates: Menno Zimmerman (3 votes), John Kurtz (6 votes), Frank Hurst (12 votes), Joseph Wenger (7 votes), and Moses Horning (2 votes). A visiting bishop from Virginia, a conservative named John Dan Wenger, was concerned that Moses Horning leaned toward allowing automobiles. Wenger proposed that the congregation require three votes for a candidate to be in the lot. But a deacon named Daniel Burkholder stood against this patent effort for human control over a divine process. If necessary, he said, he himself would add a vote for Horning in order to give him the necessary three. On ordination day, June 4, 1914, when bishop Martin asked Horning to choose his songbook from the table, the candidate was so overcome that he fainted. When he recovered and was again asked to take his book, he replied, "I can't." With one book left on the table the other candidates opened their books and discovered they were not chosen. Then Martin himself opened the remaining book and found the slip. Although conservative, he ordained the shaken Horning.[13] In the 1927 schism Horning would lead the group who accepted automobiles with black bumpers.

After such an awesome and humbling process it was important that ministers and bishops remain down on the people's level—not exalted on a pedestal or behind a proud pulpit. Silently, the architecture and arrangement of the Mennonite meetinghouse spoke an eloquent language of community solidarity. To bring everyone close, the ministers' bench stood in the middle of the long wall. The people entered the building and sat not in nuclear families but according to age, with different benches for young women, older women, young men, older men, girls, and boys. The arrangement emphasized corporate worship as communal activity in which all were brothers and sisters in Christ. In this sacred space the rituals of regular biweekly worship as well as of special occasions (baptisms, preparation services and communions, and funerals) had an ethical and legal quality rather than an otherworldly piety. Old order folk were not inclined to call any humanly created space "sacred." Their religious life was intentional, not sacramental. Members were baptized into the congregation not as infants but on the basis of personal confession of faith. They came as young adults, often after marriage. Usually theirs was a faith formed in community, not the product of sudden and emotional conversion. Church was not separate from living; instead, it provided the teaching, admonition, and discipline essential for ongoing community life.[14]

Old order daily life also was governed by written and unwritten rituals which reinforced the virtues of humility, yieldedness, and nonresistance. Members learned to speak and dress plainly and to care for each other without fanfare. There were prohibitions against military service, swearing of oaths, and participation in contentious politics. But formal restrictions affected daily life far less than did emphasis on hard, useful work by all family members, young and old. Tobacco farming was ideally suited for intergenerational family work, for it kept members working hard through much of the year. To old order folks that fact was more important than the allegedly evil effects of tobacco use. "Eliminate tobacco," said bishop Jonas Martin, "and pride comes in the congregation."[15] Young people should work at home on the farm, not be forced to seek work in the public world. Homelife, shared work, and the ritual of visiting—these knitted and reknitted the fabric of family and community.

There were rituals of active silence. Before and during worship services and before and after meals came quiet pauses. There also were more subtle silences—never speaking about any member's transgression once it had been confessed, and generally avoiding subjects that would introduce disharmony. Also, silence was often the defense when old order members were challenged or confused by outsiders. Any outsider inclined to join the group was not persuaded with words but through joining in community rituals. Momentous as it was, even the choice to become a church member became a time for silence rather than verbalizing. For both Amish and Mennonite old order groups, silence was a coping strategy and a way to remain separate and different from the world.[16]

On alternate Sundays there were no worship services, and old order folk used the time to keep in close touch. Visiting in small groups, members addressed both the momentous and the trivial. "I truly feel glad that you had paid us a visit," wrote J. S. and Maria Kurtz to Virginia bishop John Dan Wenger. "It is more natural and creates more love when we see the brethren face-to-face." And it enables us "to build up each other in the holy faith."[17] Old Order Mennonites wrote many letters to each other (typically signed with names of both husband and wife) and published many books of piety and song. But their most eloquent testimonies were in the unexplained and informal rituals of sharing in community.

THE *ORDNUNG*: BOOKS, VARIATION, AND CHANGE

Sustaining the Old Order Mennonite way of life were both written words and unreflective rituals. John Herr, Jacob Stauffer, and John Holdeman had led conservative schisms in 1812, 1845, and 1859 respectively. Each had written and published one or more extensive treatises justifying his actions and setting forth the theological rationale for holding onto his understanding of the old foundations.[18] But unlike them the spiritual leaders whom Old Order Mennonites followed in the late nineteenth and early twentieth centuries—Wisler in Indiana, Jonas Martin in Pennsylvania, Abraham Martin in Ontario, and John Dan Wenger in Virginia—published no books. Nor did they begin an old order church periodical. Wenger did produce a number of tracts, beginning about 1907 with a twelve-page item against Sunday schools; and Abraham Martin wrote an extensive but unpublished critique of Jacob Stauffer's 1850 book.[19] Yet the Old Order Mennonites gave the overall impression of a religious community whose literary foundation was already in place and who therefore saw no reason to extend theological polemics. Ritual was more important than word.

Old Order Mennonites did indeed consider some books important. First, of course, was the Bible. For them the Bible was a historic drama of redemption more than a body of specific law to govern the details of community life. The teachings of

Christ were to be taken seriously; old order people paid great attention to the Sermon on the Mount (Matthew 5–7). Along with the Bible, Old Order Mennonites used a number of books from the European Anabaptist-Mennonite tradition, especially Dirk Philips' *Enchiridion* (1564), Thieleman Jansz van Braght's *Martyrs Mirror* (1660), Gerhard Roosen's *Christliches Gemütsgespräch* (1702), and Jacob Denner's *Christliche und erbauliche Betrachtungen* (1730). Denner's sermons were a major source of Pietist influence. So were several books by a prominent Lutheran Pietist, Johann Arndt. One non-Mennonite European book found in nearly every Old Order Mennonite home in the nineteenth century offered morning and evening prayers for each day of the week—Johann Habermann's *Morgen und Abendgebete* (1567). Old Order Mennonite piety drew strength from various printed sources. Not all of them fit the shape of old order religious and social life, however. The writings of Habermann, Denner, and Arndt emphasized inward piety rather than the church as a disciplined community of believers.

Old Order Mennonites also used books written earlier by American Mennonites who had charted the way for a separate people of humility and nonresistance. They considered themselves the true inheritors of a tradition defined in such works as Heinrich Funck's *Restitution* (1763) and *A Mirror of Baptism* (1744), Christian Burkholder's *Address to Youth*, John M. Brenneman's *Christianity and War* (1863) and *Pride and Humility* (1867), and Jacob Stauffer's *Eine Chronik oder Geschicht-Büchlein* (1855). If Old Order Mennonites added anything to the tradition, their new ideas or insights were not the kind to be transmitted through the printed page. Their genius was to use the inherited values to meet the practical challenge of maintaining a counterculture—a communal yieldedness in a world of increasing individualism and aggression.

Partly written but mostly assumed, there was a structure of rules which governed old order life in community. It was called the *Ordnung*. Acceptance of the *Ordnung* was prerequisite to baptism. The baptism ritual included a specific commitment to the process of group discipline of Matthew 18, which says that offenders are to be dealt with first privately, then in a small group, and finally by the church. Ideally, the purpose of group discipline was to "gain the brother" back to the community.[20]

As new conditions posed challenges to core values, the *Ordnung* was subject to revision. Leaders did not insist that congregations in different areas keep their rules exactly uniform. Old order life included variations which helped it adapt to a changing environment. Yet within the variations old order members maintained a strong sense that order undergirded community life. So they nurtured an ability to respond to changes in technology and fashion in terms of their own values of love, humility, and simplicity.

Virginia was different from Pennsylvania. No one ever doubted that bishop John Dan Wenger of Virginia was a conservative old order leader. But he did not turn back the clock entirely on changes that occurred before Virginia's old order schism of 1900. The state's Mennonites were more scattered than those in the Pennsylvania heartland and had absorbed more influences from non-Mennonite neighbors. Virginia's old order ministers therefore preached in English from raised pulpits, and their congregations made much use of English songbooks. To instruct baptismal candidates, the Virginians also adopted a different catechism book than was used in Pennsylvania. While others used confessions compiled by Christian Burkholder and Benjamin Eby, they used an English translation of a volume by Peter Burkholder which included a version of the thirty-three articles of faith printed in the opening section of the *Martyrs Mirror*.[21]

Meanwhile Ontario's Old Order Mennonites drew still different lines. When "falling" buggy tops (more open and jaunty in style than strictly rectangular ones) became controversial across the old order communities, only Ontario held to the conservative line and refused them.[22] In 1922 another form of accommodation came in Pennsylvania with a kind of halfway covenant for automobile owners: they were held back from communion without being dismissed from membership. The use of different hymnals showed another kind of variety, which in turn reflected different degrees of evangelical influence.[23]

Nevertheless, the differences from region to region did not necessarily mean differences in the principle of *Ordnung*. The Old Order Mennonites were not a hierarchically organized denomination; they did not intend that an overarching denominational structure should exist and enforce uniformity among districts. If a given congregation became too innovative, visitors came from elsewhere to discuss matters and give counsel—not dictate. What counted was the quality of life in community. When it functioned properly, the *Ordnung* helped to guarantee community.

Old Order Mennonites often resisted new inventions or fashions which seemed, at the time society adopted them, to foster social distinction and pride. But once society had made such innovations commonplace and the changes no longer threatened the old order quality of community, the *Ordnung* accommodated. Thus, in time, old order women began to use china dishes rather than traditional metalware. They also used sewing machines, but not to make fancy ruffles. Men adopted farm machinery that did not displace hard work as family activity. "As new inventions came, old had to go, to make it so much the easier on the farm near Martindale," wrote old order farmer Menno Weaver (1887-1963) in 1927. Weaver took forty-four tablet pages to chronicle technological changes his people had accepted. The binder had displaced hand-tying of bundles of oats. The stationary motor-driven thresher had replaced the horse-powered threshing machine. The two-row corn planter and two-horse shovel harrow had replaced the one-row models. A mechanical tobacco planter had replaced hand planting. Hay loaders and side rakes had replaced one-horse rakes. The circular buzz saw had replaced the bucksaw. And gasoline engines on rubber tires had replaced engines on iron wheels.[24]

Such changes revealed a community not frozen in time but adapting at its own pace, for its own purposes. On many matters the *Ordnung* regulated the pace of change rather than serving as a fixed instrument to express God's unchanging will. It guided adaptation in ways that protected the community's core values.

Despite many marks of social and religious separation, Old Order Mennonites had to be involved in their regions' broader economic life. Menno Weaver wrote of making visits each fall to the Lancaster stockyards "to see what the Jews have to sell" and to buy cattle "as cheap as we could."[25] Letters passing between regions included information about economic life as well as about family and church. From Michigan, far away from tobacco country, Matilda Dettwiler and her daughter Susanna Switzer wrote back to Pennsylvania about the prices they received for butter, eggs, hens, potatoes, beans, and beets.[26] Always in contact with the outside world, old order folk became a people who adjusted to American society in their own way. They did not refuse to adapt.

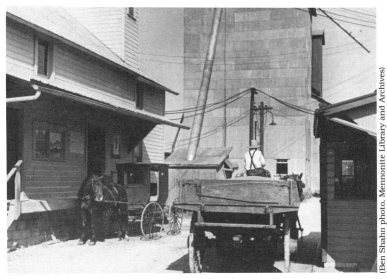

(Ben Shahn photo. Mennonite Library and Archives)

Amish farmers deliver grain at Plain City, Ohio.

PERMEABLE WALLS OF SEPARATION

"It is so deplorable that the old Mennonite ground is being lost to such an extent," wrote Jonas Martin in 1896 to a conservative minister of the Franconia conference named Jacob Mensch.[27] Mensch agreed. Had there been an old order congregation in his area, he probably would have joined. But in an 1847 division Franconia had shed its progressive "new" Mennonite wing, and in the 1890s the remaining body was still conservative enough to avoid an old order division. So while Martin led an old order departure, Mensch remained "old" Mennonite. The two leaders fellowshiped and supported one another through correspondence but would not speak in each other's congregations. Holding to "the old Mennonite ground" required walls of separation between Mennonite groups as well as between Mennonites and the world.

Indeed, the severest threats to Old Order Mennonite survival and growth came not from the secular and materialistic world but from nearby Mennonite or Church of the Brethren groups. These might offer old order members a less austere and more pietistic religiosity. The old order was always vulnerable to the charge that the *Ordnung* was a formula for seeking salvation through human works rather than God's grace. In fact, Old Order Mennonites were theologically orthodox. The third article of the 1632 Dordrecht Confession of Faith spoke of Jesus, the Savior, the Word made flesh, whose death on the cross provided redemption for all people. But they rehearsed the drama of redemption in rituals of the congregation of believers and in their life in community more than in theological argument or statements of orthodox belief.

All Mennonites in America and the old order groups in particular faced a special problem in adapting their religious understandings and rituals to the transition from persecution to toleration. Early Anabaptists' and Mennonites' identity had been forged in martyrdom. Their most important hymnbook, the *Ausbund*, was a collection of martyr verses. Their most important history book was the *Martyrs Mirror*. But relatively tolerant America crucified and burned no Mennonites. How could a suffering faith sustain vitality and relevance for a nonsuffering people? The absence of suffering had brought new understandings of Christian discipleship and identity. But in the transition, what assurance was there that the powerful forces of American individualism would not overwhelm and destroy a central Anabaptist-Mennonite commitment—commitment to the church as a community of believers responsible to each other and to God?

In subtle ways, individualistic emphases from European Pietism and American revivalism entered into old order life.[28] Pietist devotional literature, which Old Order Mennonites read, used the concept of yieldedness (*Gelassenheit*). The concept was very important to old order people. But Pietists typically put the greater emphasis on yieldedness in one's personal relationship to God, and somewhat less upon the ethical implications of yieldedness within the community of believers. A Pietist emphasis upon right living struck a responsive chord among Mennonites who believed in discipleship. The Pietist version could erode Mennonite ways. To a degree it detached right living from disciplined living in community. Pietism was more individualistic.[29]

Pietist or revivalist influences were quite pronounced in old order hymnody. Already at the beginning of the nineteenth century the Lancaster and Franconia conferences had adopted new hymnbooks which departed from the earlier *Ausbund* emphasis on martyrdom as the central symbol of obedience and yieldedness. Borrowing from Reformed and other sources, a Franconia conference hymnal of 1803 kept only two hymns from the *Ausbund*. By the end of the nineteenth century there had been further changes, and Mennonite singing showed considerable variety. Some songs and hymns emphasized the sovereignty and glory of God. But Pietist and revivalist influences had brought a shift toward a sweeter Jesus who consoled the suffering rather than a Lord who called followers to suffering discipleship. Thus Old Order Mennonites sang "Sweet Hour of Prayer," "What a Friend We Have in Jesus," and "Rock of Ages Cleft for Me, Let Me Hide Myself in Thee."

In contrast, hymns directly from the Anabaptist-Mennonite tradition had a martyrdom theme. As a typical text from the *Ausbund* proclaimed: "Christ's servants follow him to death/ And give their body life and breath/ On cross and rack and pyre." Whether borrowings from a different hymn tradition really made Old Order Mennonites vulnerable to individualistic forms of American Protestantism is impossible to prove. The songs were adapted to the old order ritual of chantlike singing. That form was probably more significant than the literal meaning of the words. The group had worked out its own balance between individual and community.[30]

Although they were known for group conformity, there were two important ways Old Order Mennonites preserved individual freedom. Unlike Hutterites and other communitarian groups, they retained private property. And they maintained the Anabaptist tradition of adult baptism. Some Mennonite groups who accepted the patterns of American revivalism began to baptize preadolescents as young as eleven and twelve years, if they could claim the experience of conversion. To Old Order Mennonites baptism was a sign of both personal faith and subordination to the body of believers; so they held firmly to the pattern of mature individuals freely choosing to live in regulated community. One cost of their high standards was that they lost quite a few young people to other Mennonite groups, groups with less stringent requirements and more accommodations to revivalism. Three generations after the 1893 schism, Jonas Martin had more descendants in the Lancaster "old" Mennonite conference than did the seven bishops who had expelled him.[31]

OLD ORDER AMISH

Although Old Order Mennonites and Old Order Amish both took on their "Old Order" designation in the latter part of the nineteenth century, they had quite different identities. Separate histories had begun in 1693, with the Amish-Mennonite schism in Europe. In America in the eighteenth and nineteenth centuries Amish immigrants settled in communities which were sometimes adjacent to Mennonites but often some miles away. By 1890 the total estimated Old Order Amish population was 3,700 persons, with the largest settlements in and near Lancaster County, Pennsylvania; Holmes County, Ohio; and Elkhart and Lagrange Counties, Indiana. Four decades later, by 1930, the population had increased fivefold, to 18,500 persons. The three largest settlements had more than doubled in size, and there were Amish districts in more than a dozen states.[32] The Holmes County vicinity eventually held the largest concentration of Old Order Amish in the world.

Mennonite and Amish old order people shared common emphases: strict group discipline, careful control of technological innovation, and a premium on humility and nonresistance. But they were not interested in union or merger. This was partly because the administrative skills and techniques of denominational organizing went against the old order ethos of humility and yieldedness. To build denominational institutions required aggressive individuals. Partly also, such union would also have had to overcome differences in church life. With rare exceptions the Amish worshiped in homes, the Mennonites in meetinghouses. Worship in homes kept Amish districts small, for no congregation could grow too large for an Amish house. Also, the Amish held onto the *Ausbund* and its martyr hymns, while the Mennonites accepted newer collections. But perhaps the greater inhibitor of broad cooperation and union was the commitment of all old order folk to humble and simple living in small primary communities. Their ethos did not invite broad denominational organization and ideas of merger.

The number of Old Order Amish grew. It did so despite individuals who chose to leave (about one fifth of family members), and despite some congregations' deciding to join other Amish Mennonite or Mennonite bodies. In the third quarter of the nineteenth century a great, though somewhat gradual, division had occurred. The Amish had divided into two groups, the more progressive Amish Mennonites and the more traditionalist

Old Order Amish. Many of the Amish Mennonites then
organized into three district conferences—Eastern, Indiana-
Michigan, and Western—which eventually joined the "old" Mennonites. Other progressive Amish groups, such as the Stuckey
Amish (mostly in Illinois) and the Egly Amish (mostly in Indiana) organized independently. In 1910 some conservative
Amish from Michigan, Ohio, and Pennsylvania met to form a
body not affiliated with Amish Mennonites but also not as conservative as Old Order Amish. This body, later known as
Conservative Amish Mennonites, organized new activities, including Sunday schools, an orphanage, and mission work.[33] The
differentiation and realignment of Amish groups varied widely
in different places and times. The Iowa Amish, for example, did
not separate as rapidly and as clearly into Old Order Amish and
Amish Mennonites as did most others.[34] Before 1927 there were
four major groupings of Amish in North America. On a liberal-
conservative continuum they ranged from left to right as follows: Stuckey Amish and Egly Amish, Amish Mennonites, Conservative Amish Mennonites, and Old Order Amish.

BEACHY AMISH

In 1927, in the Casselman River district of Somerset
County, Pennsylvania, a "Beachy Amish" division took place and
soon became linked to a new group from another division in
Lancaster County. In both cases the roots of the separation
went back to the 1890s.[35] In effect the Beachy Amish established another option on the continuum, at a point between the
Old Order Amish and the Conservative Amish Mennonites. Their
leader was an Amish bishop named Moses M. Beachy. Setting
off the schism was an issue of how to relate socially to former
Old Order Amish members who had left to join a nearby Conservative Amish Mennonite congregation at Grantsville, Maryland. The Conservatives had English sermons in nearly every
worship service and not many younger men wore beards.
Orthodox old order regulations required that ex-members be
placed under strict shunning (*streng Meidung*). Beachy refused
to comply, and old order ministers came from other communities to mediate. When reconciliation failed, the traditionalists of Beachy's congregation, choosing to stay in fellowship with the Old Order Amish, withdrew. Their leader was one
Moses Yoder. Since 1881, atypically for Old Order Amish, the
congregation had worshiped in meetinghouses. After the divi-

sion, for twenty-six years, both sides continued to use the same buildings. Meanwhile bishop Beachy's congregation became independent and gradually made other changes, especially organizing Sunday schools and allowing electricity and automobiles. But the Beachy Amish avoided other changes which would have made them no different from the Conservative Amish Mennonites.[36]

Beachy's people worked out what they considered a middle way. They actually tightened some rules; kept the traditional haircut and full beard; used only German for preaching (except for funerals); and in worship, sang in unison and only in German. Theirs was a new option which would be attractive to those who wanted to be traditionally Amish in language, worship, and appearance but who also wanted automobiles and electricity. Beachy had no grand design to found another Amish branch. But groups in other places felt drawn to his synthesis and his leadership. By 1929 his people were in fellowship with some at Bird in Hand in Lancaster County, Pennsylvania, whose leader was bishop John A. Stoltzfus. The Stoltzfus group, later known as the Weavertown congregation, was part of a segment who in 1911 had broken from the Old Order Amish over shunning and electricity yet continued to worship in homes and reject automobiles. In the 1930s and later, other groups joined with the "Beachy Amish Mennonite Fellowship." The label joined the names of three religious leaders, each from a different century.[37]

Although the issue of strict shunning had been pivotal in Beachy Amish origins, later movements from Old Order to Beachy Amish usually had to do with interpretation of the *Ordnung*. Gradually the Beachy Amish Mennonites accepted changes well beyond those the founders had envisioned. Meanwhile, it seemed to Old Order Mennonites and Old Order Amish that the urge to grasp new technologies often involved the sin of pride—*Hochmut*. The automobile appealed to the same worldly impulses that made young men want to wear mustaches and young women to wear fancy hats.

Yet more was at stake than pride. In ways Mennonites only dimly understood, the twentieth-century technological revolution in American transportation and communication threatened the underpinnings of small community. A congregation of mutually committed and disciplined believers needed to live close together and be bound together by frequent face-to-face

meetings as they made decisions for farm, home, and congregation. Horse-drawn transportation dictated that no family live
farther away from the meetinghouse than the distance it could
easily travel in a buggy. Automobiles made it possible for members to drive so far to church that the congregation would not
be sharing the week's day-to-day living. Old Order Mennonite
and Amish ways resisted such unnatural separation of worship
and daily life.

To resist the powerful lures of American industrial and
capitalist society, old order people necessarily resorted to practices which others saw as hair-splitting legalism. But their
warnings about pride were close to their mark. "If we open the
door for the auto, we are in line with the fast element, [and] . . .
the language of the Prophet Amos 6:1-6 will be disregarded,"
wrote John Dan Wenger of Virginia.[38] Had not the prophet
warned in Amos 6:1, "Woe to them that are at ease in Zion"?

OLD ORDER MENNONITE AUTOMOBILE DIVISION—1927

In 1927, just as Beachy was beginning his new Amish
group, Old Order Mennonites divided in Lancaster County. Unlike the bitter 1893 schism, this was a "friendly" separation
and did not chart new territory. Jonas Martin died in 1925.
While he lived, his church exercised firm discipline against
automobile owners. In 1910, for the first time, it expelled one.
In 1922 it relaxed the rule to the point of allowing such people
to remain as members, but in a kind of limbo, excluded from
communion and active congregational involvement. They were
called "half back" (*halwer zurick*) members.[39] After Martin's
death his successor, Moses Horning, so timid at his ordination
and always a man of quiet temperament, responded more and
more to pro-automobile pressures. He hardly thought it consistent to exclude automobile owners and yet accept persons
who regularly used others' cars.[40]

Among traditional Mennonites communion was a ritual
which not only celebrated the sacrifice of Christ but also tested
and confirmed relationships of those in fellowship. By the time
of spring communion in 1927 bishop Horning had relaxed the
discipline, and so a large number of conservative members
refused to participate. Led by a minister named Joseph O.
Wenger, the conservatives decided to meet separately. Soon they
were known as "Wenger Mennonites," the "Groffdale conference," or the "team Mennonites." Like the "Beachy" and

"Yoder" Amish in Somerset County, the Horning and Wenger Mennonites (both still considered to be part of the old order) continued to use the same meetinghouse. The "Horning" group, later known as the Weaverland conference, accepted automobiles but developed that rule whereby bumpers and all were painted black. The rule was to prevent fancy adornment. Indirectly of course, it helped draw a line of difference from more worldly people. The Horning Mennonites remained quite conservative and not inclined to support missions, Sunday schools, and other denominational activities as the Beachy Amish eventually came to do.

The 1927 "automobile split" reordered the affiliations of these Lancaster County folk with Old Order Mennonites elsewhere. The Virginia Old Order Mennonites held the line against automobiles and associated with the Groffdale conference. Among the "Wisler" Old Order Mennonites in Indiana and Ohio, there had been a telephone split in 1907, a division which had hampered relationships with the Lancaster-area folk. From 1907 to 1927 Jonas Martin's people did not want to take sides in a way that would endanger their own unity. However, after the 1927 automobile separation in Lancaster County contacts once again flourished with the Midwest. Now with two Old Order Mennonite groups in each area, each group could affiliate with a like-minded counterpart.[41]

Amish and Mennonite proliferation would continue in the coming decades; so the Mennonite-Amish spectrum would become even more variegated and confusing. The process revealed the great paradox of unity and diversity which characterized old order life.[42] On the one hand, old order people strove mightily for a disciplined unity. At the high price of socially shunning their own beloved family and congregational members who chose to deviate from the *Ordnung*, old order leaders worked incessantly to define common standards of life for their scattered settlements. On the other hand, they made way for local autonomy and variety. They did not create overarching regional, state, or national creeds, rules, or enforcement agencies to dictate styles of clothing, transportation, or worship. They visited and counseled with each other but preserved a good measure of local choice.

The largest miracle of the old order churches was not their many schisms but their ability to survive, grow, and be vital through the twentieth century. Their vitality did not include

missionary outreach; on that point they deviated from the New
Testament norm. Progressive Mennonites and Amish claimed
that they needed colleges to hold the young people and that denominational boards were necessary to carry on the church's
work. Yet old order peoples demonstrated the ongoing viability
of a humbler, more simple way.

A further consequence of the technological revolution and
the proliferation of Mennonite and Amish groups was greater
and greater cultural distance between the most conservative
and most liberal. When some groups accepted the radio in the
1930s, television in the 1950s, and many other changes along
the way, they increasingly entered a world alien to old order
folks. As gaps widened, it became more difficult for individuals
to move across them. It remained a struggle for all Amish and
Mennonites to recognize themselves as part of one family of
faith.

THE AMISH AND MENNONITE MOSAIC

Old Order Amish and Old Order Mennonites have long been
seen as being at the right-wing or conservative end of a continuum based upon attitudes toward change. In their resistance
to change, their holding onto what they called the "old Mennonite ground," they could claim to be the only true Mennonites
while other groups deviated. Of all Mennonites and Amish the
old order peoples seemed to be the least modernized, the least
Americanized, the most stubbornly traditionalist. They seemed
to be the quintessential Mennonites.

In fact, the old order peoples were part of a mosaic of Mennonite groups, all of whom had made and were making functional adaptations to life in America. Other groups were more
open to progressive change, but as long as they claimed to be
Mennonite they could never fully escape the old order definition. Each part of the mosaic had its own cultural expressions,
its own means of renewing religious group vitality, its own dis-
ciplines and rituals for maintaining identity while coming to
terms with the tolerant and pluralistic American democratic
environment. In the interdependence that gave unity to the
Mennonite mosaic, Old Order Mennonites and Old Order Amish
had a special influence upon the others—whether or not the influence was immediately recognized. They were very tenacious
in holding to their ways. They were prolific and supplied sons
and daughters for other Mennonite groups. They survived and

thrived far beyond the expectations of any melting-pot or acculturation theorists. For all those reasons, the old order people lent definition to the Mennonite experience in America.

Mennonites of the Dutch-Prussian-Russian wing were ethnically and genealogically unrelated to those old order folks, who were of Swiss and south-German background. Yet even they had to reckon with being members of a common peoplehood.

3

THE DUTCH-RUSSIAN
CONGREGATION CHRISTENDOM

For the New Alexanderwohl Mennonite church on the plains of central Kansas, August 17, 1890, was no ordinary Sunday. On that day the congregation's elders laid hands on Cornelius H. Wedel, age thirty, to ordain him minister of the gospel.[1] On the north balcony with the other unmarried young women sat Susanna Richert, Wedel's fiancée, one of Alexanderwohl minister Heinrich Richert's seventeen children. The ordination signaled not only an ordinary passing of churchly authority to a younger generation but also a transition from traditional lay leaders to leadership of a new kind: educated, prepared to guide a modern denomination. Wedel was a young man fresh from theological studies at Bloomfield Seminary in New Jersey. Control was passing from patriarch to professional. Two decades later, in 1910, he would die untimely; but while he lived he became the only educated Mennonite in America before the 1930s to articulate a modern understanding of the Christian faith and still keep the confidence of his people.

ORDINATION FOR CHURCH AND SCHOOL

Of the elder patriarchs who ordained Wedel, each belonged to a different congregation. They were Jacob Buller of New Alexanderwohl, Leonhard Suderman of Emmaus, Jacob Toews of Newton, and Christian Krehbiel of Halstead. The four were an average of thirty years older than Wedel. Each had experienced momentous transitions in his own life. In 1874 elder Buller had led his congregation from the Ukraine, to Kansas.[2] Elder Suderman had been born in Prussia, emigrated to the Ukraine and become leader of the urban Mennonite congregation of Ber-

Interior of Alexanderwohl Mennonite Church, facing the north balcony.

Alexanderwohl Church, Marion County, Kansas, built 1886.

(Mennonite Library and Archives)

dyansk on the Sea of Azov, and emigrated again to settle in 1876 among Prussian Mennonites in rural Butler County, Kansas.[3] Elder Toews had moved from Prussia to Saratov and before emigrating to America in 1884 had gone on an ill-fated trek of some Mennonites to Central Asia. The group had expected that Christ would return in the East.[4] Krehbiel, who had come to America from Bavaria in 1851, was the only elder who had been ordained by lot.[5] Unlike the Swiss and south Germans, the Dutch-Russian Mennonites did not choose leaders by lot. Wedel's ordination showed the way that Mennonites in Kansas of both the Swiss and the Dutch streams were trying to cooperate. Wedel had just been appointed to a teaching post at the Mennonite seminary, or preparatory school, at Halstead. Halstead was the Kansas town where elder Krehbiel and his wife, Susanna, south Germans, ran a government-subsidized school for Indian young people.[6]

Even though he was called to be an educator, Wedel was ordained a "preacher of the gospel" (*Prediger des Evangeliums*). An account in the church paper said he was now "called to preach . . . as much as his occupation as teacher allows. . . ."[7] But Wedel was ordained to preach more than spare time. The New Alexanderwohl congregation had helped finance his higher education. Now the church's hand of blessing and guidance was to be upon the educational enterprise itself—upon the Halstead Seminary and upon Bethel College, which followed in 1893. The school was intended to meet the needs and fulfill the purposes of the church, for education also was a way to proclaim the gospel. The relationship of the church to its institutions of higher education, symbolized here in an ordination for both church and school, would remain a point of creative tension for decades to come.

At the ordination there was one special sadness. Wedel's father, Cornelius P. Wedel, was also a Mennonite elder, who by all canons of family solidarity should have shared in the joy of helping ordain his son. But the father had to give his blessing privately. Ten years earlier he had led a breakaway from the New Alexanderwohl congregation and founded a Mennonite Brethren congregation nearby. Most of his family had gone along, but Cornelius had stayed with New Alexanderwohl. The Mennonite Brethren, emphasizing spiritual renewal through heartfelt conversion and using the rite of rebaptism by immersion as their sign of membership, had begun in the Russian

Empire about 1860. Now, both in the old country and in Kansas, their movement cut across family and congregational lines. In order to maintain family ties C. H. Wedel had to bridge a gap between the GC Mennonites and the MBs. When his father died in 1900, the funeral ceremony was in the New Alexanderwohl church and the people of both churches united in mourning.[8]

THE TRANSPLANTED COMMONWEALTH

The New Alexanderwohlers, like other Mennonites who migrated from Eastern Europe to the American plains in the latter part of the nineteenth century, had brought personal luggage, communion cups, and seeds of Turkey Red wheat. They also had brought a set of assumptions. Not least were ideas about the natural and proper ways to incorporate Anabaptist Christian values in established rural communities. Moving from the steppes to the prairies, New Alexanderwohls had set out to replicate Old Alexanderwohls. As it turned out, they were able to reproduce old-world community life only in part. As with all other immigrants, America gradually changed the Alexanderwohlers. Meanwhile, religious ritual, religious identity, and witness were very important as the group moved and resettled.

As the Dutch-Prussian-Russian Mennonites set out to re-create community on the American frontier, they followed principles somewhat different from those which guided Old Order Mennonite life in the East and Midwest. The two groups held many charter beliefs and documents in common, especially the Bible, the *Martyrs Mirror*, and the works of Menno Simons. Yet their different points of origin in Europe as well as centuries of separate historical development had produced different patterns. The two traditions had differing forms of community, identities, and ways of boundary maintenance. The normative value of *Demut* or humility so central in Old Order Mennonite life was by no means absent among these immigrants from Russian lands, but it was much less pivotal. Nor had the Russian Mennonites developed such a strong concept of *Ordnung*. In the czars' empire Mennonites took a more positive view of worldly communal responsibilities. They chose their own village mayors and area administrators. These officials made the difficult and controversial decisions about allocating land and taxes; about roads and bridges, education and benevolence; and even about whether a family would be allowed to leave and resettle. Mennonites in the Ukraine set a standard which became known among other Mennonite settlements in East European provinces. The Ukraine colonists valued not only their separation from the world but also their control of local institutions and instruments of power. Theirs was a small-scale, congregation-oriented Christendom. Some have called it a state within a state.[9]

From the 1850s through the 1870s the Russian Mennonite commonwealth underwent major upheavals which increased its pluralism but left its underlying principles intact. One upheaval was a struggle between Mennonite classes, the landed and the landless. Another was the major religious schism and reform which produced the MB church. A third was an attempt by the Russian authorities, who wished to make colonists more a part of a Russian nation, to "russify" the Mennonites (and others who enjoyed special privileges and lived apart). The authorities required German-speaking peoples to use Russian extensively in their schools, drafted Mennonite young men (albeit finally into forestry rather than military service), and reduced Mennonites' local political autonomy. These changes threatened not only Mennonites but also German Lutherans and Catholics, some of whom, like some Mennonites, emigrated and joined a wider German subculture in America. About a third of the Mennonites emigrated. But the Mennonite commonwealth in Russian-held lands did not collapse. Between 1880 and World War I it brimmed with vitality. The Mennonites who stayed showed new intellectual vigor, expanded their industries, and established new colonies. Meanwhile, emigrants to America measured themselves by Russian Mennonite models. In 1894, the first year of classes at Bethel College, C. H. Wedel observed that "schools in South Russia with similar curricula have trained their teachers for many years and have done a remarkably good job."[10]

The MB movement brought a measure of religious pluralism. Pietism and evangelicalism produced other movements, especially Adventist, Baptist Stundist, and Templar or Friends of Jerusalem. These also won members from the Mennonites and added to the pluralism. But the MBs were more numerous. Spiritually fervent, the MB minority organized alternative congregations in most Mennonite villages. Yet while they worked to reform and purify the church, the MBs did not challenge the basic terms of the Mennonite social contract. Their 1860 secession document spoke for "the entire Mennonite brotherhood [*Brüderschaft*] because the supreme government authorities consider it one true brotherhood."[11] The MB founders did not intend to withdraw from public responsibility within the commonwealth. At one point some MBs became the Mennonite majority in a new colony which they established in Kuban province in the northern Caucasus. When they did so their leaders, thoroughly capable, took up the civic posts of area administrator and school director as vigorously as mainline *Kirchliche* Mennonites were doing back in older colonies such as Chortitza and Molotschna. Mennonites of all kinds would have warned against entanglements with the world, that is, contacts with the empire's broader society. Yet they also shared a consensus that they should have a progressive spirit and assume public responsibility within the Mennonite commonwealth. Neither the *Kirchliche* nor the MB emigrants moved to America to escape the state church or *Volkskirche* implications of their colonies' commonwealth. Instead, they hoped to make their peoplehood even more autonomous and secure. Ironically, in America autonomy and self-direction were elusive, and slipped away as rapidly as they slipped from those who stayed in the lands of the czars. In America as in the homeland, village isolation yielded to the larger society's nation-building.

The American political environment offered no civic offices equivalent to those of the mayors and area administrators of the Russian Mennonite colonies and villages. In those offices Mennonites could exercise authority accountable to their own religious-ethnic commonwealth. They acted in behalf of, and subject to the sanctions of, their own Mennonite people. But in America, prior to Mennonite arrival, English-speaking Americans had organized states and counties and filled the offices. In no U.S. county did immigrant Mennonites settle densely enough to be a majority. Their concentration was greatest in south-central Kansas. But there, in Marion, McPherson, Harvey, Reno, and Butler counties, the Mennonite settlements spilled over county boundaries, and in each jurisdiction Mennonites were a minority. Thus the emigrants to America entered an environment *less* favorable than the Russian situation for using civic offices to build Mennonite peoplehood.

Citing the dangers of "worldly" involvements, many Mennonite settlers were reluctant to become involved in American politics. In 1888 an MB conference stated: "We want to have a

good government, but we also wish not to defile our consciences with political contentions." In 1893 the same conference ruled that members should not hold offices of justice of
the peace or constable.[12] The GC-related Kansas Conference was
somewhat less cautious. Many of its people had been politically
involved back in the homeland but largely on their own terms.
America dictated social and political terms more subtly than
did the Russian system. Mennonites who did participate in
state and local politics—for instance, two in Kansas, Ferdinand
J. Funk in Marion County and Peter J. Galle in McPherson
County—tended to drift from their Mennonite moorings.[13]

INSTRUMENTS OF THE
NEW CONGREGATION CHRISTENDOM

Congregations. In the absence of a viable village social
structure, the *congregation* assumed an even more important
role as the center for Mennonite identity, worship, teaching, admonition, discipline, and recruitment of leaders. In their
churches Mennonites experienced the profoundest symbols and
rituals of a community-oriented Christian faith. Congregational
rituals and activities were geared to the rhythms of nature from
seedtime to harvest, and of the life cycle from birth to baptism
to death. Rural Mennonite congregations did not distinguish
clearly between the secular and the sacred, for God's presence
was everywhere and God's guidance was to be sought at all
times. Yet there were some differences between the language of
worship and the language of the farm. The Russian Mennonite
immigrants worshiped in High German but conversed in dialect.

Some congregations showed great vitality, producing missionaries and church leaders, planting new congregations, and
stimulating new institutions from schools to hospitals, orphanages, and Sunday school associations. The largest congregation to immigrate as a body was New Alexanderwohl, and
it provided much leadership. The Halstead congregation, which
mixed recent immigrants from south Germany with others from
the Russian empire, also offered especially strong, entrepreneurial leaders in the persons of David Goerz, Bernhard
Warkentin, and Christian Krehbiel. The Ebenezer MB church in
Reno County had a special role because its leader was a man of
strength, Abraham Schellenberg. The Ebenfeld MB congregation
and an MB congregation in Corn, Oklahoma, provided many
church workers and denominational leaders. The Swiss-Vol-

hynian Hoffnungsfeld congregation near Moundridge, Kansas, of European Amish background via so-called Polish Russia, adapted quickly to the dominant Russian ethos in the Kansas Conference and produced several offshoot congregations. The town congregations related to Bethel College at Newton and Tabor College at Hillsboro were of more mixed background than most rural congregations and often led in imitating American Protestantism.[14]

Newspapers. Beyond the congregations, there emerged some institutions which tried to speak to the common Mennonite culture tying the different congregations and conferences together. Mennonite immigrant newspapers became very important for working across congregational and conference lines to integrate the sacred and the secular, and the ethnic and the American. In Kansas from 1880 through 1910, in addition to papers sponsored by churches, there were fifteen German-language newspapers which Mennonite editors and publishers either already operated, or founded newly, or reorganized and renamed.[15] In Indiana, John F. Funk's publishing house produced *Die Mennonitische Rundschau* for the Russian immigrants and for readers back in the homeland. Elsewhere there were a few other attempts—for instance, J. J. Baergen's *Unser Besucher* in Mountain Lake, Minnesota. The births, deaths, and rebirths of these newspapers reflected general economic conditions. A flurry of new, privately published papers appeared between 1885 and 1889 followed by a depression and then by another surge in the late 1890s.

PRIVATELY PUBLISHED
KANSAS MENNONITE NEWSPAPERS

Zur Heimath (Halstead, David Goerz, ed.), 1871-1881.
Farmers Anzeiger (Hillsboro), 1883.
Der Freundschaftskreis (Hillsboro, John W. Fast, ed.), 1885-1886.
Hillsboro Herald (Hillsboro, John C. Fast, ed.), 1886-1889.
Marion County Anzeiger (Hillsboro, John F. Harms, ed.), 1887-1897.
McPherson Anzeiger (Hillsboro, John F. Harms, ed.), 1887-1890.
Newton Anzeiger (Newton, Ulrich Hege, ed.), 1887-1892.
Das Kansas Volksblatt und Anzeiger (Newton, David Goerz and William J. Krehbiel, eds.), 1897-1902.

Hillsboro Post (Hillsboro, H. H. Fast, ed.), 1898-1902.
Post und Volksblatt (Newton, H. P. Krehbiel and C. E. Krehbiel,
    eds.), 1902-1910.
Das Echo (Lehigh, Jacob J. Wiebe, ed.), 1906-1908 (?).
Deutsche Westen (McPherson, H. H. Fast, ed.), 1907-1910.
Der Herold (Newton, C. E. Krehbiel, ed.), 1910- .
Vorwärts (Hillsboro, A. L. Schellenberg, ed.), 1910- .

Official German-language denominational papers also
flourished: the MB *Zionsbote*, founded in 1884 with John F.
Harms as its first editor; the GC *Christlicher Bundesbote*,
founded in 1882 with David Goerz as first editor; and somewhat
later, in 1915, the Krimmer Mennonite Brethren *Wahrheitsfreund*, with M. B. Fast as first editor. With the beginnings
of the Mennonite colleges two additional institutional German-
language newspapers made their appearance: the *Monatsblätter
aus Bethel College* in 1903, edited initially by David Goerz; and
the *Tabor College Herald* in 1912, with David E. Harder as first
editor.

By 1910 the newspapers not sponsored by churches had
been reduced to three survivors: *Der Herold* of Newton,
Vorwärts of Hillsboro, and *Die Mennonitische Rundschau* of
Elkhart, Indiana. These papers, especially *Vorwärts* and *Der
Herold*, reached for an inter-Mennonite audience as well as for
a wider German-language constituency. Such papers freely
mixed secular with religious news and commentary and thus offered a clue for understanding Mennonite immigrant culture at
its peak of progressive optimism from about 1890 to 1915. For
their readers' secular news, Mennonite editors assumed that
their newspapers would be the primary and in some cases the
only source. Often they gave the entire front page to national,
domestic, and foreign affairs, with more of the same on inside
pages.

Warnings of church conferences against political involvement did not seem to dampen Mennonite editors' interest in
American politics. In his *Marion County Anzeiger* in 1888 John
F. Harms, one of the most able and aggressive of editors, spoke
out vigorously for Republican low-tariff policies. In 1890 he
proposed that America deal with the farm depression by extending government credit to farmers.[16] His suggestion revealed an
immigrant's old-world orientation, for it proposed a system
used in Germany and Poland; yet he claimed to be an American

"in the egotistical sense of the word" (*im egoistischen Sinne des Wortes*).[17] He published this proposal, along with a critical assessment of the American Farmers Alliance movement, in the official MB church paper, the *Zionsbote.*

Henry Peter Krehbiel was the son of church leader Christian Krehbiel from south Germany. As an editor he endeavored to reach the Russian Mennonite immigrant readership and enthusiastically promoted a combined religious and secular agenda. "Wherever large settlements of Mennonites exist," he wrote in 1901, "the secular press should be chiefly in the hands of Mennonites who are in sympathy with the ideals pursued by the denomination, thus assisting in their perpetuation and extension."[18]

Of course, secular publishing had its dangers along with secular politics. Contacts with the broader publishing world moved some editors away from Mennonite associations and ideals.[19] Such was the case with William J. Krehbiel, who for several years edited the *Kansas Volksblatt und Anzeiger* of Newton. But other editors, such as David Goerz, John F. Harms, and Henry Peter Krehbiel, found ways to sustain a healthy tension among the secular and religious elements of Mennonite immigrants' Christendom.

Mennonite newspapers published letters from the scattered communities and kept the various settlements in touch with each other. An immigrant Mennonite paper would have failed if it had not been a medium for faithful and interesting correspondents from Mountain Lake, Minnesota; Freeman, South Dakota; Henderson, Nebraska; Corn, Oklahoma; and other such places. Substantial portions of inside pages carried down-to-earth reports about the weather, crops, and recent visitors. Unsigned, the news was often written by women. The reports expressed the congregational basis of Mennonite life—news about baptisms, missionary festivals, revival meetings, and new church buildings.

Exceptionally interesting were travel accounts of some who made return pilgrimages to the old country. It seems that about the turn of the century nearly every important immigrant leader took such a tour, to nourish roots and renew communal ties. Comparisons of life in the Russian Empire and in America made fascinating reading. Heinrich Dirks, an elder from the Molotschna colony in the Ukraine, traveled in America in 1895 and observed that Mennonites in Mountain Lake, Minnesota, did not keep their gardens as neat as those back home. He said this was because Mennonites in the homeland could hire labor much more cheaply. "If you do not want to work hard yourself," new-world Mennonites repeatedly told Dirks, "you should not come to America."[20]

Mennonite immigrant newspapers reflected influences from the broader German-American press, which in the 1890s was publishing nearly eight hundred newspapers and journals in German.[21] The Mennonite editors borrowed most freely from religious papers, but along with religious topics they also reproduced much news about Germany's political, social, and cultural affairs. It was an interesting time, the era in which Chancellor Otto von Bismarck was making Germany into a unified nation. In both the Russian Empire and America, German language and culture were useful allies as a people of a minority faith tried to maintain separate identity over against the dominant Russian Orthodox or American English Protestants.

Besides being a tool for separatism, German culture carried power and prestige which drew Mennonite leaders. In 1897 a writer in John Harms' *Zionsbote* wanted Mennonites to "cultivate and protect the German language" because Germany was rising to first rank in world civilization. Napoleon had humiliated Germany eighty-three years before, the writer said, but today German science, education, and theology were exercising the highest of influence.[22] No Mennonite editor became a crusading apologist for the political aims of the German Reich; yet manifestations of German nationalism, odd for a nonresistant people, entered Mennonite discourse. In 1898 William J. Krehbiel of the *Kansas Volksblatt und Anzeiger* offered a large portrait of Bismarck as a subscription bonus—saying that it "should be in every German house as a token of German power, German greatness, and faithfulness."[23] In principle, Mennonites could not put nation ahead of church. But they were tempted by a nationalist identity, as much from Germany as from America.

German Schools and German Teachers. In 1886 Mennonite teachers of German-language schools in Kansas organized a "German Teachers Association" (*Lehrerverein*). The association soon had as much stake as the Mennonite German-language press in maintaining the immigrant Mennonite Christendom.[24] The organization was largest (about seventy) and enjoyed its strongest influence from about 1895 to 1908. World War I and wartime anti-Germanism devastated it, although it continued marginally until World War II. In it MB and GC teachers cooperated, in the membership and on the executive committee. Leaders kept the agenda free of potentially divisive issues, whether of theology or of church practice. A highly formalized parliamentary procedure very different from traditional proceedings in church congregations helped the teachers find cultural definition. A constitution, occasionally revised, added to the formality. So did elected committees, who certified membership, drafted resolutions, planned meetings, reported to the press, created a school songbook, and produced model curricula. At its peak the association held general meetings twice yearly and sponsored an annual two-week teachers' institute.

The German Teachers Association saw itself as the guardian of the Mennonite religious and cultural tradition. In 1910 the name became "Mennonite Teachers Association." Members taught in several dozen primary schools, where they provided special religious instruction not available in American public schools. Meetings and institutes were forums to discuss practical questions such as how to acquire good books, examine students, and update teachers' methods. In 1898 Professor Gustav A. Haury of Bethel College reviewed educators from Socrates to Pestalozzi. The latter, he said, was "correct in many respects" but "not our complete ideal."[25] During the Spanish-American War the association struggled with such questions as: "What shall we do regarding patriotism? (Ans.: Guide it in the right paths)" and "Shall we raise the flag? (Ans.: Yes, in the right way.)"[26] Continually on the agenda were relationships with the American schools, especially as the public schools pressed the German ones for time and resources. The conference at year's end in 1897 took note of a Marion County proposal that in Mennonite areas the public schools teach German alongside English. Participants feared the plan might displace the separate Mennonite schools. This, said their report, would mean "the grave of our Deutschtum."[27] The association stood for both *Mennonitentum* and *Deutschtum*. It had a corporate cultural agenda that transcended differences between Mennonite groups.

Mennonite educators organized primary schools on a number of patterns. The German school term usually followed the American term.[28] In solidly Mennonite districts a certified bilingual teacher could teach both terms. There were problems with inadequate facilities, salaries, and community commitment. But the most serious threat came when state legislatures gradually extended the required English term, thus reducing the time available for the German. The term required by Kansas law grew from three months to five in 1903, seven in 1909, and eight in 1923.[29] Other states passed similar laws. The laws squeezed Mennonite German-language schools to the margins even before the anti-Germanism of World War I dug a grave for all *Deutschtum* in America.

Among the members of the German Teachers Association were instructors in Mennonite "preparatory schools." These schools shared the common religious-cultural task. Of the eighteen preparatory schools founded before World War I, eight were outside of Kansas, in keeping with the Mennonite community's geographical spread.

MENNONITE GERMAN LANGUAGE PREPARATORY SCHOOLS

Name of School	Location	Founded	Closed
Peter Balzer's School	Near Goessel, Kans.	1879	188?
Halstead Preparatory School	Halstead, Kans.	(1882) 1883	1893
Mountain Lake Bible School	Mountain Lake, Minn.	1886	—
Hillsboro Preparatory School	Hillsboro, Kans.	1897	1935
Buhler Vereins Schule	Buhler, Kans.	1889	1902
Mennonite Collegiate Inst.	Gretna, Mani.	1889	—
Mennonite Bible Academy	Beatrice, Nebr.	1890	—
Bethel Academy	Newton, Kans.	1893	1927
Whitewater Bible School	Whitewater, Kans.	1900	1915
Corn Bible School	Corn, Okla.	1902	—
Henderson Bible School	Henderson, Nebr.	1902	1944
Freeman Preparatory School	Freeman, S. Dak.	1903	—
Goessel Preparatory School	Goessel, Kans.	1906	1925
Hoffnungsau Bible School	Inman, Kans.	1907	1927
Moundridge Bible School	Moundridge, Kans.	1908	1918
Gotebo Bible School	Gotebo, Okla.	1910	1917
Meno Preparatory School	Meno, Okla.	1911	—
Herbert Bible School	Herbert, Sask.	1913	—
Zoar Bible School	Inman, Kans.	1915	1946[30]

Mennonites both north and south followed patterns set in the Kansas immigrant heartland. The founding of Mennonite colleges at Newton (Bethel College in 1893) and Hillsboro (Tabor College in 1908) added life and clarity to the immigrant, German-language Christendom. Both of the schools' first presidents, C. H. Wedel and Henry W. Lohrenz, had been preparatory-school teachers and were committed to traditional German-language culture. Speaking in 1901 to the German *Verein* (Association) at McPherson College, Lohrenz elaborated upon the "Value of German Education." Every German teacher, he said, should "disseminate German ways of thinking and true Christianity at the same time." And beware of those who stir their own heritage into the dirt "and spoil their Christentum along with their Deutschtum."[31]

Although in time the colleges became potent agents of Americanization, Lohrenz and Wedel wanted their people to use the strengths of German culture to fashion a Mennonite peoplehood. They were at least partly successful. The influence of these two educated leaders in their respective MB and GC denominations reached to Russian Mennonite settlements well beyond Kansas. In 1913 a Mennonite visitor from Germany reported of his Kansas hosts that "their hearts have remained German and we felt inwardly united as German Mennonites in brotherly exchange of ideas."[32]

In part, Dutch-Russian Mennonite hearts in America did indeed remain German. But even more, in America the Mennonites of this distinctive "congregation Christendom" became German in new ways. The more open and pluralistic American society gave new social and cultural functions to their Germanness. And so they underwent a double change. In some ways the new situation made them more Anglo-American and brought them closer to the mainstream of a majority, national, English-speaking culture. In other ways they were German-Americanized. Their newspapers, schools, and social contacts with other German-Americans moved them toward the German-American culture of *Auslands-Deutschtum* (the German diaspora). Long before migrating to America, Mennonites of Dutch background had been Germanized in Prussia and the Russian Empire. But there was a difference. When leaders such as Wedel and Lohrenz tried to lay a German basis for Mennonite identity, they were being German more intentionally than their grandparents had been, under the czars.

In quite a few communities a variety of German dialects shaped and complicated the double movement of Anglo-Ameri-

Chancellor Otto von Bismark, an incongruous hero for Mennonites.

(*Kansas Volksblatt u. Anzeiger.* Mar 17, 1898, p. 4)

canization and German-Americanization. For example, Hutchinson and Turner counties of South Dakota had three groups of Mennonites, each with its own speech along with High German: Low German (Dutch-Prussian-Russian), Hutterish (from the Hutterites), and so-called Swiss (a Palatinate-origin dialect spoken by the Swiss-Volhynians). As members from all three groups cooperated—especially in Freeman Academy, founded in 1903— their identity took shape not in dialect but in the use of both High German and English. Freeman Academy intended both to foster German and to adapt to English.[33] In Kansas, where even more Mennonite German dialects flourished, there was a similar movement from ethnic-dialect multiplicity to a commonality through public use of High German and English.

CRACKS IN THE CHRISTENDOM

In 1895 Heinrich Dirks of a Russian colony visited in

America and noticed overlap in the publications, education, and missions of the *Kirchliche* Mennonites and the Mennonite Brethren. He thought that in America these two groups did not clash as much as in his homeland. And he was glad, for he wanted such unity and progressive cooperation.[34] Dirks decided that perhaps in America, removed in time and space from the painful events of the original schism, the two groups might come together. And they did cooperate in important ways. But new denominational institutions also sharpened their separate identities. Each group developed its own colleges, mission boards, and publications. These institutions took cues from different forces on the American Protestant scene. Dirks' ecumenical Mennonite hopes were not realized.

Kirchliche Mennonites

The *Kirchliche* Mennonites made their institutional alliance with the General Conference Mennonite church. In so doing they cast their lot with the progressive wing of American Mennonites, the wing that pointed toward missions, education, and ecumenism. New Alexanderwohl and other congregations first joined the GC as individual congregations. In 1892 their Kansas Conference of Mennonites reorganized and became the Western District of the General Conference Mennonite church.[35] The Western District was an ethnic polyglot, including immigrants not only from the Ukraine but also from Prussia, Galicia, Volhynia, and southern Germany. Despite different origins, Western District congregations cooperated in education, missions, publications, Sunday school conventions, itinerant ministry, poor relief, and hospitals. New hospitals and deaconess homes in Goessel, Kansas (1899); Newton, Kansas (1903); and Beatrice, Nebraska (1911), offered models for hospitals established later by American Mennonites further east in Bloomington, Illinois (1919), and Bluffton, Ohio (1920).[36]

In their GC connections the Russian Mennonites from the plains had to find ways to cooperate with congregations in the East who were more Americanized. In its offices and activities the GC general conference tried to represent its various constituencies. From the East, Andrew B. Shelly of Pennsylvania served as mission board executive secretary for thirty-nine years, until 1911. In the Midwest the town of Berne in east-central Indiana became a publishing and bookstore center, and from 1886 to 1930 was the home of the official German-lan-

(Mennonite Library and Archives)

David and Helene Riesen Goerz, ca. 1900.

guage GC newspaper, *Christlicher Bundesbote.*

The most controversial issue between East and West was language. The problem surfaced in 1899 at the triennial general conference meeting. Thereupon, Silas M. Grubb, youthful pastor of the Second Mennonite Church of Philadelphia, wrote a contentious appeal for the conference to shift from German to English. He asserted that the eastern conference had been "fully German" only ten years earlier and had become three-fourths English. In only four years the Middle District conference in Ohio had shifted from little English to little German. In Grubb's view the transition to English elsewhere was inevitable and would enhance both Mennonite mission and inter-Mennonite ecumenicity.[37]

David Goerz, church leader and institutional entrepreneur among Russian Mennonites in Kansas, responded with an article making quite clear that German-speaking Mennonites in the West would withdraw from the GC body if it switched to English too quickly.[38] Though it was more than a quarter-century since he had left the Ukraine, Goerz's arguments reflected the principles of the Russian Mennonite commonwealth. He said the U.S. Constitution guaranteed that Mennonites could keep their own ways, including language. Mennonites should learn and respect English as the national language, but they had not come to America to trade Russianization for Americanization. Goerz believed that if the Russian immigrants had thought the GC branch would switch to English they would have remained independent or joined others to form an independent *German* conference. The GC general conference, he thought, must remain German in "language, character and essence [*Wesen*]." Advocates of German believed that more German-speaking Mennonites would immigrate to America in the coming years. And if the issue was mission work, there were great needs among German-speaking people in America.[39]

So ran the reasons of Goerz and Mennonite *Deutschtum*. Grubb responded that the conference mission work was among Cheyenne and Arapaho Indians. Why, he asked, should the GC Mennonites teach English to these heathen but impose German on civilized English speakers from Pennsylvania?[40]

German remained the language of GC general conference sessions for two more decades, until after World War I. But in GC Mennonite family and congregational life meanwhile, from East to West, there was a gradual shift from German to English. By 1930 few speakers used German on the floor at conference sessions. The World War accelerated the change for East and West alike. However, in the 1920s and 1940s major new groups of German-speaking Mennonites arrived from the Soviet Union, going mostly to Canada, and revived German in parts of the conference.

Mennonite Brethren (MBs)

Unlike the *Kirchliche* Mennonites, the Mennonite Brethren did not affiliate with more Americanized Mennonite groups. They stood aloof despite the hopes of John F. Funk and others to draw them into the "old" Mennonite orbit and despite Funk's publishing the MB-oriented paper *Rundschau*. Instead, they turned more to German-speaking Baptists, with whom they had associated also in the Ukraine. In the 1890s John F. Harms, editor of the MB *Zionsbote*, copied many articles from a German Baptist paper named *Sendbote*, of Cleveland, Ohio, and commented on the Baptist-related Stundist renewal movement in the homeland.[41] The *Zionsbote* reported and promoted Baptist missions in India, the Cameroons, and Kansas City. Young MB scholars studied in the German department of the Baptist

(Mennonite Library and Archives)

**John F. Harms,
Mennonite Brethren
leader.**

Theological Seminary in Rochester, New York. In 1896, with MB financial support, a former Rochester student named Peter Wedel (brother of C. H. Wedel) went with his wife, Martha Liebig, to the Cameroons under the North American Baptist Mission Society. By 1899 in India, where Russia's MBs had been sending missionaries under the Baptist Missionary Union of Boston since 1890, four MB persons from America were cooperating in Baptist work among the Telegu people. Some young MB men became Baptist pastors. For instance, in 1898 C. E. Kliewer was pastor of a Baptist congregation in Portland, Oregon. On a visit to Hillsboro, Kansas, Kliewer led a meeting in the local Baptist church, many of whose members had once belonged to the Ebenfeld MB congregation.[42]

Yet there were limits to MB-Baptist cooperation. In 1892 a Baptist pastor from Kansas City attended the MB conference and presented a case for Mennonite Brethren-Baptist union. The gathered MBs excluded the Baptist from the business sessions and rehearsed various reasons against the union: Baptist churches provided a haven for errant MB members being disciplined by their congregations; Baptist ministers engaged in "sheep stealing" of MBs in isolated outlying areas; Baptists accept military service, the oath, worldly politics, divorce, and other behavior which Mennonites forbade; and in an MB-Baptist union "our identity would soon disappear."[43] Moreover, the MBs were careful in what they borrowed from the Baptists. Editor Harms favored articles from the *Sendbote* which reinforced Mennonite emphases. For instance, in 1895 he published a conservative Baptist warning that a rush to organize parachurch associations (*Vereine*) such as youth and women's associations was endangering the centrality of the congregation.[44]

Between 1898 and 1905 the MBs cooperated in higher education with another group, the Church of the Brethren (Dunkers). They even took over the German department of a Church of the Brethren school, McPherson College at McPherson, Kansas. The department offered German-language courses in a number of subjects, including history and literature. Teacher John F. Duerksen reported that 249 students from MB congregations attended classes in the McPherson German department. But funds were short. Then in 1904 a rumor circulated that the dean of McPherson's Bible department did not believe in the divinity of Jesus. The rumor helped terminate the MB-Dunker experiment, and in 1908 the Mennonite Brethren founded Tabor College a few miles away.[45] In founding Tabor the MBs stayed apart from the GCs' Bethel also, less than twenty miles apart. The two colleges helped institutionalize the differences between MB and GC Russian-immigrant Mennonites as surely as did the separate church conferences.

In Chicago (and in Berne, Indiana) John A. Sprunger of the Light and Hope Mission offered another potential union. In 1896-1897 he and others attempted to bring three small evangelical groups—the Mennonite Brethren, Krimmer Mennonite Brethren, and Defenseless Mennonite Church (Egli Amish)—into one body. Sprunger sponsored union conferences in Gridley, Illinois, and Berne, Indiana. John F. Harms attended the first one and returned rather interested in alliance. In the *Zionsbote* of February 1896, he published the full text of an 1895 Defenseless confession of faith and noted large areas of agreement with MBs.[46] However a key difference was the form of baptism. The

MBs immersed one time backward. The KMBs immersed three times forward. And the Defenseless Mennonites used the more traditional Mennonite mode, pouring without immersion. Sprunger's union movement failed, although he continued to get support for the Light and Hope Mission from members within all these groups.

Form of baptism was a bone of contention also in the relationship of MBs with independent congregations at Henderson, Nebraska, led by elder Isaac Peters, and at Mountain Lake, Minnesota, led by elder Aaron Wall. In 1889 those congregations organized a "Conference of United Mennonite Brethren in North America" (later named the "Evangelical Mennonite Brethren"). The Peters-Wall group baptized by pouring. At first they were inclined to affiliate with the "old" Mennonites as a "Nebraska-Minnesota Conference." Later they cooperated closely with the Defenseless Mennonites. But eventually they remained separate and independent. Tendencies for exclusion and division among these smaller "Brethren" groups were a liability against efforts to build denominational institutions which needed larger constituencies. None of the smaller groups established a successful college of its own. And even Tabor College struggled year after year against limits to its resources and personnel.

MB congregations baptized new members into the church on their testimony to personal, heartfelt conversion. Spiritual revival became a critical matter not only for individuals but also for the vitality and life of the larger church community. The Ebenfeld congregation near Hillsboro found renewal in a sequence of springtime revivals which won fifty new members in 1887, fifty again in 1892, sixty-seven in 1907, and fifty-nine in 1937.[47] Each revival improved the ongoing health of the congregation. Meanwhile, MBs operated a church school in Corn, Oklahoma, which closed down in 1911 and in 1918 because of lack of student enrollment and constituency support. But in each case the school was rescued the following year by religious revival which restored community vitality. The revivals of 1911 and 1912, initiated by a fiery evangelist and candidate for mission to China named Frank J. Wiens, stimulated ninety baptisms at Corn. The revival of 1918, held in the English language and in the stressful context of the World War, led to 155 baptisms.[48] In times of upheaval, revival enabled individuals to find personal reorientation and to unite, with a sense of community.

In the three decades after the founding of the North American MB conference in 1879, elder Abraham Schellenberg's strong leadership brought a centralization of authority. In effect, Schellenberg exercised the powers of a central bishop. For eighteen out of twenty years he chaired the annual conference, and at various times he presided over the Foreign Missions Board, the Publications Committee, and the Sunday School Association.[49] In 1919, after expanding into Oklahoma, Nebraska, Colorado, Minnesota, South and North Dakota, and Canada, the MB conference reorganized into four districts, thereby dispersing authority. After that it held its general conferences triennially rather than annually.

Other, more centralized institution-building turned the town of Hillsboro into a denominational center. It became the home not only of Tabor College but also of the MB publishing house (1913) and of a thriving MB congregation. Elder Schellenberg's oldest son, Abraham L. Schellenberg, symbolized the transition from powerful patriarch to institutional-denominational professional. In the years 1907-1919 and 1923-1929, the son served as director of the publishing house and editor of various of its publications. The father, although a church leader, earned his income by farming, helped by his nineteen children (seven by first wife, Katharina Lohrenz, and twelve by second wife, Suzanna Flaming). The son drew income from effective management of a denominational press which could not occupy the labor of the ten children borne by his wife, Sarah Schroeder. He was certified by higher education at McPherson College and Rochester Theological Seminary. The elder Shellenbergs gave their children traditional, mostly biblical, names. The younger named three of their boys Abraham Lincoln, Henry George, and Theodore Roosevelt.

THE CONGREGATION-CHRISTENDOM VISION
FORMULATED

At the turn of the century nobody articulated the core values and assumptions of the Dutch-Russian American Mennonite communities on the plains more clearly than did C. H. Wedel, president of Bethel College and mentor to a generation of future church leaders. Wedel published the substance of his class lectures in biblical and church history in a series of six books, 1899-1904.[50] The volumes, which he called his *kleine Opus* (small opus), spanned the time from creation to the present and unfolded an original interpretation of the meaning of the Anabaptist-Mennonite experience. His interpretation both reflected and justified the Mennonite community life in the Russian empire and in America, the life his Alexanderwohl congregation represented.

On the one hand Wedel was a modern scholar and educator bent on making the Christian faith and the Mennonite identity winsome and persuasive as his people entered the modern world. "History," he wrote, "is the science of that which has taken place. . . . Only free creatures can have a history."[51] The scientific-historical method required that salvation history be understood in relationship to secular history, not just in isolation. That included Mennonite history. Art and science, in Wedel's view, could be allies for the church in the development of Christ's kingdom in this world. Sixteenth-century Anabaptists who responded to persecution by withdrawal had been mistaken in their excessive legalism and too-sharp separation of church and world.[52] While saying that Christ's kingdom is not *of* this world, Wedel affirmed the possibilities of a Christendom which would incorporate the Christian ideals into human community. The boundaries of Christendom, Wedel believed, should be aggressively extended both by missions to non-Christians and by active witness to Americans. Wedel's affirmation of culture, his approach to history, and his biblical interpretations were greatly influenced by Dr. George C. Seibert, a professor at the Presbyterian Bloomfield Seminary in New Jersey. Prior to his 1890 ordination and teaching career in Kansas, Wedel had studied and taught at Bloomfield.[53]

Nonetheless, Wedel qualified his modernity by a deep commitment to his people's traditional faith and self-understanding as a distinctive people over against the world. The Christendom which Wedel idealized was a *congregational* Christendom, a *Gemeindechristentum*, radically different from the official Christendoms of Roman Catholicism, orthodoxy, and state-church Protestantism. The *Gemeindekirche* (congregation church) had taken shape in history through God's revelation in Christ. Therefore it stood at the centerpoint of salvation history. Anabaptist-Mennonite history thus was not marginal to God's purposes. Mennonites were the true descendants of the New Testament church. It was Christ's will that his church be made up of believers who freely choose to follow him in discipleship.

(Mennonite Library and Archives)

Cornelius H. and Susanna Richert Wedel.

In the churches of the first century following Christ's resurrection, believers had formed independent congregations. Then the organized church had abandoned Christ's plan and grasped for the centralized power of bishops, popes, and emperors. But an underground, persecuted, alternative *Gemeindekirche* had survived through the centuries. Sixteenth-century Anabaptists had learned this alternative heritage from the Waldensians and renewed the tradition. It needed renewal in every generation; yet Anabaptists stood in a continuous tradition which had begun with Christ.

Wedel's view of church history owed much to the historical writings of Ludwig Keller, a professional German historian who did more than any other person in the late-nineteenth century to rehabilitate the tarnished reputation of Anabaptism. Keller accepted the idea that there had been a succession of groups representing the faithful remnant; for them he used the label "Old Evangelical." But Wedel went beyond Keller when he made

the *Gemeinde*, or congregation, the foundational principle of
his historical synthesis.

Like all defenses of Christian community, Wedel's vision
wrestled with the tensions between Christ and culture.[54] Wedel
did not set Christ *against* culture in sectarian fashion, for he
tried to embrace the methods and the fruits of modern learning
and civilization. He saw God's primary arena of action to be the
church—the church as local congregation—rather than being
the individual, the nation, or humanity in general. The concept
Gemeinde implied the dimensions of close fellowship in primary relationships Wedel had known as a child of the Alexanderwohl community, while the term Christentum spoke of
concern for the outside world. Wedel was an educator in two
progressive and institution-building decades between 1890 and
1910. He could justifiably hope that the uplifting influence of
school and college would draw Mennonite congregations into a
richer and more redemptive involvement in modern life.

Wedel led the education of GC Mennonite young people at
Bethel College for a generation, and influenced others as his
books circulated in both North America and the colonies of the
Russian Empire. But he had little influence upon Swiss-
background Mennonites of the East and Midwest—whether of
the "old," Old Order, or "new" Mennonite variety. "New" Mennonites of the early-twentieth century absorbed their progressive
ideas via the English language; Wedel almost always wrote in
German. "Old" and Old Order Mennonites were not receptive to
Wedel's cultural affirmations, for his ideas suggested accommodation to the world. "Old" Mennonite editor John F. Funk
did note that Wedel, "one of the most highly educated men in
the Mennonite denomination in America," did not like congregational leaders to use the term "reverend."[55] An educated
man who opposed titles of distinction was a strange paradox.
But Funk did not borrow from Wedel's basic ideas and writings,
for Funk was "old" Mennonite and Wedel belonged to the General Conference. Different Mennonite groups were developing
some of their own ideas as well as their own schools, literature,
and organizations.

Few Mennonite leaders used Wedel's *Gemeindechristentum* concept, and no one translated his opus into English.[56]
Wedel taught and wrote in German for a people who were shifting from German to English. His central vision of *Gemeinde* did
not survive the language transition, and his long-range impact

was limited. One problem was that he died young, in 1910, when he was only 49. Four years later came World War I, which smashed many German-American dreams. So Wedel's ideas did not get a hearing in the changed Mennonite world of the 1920s. Another problem was that Wedel never managed to integrate his concept of *Gemeindechristentum* into his shorter and more popular writings. And a more subtle barrier was that his ideas did not translate easily into English. It would have been very difficult to carry over into English the corporate and cultural dimensions of critical concepts such as *Gemeinde, Mennonitentum,* and *Christentum.* Translators have usually expressed *Gemeinde* as "church," but in so doing they have lost the word's German implications of fellowship in a congregation of face-to-face relationships. *Mennonitentum* was translated as "Mennonitism," implying an ideological "ism" rather than the social/cultural manifestations of the German suffix *"tum."* *Gemeinschaft* became "denomination," again losing the meaning of a corporate fellowship. In the twentieth century the very concept of Christendom went out of fashion.[57]

In the 1940s, a time when Mennonites faced a new common experience in World War II, another Mennonite intellectual—Harold S. Bender of Goshen College—projected another integrated concept which captured imaginations of Mennonites in various groups: the "Anabaptist Vision." Like Wedel, Bender formulated his vision historically around the concept of the church. That Bender never referred to Wedel's works, perhaps had never read them, was testimony to the distance between the Dutch and Swiss streams of Mennonitism and the power of separate denominational institutions to separate like-minded people from each other. The American Mennonite mosaic had a bipolar shape. The Dutch-Russians were at one pole, quite distant from the Swiss-south Germans at the other.

CHAPTER
4

SWISS-AMERICAN MENNONITISM

About midnight on July 25, 1896, Enos Barge and Barbara Hershey, ages twenty-three and eighteen, left a party and made their way by horse and buggy toward their homes near Pequea Creek in Pennsylvania's Lancaster County. At a railway crossing at the village of Bird in Hand, they failed to hear or heed an oncoming locomotive. The train smashed into the buggy. Barbara died instantly, and the next day, Sunday, Enos died in the Lancaster city hospital. In Paradise and Strasburg townships several thousand people attended the youths' funerals.

IN THE HEARTLAND: TRAGEDY AND REVIVAL

The shocking deaths came at a time of religious revival. Both Enos and Barbara were from Mennonite families, but neither had been baptized. Neither was a member of the church. Revivalist-minded Mennonites interpreted the events as "a warning sent by a kind heavenly father to all."[1] Scores of sobered young people came to revival meetings, confessed Christ, and joined the church. The Pequea District had eighty-three converts, the Groffdale congregation had forty-three baptisms, and elsewhere there were dozens more.[2] Amos (A. D.) Wenger, a gifted young evangelist who led the extended revival, later called it "the ripest field I ever saw." Thirty-six years later, Wenger thought that the Mennonite church in Lancaster County "has been different ever since."[3]

Wenger's work as an "evangelist" was part of the transition. Traditionally, the Mennonites, whose leadership consisted of ordained ministers, deacons, and bishops, did not welcome itinerant "outside evangelists" or revivalism. In 1896 Wenger was an exceptionally mobile person without firm roots in any congregation. Reared in Rockingham County, Virginia, he was baptized about 1890 at age twenty-three and joined a congregation at Elida in Allen County, Ohio. Two weeks later he moved west to Iowa. He spent some time in Chicago at Moody Bible Institute and at a new Mennonite mission. By November 1894 he was in Cass County, Missouri. There the Bethel congregation ordained him minister by unanimous election rather than by lot, only to see him leave ten months later to attend Penn College, a Quaker school in Oskaloosa, Iowa. He was the first "old" Mennonite minister in America to go on to higher education after ordination. After a year at Penn College, Wenger traveled for ten months as an evangelist in Ohio, Ontario, New York, Pennsylvania, and Virginia. He preached more than three hundred sermons and visited more than a thousand homes.[4] That such an educated, uncommissioned, and unsponsored evangelist was allowed to preach in Lancaster County, where both higher education and revivalism were thought dangerous, was a tribute both to Wenger's gifts and to a climate of change. There had been ferment in the Lancaster conference since before the 1893 Old Order schism. That separation had freed the conference from its most conservative element and opened the way for cautiously progressive renewal. The Barge-Hershey accident was a tragic catalyst.

THE IMPACT OF REVIVALISM

In eastern "old" Mennonite and Amish Mennonite communities, change came slowly and moderately. It took several decades for the great majority of "old" Mennonites to accept American revivalism, and when they did, their revivalism retained a distinctively Mennonite flavor and style. Some conferences and congregations did not let it penetrate. History spoke for resistance. Mennonites had remained steadfastly opposed to the American revivalism which historians call the First and Second Great Awakenings (ca. 1720-1740 and 1800-1830). For that opposition they had paid the heavy price of seeing many members attracted by the warmer piety of revivalist or "New Light" alternatives.[5] Now in the late nineteenth century they borrowed from Protestant revivalism but still did so cautiously. The movement passed generally from west to east. Congregations in Illinois, Indiana, and Ohio accepted revival meetings before those in Virginia and Pennsylvania. The

Virginia conference gradually accepted them in the late 1880s, the Lancaster conference in the 1890s. The Franconia conference, despite numerous converts in the revival of 1896-1897, put up a wall of resistance until after World War II.[6] Yet the revivalist movement about the turn of the century touched all of the "old" and Amish Mennonite district conferences, who formed the constituency of John F. Funk's *Herald of Truth* and *Herold der Wahrheit.*

In part, early Mennonite evangelists imitated what they saw of Dwight Moody and Reuben Torrey in Chicago or of Methodist and Baptist revivalists in rural tent campaigns.[7] But to be accepted in traditional Mennonite congregations revivalism had to be modified and adapted. Much about American revivalism ran against the grain of Mennonite humility and simplicity, for it often used manipulative emotionalism, flamboyant preaching, and prideful publicizing of one's experience or of numbers of souls saved. It emphasized individual salvation rather than discipleship in community. It separated the salvation experience from Christian nurture carried on by pastors, families, and congregations. Traditional Mennonites were quite willing to confront people with the need to decide for Christ; Anabaptists had emphasized the believer's choice from their beginnings. But traditionalists sensed an alien spirit of pride in the style of the young Mennonite evangelists. "I am not wounded because you evangelize," wrote a conservative critic to John S. Coffman, the pioneer and dean of Mennonite evangelists, "but it does wound me to see that you like to make it known so well what you are doing in this work."[8]

Coffman, an associate of publisher John F. Funk at Elkhart, Indiana, set the standard for "old" Mennonite revivalism. Like A. D. Wenger, who came after him, Coffman was a child of Virginia who moved west (1879), learned some new ideas and techniques, and spread his influence in both West and East. In the early 1880s he began holding evangelistic meetings; and before he died in 1899, at only forty-nine, he brought revivalism into the Mennonite mainstream, inspiring a whole new generation of Mennonite evangelists and their followers.

Coffman established a subdued revivalism, deliberately respectful of the scruples of the more traditional Mennonites. He preached in an earnest conversational voice, unlike either the traditional singsong of Mennonite preachers or the bombast of some Protestant revivalists. His sermons taught distinctive Mennonite doctrine as well as the "plan of salvation." He wore the plain collarless coat and even gave that sign of Mennonite nonconformity new emphasis and status. Where local tradition forbade preannounced "protracted meetings," he was willing to hold one meeting at a time, announcing the next meeting at the one before. Gentle and engaging, he won young people while deflecting criticism from elders. Coffman's mature blend of Mennonite and revivalist styles set a high standard.[9]

The acceptance of revivalism into mainstream "old" Mennonite and Amish Mennonite churches revitalized and transformed these branches of the church. In the life of each congregation there came that critical moment of the first "protracted meetings." It was as memorable as the first sermon to be preached in English or the first time a family arrived at meeting in an automobile. The result was often a harvest of young people for church membership. Frequently the revivals followed times of extended controversy, tension, or schism in the congregation. For example, the Oak Grove congregation in Ohio's Wayne County held its first revival meetings in the spring of 1890 in the wake of a painful struggle which caused a number of families to leave. The congregation adopted a sixteen-point agreement which relaxed some of the old rules while reaffirming others: buttons could replace hooks and eyes, caps of simple style might replace hats, and younger brethren who did not wear beards would be treated with "patience." Within the community such symbols of change were momentous. And none carried more impact than the acceptance of "protracted meetings."[10]

At Oak Grove such meetings began under the evangelistic ministry of two progressive Amish Mennonite guests from Indiana, Daniel J. Johns and Jonathan P. Smucker. From May of 1890 through May of 1893, Oak Grove took in 112 new baptized members, nearly all young people. The revitalized congregation, having stemmed the loss of potential members to nearby evangelistic groups such as the Dunkers, went on to play a special role in Mennonite education and missions. In 1893 and thereafter, Oak Grove was a key to forming and developing the Eastern Amish Mennonite conference.[11]

The Oak Grove experience illustrated the particular meaning and function of the revivalism of the 1890s among the Swiss and south-German stream of Mennonites in America. A typical pattern was a division between Old Order Amish and

Amish Mennonites or between Old Order Mennonites and "old" Mennonites, followed by vigorous revivalism in the non-old-order group. The schism always centered upon the extent of change and accommodation to the American environment. The sequence of schism and subsequent revival seemed especially clear in Ontario, where, after the old-order division of 1889, John S. Coffman led sweeping "old" Mennonite revivals in the early 1890s.[12] The pattern of schism and revival yielded benefits on both the conservative and the progressive sides. The separated factions were freed from fighting each other. Each could then concentrate on the positive features of its way of congregational life and discipline. In Lancaster County, for example, by 1900 the old order and the "old" factions of the Weaverland congregation each had more active members than Weaverland had enjoyed just before the 1893 division, when the two factions were in the same congregation.[13] The schisms, although universally deplored, brought new vitality by providing Mennonites with a functional way to allow greater cultural variety.

The revivalism of the "old" and Amish Mennonite churches in the late nineteenth century recruited a whole generation of new church leaders. They led local congregations as well as the rising denominational institutions, and led them for decades to come. A few examples: Samuel G. Shetler, converted at Johnstown, Pennsylvania, in 1891, became a Bible teacher and evangelist who held revivals in two hundred churches and visited in eight thousand homes in the United States and Canada[14]; Mary Denlinger (1867-1958), converted in a John S. Coffman revival, worked at Mennonite missions in Chicago (1894-1899) and Philadelphia (1899-1924)[15]; in 1891 Noah E. Byers (1893-1962) was "won to the church" at the first evening meetings held at Sterling, Illinois, and later became principal of Elkhart Institute, president of Goshen College, and then dean at Bluffton College.[16] At the Bethel congregation in Missouri, there were two especially portentous conversions.

In 1890 Daniel Kauffman was converted under Coffman's preaching. A twenty-five-year-old widower and public school teacher and county school superintendent, Kauffman would emerge in the coming decades as the most powerful leader of the largest Mennonite branch, the "old" Mennonites.[17] Then in 1895 sixteen-year-old John Ellsworth Hartzler made a decision for Christ. Hartzler later claimed to have been impressed with

MANUAL OF

BIBLE DOCTRINES,

Setting Forth the

General Principles of the Plan of Salvation,

Explaining the

Symbolical Meaning and Practical Use of the Ordinances Instituted by Christ and His Apostles,

And Pointing out Specifically some of the

Restrictions which the New Testament Scriptures Enjoin upon Believers.

— BY —

DANIEL KAUFFMAN.

"All Scripture is given by inspiration of God, and is profitable for doctrine, for reproof, for correction, for instruction in righteousness."—2 Tim. 3:16.

ELKHART, INDIANA.
MENNONITE PUBLISHING CO.
1898.

Title page of Daniel Kauffman's *Manual of Bible Doctrines,* 1898.

(Bryan Reber)

Robert S. Kreider with muslin sheet used by J. S. Shoemaker for Bible conference presentations.

evangelist A. D. Wenger's bright necktie and swallowtail coat.[18] In any case, Hartzler himself became a gifted evangelist, author, and Mennonite college president, who offended both Kauffman and Wenger with touches of flamboyance and suspect theology. In the early twentieth century both the meaning of conversion and the limits of acceptable dress were important issues as the new workers and leaders added to the growth of the denomination.

DOCTRINAL REORIENTATION

The unsettling transitions in Mennonite communities in the latter part of the nineteenth century invited a new doctrinal formulation. Life in community seemed to need a new basis of authority.[19] Sunday schools and revivals had brought new ideas and influences expressed in English. New rituals and forms had changed the ways people became Christians and joined the church. The old traditional rules, borne along by the unwritten wisdom of the *Ordnung*, were under challenge. In the face of rapid change Mennonites needed to agree on a revised code of both theology and practice and to express it in English. Codification proceeded along a number of lines. Quite a few congregations wrote new constitutions and revised their rules for behavior. District conferences produced more and more elaborate regulations to guide bishops and ministers. Aided by a new "Bible conference" movement, they defined and disseminated the meaning of the changes.

The Bible conference movement began in the mid-1890s and peaked in the decade before World War I. In its heyday its gatherings were forums for doctrinal reorientation.[20] Teachers and learners came together for a week or more. Individual congregations, district conferences, or church schools sponsored the sessions, holding them in winter when farm work was slack. Unlike in Sunday school conferences women did not appear on programs; invariably, Bible conference teachers were men. They worked at the teaching tasks most basic to evangelical Christian communities: understanding the teachings of Scripture and orienting lives around those teachings. In the life of Mennonite congregations the moment was ripe. Many, many fervent members, youth as well as older folk, responded. Volunteer leaders were eager to show the way.

Bible conference teachers followed the style of Bible institute teaching and used a number of new methods to win attention and increase comprehension. "Eighty-five per cent of all that we learn enters the mind through the eye," reported John S. Coffman.[21] So teachers drew elaborate diagrams and charts to illustrate the "plan of salvation" or the epochs leading to the millennium. They or their sure-handed wives printed lecture outlines by hand in big, inked-stamp letters on large, reusable three-by-four-foot pieces of cloth. To involve class members they opened their sessions by assigning Scripture texts in support of points in the outline and then having individuals read the texts at the appropriate times. Students busily copied the outline notes. The teaching methods were up-to-date. And the content spoke to immediate and personal experience, both religious and social. Never had Mennonite Bible teaching seemed more rational, organized, immediate, and relevant.

At the height of the movement, about 1906 to 1914, there were some twenty such Bible conferences per year. In some places the institution continued well beyond World War I.[22] Along with reorienting congregations' doctrine and lifestyle, the conferences supported education and missions at higher levels of church organization. Moreover, some evolved into winter Bible schools lasting from two to twelve weeks. In turn the Bible schools stimulated broader district or regional systems for educating young people. The Ontario Mennonite Bible School and Institute in Berlin (Kitchener), begun 1907-1909, grew from Bible conference origins to become an institution of the "old" Mennonite conference of Ontario. In 1929 the school lengthened its sessions from six weeks to twelve.[23] In Pennsylvania the Johnstown Bible School began in 1922 for the Allegheny conference area, but was independent rather than an official conference organization.[24] Urban mission stations in Canton and Lima, Ohio, and Altoona, Pennsylvania, occasionally sponsored winter Bible schools. In 1920 the Dakota-Montana and Pacific Coast conferences began "migratory" winter Bible schools hosted by different congregations.

"Old" Mennonite academies and colleges sprang up at Elkhart (1894) and Goshen (1903) in Indiana, Hesston in Kansas (1909), and Harrisonburg in Virginia (1917). In addition to regular academic programs they all sponsored short-term winter Bible schools. In the transition from Bible conferences to winter Bible school, there was a tendency to standardize curricula and program. By the end of the 1930s winter Bible school attendance increased to about two thousand.[25]

In 1898 a booklet and a book put the new Bible conference blend of Mennonitism and American evangelical revivalism into print. The booklet, with sixty pages, was *Outlines and Notes Used at the Bible Conference held at Johnstown, Pennsylvania, from Dec. 27, 1897 to Jan. 7, 1898*, by John S. Coffman. The more systematic, 272-page book was *Manual of Bible Doctrines*, by Daniel Kauffman. Both were published by the Mennonite Publishing Company in Elkhart, Indiana. The two writings exhibited three doctrinal trends: (1) to structure doctrine into concise, propositional, numbered form; (2) to separate doctrines of salvation from ethics; (3) to offer new points of doctrinal controversy, especially the doctrine of premillennialism. All three were borrowed from late nineteenth-century American evangelicalism. Beneath them was a broader shift away from tradition and nonverbal ritual as transmitters of values in community and toward more precise and written teachings and rules.

Kauffman proposed a new three-part ordering of doctrine: (1) Plan of Salvation, (2) Ordinances, and (3) Restrictions. The title page of his manual set the agenda:

Setting Forth the
General Principles of the *Plan of Salvation,*
Explaining the
Symbolical Meaning and Practical Use
of the *Ordinances* Instituted by Christ
and His Apostles,
And Pointing out Specifically some of the
Restrictions which the New Testament Scriptures
Enjoin upon Believers.

The Plan of Salvation was first and most important. Borrowed from American evangelicalism, its label was well suited to a generation trying to systematize denominational renewal and belief. The plan itself included the general Protestant doctrines of creation, fall, sin, faith, repentance, conversion, regeneration, justification, and redemption. There was little in it that was uniquely Mennonite. For example, on the topic of conversion Kauffman made no special point of the Anabaptist-Mennonite emphasis on free, adult decision-making. Although he himself had been converted at age twenty-five, he emphasized the "child-like simplicity of converted persons."[26]

Kauffman's discussion of "Ordinances"—seven religious rites or practices which the author saw as specifically commanded in the New Testament—was more specifically Mennonite. The ordinances were baptism, communion, the footwashing rite, the prayer-head-covering for women, the holy kiss, anointing with oil, and marriage. According to Kauffman these all functioned as "symbols or memorials," not as sacraments. Yet by putting them into an elevated, divinely ordained category, he seemed to give the practices a fixed and definite ecclesiastical status. The ordinances also helped to mark the boundaries between Kauffman's "old" Mennonites and other groups. The women's prayer covering, a long-established and biblically validated custom, was elevated to a class with com-

munion and baptism and took on a new and hallowed meaning
as a distinctive Christian ordinance.[27] The very idea of ordinance, an idea which does not appear often in the New Testament, became a tool to help define and consolidate "old" Mennonites over against others who did not observe the practices
in the same way. Kauffman's new definitions gave all seven ordinances the same level of biblical authority and insisted they
made up a seamless whole. If a group set aside foot washing,
Kauffman wrote, "soon all the Bible ordinances and restrictions
that call for self-denial [find] their way out at the same door."[28]

Kauffman and the other Bible conference teachers did not
intend to separate salvation and ethics. "After all, our works
are an evidence of our justification," the emerging leader wrote,
"not for the works' sake, but because a faithful heart is productive of good works."[29] Yet his category "restrictions" made Mennonite principles of behavior seem strangely negative. And his
categories separated behavior from the more primary plan of
salvation, which Kauffman stated more positively. The "restrictions"—rules designed to keep Christians from going astray—
included "non conformity to the World, that is, refusal of worldly adornment, politics, amusements, drunkenness, etc."; nonresistance (refusal of military service); rejection of sworn oaths;
avoidance of lawsuits; and nonmembership in secret societies.

Kauffman's threefold system did not abandon distinctive
Mennonite beliefs so much as relegate them to a third-level
status as points coming after the plan of salvation and the ordinances. The real gospel was framed in terms borrowed from
American evangelicalism. Old Order Mennonites and Amish
continued an Anabaptist tradition which experienced gospel in
a community context where salvation was intimately bound up
with life together from birth to death. But more and more,
revived "old" Mennonites made the relationship of salvation
and ethics a matter of sequence. First came salvation and then
came obedience. George L. Bender, a young progressive whom
John F. Funk had brought to Elkhart, began wearing the distinctive Mennonite plain coat. His revivalist-Mennonite defense
of such visible nonconformity was that "while attire has nothing to do with our getting saved, it has . . . a great deal to do
with our remaining saved. . . . There are two words that cover
all: 'Blood' and 'Obedience.' The blood of Christ saves us, and
obedience to His Word keeps us saved."[30] As he donned the
plain coat, Bender helped John S. Coffman and others create a

new bond between revivalism and nonconformity.

Along with other points borrowed from revivalism in the 1890s came the doctrine of premillennialism. This was the teaching, increasingly popular among Protestants, that Christ was returning soon to inaugurate a literal thousand-year reign.[31] At the landmark Johnstown Bible conference in 1898, A. D. Wenger—with the help of a time-line diagram—outlined and explained the stages or "dispensations" of divine history and the meaning of forthcoming events such as the "rapture" and the "tribulation." John S. Coffman was more cautious. He had been aware of premillenialism and dispensationalism since hearing Cyrus I. Scofield at the Columbian Exposition in 1893. But he warned in his introduction to the 1898 *Outlines and Notes* that this manner of interpreting prophecy was "by no means the generally accepted view of the Mennonite people."[32] For the next three decades the Bible conference method of interpreting and teaching Scripture, which insisted on literal applications, helped make premillennialism divisive and troublesome for Mennonites. Important leaders, district conferences, and church schools became identified with one side or the other.

Another influence on some revivalistic "old" Mennonites was the holiness movement, of Wesleyan origin. Holiness teaching emphasized a postconversion "second work of grace" or baptism of the Holy Spirit. Sometimes the "second work" was called "sanctification" or "second blessing." Through it the faithful attained a higher standard of Christian perfection. Two Mennonite-related groups for which holiness teaching and experience became a source of renewal and a norm for church life were the Mennonite Brethren in Christ and the Brethren in Christ. But Mennonites also learned holiness doctrine and style from other groups: Methodists, Presbyterians, and nondenominational groups such as the "Fire Baptized Holiness Association." Some holiness groups had much in common with Mennonites: lay participation, concern for practical Christian life, and separation from the world. But they seldom reinforced the traditional Mennonite virtues of humility, quietude, and nonresistance.[33]

The life of David D. Zook, a pastor of Amish Mennonite background in the Pennsylvania Mennonite church in Harvey County, Kansas, illustrated the troubled course of holiness teachings in "old" Mennonite circles. In 1890 Zook passed

through a series of momentous personal events. Some days
after hearing evangelist John S. Coffman preach and not long
before being selected by lot and ordained to the ministry, Zook
had a decisive second-work experience. The experience came
after he sought it, on the advice of Free Methodists in nearby
Newton. When it did, at first he feared it would mean a break
with his parents and his friends; but he was allowed to continue as pastor. Indeed, in 1899 and 1900, the Kansas-Nebraska
"old" Mennonite conference adopted official resolutions that
seemed to accept holiness teachings. Some young people from
the congregation attended school at the holiness-oriented
Hepzibah Faith Missionary Association in Tabor, Iowa.[34]

But Zook's own congregation lacked consensus. In 1903,
after a time of conflict, eight holiness-inspired couples and
several individuals left it. Two members named Ira and Harvey
Yoder refused medical aid on holiness grounds and died of
typhoid fever. In 1912 the conflict flared again. This time the
Kansas-Nebraska conference declared itself against "these holiness associations as well as other religious organizations"
which did not subscribe to all Mennonite teachings. David Zook
then withdrew with about fifty members and established a new
East Emmet church, with a meetinghouse a mile away from the
Mennonite one. The East Emmet group gradually drifted from
its Mennonite identity. In World War I it gave up the doctrine of
nonresistance. Zook died in 1948, and not long afterward his
congregation dissolved.[35]

The parting of holiness and Mennonite ways suggested
broader trends in the wider "old" Mennonite church. From
1890 to about 1912, while David Zook was still one of the
pastors in his Mennonite congregation, doctrine was flexible
and the church accommodated some influence from the holiness movement. But by 1912 a new generation, led especially by
Daniel Kauffman, had formulated clear interpretations of the
Bible for Mennonites and was using the district conferences
and church colleges to enforce those interpretations. Daniel
Kauffman's associate, Daniel (D. H.) Bender, moved from the
state of Pennsylvania to be the first principal of Hesston College (begun 1909) as well as a bishop in the church. Bender
brought in Jacob (J. B.) Smith, an articulate defender of doctrine, to head Hesston's Bible department. One of Zook's followers wryly complained that "about 6 or 8 Big Guns have the
ruling of the whole Conference district and if a man is not a

College man then of course what he knows is not worth knowing."[36] Zook and others were victims of the new orthodoxy and its establishment in denominational institutions.

ORGANIZATIONAL REORIENTATION

The doctrinal reorientation of Swiss-American Mennonites coincided with new patterns of organization. In a broader perspective the organizational changes reflected patterns in larger American life. The changes occurred from the mid-nineteenth through the twentieth century and shaped Mennonite behavior and mentality at all levels—from congregation to district to church-wide conference. American organizational styles first came to Mennonite congregations via the Sunday schools. Like many others, Mennonites at first held the schools not in their meetinghouses but in public school buildings or elsewhere. Young people learned not only the Bible but also how to organize—to follow parliamentary procedures, elect officers, serve as chairman or secretary and treasurer, and keep records. Sunday schools taught Mennonites new ways to mobilize and lead their people.

In addition to spawning new structures, the new methods altered old ones. In some district conferences they helped concentrate the power of leading bishops and helped leaders enforce standards of behavior. Such changes came slowly. For example, in 1885 the bishops of the Indiana-Michigan Mennonite conference began to gather separately before the yearly conference meeting to set agenda. In 1891 they first began sessions by electing a moderator and a secretary. In 1898 they chose a permanent secretary, for a three-year term, to keep more regular minutes in a special book. By World War I this conference's executive committee, led by Jacob (J. K.) Bixler, was one of the most powerful among "old" Mennonite conferences.[37] An important moment for any conference was the point at which it decided to publish its minutes, resolutions, and rules. The Lancaster conference had printed its "Rules and Discipline" as early as 1881. The Virginia conference first published minutes in 1884. In 1915 the Indiana-Michigan conference reached a new peak of prescription by publishing a "Constitution, Rules and Discipline." Published rules, directed mainly toward regulating the limits of worldly dress and association, helped shore up Mennonite resistance to outside influences. But, ironically, Mennonites borrowed the means of resistance from American culture itself.[38]

In 1898 "old" and Amish Mennonites topped their organizational development by creating an overall general conference. In the next decade they created three major churchwide boards—the Board of Missions and Charities (originated in 1892 and organized in lasting form in 1906), the Board of Education (1905), and the Publication Board (1908). The era of John F. Funk was yielding to the era of Daniel Kauffman, and the new boards were points where the new, strong leadership came to focus. The constituency of Funk's *Herald of Truth* (never quite as large as the seventeen district conferences Funk claimed) formed the base of the "old" Mennonite and Amish Mennonite organizational structure. Meanwhile, doctrinal books, which Kauffman led in developing, offered a clear, coherent, Mennonite position. The structures and the doctrine were conservative, yet stood apart from those of the Old Order Mennonites and Old Order Amish. In the other direction they stemmed loss of members and congregations to the General Conference Mennonites. After 1898 these two major branches—the "old" and the GC Mennonites—continued their competition for members from a new organizational context. The GC ecumenical dream for an all-Mennonite union faded as doctrinal and institutional differences became more distinct and rigid. At the congregational and district levels both branches allowed some diversity of church polity and practice. But the "old" Mennonites reached more vigorously for a consensus enforced by prescription, while the ethnically heterogeneous GC church allowed more leeway for congregations.

"We are now in the 'organization' period of our church life," wrote one of the ablest of Mennonite organizers, Menno (M. S.) Steiner, in 1910. "Everybody seems to have been taken with the fever throughout the Church." Two decades earlier, Steiner had helped a new Sunday school conference found a Mennonite mission in Chicago. Since that time, first in the West and later in the East, the organization and reorganization of boards, committees, conferences, and institutions had become a passion. Organization gave the church new power to set objectives and to achieve them. Yet the best of the organizers saw that organization could become a dangerous end in itself. Steiner had second thoughts about the trend he had helped to start. Said he, "the thing is being overdone."[39]

PARTIAL UNION OF AMISH AND MENNONITES

The greatest "old" Mennonite achievement was denominational union with a major portion of the Amish Mennonites. In part, this was a matter of healing a 200-year-old schism. Also, it followed a sorting out of Amish Mennonites from Old Order Amish. A series of general Amish conferences from 1862 to 1878 had left the Amish divided over both teaching and practice. Daniel Kauffman, in the 1898 *Manual*, urged Mennonite union with the more progressive Amish, the Amish Mennonites. "There is no reason," he wrote, "why these two organizations should not be merged into one organization."[40]

However, at the turn of the century the groups of ex-Amish constituted not a single organization but five major organized clusters and some smaller fragments. They were: (1) the eastern Amish Mennonite conference of Pennsylvania and Ohio, organized in 1893; (2) the Egly Amish, separated in 1866 and incorporated in 1908 as the "Defenseless Mennonite Church," with congregations in Indiana, Ohio, and Illinois; (3) the Indiana Amish Mennonite conference, organized in 1888 and strongest in northern Indiana, where it associated and cooperated with the Indiana-Michigan Mennonite conference; (4) the Stuckey Amish of central Illinois, separated in 1872 and organized in 1899 as the Central Illinois conference; and (5) the Western Amish Mennonite conference, organized in 1884 for congregations west of Indiana.

The barriers to Amish and Mennonite denominational merger were not primarily theological or social liberalism or conservatism. All groups were conservative, although with some variety. Some Amish congregations, such as the Oak Grove congregation in Wayne County, Ohio, were more progressive in matters of education and dress than were the "old" Mennonite conferences they joined. A more important barrier was difference in polity. Through history the Amish had given congregations more autonomy, whereas among "old" Mennonites the bishops, bishop boards, and conferences had exercised more authority. The difference was especially important in a time when leaders were becoming more specific about church doctrine and discipline—for instance, on a matter such as disapproving lapel coats for men. "Old" and Amish Mennonites merged their organizations deliberately, only after they had smoothed the way with decades of fellowship, association, and negotiation. The Indiana-Michigan merger finally came in 1916, the Western in

1920-1921, and the Eastern in 1927. None came until some time after 1898, when the new general conference began to bring "old" and Amish Mennonites together at a higher level. As the district conferences merged, the Amish Mennonites sacrificed their Amish name but became a major component of the "old" Mennonite church.

The merger was the greatest ecumenical achievement of any Mennonites and Amish in the early-twentieth century, and the "old" Mennonite branch gained a flow of new members from more conservative Amish sources. Yet the union did not succeed totally. From 1905 to 1927 "old" Mennonite leaders claimed the Stuckey and Egly Amish Mennonites as part of their constituency and listed them in the *Mennonite Yearbook and Directory*. But those progressive Amish went their own ways. In 1946, after half a century as the independent Central Illinois Mennonite conference, the Stuckey Amish joined the General Conference Mennonite branch.[41] Meanwhile, in overseas mission work they cooperated with the Egly Amish in the Congo Inland Mission. In higher education they were less oriented to the "old" Mennonites' Goshen College than to Central Mennonite College (renamed Bluffton College in 1913), an institution of the GCs' Middle District conference. The Egly Amish suffered a schism in 1898 when Joseph Ramseyer, bishop Egly's heir apparent, left with a large group of followers to found a new "Missionary Church Association." The remaining members eventually accepted Ramseyer's views—Holy Spirit baptism separate from conversion, baptism by immersion, and premillennialism—but the schism remained. Over the years the Egly Amish increasingly opted for American Fundamentalism.[42]

"OLD" MENNONITE/RUSSIAN MENNONITE NONUNION

The general conference formed by the "old" and Amish Mennonites in 1898 came on the scene too late to attract Dutch-background Mennonites who had immigrated from Prussia and the Russian Empire in the 1870s and 1880s. Except for the Mennonite Brethren, most of these had joined the General Conference Mennonite body, organized in 1860. The cultural differences between Swiss-American and Dutch-Russian Mennonites would have made association and cooperation difficult in any case. The fate of one small group of "Russian" origin, the "United Mennonite Brethren" (later the "Evangelical Mennonite Brethren"), is suggestive. This group originated from separate groups in Henderson, Nebraska, and Mountain Lake, Minnesota, who broke with congregations that later joined the GC branch. "Old" Mennonite leaders tried hard to attract the "United Mennonite Brethren" and from 1905 to 1918 listed them in their annual *Mennonite Yearbook* as the "Nebraska Minnesota Conference." Leaders of the "old" Mennonites such as M. S. Steiner, Noah Mack, and Daniel Kauffman attended the group's conventions. In 1896 John F. Funk apparently served as convention secretary. The United Mennonite Brethren sent their first overseas missionaries, Peter A. and Helena Hiebert Friesen, to India under the "old" Mennonite mission board. Yet the bond did not last. By World War I the so-called Nebraska Minnesota Conference broke ties with the "old" Mennonites and continued independently with the name "Defenseless Mennonite Brethren in Christ of North America."[43]

Cultural differences, not theology, separated the groups. Prior to the war the Dutch-Russian Mennonites held firmly to the German language and to their Low German dialect. Meanwhile the Swiss-Americans were shifting from their (quite different) Pennsylvania German dialect to English. The Dutch-Russian United Mennonite Brethren had their own gestures, rituals, and family networks for group identity. Those rituals did not include all of the prescribed "ordinances and restrictions" which had become marks of "old" Mennonite separation from the world. Daniel Kauffman called this failure to accept his group's formula a "general trend toward more liberal standards."[44] In fact, the separation was the product of two culturally different conservatisms, one Swiss in origin and the other Dutch. Each adapted to American conditions and absorbed elements of American evangelicalism in its own way.

"OLD" MENNONITES AND JURA SWISS INDEPENDENCE

Some Swiss Mennonites who had immigrated to Ohio and Indiana in the nineteenth century were especially independent and resisted Americanized "old" Mennonite patterns of church life.[45] The Sonnenberg congregation of Wayne County in Ohio was the earliest (1819) and served as the "mother" or way station for numerous other Jura Swiss congregations. Sonnenbergers held onto the German language until the 1930s and remained formally independent of American Mennonite conferences until 1952.[46] Other Jura Swiss joined the General Conference Mennonite church. These had been influenced by the

Wadsworth school and attracted by the GC combination of congregational autonomy and denominational mission. Especially thriving was a cluster of congregations in Putnam and Allen counties in western Ohio—Ebenezer, St. Johns, Grace in Pandora, and First Mennonite in Bluffton. The GC-related Central Mennonite College was founded in 1900 mainly to serve their area. At Berne, Indiana, Samuel F. Sprunger led another substantial Jura Swiss congregation to become a strong GC church and center of GC publication. Trained at Wadsworth in the 1870s, Sprunger served as pastor at Berne until 1903.[47]

The Jura Swiss of the GC branch gradually gave up the severe simplicity of their immigrant foreparents, yet kept a strong sense of ethnic heritage. "One characteristic of a Swiss, different from other people, is that he hardly ever goes farther afield than his cow pasture," wrote Swiss Mennonite sawmill operator and historian Peter B. Amstutz self-mockingly. If Amstutz admitted to provincialism, he also celebrated Swiss Mennonite "improvement and progress" and reported a trip he made in 1914 to Europe and the Orient.[48]

A few of the Jura Swiss did find their way into the "old" Mennonite fold. Among them was Menno S. Steiner's Zion congregation in Ohio's Allen County. A Swiss pastor had founded the congregation after he differed with his fellow Swiss by favoring the ceremony of foot washing. But that congregation was the exception. In most cases the Jura Swiss immigrants nourished a strong sense of distinct peoplehood which kept them from easy absorption into the "old" Mennonite denominational consensus.

ORGANIZATIONAL CONTROL

The "old" Mennonite general conference of 1898 moved quickly to become a central government to define orthodox teachings and control "old" Mennonite institutions. According to a preliminary meeting in 1897, the first object of the conference was "to bring about a closer unity of sentiment on Gospel principles." Such unity, resulting from closer spiritual intercourse, would mean "a weeding out of heretical doctrines, and the consequent purity of the church." The conference organizers said they did not intend to assert legislative authority over district conferences and congregations. Yet phrases such as "to centralize" and "to direct" implied that somehow the conference would exercise binding power. At least it would exert power over church institutions such as publications, homes for orphans and the elderly, and missions, plus their boards. It would also establish acceptable church doctrine and behavior.[49] Daniel Kauffman, then only thirty-three, presided over or "moderated" the first general conference meeting.

Immediately the new body appointed a committee "to investigate all organizations that wish to be considered as church institutions." The conference would recognize only those institutions which met its standards for purpose, composition, management, and character.[50] In 1900 at its second meeting it accepted several: an old people's home at Rittman and an orphans' home at West Liberty in Ohio; the forerunner of Goshen College, Elkhart Institute; a Mennonite Evangelizing and Benevolent Board at Elkhart; and a Mennonite Aid Plan, whose treasurer was in Scottdale, Pennsylvania. None of the institutions was centered in the old heartland of eastern Pennsylvania, even though the heaviest concentrations of Mennonite population were there. The conference never assumed legal control and actual direction of the institutions. But general conference approval became very important for them and for others which came later.

In an official conference sermon at the first meeting John F. Funk acclaimed the new organization to be the "consummation" of twenty-five years of planning.[51] Before the second meeting in 1900, however, Funk reversed his position and spoke out *against* the conference organization. A struggle had emerged with Daniel Kauffman and others pitted against him, most directly for control of "old" Mennonite publishing.[52] Funk now argued that the conference founders had moved too rapidly, without an adequate mandate from the district conferences and congregations. The large eastern conferences, Lancaster and Franconia, had refused to affiliate officially. In reply, N. O. Blosser of New Stark, Ohio, noted that when Funk had begun his own Mennonite publishing house a generation earlier "many of our people then living were not willing to accept it as an institution in any way connected or beneficial to the Church." Funk had won support by hard work, Blosser said, and so could the new general conference.[53] The parallel was apt. Progressive change among Mennonites had never depended upon majority support or upon the blessing of traditionally constituted authorities. Funk, although he had long been at the church's progressive forefront, was resisting the tide of history. And after

(Mennonite Library and Archives)

John E. and Mamie Yoder Hartzler, with children John and Helen.

World War I, once their organizations were established, the conference organizers would in turn struggle against challenges from yet another young progressive generation.

The generational transition at the turn of the century was stormy. Funk was not willing to yield to energetic younger men such as Daniel Kauffman, G. L. Bender, M. S. Steiner, Aaron Loucks, and A. D. Wenger.[54] In 1892 some of the younger group and evangelist John S. Coffman had set up a rival "Mennonite Book and Tract Society," another institution which in 1898 quickly asked and got recognition from the new general conference. Funk's Mennonite Publishing Company, a private corporation of shareholders, had long operated in the name of the church. Now Funk refused to apply for general conference endorsement.

Complicating the situation was a local dispute in Funk's congregation at Elkhart. Funk as bishop was charged with acting arbitrarily in a conflict involving the Elkhart Institute and the congregation, and the Indiana-Michigan conference convened a committee of five ordained men to investigate. Made up of leaders from the four district conferences of Lancaster, Virginia, Ohio, and Kansas-Nebraska, the committee recommended that Funk be suspended as bishop. He was never restored to the office. Then in 1903 a failure of a local bank put his Mennonite Publishing Company into bankruptcy. Four years later a fire destroyed half its plant. Meanwhile a rival group at Scottdale, Pennsylvania, organized the Gospel Witness Company and began to publish a periodical called the *Gospel Witness*. The new paper competed directly with the *Herald of Truth*, and by 1908 Funk sold out to his rivals.

At that point the younger leaders founded a church-owned publishing house, a churchwide publication board, and an officially sanctioned denominational paper called the *Gospel Herald*. In the judgment of one observer, Funk's *Herald of Truth* had become "an easy prey" to leaders who were "younger," "aggressive," and "well-organized."[55] Funk's leadership was finished, even though he lived until 1930.

With Funk's decline, denominational institutions shifted away from Elkhart. In 1903 the Elkhart Institute moved to the nearby town of Goshen and became Goshen College. Publishing shifted to Scottdale, attracted by the entrepreneurial energy, prosperity, and generosity of the Loucks family there. Daniel Kauffman moved to Scottdale, where he edited the *Gospel Herald*. His editorship stretched from 1908 to 1943.[56] Like Funk, Kauffman used the office for broader church leadership and initiative. These two men, the first as an innovating entrepreneur and the second as a denominational organization man, gave the "old" Mennonites nearly eight decades of continuity in leadership (1864-1943).[57] Through many changes they helped give the "old" Mennonites stability.

In the first quarter of the twentieth century the authority of the "old" Mennonites' general conference grew rapidly despite a remarkable vagueness of its institutional boundaries. It was never precisely clear which and how many district conferences belonged, for general conference leaders tried informally to include even those who had not formally affiliated. Bishops from any "old" or Amish Mennonite conference, including Lancaster, could attend and vote in general conference sessions. Conference reports reflected this vagueness. They referred at times to a constituency not of member churches but of "such churches commonly held as belonging to the Mennonite General Conference."[58] The three general church boards for missions, publication, and education were created apart from the general conference and so were formally autonomous. The general conference appointed some members to the missions and publication boards, but not until 1923 did it appoint any to the more controversial Board of Education. In addition to these three general boards, the conference created a number of committees to deal with matters such as a new hymnal, new statements of Mennonite history and doctrine, and dress regulation.

Daniel Kauffman organized with an authoritative style. An example was the way he moved to bring the three "old" Mennonite colleges (Goshen, Hesston, Eastern Mennonite School) under the Board of Education and a common constitution with consistent by-laws and centrally formed policies. That board, founded in 1905 as a successor to the Elkhart Institute Association, did not have official general conference status. Yet Kauffman acted in the name of the church as a whole. He projected a given structure, gave orders to create that structure, assigned to himself the central coordinating role, and demanded that school officials carry out their work quickly. In 1918, for example, Kauffman wrote to J. B. Smith, principal at Eastern Mennonite School:

> Our mission will be to write a Constitution for the Board which will also embody the government of the institutions under it. This combined Constitution and by-laws is to fit each institution, there being special by-laws for each institution to fit its peculiar needs. . . . I am to rewrite, combine the three, detailing the special by-laws to each institution. The committee is to have the task of then criticising and still further perfecting the writings and submitting their report for action by the Board. There is to be no attempt to write a School Policy until we have the Constitution and by-laws prepared, and will then make the Policy fit the Constitution. This means hurry up and jump committee. Do your part of the jumping.[59]

Kauffman's grand design for control over the colleges did not succeed. Its failure grew partly out of an extended upheaval at Goshen College. But Kauffman had more success elsewhere—especially in forming centrally defined doctrine.

In 1914 under Kauffman's leadership the "old" Mennonite general conference published a 701-page volume defining "old" Mennonite teachings. In content it was a revised and expanded edition of Kauffman's 1898 *Manual of Bible Doctrine*. But the new book had multiple authorship and official denominational sanction. Kauffman managed the project and gave the book its shape. He chose the chapter topics, oversaw selection of writers, edited all manuscripts for style and content, and provided the chapter arrangement and section introductions. Being from Pennsylvania, Virginia, Ontario, Ohio, Indiana, and Kansas, the writers broadly represented different regions. They came from different group backgrounds, Amish as well as Mennonite. They varied somewhat in their theology—including, for instance, both J. E. Hartzler and George R. Brunk, with respectively progressive and conservative reputations. Hartzler, president of Goshen College from 1913 to 1918, wrote the entire section on the plan of salvation. Partly because he sometimes could find no willing author, Kauffman himself wrote seven chapters. In one, entitled "From Death to Judgement," he had to skirt the controversial millennialism issue. The process of building consensus was cumbersome. From the presidential office at Hesston College, D. H. Bender complained that there were "at least 75% too many writers."[60] But broad participation ensured denomination-wide ownership.

This 1914 *Bible Doctrine* and a 1928 edition, revised by Kauffman and called *Doctrines of the Bible*, did not enjoy the status of an official creed. But they provided an accepted standard for "old" Mennonite congregations, Bible conferences, winter Bible schools, and other forums.[61] They also bore the marks of the escalating American Protestant debate between Modernists and Fundamentalists. In his 1898 volume Kauffman had simply assumed the authority of the Bible without worrying much about a theory of inspiration. "We know that a thing is true," he wrote in a passage addressed to higher criticism, "because it is in the Bible."[62] However, the 1914 book included a thirty-page chapter on "The Bible," written by J. B. Smith of Hesston College. Skillfully, Smith set forth a conservative theory of biblical revelation. A graduate of Ohio Northern University at Ada, and a true scholar, Smith introduced terms new to many Mennonites: "plenary inspiration," "verbal inspiration," "original autographs."

Thus it was that "old" Mennonite definitions of ordinances and restrictions, based directly on Bible texts, gained a more legalistic undergirding than ever before. To question the *Bible Doctrine* case for foot washing, prayer coverings, or other "old"

Mennonite patterns of nonconformity to the world became more and more like challenging the authority of Scripture and the church. To challenge *Bible Doctrine* was to be branded as favoring Modernism and modern critical ways of interpreting the Bible. Yet while *Bible Doctrine* borrowed from Fundamentalism, its purpose was to offer a pattern for conservative denominational life.

DRESS, OBEDIENCE, AND NONCONFORMITY

Day to day, no pattern affected "old" Mennonite life more visibly than did prescribed forms of clothing. Plain and simple attire was a long-standing Mennonite tradition, a sign of humility in a world of fashionable pride. Revivalism made the question of dress seem more urgent and serious. The evangelists awakened young people to religious concern much earlier in life and persuaded young as well as old to be more earnest about simplicity. Members turned with new intensity to the Bible, to its general admonitions regarding nonconformity, and to specific injunctions such as Paul's command in 1 Corinthians 11 for women to cover their heads. They wanted mainly to be obedient to Scripture, but they faced the problem that intense obedience might produce legalism rather than real transformation of the heart. Discussions and resolutions relating to dress occupied more time and attention at "old" Mennonite conferences than did any other issue.[63]

Pressure for uniformity of attire increased from the 1890s onward, as the "old" Mennonites adopted more structured and denominational forms of church life. An impulse toward written and prescribed uniform dress standards paralleled the impulse for written and prescribed doctrine. Both deeply affected church newspapers, district conference resolutions, and actions of the "old" Mennonites' general conference. In 1911 the conference created a "Dress Committee" to bring "all our people to the Gospel standard of simplicity and spirituality."[64] The committee's report, published two years later, was apparently drafted by Daniel Kauffman, whose name headed it. The report recommended a "more perfect uniformity among both brethren and sisters," a uniformity based upon "God's Word and the order of the Church." It stated its regulations more urgently for ministers than for lay people and in greater detail for women than for men. Yet in 1917 the same committee warned "against two double standards, (1) a plainly attired ministry and a fashionable laity, and (2) plainness for sisters, no restrictions for brethren."[65]

In dress as in other matters the "old" Mennonites' general conference had no formal mandate to impose its will. Nevertheless, by spelling out church authority in ever more specific and sweeping language the conference gave strength to those people at the district and congregational levels who wanted more strictness. The dress committee declared in 1921 that "the Church is vested with authority in all matters of doctrine and discipline (1 Tim. 3:15; Matt. 18:17)." Therefore, "so long as her rules and regulations do not conflict with the Word of God (Gal. 1:8, 9) her decrees are binding and her authority should not be questioned (Matt. 18:18; Acts 15:6-33; 16:14; Heb. 13:7)."[66]

Regulated and distinctive dress served to separate "old" Mennonites from the broader American society. To some extent it replaced the eroding function of social isolation and separate (German) language. Some of the most enthusiastic and aggressive denominational organizers also spoke out most strongly for nonconformity in apparel. John S. Coffman and many who followed his progressive footsteps committed themselves to the plain coat and provided a new biblical rationale for the women's prayer covering (1 Corinthians 11).[67] The common commitment to distinctive dress helped hold together "old" Mennonites of the traditionally conservative East and the denominationally progressive West. In some cases, such as in the attitude toward men's neckties, the West actually brought more conservative standards to the East, where bow ties had been long accepted. For example, in 1911, George R. Brunk of Kansas moved east to Virginia and took with him a movement against both kinds of ties—saying, reportedly, "Now we have the West plain. I've got to go and make the East plain."[68] It was said also that Noah Mack, Lancaster conference leader who had adopted the plain coat only after a long personal struggle, made a trip west and returned without his necktie—and that his wife advised against another such trip lest he come back without his shirt![69] The dress code took on fine shades of difference in different areas as members tested the limits. Prayer coverings varied in size, material, strings, and color of strings, and in whether strings were tied or hung loose. Some districts allowed neckties, others only bow ties, and some neither.

In general, Pennsylvania held to dress regulations more than did the West. Men resisted them more than did women, and lay members dressed more freely than did ministers and their wives. "Old" Mennonites never achieved absolute uniformity of attire. The Virginia conference, for example, openly acknowledged that members' practice often was quite different from conference rules. A 1918 report admitted that while the conference's Middle District had more than 700 members, only "100 brethren and 175 sisters conform to the regulation of the church."[70] Some 60 percent of the members did not fully obey the rules. Yet the conference treated that fact as a matter of concern, not crisis. Most members, "with painful exceptions,"[71] at least dressed modestly and were loyal to the church in other ways. At the same time, conformity on regulated dress did not automatically confer trustworthiness. J. B. Smith in Virginia complained that progressive S. F. Coffman in Ontario "wears the plain coat and the old kind of pants and yet fights simplicity."[72]

In "old" Mennonite circles everywhere, the trend from the 1890s was to replace traditional and informal sanctions regarding dress with more formal, written codes. In Franconia the turning point toward more literal definitions and enforcement came in 1911. In that year the fall conference resolved, among other dress regulations, that "Sisters wearing hats are required to dispense with them before Spring communion and instead wear the plain protection covering."[73] The trend to formalized, rationalized codes set off discussion and argument everywhere. There was never complete agreement or absolute enforcement. Nevertheless, the "old" Mennonites' denominational leaders were able to use dress to clarify an authoritative standard and to mark out their group's peoplehood. Regulated dress identified "old" Mennonites as separate not only from the non-Mennonite world but also from old order traditionalism on the one side and "new" Mennonites' more liberal practices on the other side. In 1927 conference leader D. H. Bender noted that despite dangers of Modernism and worldliness "we praise the Lord that we still have fairly good control over the membership generally."[74]

"NEW" MENNONITES—GENERAL CONFERENCE (GC)

In 1898, shortly before the organizational meeting for creating the "old" and Amish Mennonites' general conference, John F. Funk proposed to name the new body the "United Conference of Mennonites." He suggested that "General Conference" was improper, and perhaps illegal, since there already existed a legally incorporated body named the "General Conference of Mennonites of North America," formed in 1860.[75] But the "old" Mennonites ignored Funk's advice and created much confusion in Mennonite nomenclature. After 1898 there were two Mennonite "general conferences," sometimes referred to as "General Conference A" and "General Conference B." Both reached out for the largest possible share of the Mennonite constituency.[76] The organizers of both were from the Swiss and south-German stream of Anabaptist-Mennonite history. At least in origin, both conferences were part of Swiss-American Mennonitism.

At the turn of the century some of the key "General Conference A" Swiss-background leaders were graduates of the first and ill-fated GC educational institution, the Wadsworth Institute at Wadsworth, Ohio (1867-1878). At Wadsworth students had learned, in the words of one graduate, "the breaking away from formalism and the beginning of intelligent, aggressive work for the Master as well."[77] One Wadsworth alumnus was Nathaniel (N. B.) Grubb, pastor of the First Mennonite Church of Philadelphia from 1882 to 1920.[78] In 1885 Grubb was a founding editor of an English-language GC paper, *The Mennonite*, and he served as editor until 1892. Among other accomplishments he also initiated Philadelphia inner-city mission work, which resulted in the Second Mennonite Church of Philadelphia, where his son Silas later served as pastor. Grubb also helped to found a Mennonite Home for the Aged at Fredericksburg in 1893 and was among those who organized the Eastern District Sunday School Convention. Leaders such as Grubb demonstrated that there could be a progressive urban Mennonitism. At the large First Mennonite Church in Berne, Indiana, two other Wadsworth-educated denominational innovators named Samuel (S. F.) Sprunger and Isaac A. Sommer also brought progressive changes: Christian Endeavor, foreign and home missions, and Christian education.[79] Unlike Philadelphia and even more than rural eastern Pennsylvania, Berne was a small community where Mennonites took major roles in retail, manufacturing, and civic affairs. As it became the GC publishing center, both the German *Christlicher Bundesbote* and (after 1905) the English *The Mennonite* were edited there. Mennonite prohibitionists at Berne led a vigorous and successful eight-year battle to banish the town's saloons.[80]

By the end of the century the focus of the General Conference Mennonite church's agenda had shifted away from educational mission and Wadsworth Institute. Instead, the vision became mission work in Indian Territory, Arizona, and India. Conference identity took shape partly around aggressive denominational activity and partly around ecumenism. In 1908 the GC general conference joined the Federal Council of Churches, then withdrew in 1917 when American Protestants joined the war effort. Also, GC identity was partly a matter of what its leaders refused to do. They rejected what they considered traditional formalism and legalism. Most often this meant avoiding dress regulations, but sometimes the GCs rejected other conservative patterns of church and community life. The Dutch-Russian immigrants who gradually took a dominant role in the GC general conference had somewhat different ways of tradition and innovation from those of the Swiss and south-German stream who founded the conference.

While "old" Mennonites were centralizing authority, GCs stood for "liberty in nonessentials." That code phrase begged the questions of what was really essential and of how essentials were to be made secure. But it allowed greater variety and a great deal of congregational autonomy. The GC general conference had no single commanding leader to compare with the "old" Mennonites' Daniel Kauffman. Nor did the GCs ever adopt a formal creed or "Bible doctrine" beyond a one-paragraph "common confession" in an 1896 constitution.[81] Unofficially, the conference recommended to congregations the Ris Confession, a Dutch Mennonite document of 1766 promoted in America by Carl J. van der Smissen. The relatively noncreedal and nonregulative character of the GC general conference was a product of congregational polity and cultural diversity as well as of the deliberate decision to construct denominational life around cooperative endeavor. Official GC discussions continued to include the traditional Mennonite values of simple living and nonresistance. But the GC general conference, converging the Swiss-American and the Dutch-Russian cultural streams, was less an instrument of control than was its "old" Mennonite counterpart.

OVERLAPPING POLARITIES

The "old" Mennonites were at the center of the spectrum of those Mennonite groups which originated in the Swiss and south-German wing. On their right were the Old Order Amish and Old Order Mennonites; on their left were the "new" Mennonites who found their way into the GC general conference. The so-called Russian Mennonites of Dutch background had their own spectrum. Most of the Dutch-Russians also joined the GC general conference. Others formed their own conferences. The interplay of organizational development, revivalist renewal, and traditionalist resistance to change affected the life of these groups in differing ways.[82] The "old" Mennonite synthesis was particularly successful in enhancing both Mennonite identity and spiritual vitality.

Around the turn of the century, Mennonites of several different groups began overseas missions work at about the same time. Missionary work brought its own threats and opportunities to the balances that Mennonites groups had struck between traditional identity and threatening change.

CHAPTER
5

DENOMINATIONAL ADVANCE: MISSIONS

In the spring of 1891 on a troubled reservation in Indian Territory (Oklahoma), a Mennonite missionary named Heinrich R. Voth shared a brief but remarkable moment of spiritual talk with an Arapaho prophet. The prophet was Sitting Bull, although not the famous chief of the Sioux. Voth and Sitting Bull each spoke of a nonresistant Christ. Each had a vision for a peaceable regeneration of his people. Each was about thirty-five years old, and through his vision each had established more respect among his people than was usual for a man of thirty-five. Briefly, the two hoped to merge their visions into a common effort. But such hopes, especially those of Sitting Bull, were doomed to disappointment.[1]

PROPHET AND MISSIONARY: VISIONS FOR RENEWAL
Sitting Bull's vision was born of a people's desperation. Devastated through false treaties and military combat with westward-advancing whites, the plains Indians had lost both the buffalo herds and the freedom of movement on the land that were essential to their survival. Warfare, starvation, and disease had brought havoc. The Arapaho population had dropped by about one-third—from 2,964 in the 1870s to 1,920 at a point in the 1890s.[2] U.S. reservation and land-distribution policies had assaulted the Indian way of life. White schools were giving young people alien educations. The chiefs had lost authority, and the people were dispirited. But now Sitting Bull, with new authority after going to Nevada and visiting a famous Paiute prophet named Wovoka, announced a Great Reversal. If his people would dance the Ghost Dance, a new ceremony with

(Mennonite Library and Archives)

Artifacts from Hopi culture collected by Heinrich R. Voth, mission-ary. Some displayed at the 1893 World's Fair in Chicago.

no drums and with a Christian-influenced style of singing, the Messiah would appear and inaugurate the new age. The dead would arise, the buffalo would return, the whites would melt away, and the earth would be restored. The otherworldly, apocalyptic vision carried no clear plan for political or economic reform. The people were admonished to be honest, industrious, and virtuous—in fact, to adopt an ethical code of Christian flavor. But mostly they had to dance the dance—and wait.

By contrast, Voth's vision was born of a people's progress. The Mennonites, hard-working inheritors of the Protestant ethic, had prospered all along the frontier lands where Indians had recently roamed. Mennonite life was also changing, with traditional authorities being challenged and outside influences making manifold inroads. But to Mennonites the change meant progress, prosperity, and population growth. God had blessed the Mennonites. So missionaries were to share and extend these blessings by teaching the victims of oppression and ignorance how to build thriving communities on a Mennonite model. The vision foresaw the Arapahoes (and Cheyenne, Comanche, and Hopi—who were also targets of Mennonite missions) mastering the English language, scrubbing clean with soap, sewing and wearing modern clothing, and working hard on individual farmsteads. Mennonites called on Native Americans to "take the white man's road" in all things. They were to trade tribal communalism for private property on single-family homesteads. The Mennonite vision was this-worldly and progressive.

Mennonites had no rhythm for dancing, no time for waiting. They too expected Christ's return. Indeed, at this same moment a small band of Voth's brothers and sisters in the faith were awaiting the imminent return of their Lord in Central Asia. But when the Messiah would come, he would find most Mennonites working hard to make a better life for themselves, for their children, and for those in the "heathen" world where missionaries labored for Christ and civilization.

Mennonite missions in Indian Territory began in 1880, and their first decades were a great disappointment. Eight years passed before the first baptism and seventeen years before the first congregation was organized. Meanwhile, defeated and dispirited Indians died in alarming numbers. "It may become the sad duty of our mission," Voth had written in 1887, "to sing the funeral songs of almost the last Arapahoes."[3] Sitting Bull's message of the Ghost Dance Messiah was a ray of hope and an opportunity for teaching around common symbols. Voth visited at length with Sitting Bull, a "small, lightly built and a comparatively young man." The Indian leader alleged that his faith had much in common with that of the Mennonites, and he addressed a Mennonite mission Sunday school. In turn, Voth attended the Ghost Dance. Sitting Bull took time at the dance to admonish his people to attend the missionaries' meetings and learn the Bible. Voth was greatly impressed and hoped that the Ghost Dance could be a bridge for the Arapahoes to accept the true Christ.[4]

But the gap was too wide, the visions too different. The Ghost Dance Messiah failed to appear as predicted, and the prophet Wovoka himself repudiated the dance. So Sitting Bull lost credibility, confidence, and most of his interest in following up contacts with missionaries. In 1891 Voth took himself out of the picture with an extended furlough, a trip to his own people back in the Russia Empire. Later he took up an assignment to the Hopi Indians in Arizona, a people with a much different language and culture. In retrospect it seems that lasting accommodation between the Ghost Dance and Mennonite Christianity could hardly have been possible. The Ghost Dance, far from being a move from traditional religion to Christianity, was an attempt by Indians in cultural crisis to maintain a separate religious and cultural identity. Most Mennonite missionaries were less alert than Voth regarding native custom; they followed other Protestants in thoroughly rejecting Indians' culture. Even Voth proposed to "undermine the heathenish customs and the superstitions of this people, and open their eyes. . . ."[5]

Sitting Bull and H. R. Voth may have reached out to each other a bit in 1891, but the starting assumptions of each leader practically meant death for the other's culture. Therefore Native Americans were slow to gather into Mennonite churches and Mennonites scarcely accommodated to Native-American ways. Typical were the words of one Mennonite Brethren missionary, Henry Kohfeld, on a Comanche reservation: "Only those who by God's grace were driven into a corner were willing to listen to us."[6] Decades later, in the 1930s, Rodolphe Petter, an elderly and somewhat discouraged GC Mennonite missionary, reflected that it all might have been different if the Mennonites back in 1890 had been better prepared with language and with translated Scriptures. Petter thought the missionaries might have taken advantage of the spiritual hunger of the Ghost Dance days.[7]

PROGRESSIVE DENOMINATIONAL ADVANCE

The Mennonite missionary thrust was at the heart of progressive Mennonites' new, wide-ranging denominational activity in the years between 1890 and 1930. At the end of this era a returned missionary from China, Edmund G. Kaufman, chronicled and celebrated this impressive development in a book called *The Development of the Missionary and Philanthropic Interest among the Mennonites of North America.* Kaufman constructed a composite "missionary interest" graph which included not only home and foreign missions but also Mennonite conference organizations, hospitals, old people's homes, orphanages, schools, publishing houses, and periodicals. His data showed that in the fifty years between 1880 and 1930 American Mennonites founded sixteen foreign mission programs (including those for Native Americans) and sent more than four hundred missionaries. The missionaries and those whom they won

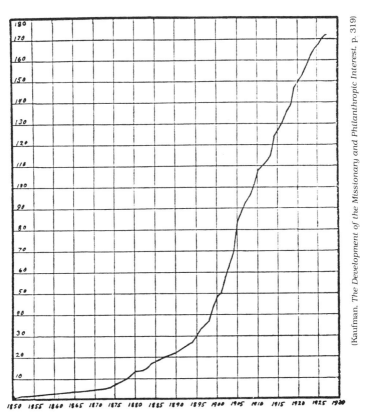

(Kaufman, *The Development of the Missionary and Philanthropic Interest,* p. 319)

FIGURE 22.   *Showing the RISE OF MISSIONARY INTEREST among Mennonites of America as indicated by the date of beginning institutions and activities at present existing, which are the result of or have influenced this interest, such as conference organizations, foreign and home missions, hospitals, old people's homes and orphanages, higher schools, publishing houses, and periodicals*

Graph by Edmund G. Kaufman of Mennonite missionary interest from 1850 to 1930.

founded some sixty new congregations, which in 1930 had about 12,500 members. The composite graph showed a gradual increase in Mennonite institutional activity until 1895 and then a steep and constant acceleration through the 1920s.[8] Kaufman was a progressive and his interpretations were open to charges of partisanship.[9] But the data was impressive. The acceleration of organized Mennonite activity bespoke a remarkable advance in progressive denominationalism.

MISSIONARY MOVEMENT

The earliest Mennonite missionaries saw their work as sparking new life in Mennonite communities at home. Samuel (S. S.) Haury was a Wadsworth-trained, south-German immigrant who in 1880 became the first American Mennonite to go out in mission work among culturally different people (Arapaho). Through mission Haury hoped to "bring new life and rejuvenation to the empty or hollow formalities our declining churches are guilty of." Growth of Protestant churches who engaged in aggressive mission work seemed to be proof of missions' "blessed reflex on the home churches."[10] Some conservative Mennonites, not convinced that their life in community was mere hollow formality, doubted that the missions reflex always brought benefits. They sensed that an outward-thrusting, aggressive mission work would change Mennonites' piety and theology. Mission brought changes in style and pace. It also brought change in the meaning and message of Mennonite community.

The Mennonite missionary movement's roots went back to the early church. The New Testament, the normative scriptural text for Mennonites, told of early Jewish Christians expanding their influence across cultural and geographical boundaries into the Greco-Roman world. Christianity was a religion dynamic enough to break through the boundaries of any tribal, national, or imperial culture. Early Mennonite missionaries took inspiration and strength from missionary stories in the New Testament book of Acts. But they responded even more to specific biblical commands. The primary texts were the great commission of Matthew 28:18-20 ("Go and make disciples of all nations . . .") and Mark 16:15 ("Go into all the world and preach the good news to all creation").[11] By responding to direct biblical commands, Mennonites reflected the ethical-legal basis of their own communities as well as the inherent dynamism of the Christian faith.[12]

American Mennonite interests in overseas missions first grew out of news from Europe, where Mennonites had earlier joined the Protestant missionary movement. Dutch Mennonites founded a mission board in 1847, established work in Indonesia, and drew support from fellow Mennonites in Germany and the Ukraine. In the 1870s some missionary candidates of the GC seminary at Wadsworth in Ohio planned to work under the Dutch board. Carl Justus van der Smissen, a German Mennonite Pietist who taught at Wadsworth and edited the first Mennonite mission journal in America, had studied in mission schools in Basel and Barmen. S. S. Haury studied in Barmen. Rodolphe Petter, a Basel graduate, worked in the GC mission to the Cheyenne Indians beginning in 1891.[13] European influences were more dominant among the GCs and MBs than among the Swiss-background "old" and Amish Mennonites. The latter took more cues from American evangelical sources.

In its motivations and strategies Mennonite missionary renewal was more Protestant than Anabaptist. In theory it might have been possible for Mennonite missions to take shape as a kind of recovery of an Anabaptist vision, for sixteenth-century Anabaptists had been aggressive in mission, as the mainline Reformers had not been.[14] However, over the centuries, persecution, dispersion, and isolation had destroyed the Mennonite missionary impulse and obliterated the memory that it had ever existed. In the late nineteenth century, there was some revival among Mennonites of interest in their own history, but not much in the Anabaptists' sense of mission. The context of mission work had changed radically. Whereas sixteenth-century Anabaptists had found their mission field within the boundaries of a Christendom they rejected, the Mennonites in the modern movement reached beyond a Christendom in which they were increasingly comfortable. As Mennonites now participated in the larger Protestant effort to carry the witness of Christendom to the far corners of the world, their traditional church-world dualism eroded. In turn, distinctive Mennonite doctrines such as nonresistance and nonconformity were obscured. For missionaries in Asia and Africa the differences between Mennonites and Protestants seemed less significant than the cultural gulf between pagan traditionalism and modern Western Christianity.

Mennonites learned the language and methods of missions through Protestant Sunday school literature, mission society journals, Bible schools, and seminaries. In every country and region where they went, Mennonite missionaries received counsel and assistance from Protestants who had been on the field for decades. From them they took their patterns: what style of mission houses and churches to build, how to relate to the imperial and the native political authorities, and how to present the gospel. They honored Protestant comity agreements designed to keep missionaries from competing and duplicating effort. To fund some of their projects they drew upon Protestant sources. Their work produced national Mennonite church congregations, just as the various Protestants created Baptist, Lutheran, and other churches.

A further source of the Mennonite missionary impulse was a climate of American expansionism, which culminated in the Spanish-American War and the acquisition of Cuba and the Philippines. From 1898 to 1900, just as Americans were in a burst of imperialism, six Mennonite and Mennonite-related groups began their first overseas missions. The "old" Mennonites, GCs, MBs, and ex-Mennonites in the Hepzibah Faith Missionary Association all began work in India. The Brethren in Christ began in the Matopo Hills of Rhodesia, and John A. Sprunger's Light and Hope Society sponsored an orphanage for Armenian Christians in Hadjin, Turkey. Meanwhile two groups began cross-cultural missions among poor blacks in America: the Lancaster conference on the Welsh Mountain in Pennsylvania and the Krimmer Mennonite Brethren at Elk Park, North Carolina. Such an explosion of mission was something quite new in Mennonite history.

Mennonites were largely an apolitical people but they did absorb ideas and attitudes from American nationalism. In 1892 the Mennonite Book Concern of Berne, Indiana, published and advertised for sale a German translation of Josiah Strong's book, *Our Country*. Strong's was an immensely popular volume which made the case for benevolent American Christian expansionism. Here Mennonites could read in German of the dangers of Roman Catholicism and the need for Protestant missionaries to counter it—and of the innate superiority of the Anglo-Saxon race and its historic mission to plant spiritual Christianity and liberty among the inferior races. In the pages of the official GC publication *Christlicher Bundesbote*, the Berne publishers repeatedly advertised their translation along with other religious literature.[15] "Old" Mennonite missions leader M. S. Steiner quoted from *Our Country* in an 1899 book, *Pitfalls and Safeguards*.[16]

Progressive Mennonites favored a kind of benevolent and pacifistic American national expansionism. U.S. president

William McKinley, commander-in-chief of America's Spanish-
American war and turn-of-the-century imperialism, was very
popular among progressive Mennonites open to outside influences. John F. Harms in the *Zionsbote* praised McKinley for
declining a $50,000 inauguration ball and instead sending the
money to oppressed Armenians in Turkey, famine victims in India, and the needy in American cities.[17] As McKinley wavered for
a time at the brink of calling for military action against Spain,
Mennonite editors praised him for humanitarian motives and
reluctance to declare war.[18] In the month that America sealed
its military victory in the Treaty of Paris, eleven young men at
the Elkhart Institute memorized and publicly presented a nationalistic speech by a former U.S. senator, Charles Sumner.
The speech said that "The True Grandeur of Nations" lay in the
pursuit of peace.[19] During the war "old" Mennonite missions
leader M. S. Steiner preached a pro-American but antiwar
sermon calling Mennonites to seize the missionary opportunities which would be opened by Spain's well-deserved defeat.
"The 8,000,000 benighted, priest-ridden, oppressed souls of the
Philippine Islands are tired of Spain's misrule," said Steiner.
"They will listen to messengers from our land. The same is true
of Cuba at our door." Steiner played upon the military metaphor so popular in wartime: missionaries, like the soldiers,
should "by the thousands go forth conquering and to conquer—
in His strength! by His command. . . ."[20]

An Amish Mennonite missions enthusiast, Charles (C. K.)
Hostetler, was not bothered by the incongruities of pacifist-
militant rhetoric. He spoke in military figures of speech and
called on Mennonites to "teach the non-resistant doctrine in
the territory lately conquered by the United States."[21] Mennonites did not send missionaries directly to Cuba and the Philippines, but they did participate in what the *Herald of Truth*
called "the generosity of our American people"; they gathered
money and goods for the suffering Cubans.[22] And they sent missionaries to other places.

Nonetheless, despite some borrowing of popular, militant
rhetoric, Mennonites did not go into missions flying the ban-
ners of American nationalism. For example, George Lambert,
the most influential Mennonite missions publicist of the late
1890s, appealed more to Christian compassion than to national
pride. Lambert came from the Mennonite Brethren in Christ
but joined the Elkhart "old" Mennonite congregation and

worked closely with the Elkhart-based Home and Foreign Relief Committee, which was mainly "old" Mennonite. He went on world tours in 1894-1895 and 1896-1897, both times publishing pro-missions travel accounts and following his trips by speaking in Mennonite communities.[23] In a book subtitled *The Horror Stricken Empire*, he drew especially graphic attention to the desperate needs of India. His work led to the founding of both "old" and GC Mennonite mission work in India's Central Province (Madya Pradesh)—work designed at first to deliver relief to famine victims. Lambert and the early Mennonite missionaries shared the spirit of American expansionism. But they did so in the spirit of missionary benevolence, not as militarists or jingoists. Nonetheless, ironically, Mennonite revitalization through overseas missions had some roots in America's surge toward national military power.

FROM HOME MISSION TO FOREIGN MISSION

For most Mennonite groups the missionary interest evolved in a certain sequence. Concern came first for scattered sons and daughters of Mennonite communities, then for lost and disadvantaged people in American hinterlands or cities, and finally for non-Christians overseas. The evolution varied. Beginning in the 1850s and 1860s "old" Mennonites of Virginia carried on a preaching circuit ministry among humble mountain neighbors in West Virginia. The first contacts had resulted before the U.S. Civil War when mountain folk came down at harvest to work in the Shenandoah Valley. Only in 1919 did the Virginia conference create a conference mission board to supervise this work. First had come the natural witness of individuals and congregations to their neighbors, with occasional marriages between the "mountain" people and persons of "old" Mennonite stock and some new family names added to the ethnic Mennonite roster. Only much later did the witness produce an agency for central planning and sending of paid missionaries.[24] In the Lancaster conference formal organization began sooner. The conservative bishops would not officially sponsor overseas missions work until the 1930s, but in 1896 they allowed youthful progressives to create a "Mennonite Sunday School Mission."[25] This group gradually extended its missions agenda to include relief for the poor, fund-raising for overseas missions, a city mission in Philadelphia in 1899, a Mennonite old people's home in 1905, and a children's home in

1911. But its first work, in 1898, was to create an educational and industrial mission for poor blacks on the Welsh Mountain, an area in eastern Lancaster County.

In the Welsh Mountain Mission—as in the urban missions which Mennonites established in Chicago, New York, Peoria, Columbus, Los Angeles, and other cities—there were vast cultural barriers to be crossed. The founders saw themselves as going into alien or heathen territory rather than as extending the Mennonite church as they knew it. Regarding city missions, Mennonite writers wrote shocking descriptions of urban life. These descriptions seemed to say that cities were fit objects for mission but not fit places for settlement.[26] No Mennonite city mission ever established a strong congregation whose life and ministries fit rural Mennonites' agenda. There remained a vast cultural gulf between Mennonite communities in relatively isolated rural areas and the Mennonite mission communities they created in North American cities. The same was true of mission communities on Indian reservations and in Asia or Africa.

NONDENOMINATIONAL INITIATIVES

Mennonite missionary efforts reflected two emerging patterns of mission organization typical in Protestant North America: independent or "faith" missions, and official denominational ones. In the late-nineteenth century hundreds of independent missionary societies formed in North America, often with women as leaders.[27] Often the independent missions arose from the Bible institute movement. Although that movement was not tied to any given denomination, it functioned almost as an alternative denomination in mission and other activities.[28] Many volunteers in nondenominational missions were sturdy individualists who felt a powerful personal call but were ambivalent toward their ethnic or denominational affiliations. They typically raised funds for themselves rather than depending upon agencies or boards. Two prominent independent or "faith" agencies were the Christian and Missionary Alliance and the Hepzibah Faith Mission. Quite a few Mennonites became involved with such groups, and as they did they tended to move away from Mennonitism. No clear statistics exist, but perhaps half the Mennonites who volunteered for overseas missions went out under such agencies. For many of the volunteers, mission was a religiously acceptable way to shift from ethnic, denominational Mennonitism to quasi-denominational evangelical

Protestantism. Like revivalistic Protestantism generally, overseas missions often served as a path to Mennonites' Americanization.[29]

John A. Sprunger was an independent Mennonite who shared the antidenominational emphases of the Christian and Missionary Alliance. He helped spur Mennonite missions in Turkey, China, and India. Like many other independents, Sprunger exuded great competitive vigor but little ability to establish institutions which would outlast his own productive years. In many cases the work of such independent pioneers passed to the stronger and more solidly based denominational agencies. In 1898 two deaconesses from Sprunger's Light and Hope Society, Maria Anna Gerber and Rose Lambert, established an orphanage in Hadjin, Turkey. At first the home operated without an organized board to give support. Eventually Gerber, one of quite a few strong and aggressive women missionaries in her time, demanded that Sprunger organize such a body. The result was the United Orphanage and Mission Board. In 1935 the United Missionary Society, which was the missions arm of the Mennonite Brethren in Christ church, took over this work. Meanwhile the work had expanded to Syria. After World War I it helped plant churches through the initiative of an Armenian pastor, Abraham Seferian, who organized an Armenian Christian church called the Spiritual Brotherhood. By 1938 the mission had workers in nine cities in Syria, Iraq, Lebanon, and Egypt.[30] The United Missionary Society also worked in Nigeria and India. Through other independent mission organizations, it reached China and South America.

In China also, Mennonite missions emerged from independent initiatives related to Sprunger's Light and Hope Society. Henry C. Bartel of the Krimmer Mennonite Brethren in Kansas and Nellie Schmidt of the Evangelical Mennonite Brethren in South Dakota were volunteers with Light and Hope in Berne, Indiana.[31] The KMBs had recently begun a mission among blacks in North Carolina, but the denomination would not accept the couple for work there because Nellie had not been baptized by immersion and did not want rebaptism. So the two went to China with Horace Houlding, an independent missionary in southern Chihli province who called for workers to replace others who had been killed in the antiforeigner Boxer Rebellion. By 1905 they left Houlding to start their own project, soon known as the Bartel Mission. The work drew money and personnel

(Mennonite Library and Archives)

The church at Puyang (Kai Chow) of the General Conference mission in China.

from the same group of small evangelical Mennonite churches which formed the loose constituency of Light and Hope: Krimmer Mennonite Brethren, Evangelical Mennonite Brethren, Mennonite Brethren, Mennonite Brethren in Christ, and Defenseless Mennonites. The Bartels struggled to get Henry's KMB group to extend official denominational endorsement. Pressed by urgent need, Nellie finally relented and allowed her husband to rebaptize her in the prescribed KMB way. Yet the KMBs in North America found other reasons to withhold denominational support. Finally in 1913 Bartel officially incorporated a separate "interdenominational" China Mennonite Mission Society and formed a board made up from a number of supporting groups.

By 1919 the China Mennonite Missionary Society expanded to a peak of thirty missionaries at seven stations with a number of Chinese assistants for work in evangelism, orphanages, education, and medicine. But then came a troubled decade. Chinese nationalism was rising, the mission and the church were in conflict, civil war disrupted work, and the mission lost personnel through death and defection. Independent missions seemed to attract strong-willed persons who would secede and start work on their own if they had any chance of separate support. As the Bartel Mission had spun off from Sprunger and Houlding, Bartel's colleagues left him to forge ahead on their own. This pattern of fragmentation, reminiscent of both Ana-baptist-Mennonite divisions and American Protestant pluralism, was frustrating and embarrassing. Missionaries claimed to serve one Lord, and Chinese believers wanted one Christian church. But the fragmentation also led to an aggres-sive, competitive scattering. On the positive side, the scattering probably mobilized more energy, raised more money, and cov-ered more territory than a centrally organized effort would have done.

Henry and Maria Miller Brown, GC Mennonites from Min-nesota and South Dakota, went to the Bartel Mission in 1909 after they were denied appointment under their denominational mission board.[32] Jonathan Schrag, a cousin of Maria, was with the Bartel Mission. But the Browns found independent support and started separate work at K'ai Chow, also in southern Chihli province. By 1914 the GC mission board officially accepted the Browns and their field. Ernst and Maria Dyck Kuhlman also used the Bartel Mission as a launching ground. Their new, inde-pendent work depended upon support from Kuhlman's home in Germany and from Maria's family and friends in Kansas. In ad-dition, in 1923 Bartel lost several missionaries and national workers to a new effort started by Bartel's own Krimmer Menno-nite Brethren, a work at Chotzeshan in Inner Mongolia.[33] The GC mission produced the largest and most vigorous national Mennonite church in China prior to the Communist Revolu-tion—2,273 members in 1940. Mennonites in that country remained a tiny fragment of the total Protestant missionary corps of nearly 10,000. In the twentieth century all the mis-sions in China felt the upheavals of a volatile sociopolitical situation and, after the communist victory, the tragedy of exclu-sion from the country.[34]

Like the Browns, Frank J. and Agnes Harder Wiens, Menno-nite Brethren from Henderson, Nebraska, were undeterred when their denominational board decided against official mission work in China. The Wienses had sufficient funds to get only halfway to that land, but they heard the Lord's word clearly: "Go! Money and maintenance I shall supply."[35] In 1910 they went to the Mennonite and evangelical communities in the colonies of Russia. It was a time when Mennonites in the Ukraine were prospering, and for a year the couple led revival meetings and collected rubles. Then they went to a field which the Baptists helped them choose, among the Hakka people of

China's Fukien Province, far south of the Bartel Mission. In 1919 the MB mission board officially accepted them and their field and began to send personnel and funds. In 1921 they reported 11 outstations, 17 schools, and a church of 450 members. In 1929, however, China's revolutionary upheavals totally destroyed the mission.[36]

Mennonite mission approaches to Africa also showed the tension between independency and denominationalism. In 1911-1912 two groups with Amish roots, the Defenseless Mennonites and the Central Conference of Mennonites, began a work in the Kasai region of the Congo. Because at the outset neither group possessed trained personnel, they turned to non-Mennonite evangelicals for vision and recruits. While keeping an all-Mennonite board they chose a nondenominational name: Congo Inland Mission. Alma Doering, a German Lutheran from Chicago who had attended Moody Bible Institute, was the mission's major recruiter of both funds and missionaries. She had a vision of expanding the mission and making it into an international effort like the famous China Inland Mission of pioneer Protestant missionary Hudson Taylor. She found recruits in Europe but saw her efforts disrupted by World War I. After the war the Congo mission suffered from fundamental disagreements. Its missionaries, a polyglot group, quarreled over infant versus adult baptism, ecumenical relationships with the Congo All-Protestant Conference, and the mission's denominational identity.

In 1925 Doering and a number of her missionaries left Congo Inland Mission and went to an adjacent region to form a separate and independent work. This "Unevangelized Tribes Mission" grew to twelve stations and numerous outstations but remained very dependent upon its founder. In the 1950s, when old age forced Doering to retire, her mission disbanded and turned its work over to stronger mission organizations, including the Congo Inland Mission. By building on a denominational base the Congo Inland Mission had built more slowly but more solidly.[37]

Aaron F. and Ernestina Strauss Janzen, missionaries with Congo Inland Mission in the Kasai from 1912 to 1920, shared the independent, entrepreneurial spirit which proliferated missions energies and organizations. They were an MB couple from Mountain Lake, Minnesota. Aaron had graduated from Moody Bible Institute and attended Rochester Theological Seminary.

After 1920 the Janzens left Congo Inland Mission to form their own private and independent work at Kafumba, supported by their own agricultural production and by gifts from MB sources. They had to struggle for a secure base, however, until the MB denomination in 1943 accepted the mission as its own.[38] The Janzens were part of a broader pattern of transition from independence to denominationalism, from charisma to routine. Early Spirit-filled and inner-directed missionaries ventured out in faith and established mission institutions which grew and soon required more adequate funding and administration. So the missionaries sought the endorsement and support of denominations. With such support came oversight and direction from North American mission boards and officials. In Africa and Asia as well as in North America the pressures of the early twentieth century dictated movement toward denominational institutionalization.

THE CAUTIOUS DENOMINATIONAL ADVANCE

Compared to the daring zeal of the independents, organized Mennonite mission boards moved into missionary work more deliberately and with institutional caution. On the one hand, their new vision compelled them to act. So did the prospect that they would lose their idealistic youth and financial contributions to aggressive outsiders. On the other hand, church conferences had to heed the fears and hesitations of traditionalist leaders and congregations. And so the three major Mennonite denominational mission boards moved into mission more cautiously.

The General Conference Mennonite church had organized in 1860 with a missions agenda, but it occupied two full decades with planning and preparation before it placed its first missionary couple. The couple were Samuel (S. S.) and Susannah Hirschler Haury, sent among the Arapahoes in Indian Territory in 1880. In 1893 this work was extended to the Hopi in Arizona and in 1904 to the Cheyenne in Montana. But it was not until 1900, two decades later, that the GC board first sent missionaries overseas: to the Central Provinces of India. The mission to American Indians was not producing the hoped-for results. Missionaries warned against overseas projects which might overextend GC resources. Before initiating their own work in India the GC leaders invited "old" Mennonites at Elkhart to make it a common endeavor. But that proposal failed.[39]

(Mennonite Library and Archives)

Edmund G. and Hazel Dester Kaufman, with Chinese Mennonite leaders, Stephen Wang (left) and James Liu (right), at Bluffton College, Ohio. 1930. Children: Karolyn and Gordon Kaufman.

The "old" Mennonites were even more cautious. In 1893, the year of the Columbian Exposition, some youthful progressives began mission work in Chicago but had trouble getting official church authorization and support. Also in 1893 a ten-year-old missions committee of the Elkhart congregation in Indiana reorganized itself as the "Mennonite Evangelizing Board of America" and got churchwide representation except from conferences in eastern Pennsylvania. In 1899 Menno S. Steiner in Ohio led a rival board, which incorporated as the "Mennonite Board of Charitable Homes."

In 1906 "old" Mennonites brought the competing boards together as the churchwide "Mennonite Board of Missions and Charities" (MBMC), popularly known as the "Elkhart board." Missions advocates among the "old" Mennonites had to contend with conservatives who sensed that Protestant-inspired endeavors were filled with dangers of pride and professionalism. The MBMC received some support in all districts, but the Lancaster and Franconia conferences were especially wary of missionary deviations from tradition. The "old" Mennonites were not tempted to move in the direction of nondenominational independence. Instead, their missions courted church-wide, denominational acceptance. The MBMC began overseas work in two countries prior to World War II—India in 1898 and Argentina in 1917. Gradually, "old" Mennonites accepted the missions movement. In 1934 the Lancaster conference opened mission work of its own in Tanganyika (Tanzania), forming the Eastern Mennonite Board of Missions and Charities for the purpose.[40]

The Mennonite Brethren had a smaller constituency than did either the "old" or the GC Mennonites. Perhaps for that reason they were cautious and attached their first overseas missions efforts to larger and more established Baptist missions. In 1890 the MBs in the Russian Empire sponsored Abraham and Maria Friesen as workers under the American Baptist Missionary Union, laboring among the Telegu people in the Hyderabad area of India. The Friesens visited in America at the end of their first furlough and in 1899 returned with the first American Mennonite Brethren missionaries to India—Nikolai N. and Susanna Wiebe Hiebert and Miss Elizabeth Neufeld. The Baptists allowed the MB missionaries to transfer their own work to MB control. By 1903 the first MB mission station had been built. By 1919 there were four more. Meanwhile, in 1894, the MB mission board had begun activity in America, among the Comanche in Indian Territory. The board had decided five years earlier to do so, again with the advice of Baptist missionaries already on the field (and, in a rare case of GC-MB cooperation, with some advice from H. R. Voth). The Mennonite Brethren also provided money for German Baptist (Berlin) missions in the Cameroons in West Africa. Four MB missionaries went to the Cameroons; three of them, Peter Wedel and Heinrich and Maria Enns, died before completing their first terms of service. In the twentieth century the MBs, who strongly preached a message of conversion, generated an overseas missions movement more extensive for their size than did either the "old" or the GC Mennonites.[41]

Missionaries working under Mennonite denominational boards were more closely accountable to their home bases for missions policies than were the independents. Yet no mission board had a coherent plan which it attempted to enforce. The world's Protestants held a landmark World Missionary Conference at Edinburgh, Scotland, in 1910, but only two Mennonites attended: Joseph (J. S.) Shoemaker, secretary of the "old"

(Mennonite Library and Archives)

Annie Funk, missionary from Pennsylvania to India, who died in the Titanic disaster of 1912.

Mennonite mission board, and Alfred Wiebe, GC missionary candidate. Distances between home and foreign field were formidable. Not until 1920, two decades after the mission was founded, did the first GC mission board member visit the field in India. The "old" Mennonites seemed to keep the tightest rein on their overseas missionaries. In 1916 India missionary Mahlon C. Lehman reported that a team of mission school students had won a "football" (soccer) game against a non-Christian team, a victory he presented as vindicating the Christian gospel. The church stood against organized sports at home, and traditionalists were aghast that their missionaries were promoting them abroad. Bishops of the Franconia conference temporarily moved to stop money from going to India. They acquiesced only when the India missionaries acknowledged "a mistake."[42]

The extent of letting grass-roots members control a variety

of issues was different from group to group. In general the distinctive denominational consciousness of the conference-based mission agencies resulted in churches overseas which eventually chose Mennonite identity; and in general the independent agencies produced overseas churches with less Mennonite consciousness. Questions of translating distinctive Anabaptist-Mennonite teachings into foreign cultures became an ongoing part of the Mennonite mission story.

CARRYING MENNONITE CULTURE

Nineteenth- and early-twentieth-century missionaries assumed it was their duty to re-create their own cultural forms among the host peoples—to create "replica churches" overseas. New Christians were to put on Western dress, adopt Western church music and architecture, sing the Western hymns, and in all ways behave by the patterns of Western Christendom. The "old" Mennonites especially discussed what it meant to teach the "all things" of Jesus' great commission: "Teach them to observe all things whatsoever I have commanded you." What, officially, did the "all things" include? The details of the "old" Mennonite *Bible Doctrine* ordinances and restrictions, such as the prayer covering and foot washing? In practice the missionaries did accommodate. For example, in India they did not require women to wear the same special headgear required of Mennonite women in North America. Instead, they followed Indian tradition and had women cover their heads with part of their regular garment. Thus the missionaries infused native custom with Mennonite meaning. The rite of foot washing did not seem to require such adaptation. Indians readily understood its religious meaning, and it did not interfere with life outside of church.[43]

Most Mennonite groups did not have as firm definitions of prescribed church behavior as did the "old" Mennonites. First-generation missionaries were often progressives at home and therefore skeptical of some of the Mennonite cultural distinctives. They were on the leading edge of change in a sending church which was itself in transition. Nor did missionaries always agree among themselves. In 1919 in the Belgian Congo (later Zaire), where the Congo Inland Mission included some non-Mennonites as well as Mennonites from several groups, a vigorous discussion on the rite of foot washing ended with a decision to institute the service—"according to the command of our Lord, beginning the first quarter after the arrival of the necessary equipment."[44] GC missionaries in China clashed over accommodations to Chinese custom in the marriage ceremony. Edmund G. Kaufman, young and progressive, conducted several marriages with elements of both Chinese and Western ritual. His action put him into controversy with some senior missionaries. As a result, Chinese believers and the missionaries created a joint committee to establish rituals for marriages and burials. A profound side effect was that the committee then evolved into a significant instrument for the Chinese Mennonites to demand more and more voice. Missionary disagreements created a margin of freedom for Chinese Christians to develop cultural self-definition and some institutional self-governance.[45]

RENEWAL AND CHANGE AT HOME

The missions movement generated a host of new activities and rituals which in the late nineteenth and early twentieth centuries sent surges of energy through Mennonite congregations and communities. Missions festivals brought people together to hear sermons on how the Bible called for mission, to listen to reports from missionaries on furlough or from visitors to the field, and to raise money. "The annual Mission Board meeting in that era was THE yearly meeting for the Mennonite Church," reported Minnie Swartzendruber Graber, who was assigned to India in 1925. "Large crowds from across the Mennonite Church attended these meetings. A kind of excitement filled the air."[46] Missionaries bore a special mystique, intensified by whatever opposition they received at home and abroad. They risked their lives in the greatest of causes and had stories to tell. They returned with exotic artifacts: foot-binding cloths from China, prayer wheels from India, fetishes from Africa. Commissioning services for new missionaries were special events, with crowds so large they sometimes required large tents. Congregations sang stirring missionary hymns, often from songbooks different from those used in their regular worship.

For Mennonite women, missions created and won approval for new religious roles. The enterprise spawned educational and medical institutions in which single women assumed responsibilities and status far beyond what church and society were likely to allow them at home. Married missionary women, while subject to the authority of their husbands, were nevertheless freed for work outside the home. Child care was available and inexpensive, the missions tasks were urgent, and the cross-cultural context did not restrict missionary women to traditional roles.[47]

Yet mission boards never had the audacity to name a woman as superintendent for any given field. A man had to hold that position. Alma Doering learned that principle in the Congo, and Maria Anna Gerber in Turkey, even though both were stronger leaders than the men around them. In India similar strength and dedication could be found in Annie Funk and Katharina Schellenberg. Funk, who later died in the *Titanic* disaster, was the founder of a girls' school in Janjgir. Schellenberg overcame formidable odds to get a medical education and a missions appointment. The oldest daughter in elder Abraham Schellenberg's family of twenty children, she got her vocational start, as did many another gifted youth in the 1890s, at John A. Sprunger's Light and Hope Society. Finally she found her position in the medical work of the MBs' India field. When she did, she was reluctant to leave for either vacations in India or furloughs at home. In thirty-eight years of mission work she returned to North America only twice.[48]

Home churches set career missionaries on heroic pedestals, but in fact they were marginal people. That was true both on the field, where they were aliens, and at home, where socio-cultural changes often passed them by. Women missionaries were especially well positioned to feel both the freedoms and strains of ambiguous roles. They gave special shape to the mission programs by going in new directions with their interests and abilities.

In the home churches also, the missions movement created new ways for women to work and organize. In local congregations they formed women's missionary societies or "sewing circles." Out of the limelight, wives of mission board officers or members often served as secretaries and hostesses. GC-related missions societies proliferated from eighteen in 1890 to eighty-seven in 1923. In 1917, to coordinate their work on a conference-wide basis, GC women organized a "Women's Missionary Association." It received an unofficial and grudging endorsement from the male-dominated GC mission board. Not until 1950 was it officially integrated as a conference "auxiliary" organization.[49] "Old" Mennonite women, who evolved their sewing

circles in a shorter time, also struggled against male authority
as they sought an approved place for their activities.[50] In 1897
the women of the Paradise congregation in Pennsylvania were
the first "old" Mennonites to organize such a circle. By 1911
Lancaster conference people had organized their circles on a
conference basis. And in 1916 Clara Eby Steiner, who had
helped her husband, M. S. Steiner, a great deal during his mission board presidency before he died in 1911, led in founding
an independent "Mennonite Woman's Missionary Society." She
did so after the "old" Mennonite mission board had refused to
let the women organize as an auxiliary. In the late 1920s the
board created its own women's committee. As a result, Steiner
and her group felt compelled to dissolve their separate and independent work.[51]

SUCCESS AND DISAPPOINTMENT

Mennonites who initiated overseas missions around the
turn of the century expected success and triumph. So their outlook was quite different from the traditional Mennonite attitudes of submission and separation. Gradually the old dualism
of church and world more or less gave way to a new polarity of
Christian civilization versus heathendom. Mennonite missionaries and missions supporters were less inclined to express
concern about keeping the church unspotted from worldly cor-
ruption than to argue that true progress of civilization depended upon the spread of Christianity. "Missions is . . . the essentially true civilization factor among all mankind," wrote Gustav
Harder, treasurer of the GC mission board in 1894. "The task of
missions is to make people into Christians. If they become
Christians, however, they become carriers of true civilization."[52]
Jacob B. Epp, a GC missionary candidate and valedictorian of
the 1905 class at the Union Missionary Training Institute of
Brooklyn, New York, spoke on the topic "The Gospel as a Means
of True Civilization."[53] Missionaries, including Mennonites
whose foreparents had fled the sword and fire of Christendom,
were now participants in a movement which fully expected to
conquer the world for Christendom and do it quickly. The
sources of Mennonite missions thinking included such books as
John R. Mott's *The Evangelization of the World in This Generation*, published in 1900, and James S. Dennis's *Christian Missions and Social Progress*, published in three volumes, 1897-
1906.[54]

Measured against their soaring objectives the first generation of Mennonite missionaries reaped a meager harvest. Before the 1930s, on all fields where Mennonite missionaries worked, native people converted to Christianity only singly or in small groups. They did not come en masse, as part of broader people's movements or large extended families. Among Native Americans the work was uniformly discouraging.

In India, the Mennonite churches took form slowly and painfully over decades, made up of people from the very bottom of the caste society: outcasts, victims of Hansen's disease (leprosy), and orphans. Persons who converted to Christianity found themselves socially excluded from their home villages and dependent upon whatever employment or other economic prospects the missions themselves could offer. The "old" Mennonite mission in the Central Provinces provided an economic and social base for converts by purchasing an 800-acre tract of land including a village settlement. Thus the requirements of Christian compassion led to a kind of institutionalization and worldly "establishment" which clashed with traditional Anabaptist concepts of church-state separation.[55] The general effort to make India Christian, an incongruous dream for Mennonites in any case, was not realized. But the hope remained. In 1929 a GC Mennonite missionary book predicted that "in the next twenty-five years we or others shall see such an ingathering as we have hardly dreamed. We are in the dawn of a new era for India."[56]

In China, Mennonite missionaries joined others in hoping for a new Christian national order. The emergence of Christian patriotic leaders such as Sun Yat-sen, Chiang Kai-shek, and Feng Yu-hsiang encouraged them. Missionary Edmund G. Kaufman attended one of General Feng's mass baptisms of his soldiers and reported that it "reminded one of Pentecost." Kaufman hoped Feng might be "an instrument in God's hand to bring order out of chaos in China."[57] It was an ironical hope for a person in the tradition of believers baptism, the free church, and pacifism. The Christian order never arrived. The Mennonite mission stations in China (the Bartel mission in Shantung Province, the GC mission in Chihli Province, the MB one in Fukien Province, and the KMB one in Mongolia) carried on aggressive work in evangelism, education, and health care. But they did so only to have the work disrupted by civil war in 1927, the Japanese invasion in 1939-1940, and eventually the communist takeover.

Africa—the presumed "dark" continent, which was expected
to resist the gospel most—in fact responded to Christian missions more readily than did India or China. By 1930, despite
the troubles of Congo Inland Mission, a native church took
shape and grew to 662 baptized members at four stations.[58] In
the early 1930s the church grew rapidly—to 3,577 members by
1935—even while the economic depression in North America
forced cutbacks in missionary budgets and personnel.[59]

MISSIONS AND GOSPEL

The missions movement affected not only Mennonite style,
numbers, and organization; it also affected core understandings
of the gospel as salvation, ethics, and church. In 1980 historian
Theron Schlabach posed this issue in terms of two sharply contrasting alternatives—a "gospel" in the biblical Anabaptist-
Mennonite tradition, and another "gospel" as worked out by
American pietistic Protestantism. The Mennonite gospel, in
Schlabach's view, saw salvation as involving the wholeness of
God's obedient people living out a way of peace in community.
The Protestant gospel, in contrast, emphasized personal salvation from sin and guilt and often used a "two-track formula" of
faith and ethics. "Old" Mennonite missionaries never fully
abandoned their distinctive gospel heritage but neither did
they generate a "well-focused vision of gospel." For example, the
teaching of nonresistance on the mission field tended to be an
addendum to the gospel rather than integral to it. Wrote
Schlabach: "The understanding of basic gospel was not much
different from that of the larger Protestant mission movement."[60] He might have written the same about other Mennonite
groups. The development among those of Dutch-Russian background was somewhat different from that among the Swiss and
south-German "old" Mennonites. Yet for Mennonites in general
the theological basis for mission was quite similar and quite
Protestant. The missions movement greatly increased the variety of cultures and nationalities embraced in the Mennonite
traditions. The presence of Native Americans, black Americans,
Asians, Africans, and Latin Americans in the Mennonite fold
also made the understanding of gospel more and more complex.

MISSIONS AND BUREAUCRACY

The organizational networks which originated and sustained missionary work fostered a modern and rational mind-

set that was new for Mennonites. Missionaries were people of profound spiritual calling, but they were also institution-builders who wanted things done in good order. "Missions is business and the more it is conducted on business principles, the better for the work," wrote Peter A. Penner from India to a mission board he suspected of sloppy administration.[61] The structures of missions organization remained quite simple through the 1920s, although signs of centralization and profes-sionalization were on the horizon. In 1915 the "old" Mennonite mission board granted a full-time living allowance to its treas-urer, George (G.L.) Bender, who had been working at the Elkhart post office.[62] (Bender had received some mission board payment for services as early as 1897-1898.) But nearly all of the sixteen Mennonite missions organizations in 1930 operated without salaried administrators and without offices other than the ex-ecutive secretaries' or treasurers' homes. Mission board mem-bers and officers sometimes received modest subsidies for travel, but they also depended on reduced rail fares for clergy-men. Their tasks were to raise funds, appoint missionaries, and keep the missions interest alive. Funds went into the work, not into administrative overhead or trips for executives to the field. Overseas missionaries had wide authority to carry on their work. And so Mennonites were able to reap the early fruits of aggressive, organized work with neither the weight nor the guidance and stability of complex bureaucracies. They had founded boards and programs, but the onset of complex denom-inational organization was not to come until after World War II.

At about the same time, other Mennonite institutions such as colleges, hospitals, and insurance societies underwent similar shifts.

CHAPTER

6

DENOMINATIONAL ADVANCE: COLLEGES AND HOSPITALS

In September 1900, Frieda Marie Kaufman entered Bethel College, but not merely as another student; she would become a symbol for a movement. Her hope was to be a deaconess, like some Lutheran women who had operated a kindergarten she had attended twelve years earlier in Haagen, Germany, near the Swiss border. When Frieda was nine years old her family had emigrated to Halstead, Kansas. That was in 1892. Eight years later her hopes caught the vision of David Goerz. The entrepreneurial Goerz, cofounder and business manager of Bethel College, wanted to start an institution of Mennonite deaconesses.[1]

HUMANE LETTERS AND HEALTH CARE

In 1900 Goerz took a world tour, and along the way he spoke of Frieda Kaufman's dream. Mennonites in the Russian Empire gave him the first seeds of money. In May 1901, Bethel's board of directors officially accepted "Sister Frieda Kaufman" as "a deaconess candidate of Bethel College." Soon she was training at the Interdenominational Deaconess Home and Hospital in Cincinnati, Ohio. In the next four decades she carried on a distinguished career as deaconess mother at the Bethel Deaconess Home and Hospital in Newton, Kansas. As her career ended, Bethel College awarded her the honorary degree of "Doctor of Humane Letters." Her life had demonstrated the linkages in Mennonite denominational developments in higher education, health care, and missions.[2]

162

Noah E. Byers, President of Goshen College, 1903-13, Dean and Professor of Philosophy at Bluffton College, 1913-38. With wife, Emma Lefevre, and sons Floyd and Robert.

HIGHER EDUCATION

Between 1890 and World War I, Mennonites in America founded seven schools of "higher" education.[3] The movement grew in the West, attracted talent from the East, and spread its transforming influences in all directions. Because of the rudimentary education of Mennonite youth of the time, the institutions all began work at a basic preparatory school level. For some years many of the students were past the normal age, as they sought opportunities earlier denied. Gradually the schools upgraded their programs. As they did they reached out for accreditation from secular agencies. But they also became centers for their denominations and helped congregations move toward having professional ministers. And they educated thousands of Mennonite youth to be leaders inside and outside the churches. Meanwhile they looked to American colleges and universities for models, and borrowed patterns of the "liberal arts." Yet no Mennonite school abandoned its religious identity and affiliation as many other church-related colleges in America had done. Some were governed directly by denominations, others by independent corporations, but all remained close to the churches.

The colleges had some imposing flaws, yet they successfully established both religious mission and social control. Religious mission meant not only joining the Protestant world missionary crusade but also working within American society to propagate Mennonite values. The main effort at social control was to stem the loss of American-educated youth from the church and to equip new leaders for guiding congregations as they moved out of rural isolation. Achievement was far from complete, yet working at religious mission and social control put new life into the Mennonite denomination, particularly its progressive wings.

Mennonite Schools and Colleges Founded 1883-1917

Name	Location	Dates
(Halstead)	Kansas	1883-1893
Bethel	Kansas	1893-
(Elkhart)	Indiana	1894-1903
Goshen	Indiana	1903-
(Central)	Ohio	1900-1914
Bluffton	Ohio	1914-
Freeman	South Dakota	1903-1987
Tabor	Kansas	1908-
Hesston	Kansas	1909-
Eastern Mennonite	Virginia	1917-

(High schools in parenthesis)

The colleges took on a creative but difficult task: to reconcile traditional, rural Mennonite values with American democratic society and its progressivism. At one level they faced a conflict between the ideals of education for indoctrination and education for liberation. Progressive prophets of liberation knew well that they were assaulting the old ways. "The whole object of education is to break up old habits of thought," said Elkhart Institute teacher C. Henry Smith in 1899, addressing students in chapel. He wanted to destroy "the ruts into which we have fallen" and to free minds from all influences which tended "to lead in a prescribed channel."[4] Even conservative apostles of indoctrination such as Daniel Kauffman were "progressives" if compared to those Mennonites, old order or other, who rejected higher education in principle. But conservatives wanted the schools to keep young people safe and loyal. In 1902, also at Elkhart, Kauffman went to the core of the matter. "The denominational school," he said, "is founded upon this one idea: That it is important that our young people be protected from the dangers of the sinful and selfish world." They should be "thoroughly indoctrinated in the principles of true Christianity."[5]

The early intellectual leaders in Mennonite colleges—C. H. Wedel and Gustav Haury at Bethel; Noah E. Byers, C. Henry Smith, and J. E. Hartzler at Goshen; Noah C. Hirschy and Samuel K. Mosiman at Bluffton; Henry W. Lohrenz, David W. Harder, and Peter C. Hiebert at Tabor—were gifted persons with strong credentials. Had they chosen to go outside Mennonite circles they surely could have had successful careers with more money and less controversy. Yet they were loyal. "Very few of our young men who have gone on to school have found employment amid our people," wrote C. H. Wedel in 1889 from the Presbyterian Bloomfield College in New Jersey, as he considered a call to return to Mennonites in Kansas. "Why should I be an exception?"[6]

Wedel chose to be an exception. Educators of his kind were exceptional in their love for the Mennonite heritage. They were committed both to the church and to the ideal of progress. In an address in 1900 upon helping to lay the cornerstone of Central College in Bluffton, Ohio, N. C. Hirschy hailed the "mighty cloud of witnesses" in Mennonite history. But he also said, "Let our college be an American College."[7]

None of the early college leaders set forth a truly coherent philosophy of Mennonite education. Overworked, they scarcely found time for systematic reflection. Nor did they finally resolve the central issues within themselves. They were like the missionaries who never settled the contradictions between traditional Mennonite teachings and the realities of being Protestant missionaries. Contradictions between orthodox Mennonitism and progressive American education were large, but Mennonite educators lived and worked within them.

In 1896 at the opening of the Elkhart Institute, "old" Mennonite evangelist John S. Coffman spoke expansively of "The Spirit of Progress." His speech was a ringing manifesto for Men-

(Center for Mennonite Brethren Studies, Hillsboro, Kansas)

Tabor College faculty and student body, 1915.

nonite progressives.[8] Progress, said Coffman, was "advancement toward a higher or better state, as in civilization," and it included various parts of life: technological, intellectual, and moral. True progress was "a grace that *makes man* BETTER." The evangelist found progress not only in biblical and church history but also in the civilizations of ancient Greece, classical Egypt, and Renaissance Italy.

Coffman discerned another, less orthodox strand of progress: a line of Catherites, Paulicans, Henricans, Petrobrusians, Waterlandians, Albigensians, and Waldensians—religious dissenters who, long before the Protestant Reformation, stood against the Catholic Church. Mennonites had often praised these groups for being the faithful, suffering remnant and the true church, but not for progress. Yet Coffman insisted that among these rejected groups, "crushed, and bleeding, and despised as they were, slumbered the spirit of progress." They had been "like the dormant fires of an inactive volcano, ready to burst forth at any unsuspected moment."

The great moment had come in the Protestant Reformation. It had come especially among the Anabaptists, and even more among highly educated ones. There had been "the learned Dr. Hubmeyer." There had been Hans Denck, "the brilliant light of

PROMINENT CITIZENS CARTOONED.

N. E. BYERS

"He was a scholar, and a ripe good one; exceeding wise, fair spoken." —*Henry VIII.*

Noah E. Byers, cartoon from unidentified newspaper.

the University of Ingolstadt." Scholars had worked to restore
the church to its New Testament simplicity. Such had been the
Mennonite spirit of progress. But alas, in the sixteenth and
seventeenth centuries persecution had virtually extinguished it.
Rural isolation had gradually turned Mennonites in on themselves. Now nearly all their youth who received advanced education in English were leaving the church. Yet Coffman was sure
that Mennonites were entering a new "epoch that marks a transition period in our beloved brotherhood." Soon one could be
both Mennonite and educated, both biblical and progressive.

Progressives among the "old" Mennonites, for whom Coffman spoke, had already moved far in crossing the cultural di-
vide from the German language to English. At Elkhart Institute
and Goshen College (as well as at Central Mennonite [or Bluff-
ton] College and then at Hesston College and Eastern Mennonite School when those institutions began), classes were in
English. Virtually all children of "old" Mennonites had attended English-language public schools, so for them an education at Elkhart-Goshen, Bluffton, Hesston, or Eastern Mennonite was a capstone to a predominantly public school education. The colleges' challenge was to teach vocational courses,
general liberal knowledge, and the Bible all in English, yet convey the religious ideals of the foreparents. Coffman saw the
dangers and warned that the "encroachments of popular opinion and world aspirations . . . will come dashing against us with
the fury of a sweeping cyclone."[9]

Mennonites often disagreed on what was worldly "popular
opinion" and what was the Lord's leading. Coffman practiced
and taught all the "old" Mennonite ordinances and restrictions
including the plain coat for men and prayer covering for
women. But quite contrary to traditionalists, he had also come
to the progressive conclusion that the church should not "legis-
late on outward forms."[10]

Often the colleges seemed to push at the boundaries of legislation and custom. For the next half century their administrators had to work amid a drumbeat of conservative criticism.
Usually a mixture of rumor and fact, the criticism said that
wayward students or faculty had flagrantly violated orthodox
Mennonite social conventions or church doctrine. In 1918, writing of the "old" Mennonites' oldest college, A. J. Bendle of
Johnstown, Pennsylvania, said that he was

grieved at heart to see that wherever Goshen lays their hand *Blight* immediately follows; the head covering begins to shrink until it is only the size of a mushroom; the bangs begin to grow; the jewelry business begins to flourish; the chickens begin to scratch the feathers off their breast and put them on their head; their clothes suddenly grow shorter and the shoes longer; the lace and ribbon stores get increased patronage and the County Commissioners have to print more ballots![11]

Hesston and Eastern Mennonite, founded respectively in Kansas and Virginia in 1909 and 1917, were built partly to offer conservative alternatives to the allegedly liberal Goshen. But genuine traditionalists knew that no higher education was really safe.[12]

Mennonites of the Dutch-Russian stream had somewhat different educational objectives and patterns. Having immigrated more recently, they designed their programs to preserve and enhance two cultures—a German-language heritage from Europe and the English-speaking culture of America. Founders of Freeman, Bethel, and Tabor wanted not only to educate their children for the American environment but also to keep their children and grandchildren German. Their foreparents had nurtured the same dream in Eastern Europe and the Russian Empire. The colleges recruited cores of Mennonite students from congregations which operated German-language elementary schools (*Gemeindeschulen*), usually as one- to three-month supplements to the English-language public schools.

A prime goal of Bethel, Tabor, and Freeman was to send forth teachers with an excellent command of both English and High German, teachers who might serve the Mennonite communities as both public and church school teachers.[13] C. H. Wedel's ideal for Bethel graduates reflected his vision of a Mennonite congregation Christendom with church and state enriching each other. The ideal graduate would be able to "teach German school, teach English district school, and also be active in Sunday School." Then, thought Wedel, "the state, church and Sunday School would all work together and would all be benefited in developing the spiritual life of our youth."[14] H. W. Lohrenz at Tabor College had a similar hope. Like Wedel, he was a former student and former teacher of both the Kansas German school and the public school. He too wanted Mennonite

education to nourish an ongoing Mennonite Germanhood
(*Deutschtum*), even as it taught the best also from the new,
English-speaking, American homeland.[15]

In his teaching and extensive writing, Wedel showed a way.
His students were to be fully conversant with Goethe as well as
Shakespeare, with modern German methods of teaching as well
as American wisdom on the "Negro problem."[16] Meanwhile students insisted on more courses taught in English even as their
elders in the congregations feared the colleges were neglecting
German. In Bethel's first year, 1893, more than one third of its
courses were in German. Gradually the percentage declined.
During World War I, under pressure, Bethel temporarily suspended its German department.[17]

On all Mennonite college campuses, students expressed
their social dreams through organized literary and debating
societies. In the "literaries" they learned American ways of
speaking and group management. The societies went by classical names such as "Platonians," "Philomatheans," or "Ves-
perians," and chose humanist mottoes such as "Master
Thyself." Their members organized civic projects, such as fund-
raising for a campus fountain or gateway, with a spirit much
like the service club boosterism in the local town. Purging
"Dutch" accents from their tongues as eagerly as they scraped
farmyard dirt from their shoes, they practiced American-style
elocution, oratory, and declamation. Sponsoring public debates,
they attracted people from both campus and town, and examined propositions such as "That the government should control the railroads," or "That Asiatic immigration should be
permitted on the same terms as Europeans." Thus they certified
that they could address the great issues of their American
society. As part of that society the students took special delight
in constitutions, elections, parliamentary drill, and other
rituals of American organization. They were learning to make
public decisions in American ways, quite different from the
brotherly and informal ways of family and congregation. And
they were learning upward mobility. One organization, begun at
Elkhart Institute and continued at Goshen College, called itself
"The Coming Men of America Debating Club."[18]

There was some dissonance between traditional Mennonite
expression and the expansive American rhetoric. Especially
loud was a clash between the German and the English pages of
the Tabor College *Herold*. A paper of sixteen pages, the *Herold*

gave equal space to each language.[19] The German section, edited by Bible and theology teacher David E. Harder, offered serious issues and *gediegenen Lesestoff* (solid reading material) in the authentic language of MB piety. But the English pages were high-spirited and reflected the world of the small American college. Students recorded which class had the prettiest flag and the "fervent glow of enthusiasm" surrounding athletics. One issue reported that a student had put the rules and regulations of the college under a laboratory microscope to see what was between the lines![20] The English also included essays and orations from the classes of Alice Hey-Friesen, "Professor of Expression," an alumna of the Columbia College of Expression in Chicago. A student named Tina Schulz wrote on the Kansas motto, *Ad Astra Per Aspera*, and asserted that "in every human soul there is a craving for success, an invincible desire to rise. . . ."[21] Another, Adolf I. Franz, who later would study at Yale and return to Tabor to teach, orated on "The Future of America." "America, proud land of the free, the home of the exiled of every race, we honor thee," he exulted. "We glory in thy strength, we love thy star-spangled banner! Thou art the young giant of promise, baptized in the sun's golden flood of morning. . . ."[22]

Thus the Mennonite colleges were crucibles of contradiction. They stood not only between traditional, German-speaking Mennonitism and progressive, English-speaking Americanism but also in the midst of the double transition from farm to town to city. There was something incongruous about farm-bred Mennonites coming to small towns to study under professionals trained in city universities in order to renew rural churches. Not surprisingly, each college developed a running conflict with its constituency. But, more remarkably, the schools did not destroy themselves through such internal contradiction. Instead they charted courses which maintained Mennonite identity while slowly educating and modernizing the church. A 1943 directory of Mennonite notables included 268 persons with A.B. degrees, slightly more than half of them from Mennonite schools.[23] Among the MB, the GC, and the "old" Mennonites, the colleges' kind of progressive Mennonitism inspired leaders for denominational development. Other groups, such as the Evangelical Mennonite church and the Evangelical Mennonite Brethren, sent their brightest sons and daughters to non-Mennonite Bible schools. And in the long run they found it harder to maintain a viable Mennonite denominational identity.

The Mennonite colleges taught professional methods which were bound to reshape traditional roles and values. In so doing they joined other American colleges and universities in creating what has been called a middle-class "culture of professionalism."[24] The key for Mennonites was lay church leadership. For generations, untrained and unpaid ministers, bishops, and elders had led Mennonite congregations with skills legitimated in the local community. But now young people sought both their skills and their credentials elsewhere. Hundreds went to the colleges and took either short-term Bible courses or a semester or more of academy or college work, then returned empowered to their home congregations. The power came from new religious knowledge, new communications skills, and new status. The new credentials could both enrich and unsettle church and community life. They could both complement and threaten traditional lay leaders. Some congregations—most often those in the towns, in the West, and/or in the GC branch—moved slowly toward salaried pastorates or what opponents called a "hireling" ministry. As they did, college-educated people were in the forefront. Even if there had been no theological issues at stake between church and college—no "higher criticism" or theory of evolution—Mennonite colleges would have been controversial for stimulating a revolution in the relation between leaders and congregations. It was a revolution in favor of a newly educated and professional elite.

Mennonite young people were especially eager to prepare in the field of education. The colleges educated more teachers than members of any other profession. For instance, a list of persons who were students at Bethel College between 1893 and 1953 named 1,799 teachers, more than five times the 333 persons who were either ministers or missionaries.[25] Many others became professionals in health-related fields, often working in or with Mennonite hospitals.

Constituents often demanded agricultural programs, yet such programs never succeeded. They failed even though Mennonites seemed to want help to pass through a scientific-technological revolution affecting America's farmers. In 1914-1919 Goshen College invested in a "School of Agriculture" which would "prepare Mennonite young people to return to the rural communities." The effort faltered. World War I disrupted it, and students were not much interested.[26] Meanwhile the charter of Eastern Mennonite School proposed to help students "choose the rural walks of life, rather than that which directs them into the commercial channels of the cities."[27] But not enough students enrolled in Eastern Mennonite's agricultural courses to justify an ongoing program.

Much more than teaching rural ways, the schools provided space for the first generation of American Mennonite intellectuals to work out new understandings of Mennonite social and religious identity. The intellectuals promoted their views in church publications. Mennonite college presidents Noah C. Hirschy at Bluffton, Daniel H. Bender at Hesston, and Noah E. Byers at Goshen, as well as teacher Henry F. Toews at Tabor, wrote and edited handbooks or lesson guides for Mennonite Sunday schools.[28] Teachers from three colleges published critical pieces on the theory of evolution and its challenge.[29] In college journals and in church conference periodicals faculty members wrote essays on topics ranging from popular science, political reform, education, or history to the peace movement, church music, and church life.[30] Most writers seemed to feel that they were youthful leaders living in an age of progress and moving in the vanguard. Hardly ever did they examine the assumptions of "progress" or integrate those assumptions well with traditional Mennonite teachings. In the first decades of the century, substantive and creative scholarly output was limited.

Mennonite teacher-scholars did produce two major historical syntheses which were genuinely creative. The first was C. H. Wedel's four-volume, German-language *Summary of the History of the Mennonites* (1900-1904). Wedel had prefaced his four volumes with two earlier and shorter ones on salvation history in Old and New Testament times.[31] His work was German-American, rooted in European scholarship and insights and focused on the idea of *Gemeinde*. The second of such creative histories was by C. Henry Smith of Goshen College. Published in 1909 and entitled *The Mennonites of America*, Smith's book was the first thoroughly Americanized study of Anabaptist-Mennonite history.[32] Its author quickly became the premier American Mennonite historian. His major works included a 1920 historical survey from Anabaptist times to the present (revised in 1941, 1957, and 1983); a study of the Mennonite migration and settlement from Russia to America; and a volume on eighteenth-century Mennonite migration to Pennsylvania.[33] Both Wedel and Smith also published numerous popular essays suitable for teaching and inspiration.

As progressive and scientific historians, Wedel and Smith had much in common. Both were committed to professional, objective historiographic standards as well as to rescuing the Anabaptist-Mennonite historical reputation from its detractors.[34] They promoted the Mennonite peace witness, aggressive mission work, and congregational church polity. But unlike Wedel or any previous Mennonite historian, Smith interpreted Anabaptist-Mennonite history in terms of American Protestantism, Jeffersonian democracy, and social Darwinism. He believed the genius of Anabaptist-Mennonitism was akin to the best and most glorious features of America: individuality and freedom of conscience. "Above all," he wrote, the sixteenth-century Anabaptists were "intensely individualistic." They suffered persecution because they were ahead of their times.[35] Like America, Mennonitism had grown from the aspirations of "the common man." It had found renewal in repeated experiences of pioneering. "Just as the westward movement of civilization has kept the race young and hopeful," Smith wrote, "so the pioneer life of the Mennonite church has kept her, with all her conservative instincts, yet a church of material prosperity and spiritual progress."[36]

 Smith found no evidence for a Waldensian-Mennonite connection, a connection claimed for centuries in the *Martyrs Mirror* and more recently by a friendly German historian named Ludwig Keller. The *Martyrs Mirror* had used the connection to legitimate an Anabaptist-Mennonite "apostolic succession" all the way from the New Testament church. Yet from Smith onward, Mennonite historians abandoned this long-held thesis. Smith sought historical identity in links to sixteenth-century Anabaptism rather than to the early church.[37] The shift brought a narrowing of focus. Now Mennonites were to find historical identity first in seeing themselves as radically Protestant and second in searching how to be Christian. To a degree, Smith set the agenda that progressive Mennonites would pursue vigorously in the twentieth century: trying to recover the "Anabaptist vision."

Smith's longer books were impressive for their scholarship. However, in briefer, more popular essays he was like many writers of his day—uncritical, nationalistic, and racist in his vision for a progressive and Christian America. He taught that a benevolent Providence had guided both Anabaptist and American development. That Providence had provided for America's discovery "in the fullness of time." It had arranged for America to be settled by Anglo-Saxons, "the choicest men then known in the world."[38] In America's greatest crisis, its Civil War, God had raised up Abraham Lincoln. Wisely rejecting constitutional and diplomatic solutions, Lincoln had "resorted to the only means possible, namely: force of arms." More recently the chief threats to America were undesirable immigrants, overly prolific blacks, and the struggles between labor and capital. Now if America were to fulfill its providential mission it had to "keep pure both its Anglo Saxon blood and [its] Christian ideals."[39] Mennonites meanwhile enjoyed a heritage of industry, self-sacrifice, love, and mutual aid. Therefore, they had much to offer to America's destiny and to modern civilization.

Both Smith and Wedel favored the American "social gospel" movement, thinking it quite consistent with the Anabaptist-Mennonite tradition. Wedel wrote that since Mennonites enjoyed a heritage of practical and communal discipleship, life in many of their communities "has been a model experiment in so-called social Christianity." Being theologically conservative, Mennonites would hardly believe in human progress apart from divine intervention. But they did believe it possible to do God's will on earth. And, Wedel wrote, they thought Christianity should "penetrate all relationships of life, [to] make them healthy and prosperous." Mennonites who affirmed a social gospel agenda did so generally in reference to their own conservative tradition. They did not attach it to a new, liberal theology.[40]

Before World War I, editors of GC, MB, and Central Illinois conference newspapers shared much of the progressivism found on the Bethel, Goshen, Tabor, and Bluffton college campuses. Abraham Schellenberg of Hillsboro, Kansas, promoted Progressive Party candidates while his colleague, Jacob G. Ewert, wrote on behalf of Christian socialism. Henry Peter Krehbiel of Newton preferred Republican ideas for reform, and served a term in the Kansas state legislature.[41] Isaac A. Sommer of Berne worked with others for "All-Mennonite" unity around a progressive denominational agenda.[42] A. B. Rutt, editor from 1910 to 1915 of the Illinois *Christian Evangel*, presided over the liveliest of Mennonite progressive denominational papers.

Before World War I only the "old" Mennonites offered a well-articulated critique of the new progressivism. They did so even as they undertook an aggressive denominational program of missions, education, and publication. Daniel Kauffman, their leading church statesman and editor of their *Gospel Herald*, called increasingly and conservatively for church loyalty.[43] In 1908 John Horsch moved to Scottdale from John Sprunger's Light and Hope Society and began to write polemically in the *Gospel Herald* against liberalism, modernism, and higher criticism. Horsch was also a gifted historian who, like C. Henry Smith, collected and studied the primary documents of Anabaptism.[44] But while Smith saw Anabaptists as champions of individual liberty, Horsch saw them much more as conservative fundamentalists.[45] A Smith-Horsch debate did not receive full public airing before World War I, but in 1911 Horsch wrote an essay on "The Anabaptist View of Toleration." In it he did not accuse Smith by name, but he certainly took aim at Smith's views. Horsch said the Anabaptists had believed that final authority lay in Scripture, not conscience. For them, to speak of congregational autonomy in faith and doctrine would have been a "slander." Though they lacked a written creed, wrote Horsch, the Anabaptists had an effective substitute creed. It lay in the Scriptures, in the "writings of Menno," and in "very deed."[46] Smith did not bother to reply. In 1911 he could believe that the momentum of history favored the progressives.

In 1913 Noah E. Byers and C. Henry Smith, respectively president and academic dean at Goshen College, wearied of battling a conservative "old" Mennonite constituency and board of education. So they resigned to accept positions at a reorganized Bluffton College in Ohio. Bluffton's president, Samuel K. Mosiman, hoped to build a new "standard seminary" or "theological and Bible school." He hoped further for inter-Mennonite support—from General Conference Mennonites, Mennonite Brethren in Christ, Defenseless Mennonites, the Central Illinois Mennonite conference, "old" Mennonites, and others. From a Goshen viewpoint the Bluffton plans seemed to be for "an all-Mennonite college which would ultimately take the place of Goshen College."[47] In subsequent years progressives continued to flow from Goshen to Bluffton, as two more prominent members of the Goshen faculty made the switch: Paul Whitmer, Goshen's dean and Bible teacher until 1917; and John (J. E.) Hartzler, who had been Goshen's president from 1913 to 1918.[48] Goshen's situation deteriorated so much that the Mennonite Board of Education closed the school for 1923-

1924 and then reorganized it with a new faculty. Meanwhile Bluffton gained an exceptionally brilliant faculty.

Yet Bluffton College realized her ecumenical dreams only partially. World War I was hard on progressive impulses; moreover, the gap between Bluffton and many "old" Mennonites was wide. One result of the changes was twin images that worked against Bluffton. The reorganized Goshen appeared to be a conservative "old" Mennonite school (though not "safe" enough to satisfy many "old" Mennonites in Virginia, Pennsylvania, Kansas, and elsewhere). Bluffton seemed to be a liberal haven for the disaffected.

In Kansas the relationship between a more conservative MB Tabor College and a more progressive GC Bethel College was more or less similar, although the progressive brain drain from Tabor to Bethel came later and with less drama. MB progressives who took posts at Bethel included Cornelius Janzen (history and social sciences, 1919-1923), David E. Harder (philosophy and religion, 1922-1925), Peter S. Goertz (dean, philosophy and religion, 1930-1948), Henry W. Lohrenz (biology and Bible, 1932-1934), and Peter E. Schellenberg (psychology, 1931-1941). When teachers joined another group's college, church leaders often lamented. In 1918 J. E. Hartzler was thinking of moving from Goshen to Bethel—prompting bishop S. F. Coffman of Ontario to ask him privately, "Is there no balm in Gilead that one must go to Damascus?"[49] At each school the faculty and the students included some non-Mennonites as well as Mennonites of different backgrounds. Nevertheless, the way in which institution and constituency had developed led each college to identify strongly with one Mennonite branch. Bethel, Bluffton, and Freeman were not formally run by any conference but became General Conference schools. Goshen, Hesston, and Eastern Mennonite were predominantly "old" Mennonite. Tabor was operated by the Tabor College Corporation from its founding in 1908 until 1935; then the Mennonite Brethren conference took formal control.

DEACONESSES, ENTREPRENEURS, AND HOSPITALS

Between 1890 and 1920 some Mennonite groups and communities developed new health care institutions by bringing together two resources: (1) volunteer labor of single women (deaconesses working for subsistence or nurses working for minimal wages); and (2) the energies of entrepreneurial, community-

(Mennonite Library and Archives)

Catherine Voth, Ida Epp, and Frieda M. Kaufman, early Mennonite deaconesses.

building churchmen. The movement produced a number of Mennonite hospitals and deaconess or nurses training institutions. They were a small reflection of a broader American Protestant movement which in the last fifteen years of the nineteenth century founded at least 140 such programs in the United States.[50] Among Mennonites the combination which both appointed deaconesses and built hospitals was strongest in Dutch-Russian communities. "Old" Mennonites founded a hospital and nurses training center at La Junta, Colorado, but without an order of deaconesses. Mennonites' new health programs went hand in hand with the growing efforts in home and foreign missions and with higher education. The hospitals also came with a broader shift in the social context and meaning of illness and health care in America.[51]

A gradual change was under way from informal, unscientific folk medicine to medicine which was professional and scientific.[52] Health care shifted from mutual aid in extended family and congregation to hospitals, which earlier had been only for the decrepit and the terminally ill. Among Mennonites a corps of trained Mennonite doctors led the movement for professionalization. Some of those leaders were Dewitt R. Good of Dale Enterprise, Virginia; H. W. Eby of Elida, Ohio; and Richard S.

Haury of Newton, Kansas. In 1900 the Elkhart Institute invited
Good and Eby to address students on the topic "Medicine as a
Profession."[53] Mission boards recruited such persons for overseas service. William B. Page, member of the first team of "old"
Mennonite missionaries to India, had studied in Chicago, as
had Good. The first Mennonite woman M.D. was Esther Elizabeth Smucker Hodel, awarded the degree in 1931 and thereafter practicing in Morton, Illinois. In 1943 the Mennonite
Who's Who listed ninety-eight medical doctors, most of whom
worked apart from Mennonite hospitals.[54]

American Mennonite Deaconess Institutions*

Founding Date		Name Location
Society	*Hospital*	
1892		United Deaconess Association	Berne, Ind.
1892		Light and Hope Deaconess Home	Berne, Ind.
			Chi., Ill.
1894		Light and Hope Hospital	Chi., Ill.
1894		Light and Hope Hospital	Clev., Ohio
1898	1899	Bethesda Hospital	Gosl., KS
1905	1905	Mennonite Hospital of Mountain Lake	Mt. Lk. MN
1906		Bethany Hospital	Gotebo, OK
1903	1908	Bethel Deaconess Hospital	Newton, KS
1909	1913	Bethany Deaconess Hospital	Am Fls., ID
?	1910-11	Mennonite Deaconess Home and Hosp.	Beatrice, NB
?	1917	Salem Deaconess Home and Hospital	Salem, Oreg.
?	1918	Salem Home and Hospital	Hlsboro., KS
?	1928	Concordia Hospital	Winni., Man.

Non-deaconess Health and Training Institutions

Founding Date		Name	Location
Society Hospital			
?	1908	Mennonite Sanitarium (sold 1924)	La Jun., CL
?	1913	Nurses Training School	La Jun., CL.
?	1920	City Hospital	La Jun., CL.
?	1919	Mennonite Sanitarium	Bloom., Ill.
?	1920	Community Hospital	Bluffton, OH

* Light and Hope deaconesses also helped staff institutions at Evansville (1893) and Indianapolis, Indiana (1894); Detroit, Michigan (1894); and Bloomington, Illinois (1896).

The organized deaconess movement which supplied willing and inexpensive laborers was something new for Mennonites. Earlier there had been some scattered instances of ordained women deaconesses serving the needy in local congregations, often gaining the office as wives of church deacons or bishops. The Middle District of the "old" Mennonites' Virginia conference, where seventeen deaconesses were ordained between the Civil War and World War I, was the only Mennonite body in America with a sustained deaconess tradition.[55] The new deaconess movement took its cues from nineteenth-century Protestant models, and other eastern Mennonites did not participate.

Protestant deaconesses were usually attached and responsible not to local congregations but to their own associations or "mother houses" adjacent to hospitals, orphanages, or urban rescue missions. Deaconesses committed themselves to high standards of spirituality and service. Although they did not take formal vows as in a Catholic order, they dedicated themselves to serve Christ and lived in poverty, chastity, and obedience. The strongest leaders among early American Mennonite deaconesses—Sister Maria Anna Gerber of the Light and Hope Society (Berne, Chicago, Cleveland) and Sister Frieda Kaufman of the Bethel Deaconess Society (Newton)—were immigrants who had gotten their first inspiration (and in Gerber's case her training) from Protestant deaconesses in Switzerland and south Germany. Mennonites of the modern deaconess movement claimed support for the office of deaconess in Scripture and in early church and Mennonite history.[56]

There was some difference between the Protestant and the

Mennonite deaconess movements. The Mennonite version was more local and congregational, the Protestant more ecumenical and associational.[57] In the formative years some women—for instance, Martha Richert of Alexanderwohl and Elise Wiebe and Tina Eitzen of the Krimmer Mennonite Brethren—served as "parish deaconesses." Their work included a variety of ministries to the needy in their homes. As the work of hospital and training institutions grew, deaconesses found themselves serving institutions.[58]

In general, as the institutions of Mennonite deaconesses and hospitals developed they passed through three stages. Each stage had its own entrepreneurs and emphases. John A. Sprunger of Berne, Indiana, traveled to Germany and Switzerland in 1889, and returned to start the first stage. In Switzerland he had recruited six Mennonites for service in America: Rodolphe and Marie Gerber Petter, who soon worked with the Cheyenne Indians under the GC mission board, plus four deaconesses who served in Sprunger's own newly formed and independent Light and Hope Society. Maria Anna Gerber, a sister of Marie Gerber Petter, was Light and Hope's mother deaconess. She was a woman so strong that a younger deaconess she had trained once said that a person who knew her well could "go through hell with her."[59]

The Light and Hope Society began with orphanage work in a new, ornate Victorian house in Berne. From there it extended outward with institutional ministries of various kinds in Chicago; Cleveland; Indianapolis; Detroit; Evansville, Indiana; Bloomington, Illinois; and Bluffton. However, Sprunger severely overextended his work and the society divided. In 1897 eighteen deaconesses seceded over doctrinal issues. Fire destroyed Light and Hope buildings in Cleveland (1895) and Berne (1899). Sprunger was too much an individualist and too inclined toward nondenominationalism to get on well with Mennonite groups and conferences, whom he needed for long-range stability. He took up with a new, nondenominational Mennonite group which formed the "Missionary Church Association." His writings were fervently evangelical but lacked Mennonite content. Although some of his orphanages, missions, publications, and other evangelistic work lasted longer, by 1903 his deaconess homes and hospital work had collapsed.[60]

Thereafter Mennonite leaders who began deaconess and hospital work were reluctant to admit that they owed anything to the volatile Sprunger's aggressive example or to his recruitment of young people out of their own communities.[61] In fact, they owed him a great deal.

In a second stage, from 1898 to 1917, immigrant Mennonites of Dutch-Russian background established deaconess and medical institutions on better foundations: three hospitals in Kansas and one each in Minnesota, Nebraska, Idaho, and Oregon. Another began at Gotebo, Oklahoma, but lasted only about six years. The first of the Kansas hospitals, Bethesda Hospital, Kansas, at Goessel, recruited a former Light and Hope trainee and worker, Katharina Schellenberg, to be its first supervisor and head nurse. In the early years deaconesses received training in Protestant centers, but then the Bethel Hospital in Newton emerged as the main training center. With a three-year training course, by 1930 the Bethel program had graduated 74 deaconesses and nurses. Twenty-three more had been graduated from a smaller training program at Beatrice, Nebraska. Two hundred women had attended these institutions for shorter or longer times. Of them, 141 were from GC congregations, thirty-five from MB, and seven from the "old" Mennonites.[62]

The boards of hospitals' sponsoring associations typically included representation from various Dutch-Russian and related groups: General Conference, Mennonite Brethren, and Krimmer Mennonite Brethren. They did not include non-Mennonites. Neither did they include women, despite the strong roles of women in the hospitals themselves. The day-to-day work, including administration, was in deaconesses' hands. The deaconesses enjoyed more responsibility and honor than Mennonite women could find anywhere else among their people except in urban or overseas missions. Sister Frieda Kaufman served almost continuously as superintendent, or "sister in charge," of the Bethel Hospital from its founding in 1908 until 1938. The theory seems to have been that for success there had to be dedicated woman for compassionate labor and businesslike men for promotion and fund-raising. In 1929 Sister Magdalene Wiebe of Beatrice confided to Sister Frieda the need for "a real 'deaconess father,' who would devote his life in the interest of the deaconess work." But she feared to publicize her idea lest it "reflect on our board."[63] In the long run men replaced women even as administrators. Hospital work was becoming professionalized, and the social and educational system had failed to prepare and legitimate young women for management.

The Dutch-Russian founders of hospital and deaconess institutions saw their work as a wholesome expression of Mennonite sociocultural development. At first David Goerz—GC editor, leader, and business manager of Bethel College—organized the deaconess training in Newton as a department of that school.[64] Franz B. Wedel, originally from the Alexanderwohl congregation north of Newton, founded deaconess hospitals in American Falls, Idaho, and Salem, Oregon. The institutions were entrepreneurial ventures which served to encourage Mennonite settlement and to establish Mennonite presence in western communities. Among the deaconesses at the two hospitals, Wedel's daughters Martha and Marie were leaders. Of their patients, only a very few were Mennonites. In 1902 Peter Richert, an MB medical doctor from Goessel, Kansas, moved to Gotebo, Oklahoma, where he raised money in the churches, bought an old hotel, and for a few years operated a "Bethany Hospital." Richert attracted no deaconesses and found himself paying what he considered an exorbitant salary—$75 per month—for a professional nurse as supervisor. The Mennonite base in the area was too small, the hospital failed, and in 1910 Richert moved to Bakersfield, California.[65] But Goerz, Wedel, Richert, and the founding fathers of deaconess hospitals in Beatrice and Mountain Lake affirmed traditional Mennonite identity and doctrine.[66] In this they were quite unlike Sprunger and his Light and Hope Society.

Of all the early hospital developers, David Goerz best understood and articulated the dilemmas of hospital work as it existed in a gray area between the church congregation and the wider community. On one the hand Mennonites constituted a congregationally based culture, which Goerz, like his Bethel College colleague C. H. Wedel, called a *Gemeindechristentum*. Goerz acknowledged that the authority of the New Testament and early church history implied a congregational base for health care and other benevolence. Having special *associations* to run programs and hospitals might fit a concept of Christendom, but it strained the "principle of *congregation* Christendom" ("*das Prinzip des Gemeindechristentums*"). On the other hand, Mennonites now faced some very practical needs and opportunities which congregations working by themselves could hardly meet. So Goerz wrote that there are times when practical considerations must override apparent biblical and historical precedents. The need for health care was clear.

Money and willing workers were at hand. Surely the modern deaconess movement had roots in biblical commands.[67]

Goerz attempted to bridge the tension between the Mennonite congregational tradition and modern benevolent associations by citing the judgment of C. H. Wedel that the Anabaptist *Gemeindechristentum* principle of voluntary membership did indeed fit the voluntarism implicit in Christian benevolent associations.[68] It was appropriate, these Bethel College colleagues agreed, for a Christendom—even a *Gemeinde* Christendom—to have Christian hospitals organized on a broader community basis. Neither Goerz nor Wedel foresaw how much the coming decades would centralize health care in hospitals and how much professionals would dominate it. They started at the point of a congregationally oriented deaconess movement and continued to prefer that ideal.

In a third stage, Mennonites in hospital and deaconess work gradually shifted their vision from congregation to broader community institutions. Even when boards of directors remained almost entirely Mennonite, hospital staffs developed wide contacts with the world outside Mennonitism. Of course such contact helped break down ethnic isolation. A deaconess committee which the Western District conference formed in 1905 never played a central role.[69] Instead, Mennonite hospitals solicited and received support from non-Mennonites, both individuals and groups. Wilhelmina Eisenmayer Warkentin was the widow of immigrant leader Bernhard Warkentin. The couple had left the Mennonites to join a Presbyterian congregation, yet she funded a new home for the Bethel deaconesses in Newton. Lists of contributors to Mennonite hospitals show broad, ecumenical, community participation. In hospital work Mennonites adapted to the outside world. But the process did not necessarily destroy Mennonite identity. To be sure, in this and other such work some Mennonites cut their ethnic ties. But most did not. The Dutch-Russian movement for deaconess hospitals successfully established Mennonite presence and identity—in ways suited to American denominational society.

Mennonites organized some hospitals and nursing schools apart from the deaconess movement. In 1902 and 1903 "old" Mennonites settled in La Junta, Colorado, and began to pass the word that their community had an especially healthful climate. Soon they opened a sanitarium for tuberculars in 1908, founded a nurses training school in 1915, and took over operation of the La Junta city general hospital in 1919. By 1928 La Junta had a new, 67-bed hospital-sanitarium, built and operated by Mennonites.[70] More than other groups, the "old" Mennonites raised questions and discussed whether hospital work was good church strategy. One issue was the financial burden. Another was whether hospitals were effective instruments of evangelism. In writing about the La Junta institution, Allen H. Erb, superintendent and promoter after 1916, referred to American Protestant precedents (Quaker, Baptist, Methodist, Episcopal) but did not mention the earlier deaconess work of Dutch-Russian Mennonites.[71]

In 1920 Mennonites in Bluffton, Ohio, led by a core of Swiss-background GC Mennonites, founded what they intended to be a "Mennonite Deaconess Home and Hospital." But they failed to find deaconesses to take charge. Soon therefore the institution became a community hospital under the leadership of a head nurse and assistant. Apart from John A. Sprunger's abortive Light and Hope efforts, then, Mennonites of Swiss and south-German background founded fewer hospitals and did not join the deaconess movement. Perhaps one reason was that "old" Mennonites, from the 1890s onward, had developed clearer and stricter understandings of women's role and garb. Such role and garb may have allowed less margin for female institutional leadership.[72]

By 1930 the Mennonite deaconess movement reached a plateau and began to decline. In a summary pamphlet Sister Frieda recognized the "stillstand" and offered several explanations: an evil spirit of the times that did not promote sacrificial service, a preoccupation with institutional details and problems to the exclusion of ideals, and failure of congregations to lay a scriptural base for the deaconess work. Despite her quarter century in a deaconess *association*, Sister Frieda still emphasized strongly, in good Mennonite fashion, that the basis of her work was *congregational*. She said that women whose congregations nurtured, blessed, and ordained them for service were in fact deaconesses whether called by that name or not. Those who were not congregationally ordained were not deaconesses in the biblical sense no matter how "Christian" their work.[73]

One great challenge, Sister Frieda wrote, was modern insistence on professional certification, external examinations, and specialized science. More and more, it seemed, faithfulness in service and success in work counted for less than did official diplomas and state recognition. Deaconesses had to "swim with the stream" and try to "meet the requirements of the authorities and of science." They seemed to have little choice. But Kaufman still called young women to Christian sacrifice. They were to lay their worldly diplomas, honors, and ambitions at the feet of the crucified Lord.[74] What Sister Frieda did not quite say was that in the future the Mennonite women who faced her dilemma would face it as professional nurses, not as deaconesses. In the next twenty years at Bethel, only two young women chose to become deaconesses.[75]

CONCLUSION: DENOMINATIONAL INSTITUTIONS AND THE SECT CYCLE

By 1930 Mennonite peoplehood had gotten a new face. From the founding and flourishing of new institutions such as mission boards, colleges, hospitals, orphanages, mutual aid societies, and retirement homes, Mennonite peoplehood took on a new appearance. Moreover, in the mid and late twentieth century, the organizational revolution would continue, even accelerate. For Mennonites and their self-understanding, what did this institutional revolution mean?

In 1930 Edmund G. Kaufman, then a returned missionary, became the first Mennonite to analyze the recent Mennonite developments using the categories of modern social science. In a published dissertation he wrote at the University of Chicago, Kaufman applied the idea of a "sect cycle."[76] If the ideas of noted sociologists R. E. Park and E. W. Burgess held true, there was a "definite and predictable" evolution of sectarian social groups from isolationist separatism to assimilation or fusion with the outside world. Kaufman claimed not to follow this sect-cycle theory to the point of predicting a "complete fusion of the Mennonite sect with the outside community." He was much more interested in chronicling and celebrating the fact that the Mennonite sect cycle had recently brought a great burst of missionary and philanthropic energy.

However, as Kaufman had seemed to foresee, sect-cycle theory had a major problem. The problem was even more evident a half century later than it was to this young progressive enamored with a new sociology. The Mennonites did indeed avoid "complete fusion with the outside world." They did in fact continue to suffer a good deal of attrition. Individual members left the body, and smaller, marginal groups such as the Mennonite Brethren in Christ and the Missionary Church Association moved away from Mennonite identity. As a whole, however, the Mennonites did not lose their identity and historical memory. They did not cut themselves from their history as, for instance, the Huguenots had done earlier in America.

Instead, Mennonites became a cluster of conservative denominations who kept a strong separate identity over against American Protestants. Sect-cycle theories could not account for the uniquely American phenomenon of denominationalism or for the dynamic ways in which ethnic groups, as they became denominations, could generate a renewed sense of peoplehood. Mennonites adapted denominational institutions to a new social synthesis that accommodated some American forms while finding new ways to enhance distinctive religious-ethnic identity. Mennonite missionaries borrowed from Protestant models, but they founded *Mennonite* daughter churches and made missionary outreach a key part of Mennonite identity. Mennonite young people attended colleges where in many ways they were Americanized, but under teachers such as C. H. Wedel and C. Henry Smith they appropriated modern historical self-definitions which still prized distinctive Mennonite values and traditions. Mennonite deaconesses and entrepreneurs combined to establish new hospitals which involved close association with the wider, non-Mennonite community. But they also helped expand a *Mennonite* ethic of service.

Moreover, sect-cycle theory, like all social theories which use a straight-line idea of acculturation, could not account for long-range successes of the more conservative Mennonites and Amish. Despite strict separatism, old order groups survived and grew in numbers. As Mennonite progressives built denominational institutions, those groups stood aloof. Nor was their choice a case of "cultural lag" which time would eliminate. The old order peoples kept their communities strong and growing in the long run by other means, not with missions, colleges, and hospitals.

The various Mennonite groups remained oriented to each other. They were one mosaic. Progressives always hoped to win people and support from groups which were more conservative. So among all groups, denominational developments had a conservative cast. No group dared to alienate its own conservative wing permanently or to jeopardize its chances of working with more conservative groups. Mennonites understood themselves to be part of a common family. This helped keep the entire group generally conservative in relationship to and in comparison with American Protestants.

In America Mennonites became more mobile, both socially and geographically, than they had been elsewhere. But theirs was a limited mobility.

CHAPTER

7

MENNONITE MOBILITY—
GEOGRAPHIC, ECONOMIC, SOCIAL

"God led the Mennonites to America," wrote C. H. Wedel in 1904. Ever since Reformation times Mennonites had been on the move, impelled by persecution or quest for new opportunities and new mission. In America, quintessential land of freedom and mobility, they became even more mobile. As Wedel said, they moved despite their "worthy association" with the "most solid element of the population of our land."[1]

MENNONITES IN MOTION

Joining the Mennonites' own subculture to the American environment practically guaranteed mobility, both geographical and social. Mennonites' large families created a population pressure which forced surplus sons and daughters to find new farms or new vocations in new places. Their practice of baptizing adults or near-adults rather than infants preserved a principle of human freedom implicit in their Anabaptist origins. Since becoming Mennonite could be a choice rather than a birthright, some in each new generation chose to leave. To such persons America offered richer and more varied choices than Mennonites had enjoyed in any other country. Cheap land on an open frontier beckoned those who did not inherit viable farms. For other Mennonites, especially any who chafed at the limits of their religiously regulated communities, educational opportunities offered another way to enter this growing industrial society. Like many other leaders, Wedel worried that some fellow Mennonites were becoming like "American adventurers," drifting thoughtlessly from place to place in quest of a profitable pioneer life and disregarding historic principles of faith.[2]

(Center for Mennonite Brethren Studies, Hillsboro, Kansas)

Elder Abraham Schellenberg performing baptism in artesian-well pool with Mennonite Brethren near Escondido, California.

To the superficial observers Mennonite farms and communities may have appeared solid and stable. In fact, they were continually being divided, recombined, and transferred. Many sons and daughters married and left, sometimes to return and sometimes not. Precarious new congregations emerged—in country, town, and city.

On the American frontier, mobility was indeed astonishing. Census records for 1860 to 1880 in Trempealeau County, Wisconsin, indicate that the rate of population turnover was more than 70 percent per decade.[3] Of household heads appearing in one census, only 25 to 29 percent remained ten years later. Most people had moved. By comparison, in the years 1875 to 1905 West Branch township of Marion County, Kansas, home of the Alexanderwohl community of Dutch-Russian Mennonites, was more stable: its turnover was less than 50 percent. Between 53 and 58 percent of West Branch heads of household in one census were still there ten years later.[4] Apparently a majority of the Alexanderwohl Mennonites stayed on the land where they had settled. Nevertheless, many Mennonites did move. They moved far more often than a popular image of Mennonite stability might suggest.

The rates of mobility among Mennonite communities may have varied in different parts of the country. The U.S. Census did not include religious affiliation, and self-effacing Mennonites in places such as eastern Pennsylvania did not keep congregational records. So it is difficult to compile reliable data or verify whether a given person on a government census list was

(Mennonite Library and Archives)

Mutual aid: Mennonites clean up after a tornado near Goessel, Kansas, 1906.

in fact a Mennonite. A study of Old Order Amish in Pennsylvania's Lancaster County, based on genealogical records and Amish informants, showed that 22.4 percent left the church between 1880 and 1939.[5] The portion who moved geographically must have been larger. Available data do not permit precise statements about Mennonite mobility, yet they clearly suggest a pattern: considerable mobility, yet greater stability than in comparable rural communities of America.

The Hutterites and the Old Order Amish, who maintained a rigorous system for socializing youngsters into their own ways of living, were more successful than other Mennonite groups at holding their own children. They planned more systematically for community growth and proliferation. Some of the Hutterites who moved from the Russian Empire to Dakota Territory in the 1870s established individual homesteads. Eventually growing apart from the communitarian Hutterites, these joined Mennonites of the General Conference or the Krimmer Mennonite Brethren.[6] Other Hutterites formed colonies of economic sharing and developed a successful system for community growth and expansion. They allowed a colony to grow to about 150 persons at maximum and then divided it.

When a colony divided, the ideal was for one fragment to

find new land about thirty miles away. The average time between such colony divisions was about fourteen years. Each new colony planned for future expansion and division. Originally in the 1870s there had been three colonies. By 1917 there were nineteen—two in Montana, the rest in South Dakota. Then conscription and a crisis of conscience in World War I set off a mass Hutterite migration to Canada. All Hutterite growth was biological rather than by winning converts. Yet no other group in the Anabaptist-Mennonite family grew as rapidly.[7]

Many Mennonites moved westward ahead of any organized Mennonite church. At least ten years passed between the arrival of the first Mennonite settlers in California and the organization in 1897 of the first congregation, the San Marcos Mennonite church, fifteen miles west of Paso Robles.[8] In the new century the rate of movement to California increased. By World War I there were GC congregations in Paso Robles, Upland, Reedley, and Los Angeles; MB congregations in Reedley, Rosedale, Bakersfield, and Lodi; a KMB congregation at Dinuba; and four small clusters of "old" Mennonites not formed into congregations. The most successful communities would be those in and around Reedley in the rich fruit-growing lands of the San Joaquin Valley. By contrast, a migration to Oregon included a higher proportion of "old" and Amish Mennonites. By World War I they had two congregations near Hubbard, two at Albany, and one near Canby. In Oregon, Mennonites settled in the Willamette Valley, 90 percent of them within thirty miles of the city of Salem.[9]

For Mennonites who scattered, the task of providing church leadership and the fellowship which would sustain peoplehood often fell to unpaid ministers. This was the pattern in Texas, Colorado, Montana, Idaho, and the West Coast as well as in places near established Mennonite communities. One self-sacrificing leader was Joseph Schlegel (1837-1913) of Milford, Nebraska, a bishop in the Western District Amish Mennonite conference.[10] Schlegel's congregation included settlers from Ontario, Ohio, Indiana, Illinois, Iowa, and elsewhere. In addition to pastoring his own congregation he visited other nuclei of Mennonites on the Nebraska plains and in the wider West. Where possible, he ordained ministers and bishops to create self-sustaining congregations. Schlegel's wife, Mary Miller Schlegel, like the wives of many other itinerant Mennonite leaders, had to take major responsibility for the economic welfare of the family and for raising the children. Oral tradition tells of one occasion when Mary followed instructions sent by telegram and met Joseph briefly at the train station as he traveled from the West to the East. She gave him fresh clothing and discussed with him the most urgent business of home, family, and personal affairs. Other congregation members also stopped by to see their bishop. The stop was an unscheduled one made at his request, and folklore says that the train crew was quite impressed with the way the Mennonite people supported their leader.[11]

INDIAN TERRITORY—OKLAHOMA

Mennonites often established new communities as a kind of religious mission. Especially in Indian Territory, the land which in 1907 became the state of Oklahoma, some settlers mixed missionary intentions with land hunger. GC emissaries began work among the Cheyenne and Arapaho Indians in 1880. Believing that the crimes of white people against the Indians were a thing of the past, they decided that Mennonites could now cooperate with government to deal with Native Americans in enlightened and benevolent ways.[12] In 1887 the U.S. government established a new law, the Dawes Severalty Act, which provided for separating tribal lands into individual plots in order that Indians might become self-sufficient and independent farmers.

The Mennonite missionaries endorsed the law. They remained silent when, under the new law, white Americans took away millions of treaty-guaranteed acres. The missionaries were more concerned that the whites who flooded the territory in one land rush after another were too often rough and violent frontierspeople who were a bad influence on the Indians. So they appealed to their own Mennonite people to join the rush and claim lands near the mission. In 1889, the year of the first rush into Oklahoma, missionary H. R. Voth wrote that a "solid Mennonite congregation, instead of a mixed frontier element," would be a great advantage for the Indians and the mission.[13] Many Mennonites joined other land-hungry Americans in the 1889 Oklahoma District run, the 1892 run to Cheyenne-Arapaho lands, and the 1893 run on the Cherokee Outlet. Other Mennonites arrived later. By the time Oklahoma became a state it had at least forty-four Mennonite congregations.[14]

Most Mennonite settlers in Oklahoma were Dutch-Russians of the 1870s migration. Twenty-two of the congregations belonged to the GC branch, twelve were MB, two KMB, and two Church of God in Christ, Mennonite (Holdeman). Five new congregations were of Swiss and south-German origin: two "old" Mennonite, two Old Order Amish, and one Amish Mennonite. For support in the face of the harsh frontier these groups turned more to aid from families and congregations they had left than to other kinds of Mennonites nearby. Moreover, attempts to include Indians and whites in the same congregations did not succeed. The cultures of the two groups remained separate and largely unrelated. Though seldom as destitute and dependent as the Indians, the Mennonites struggled with drought and poverty. Finally, in 1897 better crops began to bring prosperity.

Although Mennonite migration was not as centrally organized and coordinated as the Hutterite, settlers managed to transplant various distinctive Mennonite institutions. In 1902, in Washita County, Oklahoma, at the village of Korn (changed to "Corn" in World War I), an MB congregation started a school which in 1911 became a Bible academy. With time the community and its school produced many MB church leaders for Oklahoma and elsewhere.[15] In 1911 the New Hopedale GC congregation at Meno in Major County started a school which in time became the Oklahoma Bible Academy. Mennonite publishing and hospital efforts fared less well. In 1899 John F. Harms, as editor of the MB paper *Zionsbote*, moved his printing operation to the Medford area of Grant County. But in 1906 he left for Canada and thereafter the Medford MB congregation gradually declined.[16]

There was continuous movement of families in and out of Oklahoma. Dr. Peter Richert of the short-lived Bethany Hospital in Gotebo wrote that in trying to relate to its town his institution had two clear disadvantages compared to others in Kansas. Gotebo did not have an adequate German-speaking population in the vicinity, and there had not been sufficient time (by 1906) to prepare the "field" and develop a strong hospital interest.[17] Later, virulent anti-German attitudes at the time of World War I stimulated Mennonite migration out of Oklahoma. Still later, the dust bowl and depression disasters of the 1930s did the same. Eventually Oklahoma had about the highest number of extinct Mennonite congregations of any state in the union.[18]

Some new settlements reversed the pattern of westward migration. One example was in the Virginia Tidewater on the

Warwick River, a tributary of the James.[19] In 1897, near the spot where early settlers had struggled to establish the Jamestown colony almost three centuries earlier, Mennonites from Ohio, Missouri, Kansas, and closer at hand streamed in to build a community and develop farmlands uncultivated since the U.S. Civil War. In the fall of 1899, traveling on a covered wagon pulled by two mules, the Christian K. Miller family took nine weeks and two days to get from Cass County, Missouri, to the Warwick.[20]

At first, "old" and Amish Mennonite settlers at the Warwick met as one congregation, but in 1900 they divided. Meanwhile the settlement was close enough to the growing city of Newport News to find a good market for agricultural produce, yet far enough away to develop on its own. Mennonites served on the county school board, taught in public schools, and built a special building for their own literary society. Able leaders contributed to solid growth and Mennonite identity. This was true especially after 1910, the year a bishop named George R. Brunk, soon to be a strong leader of his denomination, moved to Warwick from western Kansas. Brunk insisted upon rigorous church discipline. Some church members did not agree, for example, a schoolteacher of Amish background, J. Harvey Yoder. Yoder gave up his Sunday school position rather than accept what he called the "circumcision" of the plain coat.[21] But Brunk was also an advocate for missions and education, and a strong community supporter who voted in political elections.[22] After World War II the rural Warwick settlement would be engulfed and transformed by the urban expansion of Newport News.

Mobile Mennonites not only established new communities; in various places they left signs of older communities' disintegration. Historian John Umble, studying Ohio Mennonite Sunday schools, wrote of "scores of lonely little cemeteries [that] mark extinct Mennonite congregations." He found such evidence "all the way from eastern Pennsylvania to Oregon. . . ." Among the forces of congregational disintegration which Umble listed were small size (typically fewer than fifty members), distance from other congregations, economic difficulties, and lack of progressive and adaptive leadership.[23] Amish historian David Luthy has identified 42 Amish settlements which failed between 1890 and 1930.[24] Another scholar, studying GC congregations, has identified seventy-eight which became extinct between 1847 and 1959.[25] In 1929 there were 159 GC congregations. If a community declined, congregational record-keepers most often identified the main cause to have been migration "for economic advantage." Extinct congregations were scattered in states of Mennonite settlement fairly evenly across the country. The decade which brought the highest number of congregation closings was from 1926 to 1935. Two of the extinct congregations, South Danvers and East White Oak at Carlock, both in Illinois, had once had more than three hundred members each. Most, however, had been small rural congregations.

VARYING RELATIONSHIPS TO TOWN LIFE

Rural Mennonites traveled back and forth between country and town, if only for what Kansas farm boy Ernest E. Leisy remembered as the "annual trip to the county seat to pay taxes and buy heavy suits."[26] Town contacts left indelible imprints on Mennonite imaginations, but Mennonites in different parts of the country responded to town life in various ways. Important varieties are quite clear in a comparison of Pennsylvania's Lancaster County, Indiana's Elkhart County, and Kansas' Marion County in 1914, the year when World War I began. Each had a sizable Mennonite population. Contributing to differences in Mennonite attitudes toward nearby towns were many influences: population density, dialect, vocational choices, congregational development, church regulations, and more.[27]

Lancaster County, Pennsylvania. In Lancaster County, Mennonites' view of the public life of town and city had been shaped and refined by two centuries of experience with other sectarian groups in Pennsylvania-German culture. Sharing a dialect with their non-Mennonite neighbors, Mennonites could not rely on language to provide sharp separation. However, most Mennonites in Lancaster County avoided political involvement. Those who became businessmen or professionals and moved to the city typically joined a more liberal Mennonite or non-Mennonite group. If young people pursued higher education at Lancaster city's Franklin and Marshall College or the state normal school at nearby Millersville, many of their fellow Mennonites assumed that they were on their way out of the Mennonite fold. The bishops who made decisions in the Lancaster conference and in the more conservative Weaverland old order branch spent much time and energy defining and enforcing rules of dress and church practice. They attempted to apply biblical standards to the small details of life so that their congregations would have a consistent corporate witness. It was largely a witness of separation from the world.

Lancaster in 1914 was a county with much farmland and a goodly number of small towns, plus a small city of about fifty thousand at the center. Its population density was 180 persons per square mile.[28] Over the decades more and more Mennonites moved off the farms to live and work, but they always knew that conservative church leaders disapproved. In Lancaster city in 1914 there was a Lancaster conference congregation on East Chestnut Street. Having met already for more than twenty-five years, it had grown to more than three hundred members before the rural bishops of the conference had allowed it to have its own resident minister—John H. Mosemann, ordained in 1904.[29] In 1918 the conference's board of bishops turned down a request for a town-based bishop district. At the same meeting they also forbade members to join the Red Cross.[30] Thus they held town influences at arm's length. The very location and architecture of plain Mennonite meetinghouses suggested how marginal Mennonites were to public, community life. If a village expanded outward to surround a Mennonite meetinghouse, Mennonites usually built their next one on the fringe or farther out in the country.[31]

Lancaster Mennonites carefully regulated and resisted public involvements in town and city. Nevertheless, in times of crisis they had more direct and intimate access to their national congressman than did Mennonites anywhere else in the country. From 1909 to 1929 the congressman was a secularized Quaker, W. W. Griest. Griest clearly understood and appreciated the semi-separatist place of Mennonites and Amish within the county's ethnic mosaic. One good friend of Griest was Israel B. Good, a former principal of Terre Hill High School who had been a minister of the Weaverland congregation since 1903. During World War I, Good solicited the congressman's help to protect Mennonites' pacifist privileges. It seems that conservative and antitown Mennonites in Lancaster County could form very comfortable and functional relations with political leaders. Within the tolerant historic pluralism of Pennsylvania-German culture, Lancaster Mennonites' rules and rituals of separation had won them a well-recognized status. Mennonites and Amish were nonconformists and outsiders to the public order, yet they had a niche in that order and were comfortable in it. Their role in an allegedly evil world in 1917-1918 produced less conflict with worldly authorities in town and city than occurred in Indiana's Elkhart and Kansas' Marion counties.

Elkhart/Goshen, Indiana. Mennonites living in Indiana's Elkhart County in 1914 were a predominantly rural people, although they had established more of an institutional presence in the towns of Elkhart (population about 17,000) and Goshen (population about 8,100) than Mennonites had done in Lancaster. At mid-nineteenth century, Mennonites had established a community on the western side of Elkhart County.

Meanwhile, Amish had settled in the eastern and southwestern parts and spilled into adjacent counties. Mennonite farms were somewhat larger and the area less thickly settled than in Pennsylvania. Compared to Lancaster County's 180, Elkhart County had 115 persons per square mile. There was one Mennonite congregation in the city of Elkhart and two in Goshen. All three had emerged along with visions of denominational renewal through institutions of publication, mission, and education as Mennonite professionals moved to town to pursue that vision. The Mennonite base in Elkhart had been laid when John F. Funk arrived in 1867. Yet at the time of World War I a half century later, Mennonites' footing in the town was not really secure. The Prairie Street congregation in Elkhart had suffered much dissension and loss of members to other denominations. Funk himself had lost out to a younger generation in both business and church affairs. In 1903 the Elkhart Institute had removed to Goshen. And by 1908 "old" Mennonite publishing had moved to Scottdale, Pennsylvania.

In town affairs at Goshen, where the church congregation had been organized after the educational institution was established, Mennonite professionals and businessmen were not very prominent. Not long before the war Dr. William B. Page, a medical missionary returned from the "old" Mennonites' team in India, set up a practice on East Lincoln Avenue. The Goshen Milk Condensery, in operation since 1909, was managed by John M. Yoder and associated with the Orrville Milk Company of Orrville, Ohio.[32] But at least some "old" and Amish Mennonites assumed that their successful professionals or businessmen in Goshen would either find their places in non-Mennonite churches or transfer to the more progressive or "worldly" Eighth Street Mennonite church. The Eighth Street congregation, organized in 1913, was related to the Central Conference of Mennonites in Illinois.[33] As for Goshen College, in 1914 it was a lively but unstable institution. Its wartime president, J. E. Hartzler, had never won the confidence of the "old" Mennonites' board of education or of their conservative bishops. In 1917-1918, in contrast to treatment of the Tabor, Bluffton, and Bethel College presidents, Hartzler's church did not trust him with any significant war-related leadership role.

The strength of "old" and Amish Mennonite culture in Elkhart County was in the rural churches. There bishops such as Daniel (D. D.) Miller of the Forks church and Daniel (D. J.) Johns of the Clinton Frame congregation taught the virtues of humility, simplicity, and nonconformity. Such doctrines reinforced the feelings of Mennonite farmers whenever they went to town, did their business with non-Mennonites, and walked the streets in an essentially alien environment. Walking about town, they sensed that they could never participate fully in community life. Separation from the world still meant staying on the rural fringes. To have a Mennonite mayor or draft board member in Elkhart or Goshen was almost beyond imagination. And even though the Elkhart County folk were displaced Pennsylvania Germans, they were less established in the civil community than were Lancaster County's Mennonites, and had no counterpart to the friendly congressman, Griest. They were more progressive than Lancaster Mennonites in starting denominational institutions, yet in many ways more separate from their local "world." In Elkhart County the cultural position of Mennonites was less secure than back in Lancaster County.

Hillsboro, Kansas. In Hillsboro, Kansas, on western wheat-growing plains, Mennonites could feel at home in both country and town. There was more land and space per person: Marion County had four times more than Elkhart County and seven times more than Lancaster County. In 1914 Hillsboro was a town of some 1,300 people at the county's eastern edge, amid the Mennonite settlement. The relatively sparse population meant that farmers typically had to drive their horses and wagons farther to get to town, and a relatively high proportion of town-dwelling Mennonites meant that Mennonites could aspire to public roles. In the boosterish words of its Mennonite-edited newspaper, Hillsboro was a "Mecca of the Germans, whose diligence and zeal [*Fleiss und Eifer*] have transformed many a wasteland into a true paradise."[34]

Welcome for "band reunion" day in Hillsboro, Kansas, 1907.

The first telephone exchange in Hillsboro, Kansas, owned by J. C. Janzen.

(Center for Mennonite Brethren Studies, Hillsboro, Kansas)

In Hillsboro, Mennonite farmers could buy farm machinery, seed grain, milk products, furniture, and other supplies from fellow members. In 1914 they could get medical remedies (Dew Drop Tablets for headaches and Blackberry Balsam "to cure stomach pains, cholera, diarrhea and summer complaint") from Dr. Jacob J. Entz. Entz, a German Baptist of Mennonite background, was a former Hillsboro mayor and current Marion County health officer.[35] Hillsboro had a Mennonite Brethren college and a General Conference preparatory school. On the drawing boards was a Mennonite hospital. The town's Mennonites read Mennonite Brethren Abraham L. Schellenberg's vigorously edited weekly newspaper, *Vorwärts*, which pushed for women's suffrage, prohibition, wages and hours legislation, referendum, recall, and reform of the railroads.[36] They had two town congregations, both founded in the 1880s or two decades before the coming of the educational and publishing interests which made Hillsboro an MB denominational center. At the county seat in Marion, Hillsboro Mennonites wielded considerable influence. For instance, in eight Mennonite school districts an arrangement of dubious legality allowed them to use public funds for German-language instruction.[37]

Hillsboro's Mennonites took part in local public affairs. Between 1884 and 1913 four different mayors were Mennonites. During the early years of the European war Schellenberg used his newspaper to raise money for German war relief via the German Red Cross. When America entered the war, Henry W. Lohrenz helped organize a local committee for the American Red Cross and for local war-related activities. He even accepted an appointment to the Marion County Council of Defense.[38] Jacob G. Ewert led Hillsboro citizens in demanding that Dr. J. J. Entz be appointed to the Marion County draft board.[39] These involvements clearly assumed that there was a legitimate public role for German-speaking religious pacifists even when America was at war—an assumption which wartime experiences often belied.

Unlike Lancaster Mennonites, who depended upon worldly political figures to protect their interests, Hillsboro Mennonites took political initiatives themselves. In both places Mennonites had found homes in America, but rather different ones. Lancaster represented the Swiss-American culture of humility and separation. Hillsboro represented the German-speaking, Dutch-Russian congregation Christendom. As America entered World War I, Hillsboro's German-American culture, still relatively new and rapidly developing, turned out to be more vulnerable than Lancaster's.

SOCIAL MOBILITY: UPWARD OR FALLEN OFF

Other ethnic groups in America normally showed great pride when someone of their number became prominent. Not so with Mennonites. They had few words of praise for sons and daughters who made special contributions, gained unusual wealth, or moved to high places in community or nation. Rather than praise, they coined unflattering expressions. Such people were, in German, the *Abgefallene* (the fallen-off)—persons who had left the Mennonite ways. In English, they had "gone high." They had traded the simple and humble ways of their people for faster, more affluent, and higher-status styles of life.

Thousands of Mennonite sons and daughters left their people. Many who left won public acclaim. For instance, in Virginia's Rockingham County several of the best and brightest got a start in the "Dale Enterprise Literary Society"—a forum for debates, parliamentary drills, lectures, and other activities of cultural uplift. Members gathered in a lyceum hall built by a man with the "Mennonite" name of David A. Heatwole. For over two decades the society flourished, with a membership as high as fifty. Most members left the Dale Enterprise community to go into professions. In 1924 the "Brilliant Sons of Rockingham" returned for a reunion. William J. Showalter, who had risen to associate editor of the *National Geographic Magazine*, gave an address tracing the "scientific progress of the world." Others at the celebration included Dr. Timothy O. Heatwole, a vice-president of the University of Maryland, and Cornelius J. Heatwole, editor of the *Virginia Journal of Education.*[40]

Only a few Mennonites who were prominent in professional or political affairs remained active in Mennonite congregations. Peter Jansen of Nebraska (1852-1923) was a successful farmer, rancher, and Republican politician who served in his state's legislature. He also served as a Republican National Convention delegate and as a U.S. commissioner to the 1899 Paris Exposition. Jansen remained committed to pacifism and reportedly turned down an invitation to run for governor because he could not enforce the death penalty.[41] Maxwell Kratz (1875-1939), a successful attorney and a member of the Second Mennonite Church of Philadelphia, has been described as "a rare example of the ability to grow in his appreciation of traditional Mennonite teaching—at least on some subjects—while he grew more sophisticated in the ways of the world."[42] In World War I Kratz worked on behalf of conscientious objectors. After 1920 he served on the executive committee of the Mennonite Central Committee.[43]

Cut from a different pattern was the extended Leisy family, immigrants from the Palatinate. Over three generations the Leisys had grown wealthy and worldly through the successful brewing of beer at Keokuk, Iowa; Cleveland, Ohio; and Peoria, Illinois.[44] In Cleveland Isaac Leisy (1839-1892) was a member and supporter of the small Mennonite group; but his ties were closer with relatives in Germany than with American Mennonites, who had been influenced by the prohibition movement. In 1915 Isaac's widow, Christine "Dina" Leisy (1841-1916), embarrassed Bethel College with a $4,000 gift. A brother-in-law named Johann J. Krehbiel persuaded Bethel's board to accept the money—although he himself was active in the Prohibitionist Party.[45] A son of Isaac and Christine, Otto Leisy, built up the family brewery at Cleveland but apparently did not belong to any church. In 1905 he and his wife, Elizabeth Geber Leisy, built a magnificent 26-room mansion, surely a mark of having "gone high." To decorate the ceiling of one room with a large mural they employed another successful ex-Mennonite of the professional, urban diaspora—Albert Henry Krehbiel of the Chicago Institute of Art. Albert, son of J. J. and Anna Leisy Krehbiel of Newton, Kansas, had studied at the Academie Julian in Paris and was an early American impressionist.[46]

Cleveland's Mennonites followed the example of failed urban Mennonitism and never established a viable congregation. Yet traces of Mennonite heritage remained. In 1910 Herman C. Baehr was elected mayor of Cleveland and used a simple affirmation instead of the standard oath of office. For his Mennonite forebears such a choice had brought painful persecution. For Baehr it was only a faint remnant of a disappearing tradition.[47]

An even sadder note in the Mennonite diaspora could be heard among some who chose to leave or were cast out in bitterness and anger. Gordon Friesen, born in 1909, was an unhappy child of an impoverished and defeated KMB family in Weatherford, Oklahoma.[48] Friesen was awed by an uncle who had fought in the Spanish-American War, returned home to marry a bar girl or prostitute, and finally turned to ecstatic religion. Too many Mennonites were experiencing Mennonitism as psychologically destructive, and for them Gordon Friesen spoke and wrote. In 1936 he published an autobiographical novel, *The Flamethrowers*, which won critical acclaim. In it a Mennonite elder, a spiritual leader of his community, was a sex-obsessed bigot. All the leading characters were maimed by their history and religion.[49] As for Friesen, he eventually joined the Communist Party and moved to New York City. But he continued to feel his Mennonite identity and sent biographical data to the 1937 and 1943 editions of the Mennonite *Who's Who*.[50] Late in life he wrote, "Running through every thing I've done is the thread of my upbringing as a Mennonite—namely compassion for the oppressed."[51]

From the point of view of Mennonites who remained in the household of faith, the Gordon Friesens were lost souls. In his diary evangelist John S. Coffman wrote about a 43-year-old brother who remained unconverted, "How often have I prayed the Lord to bring him by some means to salvation. Surely the Lord will answer my prayer, but I feel sad to think of his wasted life."[52]

NEW KINDS OF GATHERING

One mark of accelerating Mennonite mobility was the changing pattern of attendance at the district and national conferences—large meetings at which Mennonites approved the activities of common peoplehood and transacted business of their emerging denominations.[53] From the 1890s to the 1920s such gatherings shifted in both scale and focus. People traveled greater distances to attend and took part in a wider and wider range of official and unofficial events. As automobiles displaced railway transportation, Mennonites who would not take vacations for pleasure were nevertheless willing to drive across the state or nation to worship and celebrate with their own people. (For them, being with their own people surely brought much more pleasure anyhow.) Conference meetings which originally had been business meetings of important leaders now became wider events which adventuresome church members used for celebration and education.

There were different patterns of choosing representatives to attend conferences. Delegates to sessions of the "old" Mennonites' general conferences represented districts, not congregations. The conferences met biennially. All bishops were automatically delegates by virtue of their office, and a district conference could send three or more ministers and deacons as well. Bishops from conferences which had not officially joined the general conference (Lancaster, Franconia, Washington-Franklin, and Eastern Amish Mennonite before 1927) were nevertheless allowed to participate and vote, a gesture to show that such conferences would be welcomed in the larger body. As larger numbers of lay men and women began to attend conference meetings, actual delegates formed smaller proportions of those who gathered.

At the general meetings of the General Conference Mennonite church (held every third year), delegates represented not districts but congregations. Congregations could have one vote per thirty members; therefore many laypersons were delegates. However, before 1932 no women served. In 1917 when the GC general conference voted to withdraw from the Federal Council of Churches, Silas Grubb, editor of *The Mennonite*, wrote, "In a democratic organization, such as our conference happens to be, it is the duty of the minority to bow gracefully to the will of the majority."[54] This ideal of democracy was quite different from the authority of "old" Mennonite ordained leaders, many of whom

(Center for Mennonite Brethren Studies, Hillsboro, Kansas)

Mennonite Brethren Church gathering at the Ebenfeld Church near Hillsboro, Kansas, in the 1890s.

were chosen by lot. The MBs also allowed laymen to serve as delegates. Until 1909 the MB body, being small and concentrated, had only one conference organization. Then it formed three district ones and gave them responsibility for home missions. The general conference remained in charge of foreign missions, publication, and education.

As more nondelegates attended the various conferences, programs offered more inspirational speakers and music, especially in the evenings. The MBs, who encouraged families to attend at least some sessions, sometimes added an all-day Sunday missions festival and children's program. In the 1920s the "old" Mennonites sometimes held "fundamentals" conferences prior to the official meetings. Especially in the evenings, such special events drew large crowds of local Mennonites.

To enable more members to attend, leaders scheduled the conferences in different Mennonite areas. Thus delegates learned to know the communities. Moreover, conference periodicals helped them prepare for meetings, and offered extensive reports afterward. The periodicals also listed train schedules, and instructions for getting reduced fares. Some rail lines issued half-fare tickets to ministers; a Mennonite yearbook could serve for identification. In 1917 the GCs advertised a special train from Chicago to Reedley, California, including free excursions on the side to Los Angeles and San Diego. In 1923 *The Mennonite* urged people to go by rail rather than automobile in order to assure a discount which depended on having at least 250 traveling together. But increasing affluence and the automobile's convenience hastened the shift from rail to highway. By 1929, people counted more than two thousand cars parked at the "old" Mennonite general conference meeting.

Before the 1920s Mennonites invariably held conferences in relatively small, rural communities who provided food and lodging without charge. But the size of the gatherings began to be too great a burden. Finally in 1929 the General Conference Mennonite church met in a city—Hutchinson, Kansas. Delegates gathered in the public auditorium, lodged in hotels, and ate meals in restaurants. A record ten thousand people attended. By chance the conference was a stormy and controversial one—perhaps due partly to some loss of symbolic unity formerly provided by common meals and by meeting in a Mennonite church building or tent. In 1927 the "old" Mennonites first used the technological advance of the microphone. It was a success, said a report in the *Gospel Herald*, because it minimized "visiting" during the business sessions.[55]

"Every Mennonite family that can afford it should attend a General Conference at least once in their lives," wrote H. G. Allebach in 1907. "The time and money so spent will repay themselves a hundred-fold."[56] By 1929 the social benefits of church harmony gained through conference meetings were so persuasive that one Mennonite leader suggested that fellowship alone was almost sufficient reason for such meetings.[57] In a world of accelerating mobility Mennonites needed the gatherings more than ever in order to celebrate and renew their peoplehood in Christ.

When war broke out in Europe in 1914, the conferences became especially serious. Warfare always exposed the roots of Mennonite separation from the world.

CHAPTER

8

THE GREAT WAR

"I hit him. I had to hit him," insisted Sergeant John B. Poindexter at the court-martial trial of George S. Miller, a Mennonite draftee. "I hit him because he [said] . . ., 'God damn the Stars and Stripes.' " On August 26, 1918, at a U.S. Army camp at Fort Dodge, Iowa, Poindexter had broken Miller's nose and left the draftee bleeding on a mess-hall floor. Miller's court-martial was on November 11, the day that all America celebrated the end of fighting in World War I. Despite the armistice, officers at Fort Dodge continued their business with Mennonite conscientious objectors.

Miller pleaded not guilty. No, he said, he certainly had not insulted the flag. He had too much "respect for the Supreme Being, and for our Government" to ever "think of using such contemptuous words." He pleaded not guilty also to a charge that he had disobeyed an officer who had ordered him to clean up a mess hall. His position was that the order had violated an agreement with the Mennonites on what work they would and would not do; therefore it was not valid. Nonetheless, the court found Miller guilty. His sentence: life imprisonment at hard labor. Eight days later the commanding officer at Fort Dodge, Brigadier General B. T. Simmons, reduced the time to fifteen years. Along with quite a few other COs, Miller went to the military prison at Fort Leavenworth, Kansas.[1]

George S. Miller was an unmarried farmhand from Sugar Creek, Ohio, where his father edited a newspaper for the Amish, *The Budget*. At age thirty-two he was more mature than the average Mennonite draftee and more ready to accept the brutal results of resisting. On the night of August 28 he and three other conscientious objectors had received the "scrubbing and tubbing" treatment. Zealous soldiers (not officers) had scratched them raw with brooms under a cold shower. A Mennonite leader who later saw Miller in the guardhouse reported that the treatment had "just peeled the outer skin off" until in some places he "looked like a piece of raw meat." Faced with such hazing, Miller's companions had agreed to wear the military uniform. But Miller had refused, and kept refusing even after his tormentors dunked his head repeatedly into a tub of water. Such persecution was illegal, as the Mennonites and Amish knew. Secretary of War Newton D. Baker had issued orders to treat conscientious objectors respectfully and not force them to do anything against their consciences.[2]

From prison Miller wrote letters expressing both spiritual submission to suffering and a great desire for freedom. On the one hand he wrote that "it has become a glory to me that I could be counted worthy of the suffering and shame for the name of Christ." On the other hand he said that sounds from outside the prison walls—the chirps of "the robin red breast, blue bird and meadow lark"—made him yearn for freedom. He also dreamed of an even greater release. One night "Christ came in the clouds and blew the trumpet. I jumped on my feet and shouted, glory to God, but I awoke and was very much disappointed." For he was "still in the same cell." Other Mennonite conscientious objectors in the Leavenworth prison were having similar dreams, he said.[3]

In April 1919, after reviewing Miller's court-martial, a clemency board recommended his discharge. The members said they seriously doubted "that the prisoner used the language attributed to him."[4] So less than half a year after going to jail, Miller was released. His story ended much like stories of nearly all the 200-odd COs who had been unjustly imprisoned. Fifty years later Miller reminisced that the experience had strengthened his faith in God and even his respect for his country.[5]

The irony of Miller's new respect for his country was the irony of many American Mennonites' experience with World War I. Despite harassment and even some persecution, in the end the war left most of them with both a stronger sense of being separate and a new appreciation for America as a home for nonconformists. They gained a new balance between civic alienation and civic respectability. It was a balance which had not come easily. Within the Mennonite family, individuals and groups responded in different ways. For them and for all pacifists and German-speaking people in America, the war wrought both agony and challenge.

VARYING REACTIONS:
SWISS-AMERICAN AND DUTCH-RUSSIAN

The responses of various Mennonites and Amish depended on which European stream they represented and on the amount of time since they or their ancestors had immigrated. The Swiss-American groups of "old" and Amish Mennonites had been in America for many generations. Without close family ties in Europe they could view the war with some detachment. When the guns of August roared in 1914, Daniel Kauffman, editor of the *Gospel Herald* and a descendant of immigrants who had arrived in 1717, denounced the war—"this institution of iniquity"—with distinctively American rhetoric. Seeing American pacifists such as Andrew Carnegie forsaking the peace cause, he attacked them for failing to ground their nonresistance in Jesus. Kauffman did not feel close enough to European Mennonites to discuss what the war might mean for them. Instead, he reflected on what might happen if the war involved America. The war was "militarism unchained." "Is our faith strong enough," he asked, "that in the midst of trial, persecution, insults, etc., we would manifest a meek, submissive spirit, suffering rather than to inflict sufferings upon others, dying rather than to kill?"[6] Thus Kauffman balanced an antiwar mood with Mennonite meekness and submission. His words were exactly right for the "old" Mennonite synthesis, of which he was a chief author.

Among Swiss-American Mennonites, C. Henry Smith provided the most knowledgeable and progressive commentary on the European war.[7] A descendant of Amish immigrants who had arrived from Lorraine in the early-nineteenth century, and now a well-trained historian at Bluffton College, Smith displayed little brotherly interest in the impact of the war upon European Mennonites. His one main comment was a judgmental one—that "to our humiliation, even the Mennonite has raised his sword against fellow-Mennonite." Apparently he was referring to some in Germany on the one side and in the Russian Empire on the other who had joined the national armies.[8] Smith's view was typically American—that the war was Germany's fault. Prussian Chancellor Otto von Bismarck, architect of modern Germany and its nationalism, had upset the nineteenth-century's peaceable "concert of Europe."

Dutch-Russian Mennonites, who had arrived in the 1870s and 1880s or in some cases more recently, saw the European war differently. "Most of us in America are immigrants," wrote Carl H. A. van der Smissen, editor of the GCs' *Christlicher Bundesbote*. Van der Smissen had come in 1875 and had studied in universities at Basel, Tübingen, and Halle. He had deep fears about what the war might mean for Mennonites in places such as Switzerland, the Palatinate, Prussia, and the German enclaves of Russia. To him the war was "a punishment of God for the godlessness of man in so-called Christendom." As was true also of C. Henry Smith, to some degree van der Smissen thought both sides were guilty. But unlike Smith's, van der Smissen's deeper bias was pro-German. Germany's Kaiser had maintained peace "for over twenty-five years." Now he was at war because he was forced into it by Russian and French mobilization.

Of all Mennonite editors the most thoroughly pro-German was Abraham Schellenberg of *Vorwärts* in Hillsboro, Kansas.[9] France had brought on the war, he wrote. Ever since its defeat in the Franco-Prussian War of 1871, France had been crying for revenge against Germany; and she would be no more successful now.[10] When the German armies advanced to within forty miles of Paris the Hillsboro editor welcomed the news, and then made excuses when the drive stalled.[11] Over and over, anti-German bias in the English-language press moved him to complain. And when a Russian Mennonite publication named *Friedenstimme* reported that Mennonites in the Ukraine were helping in Red Cross and sanitation services to assist their Russian fatherland in its anti-German struggle, he thought the message a "sad" one.[12] When Germans sank a British passenger liner, the *Lusitania*, the English-language press treated the action as barbaric. But Schellenberg blamed the Americans and British for loading munitions on a passenger ship. "He who sits on a powderkeg," *Vorwärts* declared, "is in danger of being blown into the air when he comes to a place where sparks are flying."[13]

Like other German-American newspapers, *Vorwärts* collected gifts for the German Red Cross and published the names of contributors. Many individuals contributed, but the largest gifts were usually from Mennonite church congregations.[14] After

America entered the war the collections for the German Red Cross ceased. Yet Schellenberg's pro-Germanism continued. To early news that some American soldiers had been captured he came back with a barb: "The American soldiers were sent over that they should go to Berlin, and they are already there sooner than they expected."[15] In Kansas City, Topeka, and even nearby Marion, his comment drew a storm of protest. "LET VORWÄRTS DECLARE ITSELF," demanded the *Marion Record*, condemning Schellenberg's "disloyal" words and calling on him to support campaigns for food conservation, American Red Cross, liberty bond drives, and the YMCA.[16] Schellenberg finally grew more discreet. But during the war the U.S. government launched an official investigation of his paper.

OFFICIAL DENOMINATIONAL RESPONSES

The war caught all Mennonite groups off guard. In early September of 1914, with fighting just begun in Europe, the General Conference Mennonite church met in Meno, Oklahoma, for its twentieth triennial conference. Delegates briefly considered and then tabled a resolution which might have taken a stand on military conscription. Three years later, meeting in Reedley, California, they were still "utterly unprepared for the war crisis." Although they responded to some initiatives of Western District leaders in Kansas who were cooperating with MBs and KMBs, they again left without making a clear and comprehensive statement on war and military conscription.[17] The church formed a "Committee of Seven," later known as the Exemption Committee. But it mostly left matters to district conferences, local congregations, and strong individuals. Emphasizing congregational autonomy and personal conscience, the GC church was reluctant to prescribe belief or behavior. In 1920 chairman S. K. Mosiman, president of Bluffton College, reported his committee's position—"that neither Committee nor Conference could speak for the individual conscience of the drafted men."[18]

As an organization the GC church was reluctant to decide. Some individuals were not. The strongest GC leaders in the war crisis were Henry P. Krehbiel, Peter H. Richert, John W. Kliewer, and Jacob G. Ewert, all of Kansas. The conference had three other important centers of denominational activity and organization: Bluffton College in Ohio; Berne, Indiana, the German-language publishing center where Carl H. A. van der Smissen edited the official conference periodical *Der Christliche Bundesbote*; and eastern Pennsylvania, where Nathaniel (N. B.) Grubb, pastor of the First Mennonite Church of Philadelphia, edited the English-language conference paper *The Mennonite*. The initiatives of Kansas leaders during the war helped speed up a process whereby Newton was becoming the geographical center of the GC denomination.

The "old" Mennonite church had organized under a central conference rather recently—in 1898—less than two decades before the war. Yet by 1914 it had more organizational solidarity and uniformity than the GC branch had. In the "old" body, effective authority rested with the bishops. Bishops ran the various (and much older) district conferences, and established and enforced rules for church procedures and personal styles of life. The world war would show how successfully the "old" Mennonites' general conference might set standards for bishops to enforce at the district and local levels. In 1915 at Archbold, Ohio, the conference adopted a strong statement against taking part in "carnal warfare." Clearly, members who bore arms were to be disowned from membership. Two years later, at the Yellow Creek church in northern Indiana, the conference adopted the most comprehensive statement on military service made by any Mennonite group during the war. To seal its action it affixed personal signatures of delegates or other representatives of sixteen district conferences. One hundred and eighty-one signed. The conference did not say explicitly that violators had to be excommunicated. But it did say it expected both members and congregations to show "an attitude of submission and loyalty."[19]

No doubt the Yellow Creek pronouncement bore the imprint of Daniel Kauffman, editor of the *Gospel Herald* and drafter of numerous conference statements. Aaron Loucks, general manager of the Mennonite Publishing House ("old" Mennonite official press at Scottdale, Pennsylvania), took major responsibility as chairman of the conference's Military Committee. Loucks organized wartime activities, communications with government, and visits to the military camps. But the "old" Mennonites' general conference was only an advisory body whose counsel the district conferences, some of whom were not even members, could choose to ignore. By getting personal signatures on the Yellow Creek statement, the general conference committed leaders and district conferences much more deeply than it could have done merely by declaring a conference position.

The "old" Mennonites' general conference was rigorous and clear about what it expected of its members. It was far less clear in its information about government policies. In 1917, shortly after Congress passed the Selective Service Act, the *Gospel Herald* made the mistake of saying that "after the registration the exempted classes will not be subject to the draft." Two weeks later, to correct its error, the paper cited a letter from a Mennonite woman in Montana who had her information from the government.[20] After a personal interview with Secretary of War Baker an "old" Mennonite delegation led by Aaron Loucks put out a statement saying, once again inaccurately, that the government had promised a form of service "not under the military arm of the government." This error was corrected after an audience of Quaker and Church of the Brethren representatives with Baker.[21] The "old" Mennonites, even their leaders, had little skill for political discourse and influence. So they depended on others.

The Mennonite Brethren church, made up almost exclusively of Dutch-background immigrants who had come from the Russian Empire in the 1870s, was smaller and more homogeneous.[22] Leading it was a group of educated and organizationally aggressive men such as Henry W. Lohrenz and Peter C. Hiebert of Tabor College and editor Abraham L. Schellenberg in Hillsboro. The war tended to strengthen their roles. Through institutional skills these first-generation professionals rapidly and paradoxically recentralized MB denominational power. That power found its center in the small town of Hillsboro, Kansas. In a statement of faith written before the war, the MBs had put one sentence against wielding the sword. Beyond that they had issued no official conference statement on militarism or conscription. After the war they formed an official committee for war and peace issues, but during the war they had none. In the vacuum H. W. Lohrenz did much to set guidelines for the MB response to the draft and other wartime matters.

As Lohrenz did so, he and other leaders faced a problem that especially troubled the Mennonite Brethren: many youths of draft age identified personally and culturally with the MB community but could not claim the conversion experience required for baptism and membership. The Selective Service law required that to qualify as conscientious objectors, pacifists had to be certified as members of a well-established pacifist church or sect. How could MB sons who were not yet church members be certified? The MB conference resolved the problem with a kind of halfway covenant. They arranged that a drafted youth might receive one of two official certificates. A bona fide member would receive a "Certificate of Church Membership." A nonmember might receive a "Certificate of Church Relationship"—if he had at least one parent who was a church member, was a regular attender at worship services, and was registered in the church book as a "child of our brothers and sisters" ("*Kind unser Geschwister*").[23] The arrangement satisfied draft authorities. Meanwhile, it underlined the paradox of being part of a religious community which was culturally based and loved all its children, yet extended membership only to those who claimed a definite conversion experience. Only about half of nearly two hundred MB youths who were drafted had been baptized and received into the church.[24]

Smaller Mennonite groups which lacked educated leadership and central denominational organization turned for guidance to the more progressive and developed conferences. To quite an extent, Old Order Mennonites and Old Order Amish looked to the "old" Mennonites. Occasionally different Mennonite groups in a given region gathered for common consultations. Thus they crossed the boundaries which in other situations they tried hard to keep firm.

THE DOCTRINE OF NONRESISTANCE

Mennonites were very aware that they were a people of peace. That awareness was more decisive for their wartime experience than were their differences of denominational development, cultural background, or relationship to American town life. In at least one respect the Yellow Creek statement of August 29, 1917, spoke the common mind of American Mennonites: "We hold that Christian people should have no part in carnal warfare of any kind or for any cause."[25] Whether or not an individual Mennonite could articulate the basis for this nonresistant faith, all Mennonites in America knew it was central to their identity. Many young men from Mennonite families did accept regular military service and join the war crusade. Yet almost all Mennonites and Amish agreed that in doing so they betrayed their heritage and were less than true Mennonites.

The nonresistant heritage cut across boundaries of Swiss-

south-German and Dutch-Russian origins and across lines between early and late arrivers. Conference statements of all
groups referred to the fourteenth article of the 1632 Confession
of Faith adopted at Dordrecht in Holland: "The Lord Jesus has
forbidden his disciples and followers all revenge and resistance,
and has thereby commanded them not to 'return evil for evil,
nor railing for railing.' " For all Mennonites this was a position
rooted not only in the Bible and historic doctrine but also in
their coming to America. In almost all their conference pronouncements, letters to government, and other public statements for defending pacifism, Mennonites mentioned that they
had originally come to America for a freedom of religion which
included military exemption. Swiss-American ones referred to
the favors of William Penn, Dutch-Russian ones to the promises
of President Ulysses S. Grant.[26] Under pressure of war all Mennonites tried to define and locate their right to be in America.
They too were Americans. They too were helping to develop the
distance that American liberties might extend.

Meanwhile, Mennonites turned to Bible passages which had
to do with warfare, violence, and taxation—and often disagreed.
Were liberty bonds included under the "things that are
Caesar's" (Matthew 22:21)? Was wearing a military uniform for
noncombatants a case of being "conformed to the world"
(Romans 12:2)? But behind the differences lay a fundamental
agreement about war and military service. In many ways Mennonites in the prewar decades had been influenced in doctrine
and practice by American Protestant models. Yet when
American Protestants marched off on a military crusade and explained their action in fervent rhetoric, the Mennonites did not
produce a single statement to justify the war on Christian or
biblical grounds.[27] Leaders who visited Mennonite conscripts in
military camps had only to read the relevant Bible passages
and admonish the boys to be faithful. The core teaching was
self-explanatory.

POLICY VAGUENESS AND THE PEOPLE'S CRUSADE

The America of World War I offered a new challenge for
Mennonites. Through the centuries Mennonites had sought out
tolerant princes or governments who would offer exemption or
satisfactory alternatives. Theirs was a history bespattered with
successes, failures, conflicts, and accommodations. One point
history had taught them was that their wartime fate often

rested on official arrangements with rulers or governments. America in 1917-1918 was different. The government refused to make clear and decisive national policies on the two issues which mattered most: conscription of men and conscription of money.

Instead, President Woodrow Wilson and his officials conducted the war as a popular democratic crusade—a new kind of people's war. To do so they stirred the entire nation into a patriotic frenzy. The fever took hold at the grass roots. Draft board officials, liberty bond collectors, military camp officers, and a host of vigilant volunteer citizens sallied forth to make the world safe for democracy. Against their onslaughts religious pacifists were vulnerable, and doubly so if their accents were German.

Meanwhile, distraught and confused Mennonites came to Washington, D.C., to petition for their rights and press for clarification of national policy. When they did, officials presented an enlightened face of benevolent and paternal concern. At first they told Mennonites to wait until policies could be worked out. Later they said the government was doing all for the pacifists that public opinion would allow. What Mennonites never quite realized was that Wilson and other high officials were the authors of the policy confusion, and that they were training public opinion to be intolerant.[28]

Key people in Wilson's government, full of faith in the goodness of the people, used idealism to mobilize popular energies. To raise some of the money the war devoured, Secretary of the Treasury William Gibbs McAdoo led a series of remarkably successful liberty loan drives. The drives, he said, "capitalized the profound impulse called patriotism" and were intended to build national coherence.[29] Propagandized by massive campaigns, including emotional local ones, Americans "voluntarily" gave money for the war. Meanwhile, Secretary of War Baker authorized local draft boards to administer military conscription. In a system quite unlike that of the Civil War, which had depended upon federal registrars, Baker's plan allowed local officials much freedom to interpret draft regulations.

In another quarter a progressive journalist named George Creel headed a national Committee on Public Information, actually a committee for public propaganda. The agency undertook a huge task: to persuade Americans that their cause was righteous, their enemy the incarnation of evil. Creel was at least as successful as McAdoo and Baker. He and his people mobilized patriotic artists, writers, historians, cartoonists, and others. Through their efforts Americans came to see the German enemy ever more as a spiked-helmeted beast and the Allies as noble champions of liberty. "Slackers"—anyone who shrank from the crusade—became the scum of the earth. Of course Mennonites were among the "slackers." Even worse, they were "slackers" in a popular crusade to secure the very quality of freedom which had brought the Mennonites themselves to America. As a nonresistant or "defenseless" people, Mennonites historically had chosen to be vulnerable to worldly powers. But to suffer in a democracy on crusade was something new.

MENNONITE COMMUNITIES DURING THE WAR

Frederick Luebke, historian of German America, has concluded that Mennonites in World War I became "the most grievously abused of any German culture group in the United States."[30] Community hostility against them increased during the war, reached a crescendo in the spring of 1918, receded a bit, and then, following the November armistice, burst forth once more. Governmental and private bodies such as the War Department's Military Intelligence Division, the American Protective League, and local Councils of Defense harassed Mennonites and extensively investigated them.[31] Had the war dragged on into 1919 or had the Allies not won, American hostility and violence against them might have grown far worse. As it was, the total cost in Mennonite property and lives was quite small. It was especially so if compared to the wartime suffering of Mennonites in the Ukraine and in Prussia, or to the burdens of many others from whom the war exacted treasure and loved ones.

During the war there were several dozen mob actions against Mennonites. Some almost became lynchings; yet no Mennonite was killed in his or her home community. At least two Mennonite church buildings were burned to the ground—one at Fairview, Michigan, and another at Inola, Oklahoma. On April 30, 1918, in a suspected but never-proven case of arson, the main building of Tabor College also went up in flames. However, most of the patriotic mobs stopped at smearing yellow paint, planting American flags, or leaving threatening notes.

(Center for Mennonite Brethren Studies, Hillsboro, Kansas)

The main building at Tabor College burning, presumably set by a pro-war arsonist.

The new classical-style Tabor College building, completed in 1920 by a Mennonite Brethren constituency unified through adversity.

(Center for Mennonite Brethren Studies, Hillsboro, Kansas)

Some Mennonite communities emerged relatively un-
scathed, especially in the East. Elsewhere, individuals were
frightened into purchase of war bonds or emigration to Canada.
In most cases the pressures were less direct: threats of social
ostracism; signs in towns demanding use of English; public
"slacker boards" listing persons who had not purchased their
assigned quotas of war bonds; and insistence that schools or
colleges stop teaching German. As wars go, World War I's toll on
American Mennonites was not great. Nonetheless, the pressures
delivered a major shock to Mennonite identity.

Mennonite sympathy for the cause of Germany, modified by
the doctrine of nonresistance and the practice of separation,
had not run deep even before America entered the war. After
April 6, 1917, the day the United States declared war, the feisty
editor Schellenberg in Hillsboro was the only public Mennonite
voice in favor of Germany. Yet some pro-German influence was
still quite noticeable, not only in Shellenberg's *Vorwärts* but
also in a German-language paper at Newton, *Der Herold*. A pro-
German agency provided some inexpensive copies in English of
a book, *Germany and the Next War*, by German General Friedrich von Bernhardi. In it Bernhardi glorified war as a political,
biological, and moral necessity. Yet *Der Herold* editor Christian
Krehbiel advertised the volume as available from the (Mennonite) Herald Book Store for thirty-five cents.[32] Krehbiel held
values so blatantly different that it is hard to believe he knew
what he was promoting. The tone of his paper was generally
cautious. Upon America's entry into the war he advised that "he
who knows nothing good to say about our country and government would do best now to keep quiet."[33]

Abraham Schellenberg's pro-Germanism in *Vorwärts* was
far less careful.[34] "We wish Germany victory," he wrote in March
of 1916, before America's entry, in an article which used racist
language to advise German-Americans not to let themselves be
assimilated. About the same time, Schellenberg reacted bitterly
against Wilsonian appeals for preparedness and disparagement
of "hyphenated Americans." Was not Wilson himself a hyphenated English-American? Was not Wilson "willing to betray our
country disgracefully and to attempt to defy the Congress
which is supposed to represent the people"? To support his
case for maintaining national identity, Schellenberg drew upon
the writings of French racist Arthur de Gobineau. Racial
mixing, ran Gobineau's argument, caused racial decay.[35]

Ever since 1907 Schellenberg had officially been editor of MB church publications. Yet it is doubtful that his shrill pro-Germanism had much influence even among MBs, much less among other Mennonites. During the war *Vorwärts* came under government scrutiny, but the Post Office inspector found no clear violation of the Espionage Act.[36] Schellenberg's political contentiousness, atypical among Mennonites, became even less typical in the postwar situation. Pressure mounted, and a year after the end of the war he resigned his official church post. Events of wartime had encouraged Mennonites to move further than ever from open political activity.

Mennonites might detach themselves from lingering pro-German sympathies, but they found it harder to give up the German language. After all, language was the carrier of culture in home, school, and church. On the whole the Mennonites were ready to go part way to meet patriotic American demands. Most who still used German gave it up for English in church and business. Thus the war greatly quickened the language shift. Still, the speed varied greatly from community to community. Having most to lose were those who used a group-specific dialect to mark their peoplehood's boundaries. Less affected were those who shared their dialects with local non-Mennonites or who were successful at maintaining boundaries by other means. Thus, for Dutch-Russian Mennonites to lose Low German was a greater blow than for Swiss and south-German ones to lose Pennsylvania Dutch. Yet the more conservative Amish and Old Order Mennonites held tightly to their Pennsylvania German. For them it was an essential mark of separation from the world.

War bonds brought a more specific and problematic test of patriotic duty. The government's drives were troublesome not only because they aroused people's hostility toward anyone who remained aloof but also because the legal meaning of bond purchases was not clear. For such drives the Mennonites had no obvious doctrinal guidelines. For Mennonites, an obligation to pay taxes was just as scriptural as the need to reject military service. But were war bonds a tax? Mennonite conferences, congregations, and individuals disagreed and sometimes changed positions during the war. The Church of God in Christ, Mennonite (Holdeman), decided that members should not buy. But after meeting the Kansas Loan Drive chairman they agreed to buy after all—then give the bonds for charity.[37] From quite a different perspective the GC pastor and editor Silas M. Grubb of Philadelphia counseled readers to buy bonds as a duty.[38] From yet another, Aaron Loucks advised "old" Mennonites to purchase Farm Loan Bonds as a substitute.[39] The major conferences (MC, GC, and MB) did not adopt official positions on bond purchases, although "old" Mennonite leaders quite consistently opposed them. In most rural communities Mennonites were most reluctant to buy, yet under pressure they often did so. When they did, they eagerly passed the bonds on to war-relief agencies or Mennonite institutions.[40]

In the bond drives, intimidation varied. In Fulton County, Ohio, an enthusiastic organizer entertained a cheering crowd with instructions on how to handle the objectors with "an axe, a shovel and a halter." The idea was to "use the axe to kill the man, and the shovel to bury him, and . . . the halter to lead one of his cows to market. Then you'll have money to buy bonds."[41] At Freeport, Illinois, a noncooperating Mennonite was buried in effigy on the courthouse lawn. His mock gravestone was inscribed: "Here Lies A. J. Meck, He was born before the war and died at the time of the War Chest Drive."[42] In Kansas the state's governor, Arthur Capper, added official weight to a zealous bond drive in Harvey County. Yet he did so more gently, writing to Joseph Schrag of Burrton "not in an official capacity, and with no intention of threatening or annoying you, but . . . as one friend writing to another."[43]

Some Mennonites changed their positions as the war went on. Tabor College president H. W. Lohrenz at first cooperated in civic war-related efforts and even accepted an appointment to the Marion County Council of Defense. But then he retreated. Buying war bonds was wrong, he wrote privately, because "it is just as much against New Testament teaching to use our money for . . . war as it is to engage in full military service." Yet he did not want his views publicized, nor did he try to translate them into official MB policy.[44] Apparently Lohrenz was influenced by "old" Mennonite leaders with whom he counseled at a January 1918 inter-Mennonite conference in Goshen, Indiana.

Other Mennonites at first refused to buy bonds but later capitulated. Bishop Simon Gingerich of the Sugar Creek Amish Mennonite church near Wayland, Iowa, was the target of zealous patriotic citizens in southeastern Iowa. Brought to the office of U.S. Marshal N. F. Reed in Ottumwa, forty miles west of Wayland, Gingerich signed a statement of public apology for his intransigence. On behalf of his congregation he agreed to buy $200 of War Savings Stamps, pledge $5,000 for the Third Liberty Loan Drive, and display American flags on the church meetinghouse and on homes. Gingerich's concessions were embarrassing. They violated no official or written church policy, but of course many Amish Mennonite decisions still rested on unwritten group consensus. In the postwar years some young people who resisted codes of dress recalled Gingerich's actions and used them against conservatives.[45]

In McPherson County, Kansas, zealous citizens organized a series of mob raids to terrorize selected bond resisters in their homes.[46] One home was that of Walter Cooprider, a member of the "old" Mennonite Spring Valley congregation and a son of a United Brethren Civil War veteran turned Mennonite preacher. Since Cooprider was in poor health, the mob settled for a Cooprider son, George, and tarred and feathered him. Several days later the family went to McPherson and bought bonds. At the homes of Daniel and Charles Diener, a father and son who were ministers in the Spring Valley congregation, the mob visited on three different nights. Each time it escalated its violence. On the second visit Daniel Diener wrote a $50 check for the Red Cross; but the next morning he went to the bank and stopped payment, substituting a $75 gift to Friends Reconstruction Service. Finally on June 10, 1918, members of the mob ransacked and smeared yellow paint on both Diener houses, stripped and whipped the men with a large strap, applied carboline roofing paint and feathers, and said that if the Dieners still refused they would come back and kill them. Humiliated and afraid, the Dieners went to nearby Canton and made a token purchase of "Liberty" Bonds. Thus they helped make the world safe for democracy.[47]

Two more Mennonites nearly lynched by mobs were John M. Franz of Bloomfield, Montana, and John Schrag of rural Harvey County, Kansas. Unlike the Coopriders and Dieners, who spoke English in both home and church, Franz and Schrag were harassed at least partly because they spoke German. Franz had conducted home Bible classes in German, then quit in the face of pressure. Nevertheless, in April of 1918 a crowd of patriots abducted him, took him to a canyon in the Montana badlands, and conversed with him beside a large poplar tree with a noose dangling from a limb. At the last minute the local sheriff, named Twible, decided he did not want lynch-mob blood on his

(Mennonite Library and Archives)

John and Elizabeth Stucky Schrag and family. Front row: Daniel, Marie, Jacob, Herman. Back row: Peter, Andrew, Joseph, John, Adam, Reinhold. John Schrag was a victim of mob violence in 1918.

hands. The mob took Franz to the county jail at Glendive and subjected him to a kangaroo court trial whose judges made the extraordinary decision to release him conditionally on a $750 bond (or a $3,000 bond—the accounts differ) and good behavior but to confiscate the German Bibles and other German books from the Bethlehem Mennonite (GC) church.[48]

In addition to delivering the German books to Twible, Franz was to hold all church services in English and appear quarterly at the court. And he was to encourage church members to help with war-supporting activities such as Red Cross sewing projects for the women and bond drives for the men. After that, according to one account, Franz sold Liberty Bonds so well that a Montana state senator named McCone noticed him and intervened to get his kangaroo-court bond lifted.[49]

John Schrag, a member of the Hoffnungsfeld GC congregation and a wealthy farmer in Harvey County, Kansas, was nearly lynched on Armistice Day, November 11, 1918. A mob from the town of Burrton abducted him but could not force him to buy war bonds. Neither would he carry a flag and lead a victory parade. When the flag fell to the ground the enraged mob smeared the Mennonite with yellow paint and prepared to hang him. However, Tom Roberts, head of the local anti-horse-thief association, intervened. Brandishing a gun, Roberts got the victim into the town jail, where he would be safe. Later Schrag was taken to the county jail, cleaned up, and released.

Then the Burrton patriots, charging that he had cursed the American flag, put him on trial in a Wichita district court. The judge dismissed the case, partly because the monolingual plaintiffs could not prove that Schrag's words, spoken in German, were actually slander. In turn, the Newton *Evening Kansan-Republican* deplored "the viciousness that exists in the encouragement of the German language as a means of communication in America."[50] Schrag, like Franz earlier in Montana, declined suggestions that he take his persecutors to court. Nevertheless, area Mennonites responded. They took their business out of Burrton; and the town fell into a postwar economic depression.[51]

In general, state and national officials were failing to condemn perpetrators forthrightly and bring them to justice. So there was a climate of domestic hostility and violence against nonconformists. The climate also arose from national legislation. A Sedition Act passed on May 16, 1918, included the most severe restrictions on freedom of speech and press in American history.[52] The Act was an amendment to a 1917 Espionage Act which already forbade interference with military conscription. Now, among other provisions, it outlawed any attempt to interfere with the sale of war bonds. In Ohio and West Virginia, Mennonite leaders were tried and found guilty under the Espionage and Sedition Acts.

District Attorney Edwin S. Wertz of Cleveland, who had earlier been the prosecuting attorney in the government's historic case against socialist Eugene Debs, handled the prosecution of a Mennonite minister named Samuel H. Miller. Miller, father of George S. Miller, was editor of the unofficial Amish newspaper in Sugarcreek, Ohio, *The Weekly Budget*. He had also signed the Yellow Creek statement. On May 15, 1918, *The Budget* included a letter from an Old Order Amish bishop of near Dodge City, Kansas, Mannasses E. Bontrager, who offered some views typical of conservative Amish and Mennonites toward military service and war bonds. "Sorry to learn that some of the Mennonites have yielded and bought bonds," Bontrager wrote. "What would become of our nonresistant faith if our young brethren in camp would yield?"[53]

A grand jury indicted Miller on five counts, beginning with the false charge that he "published the letter to promote the success of the Imperial German Government." In fact Miller had been out of town; his printer had put the letter into the paper. Surely he was innocent of the charges. Yet he negotiated a plea bargain under which he and Bontrager confessed that they had attempted to cause "refusal of duty in the military and naval forces of the United States." Each accepted a fine of five hundred dollars plus costs. Miller spent several days in prison before a cousin arrived with money to secure his release. In his newspaper he reported not a word of his humiliating trial.[54]

A second espionage-sedition trial involved Lewis J. Heatwole, bishop in the Middle District of the "old" Mennonites' Virginia conference, and Rhine Benner, a home missionary of the same conference who worked in West Virginia's mountainous Randolph County. Heatwole was one of the most progressive Mennonite leaders of the East. For years he had voluntarily supplied information to the U.S. Weather Bureau. He was a schoolteacher, an accomplished although amateur journalist and historian, and author of a 1908 book entitled *Moral Training in the Public Schools*. One section of the book was "The Church and the Nation's Destiny."[55]

In mid-July 1918, as patriots were getting war bond and savings stamp drives under way in Randolph County, missionary Benner asked for advice. The public-spirited Heatwole responded. As had bishop Bontrager of Dodge City, Heatwole wrote that although some Mennonites had "yielded under pressure" it was important for people at home to be as faithful as the men in the military camps. The church's position, he said, was to "contribute nothing to a fund that is used to run the war machine." Benner and Jasper Smith, a nonethnic Mennonite minister in Randolph County, shared this information orally with as many of their scattered people as possible. Others they advised by letter. Benner's letter, and eventually Heatwole's also, came to the attention of District Attorney Stuart W. Walker of Martinsburg, West Virginia. Walker prosecuted. This time the charges were drawn up more carefully than in the Ohio case, and the Mennonites retained the able counsel of a state senator named George N. Conrad. But whatever their differences, the two cases ended much the same. Reluctantly,

Heatwole and Benner pleaded guilty and were fined a thousand dollars each. The Virginia conference paid the fines. Heartbroken and in poor health, Heatwole made two unsuccessful attempts to have his conviction reversed. Benner left West Virginia and took his family to Montana, where he became pastor for a recently formed "old" Mennonite congregation near Glendive—the community which had had its way with John Franz.[56]

One scheme to resolve the Mennonite dilemma over war bonds had some success. In the spring of 1918, during the Third Liberty Loan Drive, a representative for the Federal Reserve Bank in Cleveland, W. L. Crooks, brought an unusually pragmatic spirit to a troubled area in and around Ohio's Fulton County. Mediating between zealous bond committees and intimidated nonresistants, Crooks got both sides to agree to a plan. Mennonites as a group would be assigned a quota and would put that entire amount in local banks. In turn they would receive certificates of deposit yielding 4 percent interest, a rate slightly lower than war bonds offered. Individual Mennonites would not be solicited. The money was to be used for local purposes, but there was an implied agreement that other funds from the banks would be diverted to the national Liberty Bond campaign. The campaign would get its money while the Mennonites would avoid direct contributions to war. "It places their dollars on the same basis as their grain," explained Crooks. "Of their grain they say that their responsibility ends when they sell it to the local elevator, and their conscience is free. Therefore, their conscience is equally free when they place their dollars on deposit with the local banker for local purposes." Such was one scheme for resolving the conflict between Mennonites and Americans. Wiser than most public officials, Crooks found Mennonites to be "absolutely sincere, patriotic, and thoroughly American."[57]

Aaron Loucks became an enthusiastic advocate of the Crooks plan and proposed it for other communities. But the plan was not widely accepted. Neither the national war bond campaigns nor the Mennonite conferences had enough centralized authority to establish a coherent general policy. Local bond committees had little incentive to adopt the plan. Moreover, the plan came relatively late, in mid-1918. By then many Mennonites had already bought bonds and the government knew that its campaigns had succeeded—in Mennonite communities as well as nationally. News of mounting casualties was coming from Europe, and the nation's mood was not to increase toleration and accommodation with "slackers."

If the war had continued into 1919, no doubt the U.S. Department of Justice would have proceeded with its most spectacular antipacifist case of all: a mass trial of the 181 bishops, ministers, and deacons who had signed the Yellow Creek statement in 1917. In the superheated climate of late 1918 the amended Espionage Act cast a net so broad and the record of convictions under it was so impressive that a prosecution might well have succeeded. In August District Attorney Wertz, eager for another sensation to match his success against Eugene Debs, pressed the Justice Department for permission to proceed. He thought he might get the Mennonites to plead guilty. The department had a general policy of allowing wide discretion to its attorneys. Nevertheless, it instructed Wertz to keep on gathering evidence but delay prosecution—with the understanding that "at any time in the future" he might receive advice to go ahead.[58] Late in 1918, seeking data, federal investigators called on Mennonite leaders in Pennsylvania, Ohio, Indiana, and Iowa. Then, as the war ended, the legal threat diminished. Yet half a year later, in May 1919, Jonas (J. S.) Hartzler of the "old" Mennonite church's Military Committee wrote that he still feared there might be a mass trial of Mennonite leaders.[59]

Faced with violence, bond drives, court trials and threatened trials, ostracism, and alienation, Mennonites felt tremendous pressure to make some positive contribution. As the nation sacrificed lives and treasure and sang its armies forward for human liberty, the Mennonites heard their claims for exemption and toleration ringing hollow. To salvage self-respect and public esteem they made a number of proposals, but always fell short.[60] In November 1917, working through their patron-congressman Griest, bishops of the Lancaster conference offered to buy or lease large tracts of land for the government. On it they would employ draft-age Mennonites to raise crops and produce foodstuffs "such as the Government may deem necessary for the maintenance of the National interests." Griest noted that the Mennonites were ready to accept government regulation and management of the project, and touted it as a great "patriotic offer." He said it might be "an excellent illustration of agricultural efficiency for farmers throughout the country."[61] The government, however, did not accept.

Farther west, in the spring of 1918, Mennonites offered medical facilities to treat wounded soldiers. Henry P. Krehbiel tried to raise funds to create a Mennonite veterans' hospital in Newton. Leaders of the "old" Mennonite church proposed to rehabilitate veterans at their sanitarium at La Junta, Colorado. In Hillsboro, Kansas, the Salem Hospital offered similar services. But the government was not interested. In the opinion of La Junta administrator Allen Erb, the Mennonites were denied "an excellent chance to do something for our government that would in no sense violate our principle of nonresistance."[62] Late in the conflict the Military Committee of the "old" Mennonite church made a further proposal for alternative service. Draftees, the committee proposed, might work as teachers or agriculturists among Indians in Arizona.[63]

CONSCRIPTION AND THE ARMY CAMPS

In the spring of 1917 as America was entering the war, a number of Mennonite congregations, conferences, and institutions addressed government officials with belated resolutions and petitions against war and military conscription. The witness was not well coordinated. In 1916 an "All Mennonite Convention" at Carlock, Illinois, had appointed a committee to speak for Mennonites collectively. But this was an ad hoc voice. It did not speak for the Old Order Amish and Old Order Mennonites, who had ignored the misnamed "All Mennonite" movement. It did not even speak for the much larger Amish Mennonite and "old" Mennonite bodies, for they had specifically opposed the convention.[64]

Nevertheless, the "All Mennonite" committee made a try, "prompted," it said, by both "religious conviction and true patriotism."[65] At the end of March 1917, led by J. A. Huffman of the Mennonite Brethren in Christ, it presented its petitions in Washington, D.C. Committee members reported finding "special friends for our cause in the persons of Congressman B. F. Welty, a former Bluffton boy, and once a member of the Mennonite Church; and [in] C. W. Ramseyer, Congressman from the Sixth Iowa District, a member of the Mennonite Church from Pulaski, Iowa."[66] But in fact, Welty and Ramseyer were dubious as friends, whatever their vestiges of Mennonitism. Both voted for declaring war and later for the 1918 Sedition Act.[67] Like others in Washington they must have been quite bewildered by the multiplicity of Mennonite, Amish, Hutterite, and other groups which arrived to speak against the war, against the draft, and for their own exemption.

The fragmented Mennonites were hardly in a position even to respond to overtures from other peace churches—the Quakers and the Church of the Brethren. On May 23, 1917, an unofficial meeting of people from the three faiths met in Washington. Out of the meeting came an appeal that the various groups appoint delegates for a central committee to work with various government departments on issues of war and peace. The appeal bore the signature of Silas Grubb, pastor of the Second Mennonite Church of Philadelphia and editor of *The Mennonite.* But it failed. Grubb could speak only for a narrow constituency—English-speaking Mennonites in the East who had separated from the larger conservative groups. Not until after World War I did the peace churches coordinate their efforts regarding militarism and the draft.

The war intensified Mennonite contacts with Americans at three levels: civilian public officials responsible for drafting and administering government policies; military officials in the War Department and in the training camps; and local leaders who led war bond drives, Red Cross work, draft boards, Councils of Defense, and other instruments to mobilize communities for war. At every level it became more clear that pacifist Mennonites, especially those who spoke German, were out of step with America at large. Sometimes Mennonites were tolerated and indulged, and sometimes scorned and attacked. Seldom were they appreciated.

Secretary of War Baker, the key government official for devising and administering military conscription policies, tolerated conscientious objectors. But he did so with a mixture of condescension and duplicity.[68] He and his aide in charge of conscientious-objector affairs, Frederick P. Keppel, were true progressives. To them the war was fully consistent with the platform which Woodrow Wilson called the "New Freedom"—an altruistic extension of enlightened, humanitarian democracy. The war, said Baker, was "the purest mission that a nation ever espoused." Its idealistic goals more than offset its unfortunate need to use military conscription and violence. The secretary even implied that those who failed to appreciate this upward pattern of democratic civilization must be mentally defective, victims of cultural lag, or downright perverse.[69]

Mennonite draftees at Detention Camp #1, Camp Funston, Kansas, in 1918. Carl Schmidt,—Williams, Peter Neufeld, Albert Unruh, John Andreas, Paul Bartsch.

Conscientious objectors at Camp Funston, Kansas, May 1918.

(Mennonite Library and Archives)

In the fall of 1917 Baker held a critical meeting with twenty-six conscientious objectors at Camp Meade in nearby Maryland. He left saying that the young men were "well-disposed," but "simple-minded" and "imprisoned in a narrow environment." His judgment was that they "really have no comprehension of the world outside of their own rural and peculiar community." Of those who spoke, "only two . . . seemed quite normal mentally."[70] It probably did not help that one Mennonite, uncomfortable with English, had quoted Jesus as saying, "Give to the Kaiser what the Kaiser's is."[71] Yet Mennonites always found Baker friendly—unlike the career military man who headed Selective Service, General Enoch Crowder.

Baker's strategy was to get the young conscientious objectors out of their narrow sectarian communities and into the military cantonments. There the expansive and enthusiastic spirit might catch them up. Gradually they might catch the great war vision and agree to carry weapons. The Selective Service law of May 18, 1917, provided that members of a "well recognized religious sect or organization" could be exempt from combatant service. It did not exempt them from noncombatant service, which at first remained undefined. Early on, Baker assured concerned Mennonite delegations that their drafted young men would not be required to do anything in violation of their conscience. At the same time he issued confidential orders to camp commanders to segregate the conscientious objectors and treat them kindly—in the hope that they would volunteer to be soldiers. Soon the Mennonite draftees were on their way to camp where he wanted them. As they went, Baker received a telegram from the Central Conference of Mennonites in Illinois thanking him for his "kind recognition of non-resistant principles." In private he remarked that "I have, of course, done nothing to deserve this."[72]

Whether Baker deserved praise or blame, he had succeeded in getting most Mennonites to go along with military conscription. A few, however, did not. One conservative Dutch-Russian group, the KMBs, decided to resist. In a handwritten petition to Baker, KMB elders from Nebraska, Kansas, and Oklahoma said they could not "according to the dictates of our conscience permit our members to go to the training camps." They asked for the same privilege to emigrate which the Russian government had granted in the 1870s.[73] In September of 1917 Baker sent his reply: no exemption. By that time the first two

KMB conscripts were due to report and be sent to Camp Funston in Kansas on the fifteenth. At McPherson, Kansas, KMB leaders met with the two men and with KMB Professor D. E. Harder of Tabor College. From the meeting came a decision to resist, and church leaders informed the local draft board to that effect. On induction day the county sheriff arrested the two men at their homes and jailed them for the night. But instead of pressing charges and bringing the men to trial, local authorities delivered them over to military justice at Camp Funston. Authorities there placed them first in a guardhouse and then in a detention camp with other conscientious objectors. One of the men, Jacob N. Wiens, reported being threatened with death "before sunup."[74]

After their brave start, however, the KMBs began taking cues from larger Mennonite groups and soon abandoned their formal resistance. On October 3, 1917, *Der Wahrheitsfreund*, the KMB church paper edited by M. B. Fast, published a German translation of information and instructions put out by the "old" Mennonites' Military Committee. Dated September 1, the instructions told draftees to report to the camps and make their claims for exemption there.[75]

Another option was emigration. In 1917 and 1918 some six to eight hundred Mennonites and a thousand Hutterites moved from the United States to Canada, mostly to the prairie provinces.[76] Many Hutterites moved as groups; Mennonites went more individually, without their denominations' official approval, although Canadian friends and relatives often gave help. The migration continued into late 1918. Motives were mixed. Some persons went to avoid conscription, some fled pressures from local patriots, some pursued economics or youthful adventure. Virtually all who went were Westerners from groups which had immigrated quite late: KMBs, MBs, GC Mennonites of Dutch-Russian background, *Kleine Gemeinde*, and Church of God in Christ, Mennonite (Holdeman). Scarcely anyone went from the earlier-arrived "American Mennonites" in the East and Midwest. "American Mennonites" were more confident of making arrangements with national, state, and local officials. Also, in granting military exemption, Canadian policy favored the groups which had arrived from the Russian Empire in the 1870s and '80s.[77]

In September 1917 the first drafted conscientious objectors went to the military camps—frightened and unprepared.[78]

Signals from the government were mixed. Some members of Congress still held out hope of exemption for farm work. But General Crowder of Selective Service said the law did not allow even the president to assign draftees to civilian service. Meanwhile, Secretary Baker promised congenially that Mennonite consciences would be respected. In early July the War Department had said that noncombatant service, the only kind the law offered to conscientious objectors, would be under the military in the Medical Corps, the Quartermaster Corps, and the Corps of Engineers. Still, policy was confused, and official clarification did not come until March 1918. The frustrating nine-month delay served several purposes. First, it showed the War Department that the numbers of conscientious objectors was manageable. Also, it held the men in camps where they might easily cross over into military service. Finally, it allowed the government to devise new options, including a Farm Furlough Law by which men could be put at agricultural work.

In the camps neither officers nor Mennonite draftees were prepared for their mutual confrontation. The officers' task was to work quickly to shape raw recruits into a tough, disciplined army. Any sign of noncooperation or insubordination brought swift punishment. Secretly, Secretary Baker ordered officers to use "tact and consideration" and to let church leaders into the camps to see their members.[79] Of course his instructions ran counter to the most elementary principles and habits of military training. So officers used intimidation, ridicule, and violence. Or they looked aside while regular soldiers delivered "hazings." At Camp Funston in Kansas, General Leonard Wood wrote that the War Department's policy was "not only a menace to good order and discipline but it is putting a premium on disloyalty."[80]

Overwhelmingly, the Mennonite conscripts arrived from rural backgrounds. One survey found that at the time of being drafted, 68 percent were either farmers or farmhands.[81] The draftees were in culture shock—bewildered by the varieties of religious and secular pacifists in the detention camps, fearful of humiliation and persecution, and appalled at the excessive profanity of the soldiers. Furthermore, they were counseled by church leaders who were themselves confused. Military officers routinely assumed that they were, as one general said, "of such a low grade mentality, they are actually too stupid to form any argument against military service except ready-made biblical phrases supplied them by their preachers, lawyers, and brighter associates." To be sure, the Mennonite draftees were not all literate or articulate in English. Yet intelligence tests demonstrated that conscientious objectors scored "slightly higher as a group" than drafted men generally.[82]

One point the general implied was true: Mennonite draftees found their greatest resource in their sense of Christian, nonresistant peoplehood, rooted in biblical self-understandings. David Koehn and William Frantz wrote from Camp Greenleaf in Georgia, "you cant emagen how it is to be hated. if it wasent fore Christ it would be impossible."[83] Facing officers or chaplains brought in to refute them, a few Mennonites who had been to college sometimes attempted pragmatic arguments. When told that German victory would be tragic, Cornelius Voth of Alexanderwohl argued that there would be no victors: "The way it looks to me, we'll all lose. The winner will lose too."[84] Time would vindicate such practical indictments of World War I. But in 1917 and 1918, when American military officers were eagerly making the world safe for democracy, the arguments fell on deaf ears.

The military camps varied widely in how far they violated War Department directives and mistreated conscientious objectors. The most dramatic persecutions were in camps in the South, Midwest, and West, and in the federal prisons at Alcatraz, California, and Leavenworth, Kansas.[85] Mennonites who followed their consciences against military orders were beaten with hoses and fists, scrubbed down with stiff brushes in cold showers, forced to stand at attention for hours in the hot sun, reduced to bread-and-water diets in guardhouses, threatened with various forms of execution, and mistreated in other ways. In some cases this was normal military discipline—although Mennonites interpreted it as religious persecution. Occasionally, abused COs were able to get word of their problems to church leaders who protested to camp officials or to the War Department.

The draftees' responses varied widely. Willis Shumacher, whose grandfather had paid three hundred dollars to avoid the Civil War draft, took up regular military service at Camp Sherman, Ohio. By chance he landed in the Medical Corps. After the war he returned to his home congregation, Grace Mennonite (GC) of Pandora, Ohio, yet joined the American Legion.[86] Jonas Dietz of Hubbard, Oregon, joined the army and was excommunicated from his "old" Mennonite congregation. But his parents remained members, and when he died of battle wounds in France the funeral was held in his home church.[87]

David A. Janzen, MB draftee from California and Oklahoma, at first took part in military drill with gusto and came "to like the shine of the new stock, the smell of the leather strap and the feel of exercise with the gun in arms." But later he made his nonresistant convictions known and was assigned to the Medical Corps.[88] Enos Stutzman, Old Order Amish member from western Kansas, escaped military drill by enrolling in the bugle school and memorizing fifty-five regimental calls in twelve days. Coming from a congregation where musical instruments were forbidden, Stutzman considered this a miraculous "direct deliverance."[89]

Ura V. Aschliman, of the Amish Mennonites of Stryker, Ohio, refused military service. One night at Camp Sheridan, Alabama, a group of soldiers tied a rope around his neck and threw it over a tent rafter as if to hang him. Later, with the scars still on his neck, he was court-martialed, found guilty, and sentenced to five years in military prison. At his trial a major point was that he was twenty-four, yet had not joined the church until shortly before his induction.[90] Government officials knew little of Mennonite theology.

The conscientious objectors who had the least trouble were: those who arrived in camp after procedures had been regularized, so that they were quickly put into the conscientious-objector detention camps; those whose detention camp groups included educated and effective CO leaders; and those who were able to stay in touch with the leaders of their congregations and denominations on the outside. But neither leadership nor solidarity were guarantees. At Camp Travis in Texas in June 1918, camp authorities, having failed repeatedly to break down the men's resistance, brought forty-five men to trial in a collective court-martial. The men were mostly from Oklahoma, with one Albert Voth from Goltry as their chief spokesman. The trial violated War Department directives, yet all forty-five were found guilty and sentenced to twenty-five years of hard labor at Fort Leavenworth.[91]

Mennonite leaders protested, but Secretary Baker was trapped in an administrative mess partly of his own making. He could hardly pardon the conscientious objectors. If he did, he would alienate camp commanders who chafed under his restrictions. He would risk vigorous criticism from Congress and the public. And to acknowledge his secret orders calling for tact would be to expose his indecision and duplicity. The court-martial trials brought the War Department some success with its main objective—to convince as many men as possible to take up military service. One who did was Warren Gish, a Mennonite draftee at Columbus Barracks in Ohio. Gish took out War Risk Insurance, wore the uniform, and accepted noncombatant service. "If I am in prison 25 years I will be an old man nearly 49 years old when I come out . . .," he reasoned. "He [God] knows that I have not denied the faith and that I was really forced into it."[92]

By June 1919, the army had court-martialed 504 conscientious objectors and sentenced two-thirds of them to ten, twenty, or twenty-five years in prison. Only one such trial ended in acquittal.[93] A list of religious objectors imprisoned at Fort Leavenworth as of March 10, 1919, had 135 names. The total number of court-martialed Mennonites was probably somewhat greater, but it was a minority of the total of court-martialed conscientious objectors.[94]

Across the United States each Mennonite congregation had its own experience with conscription. In general, the Mennonites and Amish in eastern Pennsylvania were more conservative and separatist than those farther west, yet they suffered little violence or confrontation. In the Lancaster and Franconia conference areas, draft boards were remarkably generous with agricultural exemptions and put few men into camps. Congressman Griest claimed that in the first draft call, draft boards discharged 90 to 95 percent of the men on vocational grounds.[95] All through the war the Weaverland congregation east of Lancaster did not have a single young man drafted, although it was a large congregation of 640 members.

Meanwhile, the Alexanderwohl congregation in Kansas had thirty-three members drafted from a membership of 743. The entire Franconia conference (twenty-one congregations with 3,726 members) provided only twenty draftees, while the GC Western District conference in Kansas, only about 50 percent larger, provided ten times as many.[96]

Franconia and Lancaster Mennonites had reached an exceptionally satisfactory and functional accommodation with their sociopolitical environment. Of course congressman Griest had political reasons to defend the interests of his Lancaster

Mennonite constituents. In contrast, Kansas Mennonites of Dutch-Russian background were less successful at finding an accommodation with American citizenship—even though, compared to Mennonites in eastern Pennsylvania, more of them were willing to accept war-bond drives and noncombatant military service.

By early 1918 Secretary Baker was aware that the conscientious-objector problem was not so great that it would interfere with overall military recruitment. Thereupon he deceived and manipulated the U.S. Congress as surely as he had the Mennonites. To House and Senate leaders he submitted a bill to let the War Department furlough enlisted men to agricultural work without pay. In early January, discreetly and somewhat obliquely, his department informed peace-church leaders that the bill "may affect this question" of alternative service for conscientious objectors. Congress passed the Farm Furlough Bill without being aware that its intent was to provide alternative service.[97] Meanwhile, with the public in a fervor for the war, peace-church leaders kept their political profiles low. Had its members known the measure's intent, Congress probably would have defeated the Farm Furlough Bill.

On March 16, 1918, having delayed until the Farm Furlough Bill was law, President Wilson defined noncombatant service. His pronouncement reestablished the three noncombatant categories the draft might allow—work in the Medical Corps, the Quartermaster Corps, or the Engineer Corps. All involved work in military camps under military direction with military payment. Some additional conscientious objectors now capitulated and took up noncombatant service as the War Department hoped, but many still refused. The refusers had to wait. Ten weeks later, the War Department created a civilian Board of Inquiry to interview them, hoping to determine who was sincere. Men who passed this reverse muster might be granted the farm furloughs. However, the Board of Inquiry had no authority to review the court-martial cases. The board was quite generous in judging CO sincerity, although the outspoken board chairman, Major Walter Guest Kellogg, later revealed some contempt for Mennonites, saying they were ignorant and lethargic. "Civilization, apparently, has passed them by," he wrote publicly. "They remain a curious and an alien survival of an old-world people, an anachronism amid the life of today."[98]

In late 1918 events in Iowa revealed that the Board of Inquiry and the farm-furlough system had not resolved the problems. Officials at Camp Dodge worked together with a Justice Department agent at Des Moines and with local Councils of Defense in Washington and Henry counties to find ways of clamping down. They were frustrated. If they had some success at convincing Mennonite draftees to accept camp work, pastoral visits from church leaders such as the "old" Mennonites' Aaron Loucks and Sanford C. Yoder seemed to cancel that success. Against Loucks, the Justice Department prepared and documented twenty-five charges. Included was the text of a speech he gave to Mennonite draftees at Camp Dodge on March 5, 1918. After the speech some of the men had decided to stop noncombatant work they had already begun.[99]

Apparently Loucks did indeed nearly violate the Espionage Act of 1917. That law said that anyone guilty of causing refusal of duty in the armed services could be punished with a fine as high as ten thousand dollars and imprisonment for up to twenty years. According to testimony, Loucks told the men of his personal meeting with Secretary Baker and Baker's assurance that they would not be forced to engage in military activity against their will. He said they would have to make their own personal decisions, but he made it obvious that his church opposed both combatant and noncombatant work. "You still have an opportunity," he said, "of going to the other side, and obeying the commands of your officers, or you can stand by your faith, and do what your mind thinks is right, and trust in God to see you through safely."[100] Although the Justice Department and camp authorities wanted to prosecute Loucks, the War Department let him off with a stern warning. In Frederick Keppel's ironic words, the warning "put the fear of God into him."[101]

Mennonites imprisoned at Fort Leavenworth obeyed orders including work detail, even though this was technically work under military direction and within the military establishment. The Mennonite cases were not as widely known or publicized as those of other absolute objectors. Often those others were socialists or nonreligious objectors who totally refused cooperation, went on hunger strikes, and complained of prison brutality. Among religious objectors, four Hutterite draftees from South Dakota—David Hofer, Joseph Wipf, and a pair of Hofer brothers named Joseph and Michael—were the most severely treated. Court-martialed at Camp Lewis, Washington, they were imprisoned at Alcatraz. There they refused the military uniform and persisted even when placed in a dungeon on a bread and water diet and with no clothing except the uniforms. After being weakened by the ordeal they were transferred to Leavenworth. There the Hofer brothers died. In a final insult prison officials sent the bodies home dressed in uniforms.[102]

J. G. Ewert of Hillsboro, a member of the national Civil Liberties Bureau, protested this flagrant disregard for human dignity. But Jonas (J. D.) Mininger, director of the "old" Mennonite Kansas City Mission who acted as pastor to imprisoned Mennonites, maintained a low profile and was submissive and grateful for privileges which prison officials granted.[103] The contrast in approach between Mininger (a Swiss-American of the humility, separation tradition) and Ewert (a Dutch background immigrant of congregation Christendom background) illustrated differences between the groups from which they came.

Even before all regular soldiers were back from France and released from service, the War Department began to extend clemency to imprisoned conscientious objectors. A storm of public protest followed. State legislatures in both Kansas and Oklahoma condemned the action. The Kansas resolution called it "an insult to the United States Army . . . a premium upon slackerism, cowardice and mawkish sentimentality."[104] The editor of the *Newton Kansan* blasted Baker for releasing these "avaricious cowardly whelps."[105] What the outraged critics did not know was that according to War Department policy the men should never have been brought to trial in the first place. Secretary Baker contradicted his liberal amnesty policy. To officials of the Fort Leavenworth prison he said reassuringly that "the conscientious objectors, like all the other inmates of the institution, have broken laws and been adjudged by properly constituted courts to suffer certain penalties of imprisonment."[106] Baker held enlightened and progressive views of punishment and rehabilitation. But the climate of war clouded his liberality.

Conscientious objectors fortunate enough to be assigned to farms were happy to get away from the uncertainty, idleness, and pressures of the military camps. But even the vastly superior furlough system was not a total success. It began late, only about four months before the war's end. Camp officials were not consistent as they drew up work agreements with farm operators who applied. In Iowa and Ohio, local patriotic groups protested the furlough system. Some in Iowa's Madison and

Dallas counties threatened the state's governor with "breaches of the peace" if the conscientious objectors were allowed to stay. Between the towns of Wellman and Kalona a mob of about forty persons had to be restrained by a county sheriff. One group of furloughed men was sent back to Camp Dodge to calm a negative "wave of feeling" stimulated by their presence in the community.[107] In Ohio, officials at Camp Sherman reported popular outrage in Champaign, Logan, and Fulton counties.[108]

Yet other conscripts found their situations to be quite satisfactory. D. Ralph Hostetter of Pennsylvania, working for a Methodist farmer in a Catholic area, wrote: "I am on a farm of 175 acres. There is plenty to do. I feel like a new person since I am out of camp and working."[109] None of the Mennonite conscripts rejected furlough work on grounds that it contributed to the nation's military effort. Some, however, refused payment for their labor.

MENNONITES AND TOTAL DEMOCRATIC WARFARE

World War I set a pattern for twentieth-century militarism and caught the Mennonites in a permanent crisis of identity. They could not get a secure hold on their American citizenship without loosening their grip on that other citizenship which mattered even more—their place in the kingdom of Christ. A Justice Department investigator, intending to make a positive report on Peter H. Richert, elder of the Tabor congregation in Kansas, wrote that Richert would "not place his religion ahead of his government."[110] Had Richert read the confidential report he would have been heartbroken. Even though he had bought war bonds, he knew that in a conflict of loyalties he must obey God rather than man.[111]

The totality of modern democratic warfare meant that there was no escape from involvement. One Military Intelligence Division report said: "As farmers, the Mennonites are 100% efficient—as militants, 100% deficient."[112] But total warfare turned even agriculture into an agency of death. American posters proclaimed "Every Garden a Munitions Plant" and "Win the War with Wheat." How could a nonresistant people escape? Even many conscripts who were court-martialed and imprisoned did not escape. If they agreed to work in the Leavenworth prison dairy they were working in a military system under military direction.

The Mennonites were eager to be good citizens. They

tended to believe that the government's intentions were good. Had they not been received more cordially in Washington than they were treated in their home communities? In contrast to local patriots' anger and mistreatment, Secretary of War Baker in Washington seemed to offer protection. The Mennonites never did understand the extent to which Wilson and his officials were themselves responsible for hysteria at the local level. Confusion and confrontation grew out of Baker's delays and deceits, McAdoo's "voluntary" drives to help finance the war, and Justice Department actions to prosecute the conscientious instead of mob leaders and arsonists. Mennonites saw all this as local excess and temporary aberration, not as a flaw in American democracy.[113]

Mennonites were not alone in misreading the course and consequences of American militarism. In 1918 almost no one could foresee the war's true outcome—not the end of militarism and tyranny but a giant step toward an eventual threat to life on the planet. And soon, Mennonites were deep in the immediate tasks of coping with the postwar era and its new conditions.

CHAPTER
9

THE 1920s: MOVING FORWARD
AND HOLDING BACK

In 1929 Peter C. Hiebert gathered photographs to illustrate a new book on Mennonite postwar relief activities. One of his choices featured Herbert Hoover, a Quaker lad of Iowa who had become president of the United States. During and after World War I, Hoover had earned a reputation as the "Great Humanitarian." In 1914 he had organized the Commission for the Relief of Belgium. Then from 1917 to 1920 he had served first as U.S. Food Administrator and later as Director-General of the American Relief Administration (ARA) in Europe.[1] The ARA mobilized public and private American resources to rescue a great many war victims from starvation, including Mennonites in so-called Russia. In the ARA effort American Mennonites contributed right along with nonpacifist Americans. They could not join the American consensus to make war, but they could join an American effort at saving lives.

The ARA had publicized its work with a photo collage of church relief administrators with Hoover at the center. Above the likenesses ran the headline "Many Faiths United in Greatest of Humanitarian Accomplishments." In the collage—right along with leading Protestants, Catholics, and Jews—was Levi Mumaw, an "old" Mennonite who was secretary of the Mennonite Central Committee. When P. C. Hiebert selected that photo, he put Mennonites into a national context. Here was visual evidence that Mennonites had seized a war-created opportunity to serve. According to Hiebert, their benevolence was a way "to disprove the charges of cowardice and selfishness made against the conscientious objectors, and to express in a positive, concrete way the principles of peace

Many Faiths United in Greatest of
Humanitarian Accomplishments

Top row, left to right: Rev. Charles S. Macfarland, General Secretary Federal Council of the Churches of Christ in America. Dr. Edmund A. Walsh, Executive Head of Papal Relief in Russia, representing National Catholic Welfare Council. Dr. John A. Morehead, Director for Europe; National Lutheran Council. C. V. Hibbard, Associate General Secretary of the Y. M. C. A. Center row: John Barton Payne, Chairman American Red Cross. Herbert Hoover, Chairman American Relief Administration. Felix M. Warburg, Chairman American Jewish Joint Distribution Committee. Bottom row: Mrs. Elizabeth Stites Cotton, Secretary for European Interests, National Board Y. W. C. A. George Repp, General Secretary, American Volga Relief Society. Levi Mumaw, Secretary-Treasurer, Mennonite Board Y. W. C. A. ... Russian representative of Ame can Baptists

Levi Mumaw (bottom row, second from right) was the secretary-treasurer of the Mennonite Central Committee, here acclaimed for cooperation with the American Relief Administration.

and goodwill. . . ."[2] Military service and bond campaigns aside, Mennonites and other Americans could find common goals.

SEPARATION AND INVOLVEMENT

The war experience in a fully mobilized nation had re-

(Peter C. Hiebert. *Feeding the Hungry.* p. 434)

defined Mennonite identity in America. Total war had offered Mennonites new ways to understand their mission as a people. Generally, in the 1920s and 1930s, American Protestantism was troubled and depressed. On the fringe of Protestantism, Mennonites shared those troubles and on some fronts suffered heavy attrition. Nonetheless, many progressive Mennonites were focusing new visions and finding new vitality.[3]

The issue of military service had sharpened the line between the church and world, thereby strengthening Mennonite identity. Once again Mennonites knew that they were a distinctive people who refused to bear arms. The refusal could be costly, even in America. Progressives and conservatives, Swiss and Dutch, Easterners and Westerners—all had their consciousness renewed. Before the war the quintessential progressive C. Henry Smith thought that Anabaptist-Mennonitism and American democracy were twins, overlapping movements of the common people. Now he recognized that Mennonites and America were at odds. In future wars, he said publicly in 1922, the American people probably would not exempt conscientious objectors.[4] Another progressive, William S. Gottschall, pastor of a GC congregation in Bluffton, Ohio, wrote that the war had convinced him that "there must be a more distinct separation of our people from the world and politics." The separation was necessary "if we want to be recognized as different from others and stand firmly on our peculiar Mennonite Principles."[5]

The war vindicated the Anabaptist doctrine of the two kingdoms and strengthened the voices of conservatives who wanted to keep the kingdoms apart. "Since we are going through this present crisis," resolved the Franconia conference in October of 1917, "we have learned that the world expects us to be separate. We therefore consider it advisable to abstain from voting."[6] The old-order groups stood especially to gain from the renewed recognition that the world was evil. They were not sophisticated critics of modern society, but a malaise of modernity which permeated America after 1918 tended to benefit their separated communities. In both its enthusiasms and its disillusion the war affected Mennonites much as the American Revolution had affected them nearly a century and a half earlier. It made Mennonites "more than ever a people apart."[7]

Yet the war also brought many Mennonites out of their relative isolation into new contacts with the outside world. A whole generation of drafted young men received an accelerated education in worldly ways. For the moment they found themselves further beyond the control of bishops and elders than Mennonite youths previously had been in America. Some returned home with new ideas and new aspirations. Meanwhile, news of the outside world caught the attention of Mennonites at home. In the quest for military exemption, Mennonite leaders came into contact with government officials and with other denominational leaders who shared their interests. They learned the advantages of inter-Mennonite cooperation. War-bond campaigns and anti-German-language crusades brought the world to Mennonite doorsteps. "The world has become a neighborhood and we are 'in the world' " as never before, wrote a Mennonite editor in March 1920.[8]

BENEVOLENCE AND REVITALIZATION

Among Mennonites the war generated new impulses and patterns of benevolence, setting the stage for new acts in the tradition of mutual aid. From common Americans, World War I called forth heroic sacrifices. Even before America entered the war, Mennonite agencies began using the military model of idealism and self-sacrifice to inspire greater giving for church programs. "If whole countries fight themselves poor for their country," reasoned the GCs' board for foreign missions in 1914, "is it a great thing for us to give ourselves poor for Christ's kingdom?" The board proposed a self-imposed "voluntary *war tax* . . . for the holy war of missions."[9] The example of a sacrificing world took a place alongside the example of a sacrificing Savior. In May 1918, L. Oliver King of Hesston, Kansas, wrote a letter to the "old" Mennonites' Kansas-Nebraska mission board urging self-denial. "These are days of sacrifice and suffering," he wrote, "and it is not right that the followers of Jesus who sacrificed and suffered more than any man for our sakes . . . should live in pleasure and ease as long as our fellow men are in untold misery."[10] The nation conscripted people and money. Could Mennonites get their own members to give time and treasure voluntarily?

Even as wartime persecution sent Mennonites to seek a moral equivalent to war's sacrifices, wartime prosperity enabled them to increase their giving. Only the generous could be worthy of American citizenship. The prices of farm commodities skyrocketed. Tobacco, important for the large Mennonite communities near Lancaster, Pennsylvania, nearly tripled its price from 1914 to 1918 (going from $.097 to $.279 per pound). In the same years, for western Mennonites, the price of wheat more than doubled, from $.98 per bushel to $2.05. Meanwhile, prices of corn, hogs, cattle, eggs, and butter also climbed. By 1918 and 1919 the financial resources of rural Mennonites were greater than ever before. After 1919 farm prices began to drop, yet in general the prosperity of Mennonites continued through the 1920s.[11]

Neighbors who had sent their sons to war put pressure upon Mennonite families whose sons had not fought, yet whose pocketbooks bulged with war-induced income. Under the pressure and for other motives Mennonites poured unprecedented amounts into a great variety of agencies. Income of the "old" Mennonites' Board of Missions and Charities doubled from 1917 to 1918 and the next year doubled again (from $86,200 to $197,800 to $391,000).[12] Total reported contributions to the General Conference Mennonite church jumped from $363,494 in 1917 to $734,873 in 1920.[13] Besides, Mennonites gave hundreds of thousands of dollars to outside agencies such as the Red Cross and Protestant relief bodies. Some of the increase was due to inflation; but fledgling Mennonite agencies received more than they could easily disburse. Even before deciding how to spend it, Franconia conference bishops appointed solicitors to "collect an amount of money for Relief purposes that would seem consistent with the sacrifices that some of the other people are making."[14]

Out of such financial windfalls Mennonite relief programs emerged. And while adults gave money, young people gave of themselves. Clayton Kratz of Perkasie, Pennsylvania, wrote on an application form for overseas Christian service that he wanted to help the suffering. After all, he said, "this great world catastrophe has not caused me any inconvenience."[15]

Some of the giving was in the form of war bonds which Mennonites had purchased with uneasy consciences. "I receive bonds continually for different funds," wrote G. L. Bender, treasurer and financial agent of the Mennonite Board of Missions and Charities.[16] Some people sent their bonds directly to a favored mission; for instance, Iowa Mennonites contributed bonds to J. D. Mininger, head of an "old" Mennonite mission in Kansas City.[17] Educational institutions benefited as well. In 1920 the Western District GC conference completed a drive to raise $100,000 for Bethel College—successful because of war-induced prosperity plus donors' willingness to part with Liberty Bonds they had never wanted in the first place.[18] The MBs' Tabor College received extraordinary contributions, including bonds, to replace its burned-out administration building.[19] Along with enhancing Mennonite separation, the war fostered generosity toward Mennonite institutions. It, too, helped Mennonites build the denomination.

ORGANIZING TO GIVE

Before the war Mennonites were not well organized for benevolence beyond their own circles. In the late 1890s two groups had created agencies to respond to famine in India. From 1897 to 1906 the "old" Mennonites had an active "Home and Foreign Relief Commission" (HFRC). Partly through the *Mennonitische Rundschau*, a paper that the "old" Mennonite church's publisher John F. Funk had founded to serve them, Dutch-Russian Mennonites gave the agency some unofficial cooperation.[20] Nevertheless, GC Mennonites formed their own "Emergency Relief Commission." From 1899 until 1914 the GC agency disbursed an average of about $2,000 per year to meet needs such as famines in India, China, and Russia.[21] Also, like the *Rundschau*, other German-language newspapers occasionally served as collecting agencies among the Dutch-Russians. In 1895 the MBs sanctioned this role by appointing editor John F. Harms of the *Zionsbote* to be treasurer of relief funds collected annually on Thanksgiving Day.[22]

Editor Martin B. Fast of the *Rundschau* said that raising money for the poor was one of the greatest satisfactions of his editorship, and reported in October 1910, that the paper had raised a total of $19,445.55 for relief of struggling Mennonite colonies in the Russian Empire.[23] As World War I got under way in Europe, Kansas editor Abraham L. Schellenberg used his *Vorwärts* to collect funds for the German Red Cross.[24] After the war, in the summer of 1919, M. B. Fast, then living in California, organized a collection and expedition for Mennonite war sufferers in Siberia. He collected and disbursed some $44,000.[25] In 1920 Kansas Mennonites helped send eight hundred cows to Germany in a highly publicized project organized by the German Red Cross and the Chicago-based American Dairy Company.[26] An "old" Mennonite "Relief Commission for War Sufferers," organized December 26-27, 1917, worked with the Quakers for postwar reconstruction in France, and with

(Center for Mennonite Brethren Studies, Hillsboro, Kansas)

Medal of thanks from Chortitza Mennonites in the Ukraine to American Mennonites for their relief aid in 1922.

Near East Relief to aid refugees in Turkey. A confusing variety of agencies benefited from relief monies which flowed out of Mennonite communities. The confusion reflected both the suddenness of the crisis and the rudimentary state of Mennonite denominational organizations.

BIRTH OF MENNONITE CENTRAL COMMITTEE

In 1920 external events triggered a beginning of centrally coordinated, inter-Mennonite relief effort. Mennonites in the Ukraine, devastated by civil war and famine, sent a delegation (or "study commission") to seek help in Europe and North America.[27] Frustrated by the chaos of eager but separated groups, the "Russian" Mennonite delegation asked to deal with one central Mennonite committee. In January 1920 Mennonites of Dutch-Russian background (Mennonite Brethren, Krimmer Mennonite Brethren, General Conference) had cooperated to organize a common Emergency Relief Commission. The "old" Mennonite Relief Commission for War Sufferers was more ambivalent about such cooperation and about the burgeoning overseas relief effort in general. One problem was the difficulty of controlling standards of behavior and dress for workers far away from home.[28] Inter-Mennonite units compounded the problem, of course: other groups did not have clear rulings on matters such as the collarless coat or puttees (legwear of a kind often used with military uniforms). In August 1919 the executive committee of the "old" Mennonite commission resolved to disband its agency as soon as it had fulfilled its postwar relief task. It expected to do so by the spring of 1920.[29]

The emergency needs of starving Mennonites in the Ukraine finally convinced the separate agencies to expand and cooperate. Out of delicate negotiations in meetings at Newton, Elkhart, and Chicago, there gradually emerged a new "Mennonite Central Committee" (MCC). For Mennonite ecumenical relationships, MCC's birth was a high moment. The new agency accepted "old" Mennonite workers already appointed to begin work in Russia. Part of the compromise was to choose Peter C. Hiebert as chairman—as a Mennonite Brethren he could be a tie between the two larger groups, the "old" and the GC. Two other parts were to locate the MCC executive office at Scottdale, Pennsylvania, and to appoint the "old" Mennonites' Levi Mumaw to be administrative secretary.

It was a masterful improvisation. From the viewpoint of the Dutch-Russians, other Mennonites in America were now joining them in a long-standing tradition of mutual aid to cousins in the homeland. Yet the "old" Mennonites could claim cooperation from Dutch-Russians for work projected and begun from Scottdale.[30] Meanwhile, GC Mennonites could see a partial fruition of their longtime agenda, inter-Mennonite cooperation. Daniel Kauffman, guardian of "old" Mennonite separatism and critic of inter-Mennonitism, was more than a little disgruntled. Only with reluctance did he report MCC news in his *Gospel Herald*.[31] Wartime and postwar upheaval had set in motion some new forces which the old guard could not fully control.

Contributing to the climate of change was an aggressive stirring of "old" Mennonite youths. In December of 1918, convinced that their leaders lacked vision to meet postwar challenges, some of them organized a new "Young People's Movement" and began to pressure the church for more aggressive programs of relief and service. Among the insurgents were Jacob C. Meyer as chairman, J. Roy Allgyer as executive secretary, and Orie B. Gerig as corresponding secretary. Fifty-four Mennonite volunteers joined a reconstruction unit operated by the American Friends Service Committee in France. The "old" Mennonite Relief Commission for War Sufferers contributed $291,000 for the French work, yet among conservatives the effort remained controversial. Through the 1920s an exceptionally sharp struggle of the generations plagued the "old" Mennonite church.[32]

To go overseas in relief work was to have one's Mennonite horizons broadened. This was true both of youthful MCC volunteers and of older church leaders sent out to investigate. Cross-cultural comparisons yielded new insights. Vinora Weaver and Vesta Zook, who went to Turkey and were the first two women to serve under MCC, observed that the Muslim women in Constantinople were pushing against regulations regarding veiling of the face. Wrote Weaver, "The Turkish women must be going through a process of liberation much as our Mennonite women have." Weaver and Zook had been careful to wear their regulation bonnets when meeting the Mennonite "higher-ups" at Scottdale who approved their going, but halfway across the Atlantic Ocean they declared independence by throwing their bonnets overboard.[33]

For relief work in the new Soviet Union, or USSR, MCC joined hands with the ARA—the organization headed by Herbert Hoover, who also was a new Republican administration's Secretary of Commerce.[34] In late 1921 the Central Committee of the Soviets authorized the MCC to carry on its own work, but for practical reasons MCC leaders chose to distribute most of their goods via the ARA. Between March 1922 and August 1923, MCC aided 75,000 people in the Soviet Union, including 60,000 Mennonites. By 1924 total Mennonite relief to the USSR's people, including tractors and horses as well as food, amounted to $1,200,000. MCC operations continued in Siberia until 1926. It was estimated that the effort saved nine thousand Mennonites from starvation. Mennonites considered this work to be their own, but the ARA connection hooked it into a national program bound up with the U.S. government's foreign policy.

The cooperative, inter-Mennonite effort riveted the attention of the various Mennonite groups in America. Leaders made trips to organize or see the work, then came back to fill Mennonite newspapers with reports. An early martyrdom added to the drama. In the fall of 1920 the same Clayton Kratz who had said the war caused him no inconvenience was administering relief in Halbstadt, a formerly Mennonite village in the Ukraine. The advancing Red army was overwhelming the White army of General Wrangel in the area, but Kratz chose to stay. He was arrested and never heard from again.[35] Mennonites etched Kratz's name in their historical memory just as nonpacifist Americans made heroes of their military dead. The Franconia Mennonite conference organized a Clayton Kratz Fellowship.

Not all Mennonite relief to the USSR went through the MCC. Many Mennonites helped friends and relatives through a "food draft" plan run by the ARA quite apart from any Mennonite agency. Individuals could fill out applications, contribute in multiples of ten dollars, and identify names and addresses of beneficiaries in the Soviet Union. The ARA distributed the food accordingly. Because knowing both English and Russian was necessary for filling out applications, donors needed expert assistance. Before the program closed on March 15, 1923, Jacob G. Ewert of Hillsboro, Kansas, a bedfast paralytic with partial use of only one hand, exhausted himself by completing applications worth $89,000. Several days later he became ill and died. He had sacrificed himself as surely as had Clayton Kratz.[36]

Mennonites in the USSR needed not only emergency relief but also help to emigrate. In November 1921, American Mennonites created a second inter-Mennonite central committee for that purpose, calling it the "Mennonite Executive Committee for Colonization" (MECC). A major immigration from the USSR to the United States such as took place in the 1870s and '80s would have greatly changed Mennonitism in America. From 1921 through 1923 some 350 to 400 Mennonites did manage to get from the USSR to the United States.[37] Many more got to Canada, but the United States closed its doors. In 1921 Congress passed an Emergency Quota Act and in 1924 the nativist National Origins Act. Assigning very different quotas to various nations, the two laws were highly biased against immigration from Eastern and Southern Europe. The quota for the Soviet Union was simply too low to allow many Mennonites to come. The MECC never got under way. In addition to national policy it had problems of weak leadership, disagreements over which country the "Russians" should go to, and priority for the emergency MCC relief program. One historian has written that in 1922 and 1923 American Mennonite "procrastination" cost thousands of Mennonites in the Soviet Union the opportunity to emigrate.[38]

Canadian Mennonites seized the initiative. A "Canadian Board of Colonization and Mennonite Land Settlement" took advantage of immigration policies more liberal than in the United States, and of generous credit advanced by the Canadian

Pacific Railway. Some twenty thousand Mennonites left the Soviet Union to settle mainly on the Canadian prairies.[39] U.S. Mennonites gave some money, but by MCC's original mandate of 1920 their first priority was relief. Finally in 1929 MCC took up the new task. A five-year plan under the ruthless Soviet premier Josef Stalin was devastating the class to which most Mennonite farmers belonged. The doors to Canada were being closed. So MCC helped emigrants resettle in Paraguay.

Postwar relief work in Europe brought American and European Mennonites together in new ways. In turn, the new cooperation provided an agenda for Mennonites to organize a "Mennonite World Conference." Its leading founder was Christian Neff of the Weierhof in the German Palatinate. In Basel and Zurich, Switzerland, in 1925, and in Danzig, Germany, in 1930, the conference held its first meetings. As for mutual aid, the 1925 gathering considered (and tabled) a Russian-Mennonite proposal to create a worldwide relief treasury to which emigrants might pay back what they had received.[40] By the time of the 1930 conference in Danzig, the U.S.S.R.'s Mennonites were in the new crisis which Stalin and his collectivizing produced. That meeting dealt exclusively with relief issues. Reports of work accomplished by Mennonites from Germany, Holland, and North America revealed dramatically how the center weight of Mennonitism had shifted to the North Americans. Their totals dwarfed all the others. As surely as World War I had helped the United States come into world power, it also helped the Mennonites of North America to dominate world Mennonitism. For them the war era was a time of membership growth, prosperity, and eager effort to meet world needs.

In 1930 one of six North Americans present at the Danzig meeting was a thirty-three-year-old named Harold S. Bender. European-educated and dean of Goshen College, Bender spoke officially on behalf of the Mennonite Central Committee. He lavishly documented and praised the American Mennonite relief effort in the Soviet Union as "unique in our Mennonite history."[41] The Soviet government, Bender said, actually found MCC's work to have been better than that of the ARA. In a brief European response the session chairman, an Amsterdam pastor named Pieter Bernard Westerdijk, quickly punctured such American self-congratulation. To cite so many statistics was "typically American," Westerdijk said. The quality of the giver's heart counted for more than the amount of the gift. Westerdijk also observed that Bender's struggle to speak in German showed him also, like the Dutch, to be a "brother in need"![42]

THE ROOTS OF BENEVOLENCE

Whether or not he intended to, Westerdijk had questioned the underlying meanings and motivations of American Mennonite relief. Was such benevolence rooted in a heritage of faith or was it a case of Americanization, in typically American style? Did it grow from spiritual depth or simply from American organization? There is much evidence that American Mennonites were indeed acting from a desire to be part of the national community which had so recently rejected them as religious pacifists. Relief work was a thoroughly national endeavor; Americans considered themselves "an unusually philanthropic people."[43]

"Combine Patriotism and Philanthropy," said the bright red letters on the stationery of one relief committee through which Mennonites sent funds and personnel.[44] The first workers to go out under the "old" Mennonites' relief commission were called "our first expedition." The phrase echoed the military language under which American troops had gone to Europe as the "American Expeditionary Forces."[45] Later, whenever Mennonites petitioned the government for the privilege of refusing military service they mentioned their relief and benevolence programs. Sometimes the used the explicit label "Our Substitution for War."[46] They were worthy of American citizenship.[47]

However, the roots of Mennonite benevolence also reached for deeper and more steady nourishment. As Mennonite leaders challenged their people to give generously, they referred often to two other sources: the Bible and Anabaptist-Mennonite history. No single biblical text dominated in relief work as the "great commission" dominated the call to missions. But the constitution of the Mennonite Relief Commission for War Sufferers cited Matthew 25:35-36 ("For I was an hungered, and ye gave me meat: I was thirsty and ye gave me drink. . . .") and Galatians 6:10 ("As we therefore have opportunity, let us do good unto all men, especially unto them who are of the household of faith").[48] In 1920 Aaron Loucks of Scottdale quoted 1 John 3:17: "But whoso hath this world's good, and seeth his brother have need. . . ."[49] Often such references implied that to give relief was to carry on the work which God had begun in

Christ. That is, they carried the message of incarnation. Eventually the MCC motto became, "In the Name of Christ." No Mennonite leader in the postwar years produced a major new theological statement to incorporate benevolence into Mennonite self-understanding. But Mennonites never doubted that when they gave to relieve suffering they were fulfilling a biblical mandate.

Anabaptist-Mennonite history also provided a mandate. Historical references were far fewer in the 1920s than they would be later, following World War II. In the 1920s some people said that it was important to help fellow Mennonites from the USSR because Mennonites had helped each other across national boundaries many times in the past. "Old" Mennonite historian John Horsch chronicled how past Mennonites had been both givers and receivers.[50] In the 1870s the Americans had helped the Russians immigrate. In the early 1700s the Dutch had helped the persecuted Swiss. In the 1660s the Dutch had sent aid to suffering Hutterites in Austria-Hungary. So in the 1920s Mennonites saw their giving as a renewal of their own mutual aid tradition. In their view, benevolence was not so much an American activity as it was a Mennonite heritage. This time the heritage also helped to win respectability in America.

Some progressive Mennonite leaders worried that the flowering of benevolence and inter-Mennonite cooperation would fade with the memory of the great war and the famine in Russia. Orie O. Miller, relief worker in the Near East, noted in 1919 that Mennonites gave generously in wartime "because of our unpopular attitude on the war question." Now it was necessary to find "new stimuli."[51] From 1920 to 1925 the crisis in the USSR gave Mennonites the opportunity to match their wartime ability and eagerness to give. In the longer run, the powerful new stimulus Miller sought came with World War II and America's permanent militarization. In the 1940s and '50s Mennonite giving and inter-Mennonite cooperation reached new proportions.

From about 1925 to 1929, however, MCC barely survived. In 1923 chairman P. C. Hiebert issued a general call through the church papers for a more permanent inter-Mennonite "Relief Machinery."[52] All groups seemed willing to cooperate except the largest body, the "old" Mennonites. In May, 1924, the "old" Mennonites' commission officially turned down Hiebert's proposal and recalled its earlier pledge to disband "when the cause for which the Mennonite Relief Commission was called into existence ceases to exist."[53] Without official "old" Mennonite participation MCC seemed destined to die. So in December of 1924, at an adjourned session of MCC, Hiebert and others created a new organization called the American Mennonite Relief Commission. "Old" Mennonites Orie Miller and Levi Mumaw were present but not able to represent their group officially. So they were "accorded the privileges of the meeting," and Mumaw was elected secretary.[54] The new body adopted a rudimentary constitution but never became an active or viable alternative to MCC. The new commission's last official meeting was in December of 1926.[55]

Meanwhile, MCC, instead of expiring, kept up some work in the USSR until 1927. Then Stalin's first five-year plan (1928-1933) generated a new crisis, and in 1929 MCC took on new life aiding emigrants. Patient work behind the scenes by Miller and others won "old" Mennonite cooperation for a permanent MCC. The 1929 publication of the book *Feeding the Hungry*, which told of the marvelously successful Russian relief program, helped create a climate for MCC to move forward.

THE MEANINGS OF BENEVOLENCE

The rise of MCC had somewhat different meanings for the three general groupings of Mennonites in America. For the Dutch-Russian immigrants of the 1870s the work in the Ukraine renewed ties of mutual aid among kinspeople, ties still quite strong after two generations. The influx of Dutch-Russian immigrants, mostly to Canada, enriched the Dutch-Russian portion of North American Mennonitism and established new bonds between people of that portion in the United States and those in Canada. For American Mennonites of Swiss and south-German background, the new relief work also constituted the renewal of a mutual aid tradition. But it reached back further to recapitulate their 1870s aid to immigrating Dutch-Russian Mennonites who were not expected to integrate smoothly with American Mennonites. The inter-Mennonite cooperation of MCC was especially momentous for the developing self-identity of the "old" Mennonites. The crisis drew them closer to other Mennonites than they had anticipated or desired. Finally, Old Order Mennonites and Amish, being more separated from the world, did not participate directly with MCC and were not much affected by its ecumenism. Secure in their identity, they felt little need to prove their civic worth or acceptability. Moreover, the charter of values which guided old-order life in community was skeptical of programs and did not put a premium on outward witness and mission.

Fitfulness and hesitation in the early years of MCC should not obscure the importance of postwar benevolence. It was a creative and critical development in the regeneration of progressive American Mennonite peoplehood. American Mennonites raised some two and one-half million dollars for relief in war-torn Europe, the Near East, and the USSR. Money came from a broad base of small contributors in congregations across the country.[56] Hundreds of church members busied themselves in the effort at home and abroad. As one Mennonite draftee who later volunteered to work in Turkey said, he had "to do something to justify my existence."[57] In the process Mennonites found both a new hold on their distinctive faith and a more secure place in America.

MCC was a borrowing from American society, but it borrowed selectively in a way that renewed Mennonite peoplehood. Chairman Hiebert wrote that Mennonites "should endeavor to make ourselves known as a people whose most conspicuous trait, next to piety, is benevolence. In order to acquire this reputation it is necessary that with all diligence 'We work the works of Him that sent us.' "[58] Hiebert's summary was apt. The key elements in this new Mennonite ethos were piety, benevolence, reputation, diligence, and following Christ. These virtues and more were needed in abundance, for in these same years Mennonites struggled with tensions related to a wider conflict between Modernism and Fundamentalism.

ANTI-MODERNISM AND CULTURAL CHANGE

For Americans generally, the crusading idealism and unity of World War I quickly gave way to disillusionment and polarization. The holy war soured almost overnight. In the immediate postwar years Americans found many ways to vent frustrations: a rejuvenated Ku Klux Klan, a hysterical "Red Scare," an anti-immigrant movement, urban race riots, labor strikes, and controversy between Fundamentalists and Modernists. Mennonites, even many who thought themselves quite separated from the world, reflected the national mood. Early in 1919 the "old" Mennonite leader Daniel Kauffman compiled a list of things "most to be feared." Kauffman's nomination for the most fearful force of all—ahead of the "curses" of Prussianism, Romanism, alcoholism, selfishness, idolatry, and indifference—was ("modern LIBERALISM."[59]

In their quest for identity and mission during the rest of the twentieth century, Mennonites would borrow language from American Protestantism and its quarrel of Fundamentalists against Modernists. Yet they also were preoccupied with the agendas of their own peoplehood. Since they were preoccupied with their own issues, it may be that none of them really deserved the label either of Fundamentalist or of Modernist.

The Modernist-Fundamentalist struggle climaxed publicly in 1925 in Dayton, Tennessee, in the oft-mentioned Scopes trial with its debate between Fundamentalist William Jennings Bryan and the irreverent attorney Clarence Darrow. Formally, that debate had to do with teaching evolution in public schools. More broadly, it was about changes in American culture. Various conservative groups drew up lists of biblical doctrines they considered "fundamental" and under immediate attack, such as the virgin birth, the bodily resurrection, the substitutionary atonement, and the inerrancy of Scripture. But such "Fundamentalists" never settled on one single list to consider normative. In 1970 church historian Ernest Sandeen described the intellectual "Roots of Fundamentalism" as running back to a dynamic joining of two doctrines. One was a version of millenarianism, which had long been an American Protestant theme. The other was a new, strict doctrine of biblical inspiration taught at Princeton Seminary. By Sandeen's analysis, people—presumably including Mennonites—were Fundamentalists if they believed in (1) the dispensationalist or premillennialist doctrine of Christ's imminent return to inaugurate a thousand-year reign on earth; and (2) the "Princeton theology" concerning biblical inerrancy.[60]

But Fundamentalism as it developed in history was more than doctrine. In a 1980 book, church historian George Marsden explored its cultural and organizational context and saw Fundamentalism as an uneasy coalition of militant Protestant evangelicals. Included were holiness fellowships of Methodist origin, Bible school people, some conservative denominations, and other revivalists and millenarians. Such groups differed widely and spoke in various voices, yet came together enough to join in a historic movement. Their unity lay not in doctrine but in their militant opposition to "both modernism in theology and the cultural changes that modernism endorsed."[61] A religious leader who shared that militancy was a Fundamentalist by definition, whether or not he claimed the title. One had only to be part of the crusade against certain encroachments—encroachments such as violation of the Sabbath, worldliness in the theater, the teaching of evolution, and especially historical-literary criticism of the Bible. In 1924 a crusading Mennonite, John Horsch, put it succinctly: "Fundamentalism is antimodernism."[62] Following Marsden and Horsch, any Mennonite who was militantly anti-Modernist could well be called a Mennonite Fundamentalist.

Yet most "Mennonite Fundamentalists" were still Mennonites first of all. Like historic Fundamentalism, Mennonitism itself was an uneasy coalition of diverse groups who found it difficult to cooperate or to speak with a common voice. Mennonites were ethnic denominational conservatives, and each group had its own conservative means of maintaining its particular identity. For nearly all of them the particular Mennonite identity and its cultural expressions were more important than Fundamentalist doctrine. Especially for the old order groups, traditional identities served as protection against absorption into America's Protestant contentions. For Mennonites generally, the commitment to nonresistance, tested so dramatically in 1917-1918, marked a separation from other main elements of the Fundamentalist coalition. To be sure, some Mennonites moved toward a Fundamentalist-style evangelicalism in reaction against their ethnic heritage. But most Mennonites who seemed to join the historic Fundamentalist movement, and who used its language and teachings, actually did so in order to shore up their conservative Mennonite traditions.

"Old" Mennonite leaders in particular were less concerned about Modernist ideas than about the "drift" away from traditional standards. For example, in 1920 John L. Stauffer, anti-Modernist Bible teacher at Eastern Mennonite School, attacked Mennonites of the postwar reconstruction unit in France. In a new "Youth Conference" held in France, the reconstruction workers had proposed a progressive church agenda. The attack included premillennialist language aimed to discredit the social gospel. "The signs of Christ's coming, the more sure word of prophecy, and the evidence of the coming dissolution of this age," Stauffer wrote, "are too ominous and imminent to turn aside and accept a social program for the world, political reconstruction or any other extra-biblical benevolent propaganda."[63] But Stauffer's fundamentalistic statement was buried in a fourteen-paragraph article which was preoccupied with alarm over cultural changes in traditional Mennonite patterns of dress and churchly authority.[64]

Mennonite anti-Modernism attempted to serve the primary cause of conservative denominationalism. Whether a person such as Stauffer should be counted as within the Fundamentalist coalition, on its fringes, or outside of it, is a matter of definition. By Marsden's definition, Stauffer and others like him would qualify. They were militant anti-Modernists and hence belonged to the conservative denominational wing of Fundamentalism. Mennonite historian Rodney Sawatsky has distinguished four categories of "old" Mennonite Fundamentalists: Radical Fundamentalist, Moderate Fundamentalist, Conservative Fundamentalist, and Fundamentalist Conservative. In Sawatsky's view John L. Stauffer, committed to biblical inerrancy and to nondispensationalist premillennialism, was a Moderate Fundamentalist.[65] However, the label "Fundamentalist" is so indefinite and easily misunderstood that for Mennonite leaders—"old" Mennonite and others—it may be best to avoid it entirely. It may be better to speak simply of conservative Mennonite anti-Modernists.

WEDGES OF MODERNITY

When Mennonite anti-Modernists borrowed Fundamentalist doctrine and copied the style of Fundamentalist militancy, they were generally not aware of how deeply they were deviating from their own heritage, with its humility and quietism. The cultural and intellectual changes which alarmed them were not mere phantoms. Mennonitism was in transition from traditional sectarianism to more modern denominational forms of church and community life. The entering wedges of modern thinking came by way of those persons, usually of the younger generation, who had encountered the outside world (and other kinds of Mennonites). The encounters had come in military camps, in overseas service work, or in college or graduate school. John L. Stauffer was quite correct when he assumed that the youthful Mennonites in the French reconstruction unit stood for change, for inter-Mennonite ecumenicity, for aggressive church outreach, for more democratic church structures, and for less concern about distinctive dress. The entering wedges even included some more modern ideas about biblical interpretation and natural science—ideas which would grow stronger in future years. In the 1920s American Protestantism was polarizing over such ideas. The challenge for a healthy church was selectively to accommodate the new forms and ideas without compromising the faith or succumbing to such destructive division. Some Mennonite anti-Modernists opted for alarmist repression and polarization. As a result their churches suffered.

Until the 1930s, no Mennonite leader adopted the cause of Christian Modernism or became a crusading anti-Fundamentalist in the manner of Harry Emerson Fosdick of New York or Shailer Mathews and Shirley Jackson Case of Chicago. Yet already by the turn of century, a few Mennonite educators and editors were cautiously open to more modern ideas. Noah C. Hirschy was a graduate of Oberlin College and Seminary and soon would be president of Central College in Bluffton. In June 1899 he welcomed biblical higher criticism, confident that that the Bible would stand the test of truth.[66] In April 1900 C. Henry Smith addressed the "old" Mennonite Elkhart Institute in favor of the "Nebular Hypothesis" as a scientific means to explain how the universe began.[67] In October 1902 a GC meeting had recently passed a resolution against "the injurious teachings of the so-called higher critics." Despite the resolution, H. G. Allebach, who had studied at Ursinus College and the University of Pennsylvania and now edited the GC paper *The Mennonite*, published two articles proposing that readers should find ways to accept the theory of evolution. Allebach said he wanted to "look at the truth from every side, with the ultimate purpose of discovering that the revealed Word of God still stands supreme. . . ."[68] At Bethel College, Cornelius H. Wedel adopted modern methods of historical and biblical study in his own way. In 1904 he endorsed a scientific method of "New Testament textual criticism" for determining which ancient biblical texts were oldest and most accurate. While he rejected the more extreme forms of higher criticism, Wedel believed in studying texts precisely. Doing so would help correct some misleading interpretations of state-church apologists and would vindicate the Anabaptist understanding of the church.[69]

Before World War I such wedges of modern thinking normally elicited no more than restrained refutation and polite dialogue. In 1910 John W. Kliewer at Bethel College wrote that the cause of "progressive orthodoxy" might prevail despite misguided voices who sounded the "effective alarm of 'higher criticism.' "[70] After 1918, as though the war had poisoned the atmosphere, the exchanges became more bitter and fearful.

"OLD" MENNONITE CONTROVERSY

Among Mennonites, the Fundamentalist-Modernist controversy took its clearest shape in the "old" church. This group had its own blend of conservatism and modernity—different from the blends of the Old Orders, the Dutch-Russians, or the smaller evangelical groups. In certain ways the "old" Mennonites were rather Americanized. They had taken on the English language; adopted revivalism and missions for church renewal; founded colleges in Indiana, Kansas, and Virginia; and developed conference organization quite fully. On the other hand they endeavored to use the instruments of denominational organization and education to maintain a separate and conservative lifestyle over against the world. Modernism seemed to threaten the prescriptions underlying doctrinal and social separation. "Old" Mennonites tried to maintain a balance, but the balance was precarious. College students and faculties could not be kept from new knowledge. Revivalism brought an experiential test to religious life that could function as an alternative to tradition. In about 1908 "old" Mennonite official publications and conference statements began to be more anti-Modernist in emphasis and mood.[71] In that year the new *Gospel Herald* became the "old" Mennonites' official paper. With Daniel Kauffman as editor it published numerous antiliberal articles, from both Mennonite and non-Mennonite sources.

The "old" Mennonites also produced some Fundamentalistic official pronouncements. Principal author of such statements was Jacob B. Smith. Smith, from 1909 to 1917 a teacher at Hesston College and from 1917 to 1922 president of Eastern Mennonite School, claimed to "owe much of my Bible knowledge" to Cyrus I. Scofield, author of a popular dispensationalist Bible commentary and study course which Smith had taken as a young minister.[72] In language which echoed anti-Modernism in other denominations he vigorously criticized the "old" Mennonites' oldest college, Goshen. From Hesston he wrote to fellow conservative George R. Brunk in Virginia, "Do you know that at least four denominations have started movements opposing the new theology (Pres. Meth. Cong. & Bap.). Papers are drawn up and signed by volunteers in defence of the orthodox view. . . . Would it not be timely for us to do something similar . . . ?"[73]

In 1911 Smith was on the resolutions committee of the Kansas-Nebraska "old" Mennonite conference and was probably author of resolutions which it adopted. For the first time the conference used language of "verbal inspiration of the Bible in the original"—code language of Protestant Fundamentalists.[74] Soon Smith also wrote a chapter on "The Bible" for a new version of the "old" Mennonites' official doctrinal book, published in 1914 as *Bible Doctrine.* In his chapter he elaborated more fully the Fundamentalist view of biblical authority and inspiration. In 1919, shortly before that year's meeting of the "old" Mennonites' Virginia conference, Bishop George R. Brunk admonished Smith to "get your fundamentals drafted good clear and strong [sic] so no liberalist can hide under them and we will put them thru at our district conf." The conference adopted Smith's eighteen-point statement as the "Articles of Faith of the Virginia Conference of Mennonites."[75]

In 1921, with only minor changes, the "old" Mennonite general conference accepted the same, as a report of its own Committee on Fundamentals. The statement's very first article was: "We believe in the plenary and verbal inspiration of the Bible as the Word of God; that it is authentic in its matter, authoritative in its counsels, inerrant in the original writings and the only infallible rule of faith and practice."[76] Putting that article first, before any statement about God or Jesus Christ, was clear evidence that the new Fundamentalist theory of biblical inspiration had become the primary issue.

Probably no conference report on paper had as much impact as did exercising church discipline over allegedly liberal individuals, congregations, and colleges. Other "old" Mennonites launched sharp attacks against Goshen College. George R. Brunk even wrote letters and spoke in conferences scolding *Gospel Herald* editor Daniel Kauffman, although Kauffman was thoroughly conservative and anti-Modernist. Brunk's complaint was that Kauffman consorted with liberals and allowed the denomination's publishing house to be "three fourths Goshenized."[77] Brunk later adopted the word "Laxitarian" to label those who sought a middle ground of fellowship with both "Loyalists" and "Liberals."[78] Other issues such as the world war and the Communist Revolution provided anti-Modernists with

militant rhetoric. In his characteristically emphatic style Brunk
once wrote to Daniel Kauffman, J. B. Smith, and A. D. Wenger:
"Our Lenines and Trotzkeys [*sic*] even if honest and sincere
must not be permitted by rose tinted speeches of Peace to dis-
arm the army of conservatives and open the gates of defence to
the spiritual HUNS who plunder home, churches and the very
word of God itself!!!"[79]

From the more liberal side, the evangelist and college president J. E. Hartzler also wrote and spoke with a flamboyant
style which ran against the Mennonite grain. For anti-Modernist "old" Mennonites, Hartzler became the favorite whipping
boy. Already in 1910, as he wrote a book called *Paths to Perdition*, Hartzler had drawn conservatives' fire. In their opinion he
was not coming out strongly enough against worldly clothing,
games of chance, and harmful art and poetry. On the other
hand he wrote too strongly against tobacco, thereby offending
tobacco-growing Mennonites in the East.[80] In 1913 Hartzler was
made president of Goshen College. In his inaugural address he
hardly ingratiated himself to conservatives, for he lavishly
praised "liberal education and culture." And, in fact, he failed
to integrate his views of liberal culture with the Bible or the
Mennonite heritage. Moreover, he seemed to go out of his way to
oppose "old" Mennonites' increasing emphasis on doctrine.
Said he, "The most erroneous view one can take of religion is
that it is one unchanging body of dogma." Hartzler's views
reflected the experiential dimensions of his work as a revivalist.
"Religion," he said, "is a matter of experience."[81]

Daniel Kauffman, meanwhile, was trying to unify the various strands of "old" Mennonite opinion. So for the 1914 *Bible
Doctrine* book he asked Hartzler to write the nine-chapter section on the "Plan of Salvation." Hartzler's chapters were
orthodox in the evangelical sense, and Kauffman edited them
carefully to eliminate any trace of liberalism. Nevertheless, conservatives would long insist that the section was "splotched"
with Modernism.[82] In 1918 Hartzler resigned from Goshen,
forced out in part by doctrinal controversy but also by the consequences of unwise overexpansion. He took a teaching position
at Bethel College, but first studied for a summer at the University of Chicago. J. B. Smith opposed the Chicago connection.
It was, Smith said, a matter of "maintaining our denominational identity."[83] In 1920 Hartzler's relations with fellow "old"
Mennonites reached a breaking point when he was not allowed

to share in the ceremony of the Lord's Supper with the "Pennsylvania" Mennonite congregation in Kansas, not far from Newton, where he was teaching. The man who finally refused him was the rather prominent local bishop, Tilman (T. M.) Erb; however, to a degree Erb's hand was forced by certain actions of a militantly anti-Modernist bishop named Jacob (J. K.) Bixler back at the Elkhart congregation in Indiana. In a struggle against persons in his congregation whom he considered too liberal, Bixler was making it difficult for Hartzler to receive a congregational letter of good standing which Erb felt he could honor.[84] In 1921 Hartzler accepted a position as president of Witmarsum Theological Seminary in Bluffton, Ohio. For the rest of his life he worked and fellowshiped within the GC branch.

In 1923-1924 the "old" Mennonite crisis came to a head at Goshen College and among congregations in Indiana and Ohio. Wanting to remove Modernist influences and to reorganize on a new basis, the Mennonite Board of Education closed Goshen College for one school year. Dozens of Goshen students transferred to Bluffton College. With key "old Goshen" persons already on its faculty, Bluffton seemed poised once again to gain at Goshen's expense. A committee of the Indiana-Michigan "old" Mennonite conference revoked the ministerial status of six ministers, and about four hundred of the conference's people withdrew to join either the Central Conference of Mennonites or the GC branch. The Ohio Mennonite and the Eastern Amish Mennonite conferences also took action to exclude certain congregations who resisted conference rules.[85]

At work were complex forces—very evident, for instance, in the fates of the Walnut Creek Amish Mennonite congregation of Holmes County, Ohio, and of a young minister there, a local son named Lester Hostetler. As with many other congregations, the coming of revivalism around the turn of the century had helped Walnut Creek to grow rapidly. In 1915 the congregation ordained Hostetler by vote rather than by the traditional lot. A graduate of Goshen College, Hostetler was the first pastor at Walnut Creek to have professional training. He even studied for three years at Union Theological Seminary. However, the congregation could not offer him a salary without violating a long tradition of lay leadership. Hostetler's wife was Charity Steiner, daughter of Menno S. and Clara Eby Steiner and herself an intellectually inclined graduate of Goshen College. Yet the two earned their living and covered school debts by raising fruit and vegetables on a twenty-acre farm the church provided, a scruffy property with old buildings and depleted soil. Nonetheless, the energetic young man exulted in his ministry, both at Walnut Creek and at a satellite congregation at Sugar Creek.

Backed by a senior minister named Samuel H. Miller, Hostetler introduced many deviations from old, time-honored ways: worship services every Sunday instead of every other Sunday, compilation of a church roll and publication of a yearbook, special music classes and a church choir, change in pattern of communion services, offerings in the church, removal of the traditional hat rack above the pulpit for ministers' hats, and more. Meanwhile, he hesitated to preach in favor of simple clothing or to exercise the Eastern Amish Mennonite conference's discipline against members who held life and property insurance. Soon the congregation divided over these issues. Many members favored change. For example, it was said that some fifty members held the forbidden insurance. Discipline finally came from the outside, and the congregation split.[86]

The outside discipline came through various moves of the conference, from Bishop Elias Frey of Fulton County farther west in Ohio, and from J. B. Smith in Virginia. In 1917 the Eastern Amish Mennonite conference officially acted to discourage Hostetler from returning to Union Biblical Seminary, a resolution the young pastor disobeyed. In 1920 the conference appointed an investigating committee, including bishops from other conferences, to examine whether Hostetler was orthodox on six points—creation and evolution, the virgin birth, bodily resurrection, biblical inspiration, the devotional covering, and conference authority. Hostetler "willingly subscribed" to the conference position on these teachings. His stand led an important committee member, Hesston College president D. H. Bender, to suggest rather ambiguously that the problem was less doctrinal than attitudinal: "He would not be so flatly unorthodox if it were not for the attitude he takes."[87]

In 1924 yet another conference-investigating committee came to Walnut Creek. Following the visit came a showdown, in the form of a congregational vote on Hostetler's resignation. Later the young minister felt sure that with a secret ballot he would have won, but the bishops collected each vote personally. That procedure made every negative vote an open statement against the bishops' authority, and Hostetler lost 139 to 101. The following year the conference revoked his membership because he had associated with some Indiana congregations who were out of fellowship with the Indiana-Michigan conference. Eventually Hostetler became minister of an independent congregation in Sugar Creek which later joined the GC branch. Many progressive members from the Walnut Creek congregation joined at Sugar Creek. Walnut Creek returned to more traditional ways, conformity to conference, and a ministry without professional training.

In January 1924 some insurgent "old" Mennonite progressives struck fear into the hearts of denominational conservatives by founding a new religious periodical, the *Christian Exponent*.[88] The progressives were not satisfied with the *Gospel Herald*, and for several years some talk of needing "a different church paper" had been in the air.[89] Nearly two decades had passed since Daniel Kauffman and others had wrested denominational authority from John F. Funk in Elkhart by establishing the *Gospel Witness*. That paper had soon absorbed Funk's *Herald of Truth* and become the *Gospel Herald*. Now Daniel Kauffman, *Gospel Herald*'s editor, was fifty-nine years old, about the age Funk had been in 1905. The editor of the new *Christian Exponent* was Vernon Smucker, who left his position as editor of the *Christian Monitor*, an official "old" Mennonite family and community paper, to accept his new role.

At age thirty-five Smucker was only a few years younger than Kauffman had been in 1905. If history were to repeat itself, a new generation would come to power and "old" Mennonite authority would shift away from Kauffman and Scottdale to new centers—perhaps to Bluffton in western Ohio. Daniel Kauffman and his generation of conservatives would not rest easily until this "anti-church publication," as Kauffman called it,[90] went out of business. There appears to have been an intergenerational struggle for power as surely as for orthodoxy and cultural stability.

The *Christian Exponent* was a mouthpiece for the "old Goshen" group—leaders who had studied at Goshen College before its closing and reorganization in 1923-1924. Among the writers were three former Goshen presidents (Noah E. Byers, John E. Hartzler, Irvin R. Detwiler), four former Goshen deans (C. Henry Smith, Paul E. Whitmer, Daniel S. Gerig, John J. Fisher), and many active Goshen alumni (including editors Vernon Smucker and Lester Hostetler, Harold S. Bender, Amos E. Kreider, and Chrissie Shenk). In their first two issues the editors laid claim to recent Mennonite history by publishing evangelist John S. Coffman's 1896 address "The Spirit of Progress."[91] Writers interpreted the Anabaptist heritage in liberal democratic terms, arguing that their sixteenth-century forebears had championed liberty of conscience over medieval Catholic despotism as surely as progressive Mennonites were now fighting against the unwarranted authority of bishops.[92]

In an effort to demonstrate the paper's orthodoxy and refute popular charges, editor Smucker stated a number of nondebatable theological points, the "principles of the Christian faith."[93] This list of fundamentals included Christ's deity, the atonement for sin, the new birth, the reality of punishments and rewards, and the "Bible as the authoritative revelation of God to man and the guide for the conduct of the believer." But Smucker had not used Fundamentalist code language. The theology of the *Exponent* was thoroughly moderate and evangelical. To be sure, careful study has revealed that many *Exponent* writers were influenced by the "liberal," "moral influence" view of Christ's atonement even as they also used the orthodox language of "substitutionary" atonement.[94] But the more radical challenge lay in the *Exponent's* sociocultural critique of their church and its leaders. Moreover, the new paper offered the church's youth an attractive alternative.

In September of 1928 the *Exponent* expired, before it was five years old. One reason it never established an alternative center of denominational power was that its editors had no clear plans to do so. They did not intend to absorb the *Gospel Herald* as the *Gospel Witness* had once absorbed the *Herald of Truth*. They never had a financial base equivalent to what the Loucks family had provided for the *Gospel Witness* in Scottdale. Many *Exponent* writers and sponsors were able to find new arenas for church work in the GC or Central Conference branches, while some decided to leave the Mennonites altogether. Vernon Smucker later joined the Presbyterians, albeit with a written proviso that let him continue to be a conscientious objector to military service.

Another reason for the *Exponent's* demise was that its program for progressive change was too far ahead of most of the "old" Mennonite church. With the nation's Protestants in an overheated Fundamentalist-Modernist debate, conservative Mennonites were ready to hear anti-Modernist attacks on progressives. In 1924 and 1926 John Horsch wrote two hard-hitting tracts which attacked the *Exponent* and the Bluffton-Witmarsum "traitors" by name. Although the controversy had little to do with Mennonites of Dutch-Russian background, even some of them responded favorably.[95] Horsch's intemperate attack helped alienate Bluffton from its established Central Conference and GC constituencies, hamstrung it from hoped-for support among "old" Mennonites, and gained time for Goshen College to reorganize on a more conservative basis. "Let us who believe in prayer not forget Goshen College," wrote Horsch.[96]

COLLEGE STRUGGLES

With its crosscurrents of theological and cultural issues, the Fundamentalist-Modernist controversy had varying consequences at the different Mennonite schools. Under a new president, Sanford C. Yoder, Goshen College did reorganize and offer a program convincingly "safer" than that of the discredited and scattered "old Goshen" crowd.[97] Bluffton College enjoyed considerable vitality in the 1920s, with its outstanding faculty and the presence of Witmarsum Seminary until it (Witmarsum) closed in 1931. After J. B. Smith's departure in 1917 Hesston took a moderate and conservative position. A leading intellectual force on its campus was a science teacher named John D. Charles, author of a booklet called *Fallacies of Evolution.*[98] At Eastern Mennonite School millennialist theories were strong, although an amillennialist named Chester K. Lehman kept a key post on the Bible faculty. Meanwhile, J. B. Smith resigned from the school's presidency rather than bow to insistence from George R. Brunk that he get rid of a piano in his home; in his place the institution appointed conservative evangelist Amos (A. D.) Wenger.[99]

In Kansas, Tabor College avoided a Fundamentalist-Modernist upheaval in the 1920s, in part by cultural isolation and theological restrictiveness. Nonetheless, it lost four teachers who had graduated there between 1912 and 1918 and had gone on to Yale Divinity School before returning to Hillsboro: M. H. Schlichting, Adolf Frantz, Abraham J. Harms, and Peter S. Goertz.[100] In 1919-1920 Bethel College underwent a major crisis which forced the resignations of four progressive faculty members and president John W. Kliewer. Liberal insurgents there seemed especially attuned to the "New Freedom" Progressivism of Woodrow Wilson and John Dewey. Following such leaders in World War I, they even seemed ready to compromise their nonresistance. In the troubled 1920s Bethel floundered.[101] More-

(*Sword and Trumpet*, April 1929, p. 13)

Cartoon from *Sword and Trumpet* magazine portraying concerns of anti-modernist Mennonites.

over, at no Mennonite college did biblical scholarship flourish. Mennonites were a deeply religious subculture, but their college science departments were usually stronger than their Bible and religion departments. Students learned quickly that the Bible was a contentious battleground; a career in Bible teaching was precarious. The conflicts of the day delayed Mennonites' coming seriously to grips with modern ways of Bible scholarship.

The impact of the Fundamentalist-Modernist upheaval on Dutch-Russian Mennonites in the West was different from its impact on their Swiss and south-German coreligionists in East and Midwest. That was because Mennonites of these two broad streams were at different points in their Americanization. As immigrants of more recent origin the Dutch-Russians had a less secure hold on America's religiocultural identity. During the war and in the 1920s they were still speaking German and were uneasy participants in a broader German-American ethnic cluster which the war had put to rout. The cultural supports of their *Gemeindechristentum*, of their "congregation Christendom," were shaking. Those supports lacked something which Daniel Kauffman and the *Bible Doctrine* synthesis had provided for "old" Mennonites and progressive Amish Mennonites: a coherent, English-language denominational system of thought and organization well adapted to American conditions. Thus a psychic and institutional crisis of Dutch-Russian Mennonites in the 1920s had its own shape and meaning.

For Mennonite Brethren life, a great religious revival at Hillsboro, Kansas, in January and February of 1922 signaled the dynamics of the postwar period. It was one of the first MB revivals in the English language. Its leading preacher was not a Mennonite but Reuben A. Torrey, creator of the first Bible institute curriculum at Moody Bible Institute in Chicago. Widely copied and adapted, Torrey's curriculum influenced various Mennonites, some who studied at Moody and others who attended Bible colleges in Minneapolis, Toronto, Los Angeles, and elsewhere. In 1920 Torrey was president at the Bible Institute of Los Angeles, and some ninety Mennonites were attending there.[102] In the same year, Tabor College president Henry W. Lohrenz met Torrey at the World's Conference on Christian Fundamentals in Chicago. The Fundamentals conference impressed Lohrenz more than did either some *Sunday School Times* contacts he had been cultivating or certain inter-Mennonite contacts he had made during and after the war.[103] So English-language revivalism did not come to the Mennonite Brethren from "old" Mennonites or their Mennonite-revivalist synthesis. It came quite directly from American Bible institute Fundamentalism.

Hillsboro's response to Torrey's messages was overwhelming. Crowds packed the halls, hundreds responded to the altar calls, and the evangelist spent hours counseling seekers. Various downtown businessmen supported a move to close the town's shops on a Friday morning so that everyone could hear a message on Jesus' resurrection. After Torrey's departure the harvest continued, with Mennonite evangelists Frank J. Wiens, J. E. Schmidt, and George P. Schultz leading the work. The *Tabor College Herald* for February counted a total of 214 converts with ten or twenty still seeking.[104] The publicity chairman of Tabor's YWCA reported that "every girl in our school is saved," and gave the names of the last eight to be converted.[105] MB editor John F. Harms wrote quite accurately that the revival marked "an epoch in Hillsboro's history."[106]

For the Mennonite Brethren, revival was the normal and desired means of renewal. For example the rural Ebenfeld MB congregation near Hillsboro had experienced major revivals in 1887, 1892, and 1907, each time harvesting fifty to sixty-seven souls.[107] But earlier evangelists had preached in German, and had been homegrown. Now in 1922 an English-speaking, non-MB evangelist was preaching. A religious leader who had supported America's role in the war was winning pacifists whose mother tongue was Low German. The war crisis, symbolized most dramatically in Hillsboro by the burning of the main Tabor College building, had made the shift in language urgent. The 1922 revival was like previous ones in that it transformed lives and brought renewed commitments. But this one also authenticated a certain Americanization. Some older German-speaking Hillsboro citizens resisted the transition. They used the town's newspaper to grumble about outside evangelists who came "in order to make us acquainted with the language of the country."[108] Some other citizens welcomed the revival but shifted the attention from individual to community salvation: "Oh, if it could happen that all unconverted souls in Hillsboro could be won for Christ. *Hillsboro für Christus!*"[109]

In Mennonite communities on the great plains after World War I, one sign of the shaken public self-confidence was that Mennonite newspapers did not comment very vigorously on public affairs.[110] The sign also showed a sharpening of two-kingdom-style separation. Before the war German-language editors such as A. L. Schellenberg, H. P. Krehbiel, and J. G. Ewert had offered constant counsel on leading political and social questions, including which state and national politicians to vote for. After the war these voices were subdued or silenced, and new ones rose in their places. In the 1920s Kansas Mennonites (the only group whose political behavior has been extensively researched) were less active in voting and local officeholding than before the war. Those Mennonites who did vote tended to support candidates whose platforms challenged regular party politics. Thus Kansas Mennonites voted in distinctive numbers for Progressive Robert LaFollette in 1924, aware of his antiwar stance of 1917-1918; for William Allen White's campaign against the Ku Klux Klan in 1924; and in 1930 for an independent candidate for governor, a quack doctor named John R. Brinkley.[111]

Mennonites also provided substantial support for the right-wing Fundamentalist Gerald B. Winrod, founder in 1925 of an organization called The Defenders of the Christian Faith.[112] Winrod's monthly magazine *The Defender* was job-printed on Mennonite presses, first at Hillsboro and then at Newton. Many Mennonites subscribed to the journal or heard Winrod preach in their churches. In the late 1920s and 1930s his preaching and writing became increasingly politicized, anti-Semitic, and pro-Nazi. To some Mennonites the outright bigotry was an embarrassment. Yet Winrod's influence revealed how postwar Mennonites—with their Anabaptist heritage, their rejection in the war, and their bitter experience with Soviet communism—could find a path through religion toward right-wing nationalism. Mennonite anticommunism, which eventually included some support for German National Socialism, or Nazism, was strongest among Mennonite migrants of the 1920s to Canada.[113]

American Mennonites of Dutch-Russian background did not respond to the influences of Fundamentalism in the same way as did those whose ancestry was Swiss and south-German. Some of the latter, particularly "old" Mennonites, made anti-Modernism work on behalf of Mennonite identity. For the Dutch-Russians the timing of the language transition, the war experience, and other stresses of cultural change in the 1920s made that strategy impossible. The Fundamentalisms of Winrod and Torrey and Scofield tended to fragment and erode the basis of Dutch-Russian Mennonite community identity.

Whatever the contrasts, nearly all Mennonites were caught in social and cultural transition. And in the transitions the controversy between Fundamentalists and Modernists troubled and complicated the processes of change. The language and spirit of anti-Modernism helped some conservative Mennonites to dig trenches and hold fast to what they thought were older ways. In fact, however, both those Mennonites who were proponents of anti-Modernism and those who espoused "progressive orthodoxy" were borrowing richly from American Protestantism. The denomination suffered divisive conflict at some levels, but vigorous advances on other lines. The success of the denominational advance depended in part upon Mennonite ability to recruit new leaders whose abilities would not be wasted upon destructive controversy.

10

LEADERS, WOMEN, PEACE

In 1920 when Warren G. Harding was elected to be U.S. president, Henry Peter Krehbiel grasped a hope for a new era of peace. Less than three years earlier some prowar outlaws had vandalized the bookstore and press of this pacifist editor in Newton, Kansas, and local officials had done nothing to find and punish the culprits. But now Krehbiel took heart that the president-elect's wife, Florence Kling Harding, was of Pennsylvania-German Mennonite descent (*Mennonitischer Abstammung*). Krehbiel hoped that through her husband she might be "a noticeable influence in the direction of peace."[1]

FRAU HARDING MENNONITISCHER ABSTAMMUNG

If Krehbiel saw that women indirectly helped to govern the nation, he saw the same for Mennonites. Ever since William Penn first brought Mennonites to America, descendants of these peaceable people had scattered to farms and cities across the land. With them had gone the "Mennonite view of life and direction of mind," which continued to have an influence even among those who had given up any Mennonite affiliation. So Krehbiel thought that Mennonites (along with the Quakers and Dunkers) were part of the reason for a deeply rooted tradition of antimilitarism among the American people. Perhaps Florence Kling Harding could make an important difference.[2]

The straw Krehbiel was grasping was a weak one. Whatever unknown marks of a Mennonite heritage she may have carried, the new first lady was estranged both from her Mennonite-descended father and from her philandering husband. Through no fault of hers, her husband's presidency turned out to be among the least reputable in American history.[3] Nonetheless, Krehbiel had touched upon three of the most important themes for Mennonites in the postwar era—the importance of leadership, the role of women, and the commitment to peace.

RECRUITING LEADERS

In the decades following World War I, not many Mennonites who had been drafted became denominational leaders.[4] Rather than preparing strong persons to lead, the difficult experiences in army camps or prisons seem to have alienated them from the church. Then came a time of conflict between progressive youth and their elders. The conflicts grew out of the peculiar conditions of the Mennonite subculture, but also from the American mood in the 1920s with its own conflicts between generations.

Many Mennonite youths caught in the World War I draft felt that their church had responded poorly. It had not prepared and supported its youth well enough in the war, and afterward it had not given them an adequate welcome back. Jacob C. Meyer, a feisty draftee of above average experience and education, complained of "how a man feels working under incapable leaders."[5] The war had been a great embarrassment for Mennonites, and the draftees' presence reminded people of the time of troubles. Psychologically, some draftees left home and never returned. Many others came home but kept their wartime experiences to themselves, often withholding their stories even from their wives, children, and grandchildren.[6] World Wars I and II were quite different in their effects upon Mennonite draftees. During World War II the Civilian Public Service program became a rich crucible for training new leaders. But being a World War I draftee was almost a death knell for future church leadership, especially in the large "old" Mennonite branch.

The dynamics of recruiting leaders in the 1920s were especially interesting in the cases of Orie O. Miller and Harold S. Bender. In the following decades these two men from Elkhart County, Indiana, made extraordinary contributions to the definition and organization of the denomination.[7] Both were graduates of the "old Goshen" (1915 and 1918 respectively). Both carried a Goshen-style vision for progressive church work. Both conflicted with older, conservative leaders. But both also had some special advantages.

Somehow, both Miller and Bender had escaped the draft.

Both were oldest sons in families well positioned in the church. Of course to be from the right family was no guarantee of Mennonite acceptability, and in each family there were members who struggled against Mennonites' prescriptive authority and eventually left the fold. But in the cases of Orie O. and Harold S., both had solid relationships with their fathers, who were denominational leaders. Miller's father, Daniel D. Miller, was bishop in the Amish Mennonite Forks congregation east of Goshen, moderator of the "old" Mennonite general conference, and officer on numerous important committees and boards. Bender's father, George L. Bender, had been a protégé of John F. Funk, was a pillar of the notable Prairie Street congregation in Elkhart, helped administer the "old" Mennonites' Board of Missions and Charities, and was active in other agencies and committees. Both sons made strategic, career-enhancing marriages. Bender married Elizabeth Horsch. College-educated, and daughter of John Horsch, Elizabeth Horsch Bender became her husband's highly effective editor and scholarly collaborator.[8] Miller married Elta H. Wolf, whose father took him on as a business partner. The thriving business, a shoe factory in Akron, Pennsylvania, in prosperous Lancaster County, gave Miller an economic base to pursue church work at will.[9] Meanwhile, neither Miller nor Bender was convinced that every official ordinance and restriction set forth in the "old" Mennonites' *Bible Doctrine* had a biblical basis. Their means for winning confidence and gaining space for leadership in the church were not mainly doctrinal.

Miller's and Bender's stories were remarkable in an era when the church and many of its most gifted young people were much at odds.

HAROLD S. BENDER

Bender's position was the more precarious. He deeply identified with and supported the youth movement which emerged among Mennonite postwar reconstruction workers in France. His father, knowing what a liability having been in the French unit could be, told Bender that he thanked the "dear Heavenly Father" that his son had not gone. "It looks," he said, "like divine intervention." Nevertheless, the young Bender became chairman of the Young People's Conference which held conventions in 1920, 1922, and 1923. In 1920 conservative Eastern Mennonite School teacher John L. Stauffer wrote a

Gospel Herald article criticizing the youth movement. Bender, then teaching at Hesston College, responded with a personal letter vigorously defending it and counterattacking Stauffer's premillennialist position. Thereupon Stauffer put the young man's future in jeopardy; he distributed Bender's letter, together with his own reply, to church leaders Daniel Kauffman and George R. Brunk—men who could make or break an aspiring young man's career in the denomination. Stauffer told Bender to decide which side he was on—the loyal conservatives or the disloyal liberals—and implied that Bender's unorthodox doctrinal positions should disqualify him from teaching at Hesston. Offended and trapped, Bender agonized—and drafted a statement sorting out his personal position on the question of regulated dress and separation from the world. In principle he rejected the case for regulated separate dress—yet he consented to wear the plain coat as a practical concession. He then wrote a long and carefully drafted and redrafted letter to Stauffer, asking that it be shared with all who had received the earlier exchange. For the future he requested the "courtesy accorded all personal correspondence."[10]

In his careful statement to church leaders Bender wrote that he was orthodox in doctrine and progressive in method. Among his points was a strong statement of faith which affirmed "the trinity of the Godhead, divinity and humanity of Christ, His substitutionary atonement and bodily resurrection, the supernatural divine and plenary inspiration of the Holy Scriptures with their supreme authority, [and] the authenticity and reality of the supernatural and miraculous." But Bender warned against a "dead orthodoxy" and accused Stauffer of ignoring the "love and service side of the Gospel." He said he wore the plain coat "because I choose to do so—under no compulsion and because the ["old" Mennonites'] General Conference and this school expects their teachers to wear it." He continued with a defense of the young men in France and argued for greater democracy in the church.[11]

Stauffer's response was defensive. He seems to have been somewhat intimidated by Bender's thorough arguments, and to have sensed a failure to discredit the younger man in the eyes of Kauffman and Brunk. Stauffer said that even though Bender had left out the term "verbal" (a key Fundamentalist code word) in describing biblical inspiration, his statement of faith was the clearest ever given by a graduate of Goshen. In passing this test Bender hit upon the formula which he would use in the future: a strong affirmation of evangelical fundamentals; a thorough counterattack against his opponents; and a blurring of the dress issue, by accommodating to church rules in practice while hiding or deemphasizing his dissent in principle.

From 1922 to 1924 Bender pursued graduate studies at Garrett Theological Seminary, Princeton Theological Seminary, and the University of Tübingen. While he and his bride were in Germany, word drifted back that Harold had grown a mustache and Elizabeth had worn a fancy hat instead of a prayer covering.[12] Despite the rumors the newly appointed president of Goshen College, Sanford C. Yoder, offered Bender a place on the purged and reconstituted Goshen faculty for the 1924-1925 school year.[13] Since Bender's reputation was shaky, Yoder's offer was for him to be a history teacher and librarian, not a Bible teacher—at least not until Bender might win the confidence of conservatives.[14] Yoder specified that to gain such confidence the couple should conform to the dress codes and write no more articles for the *Exponent*. Harold agreed, but under protest; and the two signed a statement that they would "work in harmony with the rules and regulations of the Indiana-Michigan Conference." Elizabeth later said that signing it was "half way against our conscience."[15]

Bender agreed to wear the plain coat but not to defend it publicly on biblical grounds. And he complained that to stop writing in the *Exponent* would cut him off from "most of the thinking people of the church and a lot of the young people who often pay little attention to the [Gospel] Herald."[16] Yoder, Goshen's president, was an Amish Mennonite from Iowa who had once planned a career as a lawyer—and who had accepted his new assignment reluctantly.[17] Now that he was president of the reorganized Goshen, he took quite a risk in recruiting Bender. His decision was vastly important for developing the next generation of leaders for Mennonites in America. In general, Yoder showed a great ability to keep reins on youthful progressives even as he gave them the encouragement and institutional positions they needed for their work.

Once settled at Goshen, Bender moved decisively and soon established a new base for Mennonite denominational renewal. He staked out middle ground, neither on the territory of the so-called liberals of Bluffton and the *Exponent* nor on that of the conservatives and the anti-Modernists. Rather than traditional

Bible doctrine, the ideological foundation for the renewal was to be Anabaptist-Mennonite history. At Princeton Seminary, especially from Professor J. Gresham Machen, Bender learned to appreciate a conservative (and amillennial) theology. But his studies in Europe drew him into a quest for the genius of sixteenth-century Anabaptism.

Bender believed that Anabaptist *history*, especially the Conrad Grebel and Swiss Brethren story, contained a central core of values and witness which could help modern Mennonites to revitalize. In history Bender could use modern methods of critical analysis which he dared not use in biblical studies (a field he had once considered). To dispute the authorship of Genesis or Isaiah was dangerous to one's reputation. To critically evaluate sixteenth-century documents was much safer. Throughout a brilliant career Bender simply ignored the thorny problems of biblical higher criticism. He sidestepped such questions, much as he sidestepped the issue of whether the Bible called for regulation attire.[18] By turning to history he bypassed the issues which Fundamentalists and traditionalists meant to pose.

Instead of addressing such questions, Bender turned his keen mind and prodigious energies to researching and documenting Anabaptist-Mennonitism, to developing a Mennonite historical society, to collecting books and documents, and to starting Mennonite-history publications, most notably *The Mennonite Quarterly Review*. He intended the *Review* to be an alternative to both the *Gospel Herald* and the *Christian Exponent*. In 1926, in its first issue, he wrote a ringing manifesto addressed "to the youth of the Mennonite Church." He called them to remain in his branch of the church and to attend his college. For, he said,

The coming generation in the Mennonite Church is being given a carefully built, well-knit, efficient organization of activities. This organization is the equal of that in any Mennonite group and is quite compact, has rich resources and experience behind it. It covers the field of publication, education, missions, Sunday School, church music, and church history. . . . The heritage of the coming generation in faith and practice is sound. The faith has been kept.[19]

As he established himself at Goshen, Bender gradually

moved away from his friends in the youth movement. Some began to mutter that he had betrayed their cause and fallen under the influence of his father-in-law John Horsch.[20] In 1926 he clearly broke with the progressives. His medium was a scathing ten-page review of a new book by J. E. Hartzler. Hartzler's *Education Among the Mennonites of America* was indeed flawed in its scholarship. But it also was a pioneering effort to bring the variety of Mennonite groups in America together into one history.[21] In it, to explain the problems of Mennonite education, Hartzler blamed conservative bishops. Bender's response was probably the most devastating and condescending sustained review of a Mennonite book any Mennonite scholar has ever written. The younger man had been Hartzler's student at Goshen College. In 1918 he had signed an unsuccessful petition to have that year's college yearbook be dedicated to Hartzler. But now his tone was different. He indicted this lapsed "old" Mennonite for misleading interpretations, historical errors, and extensive "minor inaccuracies."[22]

No doubt Bender's youth contributed to his lack of restraint. But surely the vigor of his attack also served a double purpose. At one stroke he defended the bishops against Hartzler's charges and counterattacked the Bluffton-Witmarsum ideal of winning united Mennonite support. Bender discredited Bluffton as a rival to Goshen and, among conservatives, secured his own reputation as an able opponent of the so-called liberals. John H. Mosemann, conservative bishop of Lancaster, wrote that in the East the review had been "received with joy." It seemed to Mosemann that "the good Lord has raised you up for a special purpose among us, a sort of John the Baptist, 'To prepare the way of the Lord and make His paths straight.' "[23]

By late 1926 Bender had gained confidence that Goshen could be the center for a 25-year, international, inter-Mennonite program of Anabaptist-Mennonite historical studies. The first priority would be to collect, edit, and publish Mennonite-history sources—"a sort of Corpus Mennoniticorum."[24] Until well into World War II, Bender's program remained hazy. No doubt it stayed that way due to the stresses of liberal-conservative quarrels, to economic depression in the 1930s, and to the incompleteness of Bender's own "Anabaptist vision." Moreover, it hit barriers on both sides. The premier Mennonite professional historian of the 1920s, C. Henry Smith of Bluffton, was under attack by Bender's father-in-law. Not surprisingly,

Smith claimed that among Bluffton's constituency it would be hard to arouse interest in a Goshen-directed historical effort.[25]

Conservatives could be equally adamant, as Bender learned in 1929 when he proposed that his historical series might include a history of Mennonite mission work by GC scholar Edmund G. Kaufman. The idea was bold, for it would have built a bridge between Goshen and Bethel colleges and between "old" Mennonites and western GC Mennonites. But church leaders at the Mennonite Publishing House in Scottdale vetoed it.[26]

Nonetheless, despite the barriers, in the 1920s Bender found an institutional base at Goshen and began to clear some intellectual space between the options the so-called liberal and conservative factions were offering. His effort would serve not only "old" Mennonites; eventually quite a few other Mennonites (and others) drew inspiration from Goshen's "Anabaptist vision."[27]

ORIE O. MILLER

Orie O. Miller's recruitment to church leadership was different from Bender's. So was his way of responding to conservatives who resisted his progressive ideas. But he was equally successful. In 1915, the year he graduated from Goshen College, Miller married Elta H. Wolf, a classmate, and moved to her home in Lancaster County, Pennsylvania. He hoped, in addition to joining his father-in-law's shoe firm, to become a minister and church leader like his father.

In 1918 he was in a class of seven candidates for ordination. To his deep disappointment, the lot, used among Swiss-background Mennonites so that God might make a direct choice, passed him by.[28] In the coming years he was in the lot twice again, and not chosen. Miller was a gifted leader. In a rational procedure he surely would have been selected. Instead, he became an active lay leader in new denominational institutions. For them, the recruiting of leaders had more place for individual initiative and human discernment of gifts. An effective administrator and businessman, Miller used his shoe business as an economic base to support extensive part-time church work in relief, missions, and mutual aid. His leadership in the Mennonite Central Committee, largest and most successful of the inter-Mennonite agencies, brought the MCC administrative headquarters to Akron, Pennsylvania, and to his own home property.

The thickets along Miller's path to leadership were not only the vagaries of the lot. He was an "old Goshen" progressive living among Lancaster conference conservatives. In the face of substantial traditionalist and Fundamentalist resistance he supported inter-Mennonite cooperation, association with the wider peace movement, and aggressive denominational organization for mission. "I am more convinced than ever that Orie is a dangerous man," wrote Bishop Mosemann to John Horsch in 1927. "That man gets machinery set in motion that will take some power to stop."[29]

The dangerous 1920s "machinery" which Miller helped organize and direct did indeed foster a lot of unsettling change. It included not only MCC but also the "old" Mennonite church's Peace Problems Committee and the Lancaster conference's Eastern Mennonite Board of Missions and Charities. Mosemann resisted mainly on two grounds. First, wider association with different groups of Mennonites and others would break down "old" Mennonite separation from the world. The next step would be compromises with Modernism. For example, in 1926 Mosemann demanded that Miller resign his post on the Continuation Committee of the Conference of Pacifist Churches. Second, Mosemann was a strong premillennialist who believed that efforts to improve the world through political and humanitarian activity contradicted the Bible and might even delay the return of Christ.[30] Mosemann's views suggested that Miller might face a conservative backlash. If he kept up his innovations, he might well "lose out in Lancaster County."[31]

Miller's approach to such criticism was more patient and irenic than Bender's, but equally unwavering. The young man submitted to criticism by withdrawing from the Continuation Committee of the Conference of Pacifist Churches and by openly admitting other transgressions against the separatist standards. Not a trained Bible scholar or theologian, he avoided disputes over doctrine and biblical interpretation. His language in writing to Mosemann was perfectly keyed to the "old" Mennonites' traditional ethos of humility:

> I am sure I want to do right, and try to serve obediently and submissively the Master and His Church. Will you pray for me that I may be kept more faithful and more watchful yes and more humbly submissive in life, attitude and mind? I appreciate the confidence that fellow workers

in the Church have and have had in me, and certainly pray that I may merit its continuance.[32]

Although submissive in word and demeanor (and clothing), Miller steadfastly continued to attend peace-organization meetings, urge the Peace Problems Committee to give an aggressive witness to government, and help lead the Lancaster conference to more effort in mission. One way was to attend and participate in ecumenical meetings as an unofficial "observer." That way he might satisfy both the organizations' desire for "old" Mennonite participation and the conservatives' insistence that Mennonites not be unequally "yoked." He must have been greatly disappointed in 1924 when the "old" Mennonites' Relief Commission for War Sufferers chose not to join with other Mennonite groups in a permanently based Mennonite Central Committee. But his style was not to lash out in anger or marshal a lot of persuasive arguments. Instead, he bided his time, kept his eye open for practical ways to proceed, and worked to gain the confidence of everyone involved. These techniques let him take advantage of changed situations or new crises—such as the 1929 events in the USSR which brought MCC back to life.

Lancaster conference congregations included other progressives, who looked to Miller for leadership. Still others, from Goshen or from other Mennonite conferences and groups in the Midwest and West, were eager to win Lancaster backing. (Conservatives tended to have greater bargaining power in Mennonite ecumenical discussions and decision-making because they did not need or desire such cooperation as much as the progressives did.) Miller's potent combination of personal and organizational gifts enabled him to bring Lancaster into wider inter-Mennonite cooperation and more aggressive denominational witness. That the progressive Mennonite Central Committee located its offices in the area of conservative Lancaster "old" Mennonite conference was quite an anomaly.

As for leadership, each different Mennonite group had its own style and techniques of recruiting and developing leaders—and of empowering and restraining them. Each had its own pattern of relationships between leaders of local congregations who dealt with daily life, and leaders of institutions and the total denomination who pursued visions for Mennonite peoplehood as a whole. The "old" Mennonites, in part because they had a semi-episcopal church polity, tended to produce leaders more influential and dominant than did the GC and the MB branches. It was common for the broader denominational leaders to find themselves nearer the margins than the centers of their traditions.[33]

Leaders such as Bender and Miller among the "old" Mennonites, John W. Kliewer and Samuel K. Mosiman among the GCs, and Henry W. Lohrenz and Peter C. Hiebert among the MBs, all learned certain ideas and techniques from the outside. However, they worked to graft their borrowings from the American environment onto a received Mennonite tradition they loved and wept for. Somehow, they hoped, the combination would renew and revitalize the Mennonite tradition. In the 1920s, more than in other decades, such leaders felt a sense of alienation (although apparently it was less acute than for leaders of many other American ethnic subcultures).[34] Mennonite leaders were in fact quite successful in forging a denominational synthesis of traditional and modern elements. For Bender and Miller this meant a transition from the Daniel Kauffman *Bible Doctrine* era to a new era of wider ecumenical and progressive concerns. One disciple of the new era, Paul Erb, has claimed that this shift had already taken place by 1925.[35] However, the fruits of the new leadership did not fully ripen until after World War II.

WOMEN IN THE TRANSITION FROM TRADITIONALISM TO DENOMINATIONALISM

The late nineteenth and early twentieth centuries' new denominational institutions offered new possibilities for leadership and public activity by some Mennonite women. Women whose mothers had been kept silent in church could now serve as Sunday school teachers, missionaries, college teachers, deaconesses, writers for religious periodicals, and activists in women's missionary societies. Yet such roles were carefully limited and circumscribed. In the 1920s the pace of change slowed. In some cases women leaders lost control of church-related activities to men. It became clear that denominational institutions and attitudes could be used not only to expand and redefine women's roles but also to set new limits. The mosaic of Mennonite groups produced no clear, single pattern for changing women's roles. In the late nineteenth and early twentieth centuries those groups which actively developed denominational institutions (especially "old" Mennonites, Amish Mennonites, GC Mennonites, and Mennonite Brethren) showed

(Mennonite Library and Archives)

Ann J. Allebach (1874-1918), ordained to the ministry in 1911 in the First Mennonite Church, Philadelphia.

a general pattern of development. At first, traditional patriarchy gave way to limited progressive change. Then came conservative counterdevelopments which checked such change. The pattern followed broader currents in American society.[36]

Traditional rural Mennonite and Amish society was built on an intricate blend of both "masculine" and "feminine" characteristics. On the one hand, Mennonites constituted a patriarchy in which men held all public positions and oversaw relations with the outside world. Mennonites read male priority in the Old Testament story of creation and in New Testament injunctions for women in the church to be subordinate and silent. On the other hand, Mennonites were a nonresistant community in which men as well as women were taught to be humble, submissive, and obedient. There were traditional informal sanctions against evidences of pride, exercise of power, or open pursuit of high position. It cannot be known for certain whether this ethos of humility, which was most pronounced in the Swiss-American groups, produced exceptional gentleness in male-female family relationships. Male power and priority surely had its uglier side. In 1917 one young Kansas Mennonite charged that "too often marriage is regarded as a license for sexual liberty, and the woman the slave of the man's desires."[37] Yet Mennonite males, socialized to nonaggressive behavior and denied the catharsis of military service, grew up in a subculture which moderated the "machismo" influences of American male violence and militarism.[38]

For both men and women, there was some tension between the new mood of progressive missionary and educational work and the traditional Mennonite values of humility and submission. Those once labeled the "quiet in the land" were now less quiet and more aggressive. As they changed, they shifted the meaning of obedience to Christ from a living of ordered relationships in community to working for heroic Christian causes.[39] "Every normally endowed person has something of heroic valor in his being," wrote progressive John W. Kliewer in a missions article of 1901. "He wants to be able to fight to win." Kliewer wrote of "missions battles" which would produce "missions heroes."[40] Women shared the rhetoric. In 1894 Barbara Sherk of Ontario called for "soldiers of Christ" who would be just as eager as volunteers for a "dangerous military expedition."[41] To Mennonite traditionalists such rhetoric and spirit could be doubly threatening. It placed women in new roles and it expressed an aggressive style that was new to Mennonites, men as well as women.

One of the most aggressive and talented of all Mennonite women before World War I was Ann Jemima Allebach. Originally from the GC Eden congregation at Schwenksville, Pennsylvania, she went to New York and became a scholar, schoolteacher, and church worker. Then in 1911 she requested ordination as a minister at the First Mennonite Church of Philadelphia. The church said yes. Her home pastor, John Wenger Schantz, preached the ordination sermon and explained that social customs of Bible times should not be used to confine women in the twentieth century.[42]

At Bluffton, Ohio, the 1911 triennial GC meeting took up the question of women's ordination. It was an issue, the conference said, "that seems to be approaching our people." J. W. Kliewer, newly appointed president at Bethel College, summarized the biblical arguments pro and con. He noted Old Testament judges and prophetesses (Deborah, Huldah, Miriam) and the role of women in the ministries of Jesus and the early church. The conference, he argued, should not judge severely against women ministers "in churches where the membership is largely composed of women and the work largely done by them." But Kliewer also concluded that the Bible, in both the Old and the New Testaments, did not allow woman "a position of commanding over man"; so he reasoned that women's ordination was "not biblical."[43]

There were no further ordinations. Allebach's occasional sermons were well attended, but she never became pastor of a Mennonite congregation. The First Mennonite Church of Philadelphia continued to be open to women's leadership. For half a year in 1929-1930 Mary E. Bakewell served the congregation in pastoral ministry.[44] But for rural and small-town Mennonite congregations the "approaching" matter would have to wait three generations or more.

For what, then, did women prepare when they flocked to Mennonite colleges? The numbers who attended were impressive. In typical years at Elkhart Institute and Goshen College from 1893 to 1930, women were 40 to 50 percent of the student body.[45]

To project a vision for such women's lives, progressive Mennonites tended to borrow images from American liberalism. The images did not reflect traditional understandings of community nor did they focus on careers as teachers, nurses, or missionaries. Instead, the central concepts were "motherhood" and "home." Those values surely were implicit in traditional Mennonite culture, but the progressives expressed them differently. Women needed education, they said, to provide high-quality nurture for the young children (boys), who would one day be responsible to build a better nation and world. In 1901 Olivia W. Good of Elkhart Institute made a fervent appeal for women's education. She said she expressed "natural and rightful longings" which hitherto had been crushed. But in her appeal she asserted that woman's "highest duty and her holiest position is in her home, through which she is really the ruler of the world."[46] J. E. Hartzler agreed. Expanding the rhetoric of an old adage, he said that "the power that moves the world is not in standing armies and navies; not in political bosses; not in millionaires but in the maternal hand that rocks the cradle at midnight."[47]

This image of an educated motherhood ruling the world by rocking the cradle not only justified women's attendance at college. It also reasserted that women's place was in the home, subordinate to men. "She has a mind of her own, as well as man," wrote progressive M. S. Steiner in 1899, "and minds are not to be crushed, but trained and educated." At the same time, however, Steiner also wrote: "America needs better homes and more of them, and any trade, or position, or calling that disqualifies a woman for domestic happiness and usefulness is a curse to the woman that enters it."[48] Single women who exercised genuine institutional initiative, such as Alma Doering of Congo Inland Mission or Katharina Schellenberg of the MB mission in India, had to be seen either as potential mothers or as exceptions to the ideal. Only in the deaconess movement was there a religiously approved role for single women. Restrictions on women came not only from traditionalists. Progressives also imposed limits as they tried to adapt Mennonite principles to the modern world.[49]

Lewis J. Heatwole, Virginia "old" Mennonite conference bishop and one of the founders of Eastern Mennonite School, referred to his wife, Mary A. Coffman Heatwole (sister of evangelist John S. Coffman), as "the queen of my home on earth." In an essay composed about 1908 Heatwole pictured woman as an idealized "connecting link between men and angels." Her role was to ennoble the man. "With her garments in white and her character unsullied, she stands as the balance in power that turns the very wellspring of a man's life into all ways of the true, the good, and beautiful things of this world."[50]

Such idealized images of women's purity, piety, and nobility stood over against alternative images of women as fallen and corrupted, victims of "lustful villains" in the cities. M. S. Steiner, acquainted with the city as founder of "old" Mennonite missions in Chicago and in Canton, Ohio, told of the awful fate of maidens who lost their purity and virtue.[51] J. E. Hartzler, acquainted with New York City through his year at Union Theological Seminary, gave space in his 1910 *Paths to Perdition* for graphic description of the ways unscrupulous men "spoiled" helpless women and led them downward from dance to drink to adultery. In a section on the "White Slave Traffic" Hartzler wrote that there were "four times as many immoral men as there . . . [were] women."[52] Steiner and Hartzler's books of modern moral exhortation borrowed the language of the Christian Endeavor Society, the Young Men's Christian Association, and the Evangelical Alliance. But they adapted such language by mingling it with Mennonites' favorite Scripture verses and preoccupation with regulated dress.

In 1906, also in a book of moral advice to Mennonite young people, Cornelius H. Wedel of Bethel College developed a similarly idealized image of woman.[53] A woman, he said, could benefit from education not only to become the object of the noblest interests of a man, but also to develop an elevated consciousness of her own worth.[54] As had Steiner, Wedel bemoaned modern tendencies for women to go into occupations inappropriate to their nature.[55] But Wedel's point of reference was German culture and literature rather than the American home or womanhood. In a list of good sources of information about marriage he cited eight German writers, including two literary works by Goethe.[56] He praised the depth of feeling of "our German people" in terms that reflected romantic German nationalism as surely as Steiner and Hartzler reflected American liberal democracy. The purity of German family life, Wedel said, contributed much to the honorable achievements of "our people" (*unserm Volk*) in history. Some critics complained that he slighted the Bible and quoted too much from poetry and novels. To them Wedel responded that his audience was already familiar with biblical foundations but needed excellent Christian literature for growth and development.[57]

Thus, whether they found their extrabiblical inspiration in American democracy or in German nationalism, progressive Mennonite leaders gave reasons for educating women. Yet they limited women's legitimate role to a newly idealized home or family.

Mennonite women provided a good share of the material which appeared in Mennonite newspapers and religious periodicals. Many unsigned community and church reports were from their pens. So were quite a few signed articles, and articles borrowed from other publications. The *Herald of Truth* of October 1892 was full of articles by women, and in one issue editor John F. Funk reproached men for allowing the women to seem "more earnest in the good work" and to appear "more spiritually minded." Referring to the "old" Mennonite "awakening" or "quickening," he said that men should be producing more "now that seeding time is over."[58] The fact was that in the *Herald of Truth* and its successor the *Gospel Herald*, the number of contributions by women was growing dramatically—from 42 in 1884, to 173 in 1904, to 360 in 1910. Around the turn of the century their articles mixed the traditional view of women's quiet virtue in church and family with the newer ideal of true womanhood and women's civilizing influence. But there was no deviation from the theme of women's submission to men, or from the importance of the prayer covering as symbol of submission.[59]

The most prolific of "old" Mennonite women writers was a schoolteacher and rural missionary in Missouri named Clara Brubaker. Between 1886 and 1927 she wrote some seventy-eight articles. In 1893 she was one of five women speakers at the first "old" and Amish Mennonite Sunday school conference held in the Missouri-Iowa district. A disciple and correspondent of evangelist John S. Coffman until he died in 1899, she attended Elkhart Institute in 1895-1896 and stayed more in the Mennonite mainstream than did the more aggressive Ann Allebach. In her remarks at that Sunday school conference she supported the evangelical plan of salvation but also emphasized simplicity, service, and nonresistance. She wanted both men and women to abide by high and uniform standards of Mennonite nonconformity to the world. From her experience at Elkhart Institute she boldly suggested that more be done to keep its Literary Society true to gospel simplicity. Yet, as was traditional for Mennonite men as well as women writers, she asked for pardon if she was wrong. Meanwhile, as the oldest daughter in her family she cared for her aging parents and did not marry until they died.

In 1925, at age fifty-five, Brubaker married John Shank, seven years her junior. The two did outstanding rural missionary work in the Ozarks.[60] After marriage her visible role, at least as a writer, declined, while her husband's writing and public leadership increased. Clara Brubaker stands for the legion of Mennonite women who willingly accepted subordination, yet found ways to put their talents to use in family, church, and community.[61]

Although women did not hold church positions over men, they could use moral power to challenge the bishops on specific issues. Barbara Freed of the Line Lexington congregation in the Franconia "old" Mennonite conference was an outspoken opponent of tobacco and alcohol. Offended that her bishop, Jonas Mininger, smoked cigars, Freed informed him that she would not take communion from his hand until he gave up his filthy habit. Mininger gave it up.[62] In some cases Mennonite women bent or bypassed church rules restricting their behavior. For example, in 1926 a male Mennonite in Pennsylvania's Lancaster County sent a newspaper clipping to an influential Franconia conference leader, Jacob C. Clemens. On it, unsure of whether to be alarmed, he had checked the names of fifteen female Mennonites who had attended a meeting of the "Society Farm Women" in the town of Paradise.[63] Conservatives held that both men and women should avoid the unequal yoke and stay away from farm organizations, labor unions, and other worldly association.

There also were families in which the wife had a stronger personality than the husband. In 1919 Noah Byers of Bluffton visited one such family in behalf of a proposed Union Mennonite Seminary. Reflecting later, he observed that even though the husband would not commit himself to attend an upcoming meeting, his wife was obviously interested. He was quite sure she would see that her husband attended.[64]

As for women's suffrage, Mennonites had double reason for not supporting it: their religious views regarding women's subordination and their traditional avoidance of politics. In 1917 two "old" Mennonite conferences, Alberta-Saskatchewan and Missouri-Iowa, adopted resolutions against women voting.[65] In the *Gospel Herald* Daniel Kauffman agreed.[66] The *Christian Exponent* at its outset in 1924 listed four women on an editorial staff of sixteen, a female contingent unprecedented for Mennonite periodicals. Yet despite its liberal or insurgent flavor the *Exponent* carried surprisingly few articles on women's rights.[67] In the more liberal GC branch, women's suffrage received more attention. In 1911 Clara Rupp Welty, former piano and organ teacher at Bethel College, argued that women voters could help protect family life and the home. In any case, she wrote, "a woman's place is at the side of a man, not beneath him."[68] In 1912 female suffrage was up for vote in Kansas, Christian E. Krehbiel, editor of *Der Herold*, drew attention to the achievements of women such as Marie Curie, Florence Nightingale, and Anna Howard Shaw and endorsed female suffrage.[69] *Der Herold* correspondents wrote on both sides of the issue.[70]

Financially, a few Mennonite women who inherited or accumulated property and money made significant individual contributions to the church and to developing church institutions. In 1907 the *Bluffton* [Ohio] *News* reported that the late Louisa Kunkleman Wohlford Snavely had contributed more than $50,000 to the church.[71] At Hillsboro, Kansas, Mary J. Regier contributed savings of $20,000 to build a dormitory for women at Tabor College, where she became the first matron in 1920.[72] In nearby Newton in 1910 Wilhelmina Eisenmayer Warkentin, widow of the wealthy Mennonite-turned-Presbyterian entrepreneur Bernhard Warkentin, funded a building for the Bethel Deaconess Society. In 1916 she paid to have it enlarged. She was the society's largest donor.[73]

In the postwar years the "old" Mennonites' Board of Missions and Charities moved to extend organizational control over the Mennonite Woman's Missionary Society (MWMS). The MWMS had been founded by Clara Eby Steiner in 1911-1912 as an independent women's organization for financial and material support of missions and women's education. When the board began trying to extend control, the women sensed a threat and for a time managed to stall a proposed new constitution. That was in 1920. But by 1926 they acquiesced as the board took over local sewing societies, which were the bases of the MWMS organization. In 1929 the board created a central sewing circle committee under its own jurisdiction, and the independent MWMS went out of existence.[74]

A denomination which was ideologically committed to women's subordination had little place for a separate organization in which women exercised executive authority and handled large funds. In fact, however, the denominational board undermined the MWMS more for organizational than for antifeminist reasons. The men who engineered the takeover, particularly the board's executive secretary, S. C. Yoder, had in mind more centralized and more efficient organization. There were bureaucratic reasons for change, much as in the Presbyterian church. In 1922 that denomination restructured its boards and agencies, and in doing so absorbed an independent Woman's Board of Home Missions.[75]

Clara Eby Steiner and her friends were victims of "old" Mennonite reorganization in the 1920s. Carried out by the Daniel Kauffman generation, the reorganization not only co-opted the women's organization but also reconstructed Goshen College, phased out the relief commission, disciplined and excluded change-minded congregations, and successfully opposed the Young People's Conference and the *Christian Exponent*. In other Mennonite branches also, the 1920s were a time of conservative consolidation rather than of progressive change. A side effect was that the times were not friendly to women's organizations or to radical changes in women's roles.

POSTWAR PEACE ISSUES

In the 1920s the Mennonites groped to reorient on issues of war and peace. The great war been a powerful lesson which taught that even in America, the land of freedom, pacifists needed to be prepared for war crises. Mennonites resolved never again to be caught unaware. Preparation for another war required that the different groups of Mennonites work together, and together define policies and programs for wartime conscientious objection. Working together implied some degree of consensus on the essentials of Mennonite peace doctrine. Yet the postwar era was scarred by inter-Mennonite tensions and intergenerational hostilities which made such cooperation difficult.

Moreover, leaders of the major Mennonite groups disagreed among themselves. How closely should Mennonites relate to the broader secular and religious peace movement in the country? How far should the Mennonite peace position move beyond basic refusal to do military service? Should Mennonites urge the U.S. government to turn away from militarism and armaments? Cluttering such questions was the fallout from controversy between Fundamentalists and Modernists. By 1930 some new Mennonite positions and realignments were emerging. On issues of conscription the trend was toward cooperation among Mennonite, Quaker, and Church of the Brethren groups—the three "historic peace churches," which together had provided a large majority of the conscientious objectors during the war. In addition, some Mennonite groups made a limited "witness" to government through letters and statements which expressed earnest moral concerns on peace issues—although even such statements showed little interest or capacity for effective "political" action.

In the early 1920s Mennonites who wanted to cooperate on war-peace issues converged especially in two inter-Mennonite agencies. However, neither agency had enough authority to make much progress. Later, during and following World War II, MCC would be a major vehicle for inter-Mennonite effort on peace issues; but in the 1920s its scope was more narrowly relief. The second agency was an All-Mennonite Convention—whose first meeting had been in 1913, at Berne, Indiana. Five meetings between 1919 and 1930 provided opportunities for progressives to appeal for cooperation and rally inter-Mennonite interest. While they spoke of education, missions, publications, and relief, the progressives especially emphasized peace issues.[76] In 1913 conservative Daniel Kauffman had addressed the meeting, but thereafter he stayed away. He decided that "through the emphasis on 'unity' " such meetings "foster the spirit of compromise," and did so "at the expense of things which are essential."[77]

After the war the All-Mennonite Conventions called for greater attention to the "historic principles of nonresistance" and for opposing "the use of government mail service for the advertising [*sic*] of Citizens Military Training Camps." They also favored causes such as "the unification of our church papers."[78] Mennonite speakers dominated the programs; yet in 1925 Frederick J. Libby of the National Council for the Prevention of War addressed the group, and in 1930, Clarence E. Pickett of the American Friends Service Committee. The meetings could not take decisive action because they were nonofficial. Many of the meetings' key leaders and speakers were "old Goshen" people, notably C. Henry Smith, Noah E. Byers, Amos E. Kreider, and Lester Hostetler. Such persons were not likely to attract the cooperation of "old" Mennonite leaders. In 1930 Lester Hostetler blamed "entrenched leadership" for blocking progress toward unity—a charge not likely to please any group's established leaders.[79] To be successful, inter-Mennonite proposals would have to come from persons not so scarred by the 1920s' theological and cultural battles.

How much should Mennonites cooperate with pacifists outside the historic peace churches? For some decades before war, progressive Mennonites had been developing such contacts. In the 1890s John F. Funk had been a member of the Christian Arbitration and Peace Society and had, of course, served as an official representative at the World's Peace Congress in Chicago.[80] In 1906 the wider peace movement honored Noah Byers for efforts toward an Intercollegiate Peace Conference.[81] World War I decimated the peace movement. And because so many worldly pacifists abandoned the peace stance once their nation was involved, the war reinforced Mennonite mistrust. However, the 1920s saw the American peace movement come back to life with scores of new religious and secular groups.[82] In 1923 a Commission on the Coordination of Efforts for Peace listed 71 peace organizations operating in the United States—33 international ones and 38 local ones—plus many other groups, including the Mennonites, who had peace committees or sections.[83]

Mennonites were particularly active in the Conference of Pacifist Churches. The organization began in 1922 at Bluffton, Ohio, and continued with yearly meetings through 1929 before losing momentum in the early 1930s.[84] It included religious pacifists from groups other than Mennonites, Church of the Brethren, and Quakers. Because quite a few of its participants seemed theologically "liberal," John Horsch of Scottdale and John H. Mosemann of Lancaster actively opposed "old" Mennonite involvement. The critics had some limited success. In response to Mosemann's protests, Orie O. Miller declined to serve on the conference's Continuation Committee. But he still attended the meetings and received mailings from various pacifist organizations.[85] Even John Horsch attended a 1926 meeting of a "World Alliance for International Friendship Through the Churches" and found it "eminently worthwhile"—although he did not want his attendance to be known in Mennonite churches.[86]

In mid-decade the GC and the "old" Mennonite general conferences each appointed a new peace committee or reorganized an old one to become more aggressive for peace education and witness. In the committees' early years no college leader or teacher from Goshen, Bluffton, or Bethel served on these committees. Apparently, lack of college connections made such activity more acceptable in the congregations. Two members of the GC committee, Henry Peter Krehbiel of Newton and Andrew J. Neuenschwander of Philadelphia, disagreed about agenda.[87] Neuenschwander, who was the more activist and ecumenical, urged Mennonites to write letters to U.S. representatives to support the antiwar Kellogg-Briand Pact (signed by the United States and various other nations in 1928) and to oppose further construction of battleships. He also wanted to keep in contact with such groups as the Committee on Education for Peace.[88] Krehbiel in turn warned against becoming too political, and was quite concerned that the Committee on Education for Peace was associated with the Federal Council of Churches. But Krehbiel also was an activist in his own way. He attended and addressed numerous pacifist meetings and kept in touch with such agencies as the American Civil Liberties Union. The ACLU took up the case of Martha Graber, a French Mennonite immigrant of Lima, Ohio, who had been refused citizenship due to her pacifism.[89]

In their own separate camps, neither the progressive nor the conservative Mennonites agreed on a coherent theological basis for peace witness. John H. Mosemann was a premillennialist who believed wars would continue "until the end of this dispensation, when he [Jesus] himself will come."[90] John Horsch grounded his peace ideas not in millennialism but in a distinction between "pacifism," a dangerous movement for world improvement outside of Christ, and "nonresistance," the true teaching which was both biblical and Anabaptist.[91] Henry J. Krehbiel, chairman of the GC Board of Publication, was an enthusiastic pacifist who called for an aggressive Mennonite contribution toward the "abolition of war."[92] Henry Peter Krehbiel, a prewar progressive who had served a term in the Kansas State House of Representatives, preferred the term "amity" to either "pacifism" or "nonresistance." Unlike the premillennialists, Krehbiel believed in the power of education (specifically education in Christ) to turn the world away from war. But like many premillennialists, he rejected political solutions and insisted that peace depended upon the transformation of the heart.[93]

So neither camp put forward a clear Mennonite theology of peace. Peace-minded individuals and committees moved forward pragmatically within the boundaries their constituencies set. The issues came to focus only later, when the coming of another war and another conscription crisis forced them on the churches.

Late in 1927 Henry Peter Krehbiel returned from a world tour quite enthused with a new vision: Let there be an international peace coalition of "Non-Resistant Old-Evangelical Groups."[94] He had learned that Waldensians in Italy and elsewhere were "definitely returning to the position of practical Christian Non-Resistance." Also interested were some Dutch Mennonites, English Quakers, and others. The name "Old-Evangelical" was an echo from historian Ludwig Keller's designation for sixteenth-century radical movements, notably Anabaptism, and for earlier ones such as Waldensianism. Eventually, however, Krehbiel chose the name "Historic Peace Churches."

In 1929, apparently acting privately rather than as a member of the GC Peace Committee, he sent out an "Overture to the Historic Peace Groups of the World." It seemed to him that

(Mennonite Library and Archives)

Henry Peter Krehbiel (1862-1940), General Conference Mennonite editor and church leader.

"among Christian people at large" there was an "increasing sway of the Spirit of Jesus." The movement was bringing new freedom to "absolutist followers of Jesus" and new opportunity for united peace action. A theological basis for cooperation would be the Apostles' Creed and Jesus' teaching of love of enemy. Although the movement would be nonpolitical, a major aim would be to secure "unity of procedure in time of stress."[95]

Krehbiel's "overture" received only a polite but lukewarm response. Moreover, economic depression and the death of his wife, Matilda Kruse, stalled the plan. In the early 1930s he revived it, with its international intentions trimmed. The result was a new incarnation of the inactive Conference of Pacifist Churches. The first Historic Peace Churches meeting, held in Newton, Kansas, in 1935 at Krehbiel's invitation, laid groundwork for peace church cooperation in World War II.[96]

Mennonite progressives never realized their optimistic pre-World War I dreams of putting their denomination in the vanguard of a national and world peace movement. In the 1920s, to act even as mildly as to write a few polite propeace letters to public officials, Mennonite peace committee leaders had to circumvent their watchful constituencies. The eventual choice of Mennonites to work with peace groups of *historic* tradition suggested a conservative outcome for a generally conservative decade. During the decade there was a good deal of casting about for alternatives. Although no Mennonite fashioned a convincing peace witness theology, various contacts with the broader peace movement at home and overseas did lay effective groundwork for proposals that eventually produced the Civilian Public Service program in World War II. That program satisfied the needs of religious conscientious objectors far better than did the draft system of World War I.

CHAPTER
11

IRONIES OF ACCULTURATION
AND ACHIEVEMENTS OF AN
EMERGING DENOMINATION

On July 30, 1893, the Sunday after John S. Coffman heard evangelist Dwight Moody preach near the Chicago World's Fair, Edward M. Yoder was born some seven miles northwest of Kalona, Iowa, south of Iowa City.[1] His parents, Mahlon T. and Mary C. (Yoder) Yoder, were members of the Lower Deer Creek Amish congregation, a congregation still in fellowship with the Old Order Amish but more or less shifting to the Amish Mennonites.[2] Thirty-six and a half years later, on January 2, 1931, Edward Yoder made his first entry in a personal diary. By then he was in Kansas, living at Hesston and serving as dean and acting president of Hesston College.[3] Although a brilliant scholar of classical languages, he was publicly shy. Yet in his diary he wrote boldly—too boldly for public eyes. There he left a fascinating chronicle and analysis of the Mennonite church he loved, worked for, and grieved over.

EDWARD M. YODER

In his brilliance Yoder captured a central irony of "old" Mennonite church development: The heirs of John S. Coffman worked hard to achieve a faithful, biblical simplicity and nonconformity to the world—yet had created a denominational system which unmistakably conformed to main currents of American life. A quiet and humble people trying to preserve the genius of their peoplehood had pursued a "feverish craving for organization, the multiplication of boards, etc." Yoder noted in 1931:

The generation now growing up is being taught to think of Christian activity and of witnessing for Christ solely in terms of organized boards and authorized committees, a conception that is sure to be deadening to the idea of personal responsibility. Can it be a good sign for the perpetuation of our ideals of simple obedience to God and the simple guidance of His Spirit when even church leaders seemingly think of problems and their solution in terms of special committees and conference legislation rather than in terms of prayer and the leading of the Spirit?[4]

In his complaint Yoder had his eye on the General Problems Committee which the "old" Mennonites' general conference had created in 1929.[5] Chaired by none other than Daniel Kauffman, the committee seemed to be moving toward a "specific and detailed program of discipline." The purpose was to control the church's drift in many areas—dress, amusements, secret societies, insurance, paid ministry, school problems, and more.[6] But the General Problems Committee did not seem to notice that the very means of regulation might also be a form of worldliness. Yoder's critique reflected both his Amish heritage and his personal experience. The Amish had always been more congregational and less inclined to centralized institutional authority than had the "old" Mennonites. Amish conferences were truly advisory and not legislative. Even the plain coat was something many Amish Mennonites had to adopt as they merged with Mennonites. At the University of Iowa in 1923-1925 and the University of Pennsylvania in 1925-1926, Yoder found that his plain coat, intended by its advocates to open opportunities for witness, mistakenly stamped the wearer as a clergyman. He wore it without joy. It seemed to interfere with his own ideal of "touching other lives in a positively uplifting manner."[7]

As Yoder watched Mennonite anti-Modernists, he was both amused and chagrined. They were so earnest in their quest for biblical truth, yet their reliance on stated propositions and proof texts buried the profounder knowledge in a mountain of literal "facts." Those who relied on proof texts ignored historical context, he wrote, "using the Bible as a book of oracles much in the same spirit that ancients used the Sibylline Books at Rome. . . ."[8]

Whatever its pagan antecedents the proof-text method could be immensely popular with students. When master-proof-texter J. B. Smith rejoined the Hesston faculty in 1928, Yoder observed that students fell "at his feet in awe and wonderment." But the adoration did not last. Yoder perceived that students "began to sense the stifling smallness of his horizon and to become encouragingly aware of his limitations."[9] Nonetheless, Yoder was cautious, for "in the hands of the unspiritual" the historical and critical method of interpretation could be dangerous. So Hesston's classicist preferred a "judicious combination" of the historical and the propositional.

Where the Mennonite way was to be extremely straightforward, Yoder had a rare appreciation for irony. He was, after all, a reader of Greek and Latin classics. Even as he penned his thoughts about Mennonite foibles he spent spare time reading *The Metamorphoses of Lucius Apuleius*—a book remarkable, he noted, "for its rather artistic presentation of foolishness and nonsense."[10] Yet apart from his diary Yoder did not carry the ironic mode over into his Mennonite world. As a Mennonite teacher, administrator, and writer he contributed seriously and purposefully to Mennonite goals of Christian discipleship and nonresistance. His mastery of Latin made it possible for him to provide accurate scholarly translations of Anabaptist documents.[11] He wrote excellent Sunday school literature for congregations, which had no place for irony. Meanwhile, he took special interest in Anabaptist founder Conrad Grebel as a fellow humanist. Unlike historian Harold S. Bender (who used Yoder's translations for his own Anabaptist research), Yoder welcomed the notion that humanism may have influenced Anabaptist origins. Yet he modeled himself not after the zealous Grebel but after the Catholic reformer and ironist Desiderius Erasmus.[12]

In 1945, before his fifty-second birthday, Yoder died of cancer. A Mennonite historian eulogized him as one among "the men who become peers in the halls of Athens and who do not forsake the courts of Jerusalem."[13] Like many Mennonite leaders Yoder indeed lived in two worlds. He carried a vision informed by classical scholarship and interpretation, yet he accepted the task of building up the Amish and Mennonite people in biblical faithfulness. In his personal diary the classical themes were prominent. In his public teaching and writing he reinforced the foundations of the Mennonite Zion, even as his understanding of the church remained more Amish than Mennonite.

DENOMINATIONAL GROWTH

If membership growth was a significant measure, the Mennonite Zion had great vitality into the 1930s. Special decennial surveys of religious bodies done by the U.S. Census Bureau show that between 1906 and 1936 the Mennonites in the United States more than doubled their numbers, going from 54,798 to 114,337.[14] Examination of a growth chart of Mennonite groups (see below) reveals significant patterns.

1. The largest Mennonite groups generally enjoyed healthy membership growth, characteristic of a take-off stage in denominational development. In the three decades five of the six largest bodies ("old" Mennonite, GC Mennonite, Mennonite Brethren in Christ, Mennonite Brethren, and Central Conference of Mennonites) each more than doubled its membership. Among smaller groups the patterns of growth or decline were less uniform. Actually, numbers for the smaller traditionalist groups, especially the Hutterites and the old-order fellowships, are not reliable. Those who intentionally separated themselves from the world did not bother with prideful statistics of membership. In 1936 the Census Bureau confessed that its returns were not complete, and its words must have applied especially to the groups most separated from the world. The Hutterites and the Old Order Amish probably grew more rapidly than statistics suggest.[15]

Membership of Mennonite Bodies

	1906	1916	1926	1936	% rural
Swiss and south-German					
Predominantly Mennonite:					
"Old" Mennonite*	18,674	34,965	34,039	46,301	84.5%
Reformed Mennonite	2,079	1,281	1,117	1,044	83.0
Menn. Breth. in Christ	2,801	4,737	5,882	7,841	47.6
Old Order Mennonite	655	1,608	2,227	1,822	94.7
Stauffer Mennonite	-	209	243	161	-
Predominantly Amish:					
Old Order Amish	5,043	7,665	6,006	9,887	94.2
Amish Mennonites**	7,640	-	-	-	
Conserv. Amish Menn.	-	1,066	691	2,538	94.8
Central Conf. of Menn.	1,363	2,101	3,124	3,434	76.3
Evang. Menn. church	967	854	1,060	1,432	96.5
Other:					
Hutterian Brethren (Hutterites)	982	700***	501***		95.0
Dutch-Prussian-Russian					
Mennonite Brethren	1,825	5,127	6,484	7,595	76.9
Krimmer Menn. Breth.	708	894	797	1,283	85.9
Evang. Menn. Breth.	545	1,171	818	1,184	65.5
Kleine Gemeinde	-	171	214	275	76.3
Swiss-Dutch combined					
Gen. Conf. Menn. Ch.	11,661	15,407	21,582	26,535	78.9
Holdeman	562	1,125	1,832	2,024	98.1
Unidentified or Unaffiliated	-	-	348	480	-
Total	54,523	79,363	87,164	114,337	

*Affected by absorption of Amish Mennonites.
**Largely merged with "old" Mennonites from 1916 to 1927.
***Affected by mass movement to Canada.

(From United States Department of Commerce Bureau of the Census, *Religious Bodies: 1936* [Washington: Government Printing Office, 1941].)

2. The chart reveals that there were no schisms in the larger Mennonite bodies, and little proliferation of Mennonite groups in these decades. Two of the apparently "new" groups on the chart, Stauffer Mennonites and the Kleine Gemeinde, had in fact begun many years earlier, in the nineteenth century, but had been missed in the census of 1906. The most important new Amish groups to appear in these decades were the Conservative Amish Mennonites, organized in 1910, and the Beachy Amish, who slowly took shape after 1927. As we have seen, in 1927 there was also an "automobile split" among the Old Order Mennonites of Lancaster County, Pennsylvania. Even so, the four decades from 1890 to 1930 brought fewer schisms and new groups than did many other four decades in American Mennonite history. Proliferation among small groups was more than balanced by the consolidation of the larger ones, especially the merger of the "old" and Amish Mennonites.

3. The numerical strength of the Mennonite groups in relationship to each other remained quite stable. Together, the two largest groups ("old" and GC Mennonite) held a gradually increasing majority of the total membership—up from 55.6% in 1906 to 63.6% in 1936. Taken by itself, the GC percentage of the Mennonite total rose from 20.4% in 1906 to 23.2% in 1936. The "old" Mennonites increased from 34.4% in 1906 to 40.4% in 1936, primarily because they absorbed most Amish Mennonites. Between 1916 and 1926 "old" Mennonite numbers temporarily declined, reflecting the crisis in that body immediately after World War I. After 1906 the Amish Mennonites disappeared from the chart, claimed by the "old" Mennonites, even though the Eastern Amish Mennonite conference was separate until 1927.

4. The census records do not sort out members by European origins and so do not provide a basis to calculate accurately a ratio of Swiss- to Dutch-background Mennonites. But apparently between a quarter and a third of the total were Dutch, and Dutch-origin Mennonites were increasing at about the same rate as the Swiss. However, in North America as a whole, a migration of Dutch-Russian Mennonites from the USSR to Canada in the 1920s increased the proportion of Dutch to Swiss. (After World War II the proportion of Dutch-Russians would jump again with another such migration.) Lively interchange continued among Dutch-Russian cousins in the faith, extending the community dynamics of "congregation Christendom" across the Canadian-U.S. border.

5. The data offer some indication of both the extent and the limits of Mennonite diaspora. For example, by 1936 the "old" Mennonites had at least one congregation in each of twenty-seven different states of the union. But the heartland settlements of Pennsylvania and the Midwest still dominated. In 1936 44.4% of "old" Mennonite church members lived in Pennsylvania and another 26.6% lived in Ohio, Indiana, and Illinois. Together these four states had 71%. The Old Order Amish had an even higher concentration: 77.9% in those four states. The General Conference Mennonite church had 32.4% of its members living in Kansas. Members outside of Kansas were more evenly scattered, with more than a thousand members dispersed in Pennsylvania, Ohio, Indiana, Minnesota, South Dakota, Nebraska, Oklahoma, and California. The smaller groups tended to be more concentrated. In 1936 the Mennonite Brethren had 87.9% of their 7,595 members in the three states of Kansas, Oklahoma, and California. They were the only group for whom California was the state with the highest membership.

6. In 1936 the overall percentage of Mennonites living in rural areas was 82%. (Rural areas, according to the census, were townships or municipalities with a total population of less than 10,000.) By way of comparison, in 1930 the rural percentage of the whole U.S. population was only 52.5.[16] Mennonites remained a rural people. Yet they were being urbanized in many ways. In 1930 Peter P. Wedel, president of the GC Mennonites, visited Eastern District churches in Pennsylvania and was astonished at how scattered were their members compared to those in congregations he knew in Kansas. Some people living twenty and thirty miles from Philadelphia actually commuted to work in the city, Wedel wrote, and congregations had to publish church newsletters to keep their members informed.[17]

Other Mennonites noted that modern developments in transportation, communication, and industry were bringing the city to the country. "The country has become urbanized," wrote Joseph B. Cressman, a businessman in the East in 1930. Telephones, automobiles, and radios provided access to urban life, while modern agricultural equipment caused farmers to depend more and more on urban suppliers and markets. Cressman thought that "old Mennonite community life . . . has almost disappeared." His judgment may have been too sweeping for 1930, but it signaled the way of the future for all but the old-order churches. Old-order folk were willing to pay the costs of resisting or at least moderating and controlling the shifts to new technologies.[18]

THE DENOMINATION ABOUT 1930

Missions. As the 1920s ended, no cause captured the Mennonite imagination more than did overseas or foreign missions. In church periodicals, missionaries in India, China, the Congo, Argentina, and other countries gave detailed reports of their work, often in special issues or supplements. Other authors also wrote on missions. The year 1930 was the fiftieth anniversary of the first organized Mennonite mission work—a mission to Cheyenne and Arapaho Indians in what was later Oklahoma. GC Mennonites celebrated by publishing a history, a common medium Mennonite institutions adopted to mark important anniversaries. Anna Hirschler (Mrs. G. A.) Linscheid wrote the history in German, the first language of nearly all the missionaries since the work began.[19] In her summary she emphasized four achievements: missionaries sent, stations established, converts won, and literature translated.

GC missionaries had baptized a total of 512 American Indians. Many baptisms had occurred shortly before death, and many other new Christians strayed away; so the number of living Cheyenne and Arapaho Mennonite Christians was only 270. Missionary linguist Rodolphe Petter had reduced the Cheyenne language to writing and published chapters of the Bible, *Pilgrim's Progress*, a songbook, and other literature in Cheyenne. In 1930 the American Bible Society published Petter's Cheyenne translation of the Acts of the Apostles.[20] Petter himself reflected optimistically despite the apparently small number of converts. If missionaries in India and China had won as high a proportion of their native populations for Christ as was true for the Cheyenne, he wrote, China would have eighty million Christians and India sixty million.[21] Petter had strong faith in the ultimate triumph of God's Word. Translation of Scripture contributed to the divine plan.

Another missions milestone of 1930 was the arrival of the first overseas Mennonites to train in an American college. James Chung-fu Liu and Stephen Hsin-fu Wang, teachers at a Mennonite school at Kai Chow in China, had spent the previous two years at the Christian University of Peiping. Now in 1930 they enrolled for a term at Bluffton College and then at Bethel. Former China missionary Edmund G. Kaufman, then teaching at Bluffton, acclaimed Liu and Wang's arrival as "evidence of the new day in missions."[22] He believed that as the national demands for self-determination escalated, mature and educated Mennonite overseas leaders would transform the relationship between sending and receiving churches. National churches would help decide how to spend missions funds and help shape the work and choose missionaries. Already the Mennonite church in China had asked to be represented on the sending board.[23]

In 1930 also, the Lancaster conference, a relative latecomer to overseas mission work, decided it would start its own missions in Africa.[24] In addition to its numerous home missions projects, the Lancaster board had been sending money for mission work in India and Argentina sponsored by the Elkhart-based Mennonite Board of Missions and Charities—that is, by the "old" Mennonites' general, denominational board. This support gradually increased during the 1920s, reaching $6,000 to $7,000 for the India mission during 1930, even though Lancaster conference bishops were increasingly critical of the central board's missionaries in India.

In May 1930 the bishops challenged the central board to answer a list of ten issues regarding the India mission. They were concerned that ten of the fourteen ordained missionaries in India had been trained at Goshen College before its re-organization, that is, in what the bishops considered to be a school tainted with Modernism. The bishops also feared the mission emphasized institution-building, especially schools, at the expense of evangelism. Furthermore, missionaries had close associations with non-Mennonite missionaries and agencies. They also believed that Indian Christian women should wear distinctive head coverings while men should not wear mustaches.[25] In Africa, where they chose Tanganyika (Tanzania) as their first field, the Lancaster conference would have opportunity to try out its own standards. Their forward thrust came at a time when the national economic depression and declining revenue was forcing other Mennonite missions—such as the Congo Inland Mission, which had been in Africa for two decades—to reduce operations. Lancaster's decision to begin separate overseas work implied that the conference would be even more aloof from the "old" Mennonites' general conference and its "church-wide" Mennonite Board of Missions and Charities. The "old" Mennonites were the only Mennonite body in which district conferences developed their own overseas missions.

By 1930 the overseas missionary enterprise, once championed by progressives and disparaged by traditionalists, had taken on a more sober and conservative cast. In the first flush of enthusiasm missionaries on all fields had founded stations, built churches and schools, and begun a variety of social and evangelical ministries. Then had come the less dramatic challenges of keeping the institutions alive and finding ways by which small, poor national churches might perpetuate the institutions which the mission had created. Protestant missions generally had not come close to their earlier, much-touted goal of winning the world for Christ in a single generation. That failure had a sobering effect.

Moreover, in some cases, as new generations of missionaries came to the field, old tensions between progressives and traditionalists seemed to give way to new ones perceived as Modernist versus Fundamentalist. In 1925 China missionary Edmund G. Kaufman, hoping to return as a university teacher, used a furlough to study at the University of Chicago. But that university was anathema to anti-Modernists. William S. Gottshall, pastor of the Swiss Mennonite Church near Bluffton, Ohio, and executive secretary of the GC Home Mission Board, worked to keep Kaufman from speaking in local churches. And Henry J. Brown, senior missionary in China, tried to block his return to the field.[26] Kaufman did not return to mission work. Instead, he put his expansive vision and leadership skills to Mennonite education.

Earlier, Mennonites had lagged behind American Protestants in missionary interest. But by the 1920s, for their size, they outstripped most Protestant denominations in mission contributions. A 1929 study entitled *Trends in Protestant Giving* showed that compared to leading Protestant groups, Mennonites consistently gave twice as much per member for overseas missions.[27] They in turn gave substantially less to maintain their local congregations, partly because most did not pay salaries to their pastors. Between 1920 and 1927, according to the reports, per-member contributions for all purposes declined both for Mennonites and for Protestants generally—an apparent reflection of a broad religious recession in the country.

Denominational Activity. In August 1929 the GC general

conference, meeting at Hutchinson, Kansas, exchanged greetings with its "old" Mennonite counterpart meeting near Goshen, Indiana. These two largest Mennonite bodies expressed subtle contrasts in their messages. The GC greeting spoke of a "common heritage" and called for "development and growth of the spiritual life and character of the people." The "old" Mennonites spoke in turn for "the promulgation of the full-Gospel standards and fundamental doctrines. . . ."[28]

Minutes of the two gatherings revealed other differences. The "old" Mennonite organization was well regulated and controlled, while the GC meeting was more open and boisterous. The "old" Mennonites spent most of their time hearing and adopting reports of committees and boards, and passed only three resolutions. The GC gathering adopted an unmanageable 137 resolutions, of varying significance. For both groups the resolutions were advisory rather than binding, and some leaders questioned their value. GC conference president Christian E. Krehbiel observed that "conference resolutions are frequently the grave-clothes in which pious hopes are gently laid to rest."[29] Despite the frustrations of organizational development, however, both bodies were strong and growing stronger. In response to changing realities each was adopting a new constitution.

After the Goshen conference a writer in the *Gospel Herald* noted that factions at the "old" Mennonites' conference had switched roles. Earlier, the most outspoken critics of conference positions had been the conservatives. Now it was the turn of the "liberals."[30] The progressive activists of 1910 had become the conservative guard of 1930. Once, Daniel Kauffman's generation had been in the vanguard of aggressive denominational organization and activity. Now it was working to consolidate its organization and win members' loyalty. No longer was that generation seeking out new frontiers.

One frontier was to revive the Mennonite Central Committee and cooperate to aid fellow Mennonites fleeing from Stalin's policies. But Kauffman's *Gospel Herald* gave far less space to that effort than did other Mennonite papers. It downplayed the story even though many of the available reports originated with MCC secretary, Levi Mumaw, Kauffman's Scottdale, Pennsylvania, neighbor. Compared to his MCC coverage, Kauffman gave greater attention to the work of his Mennonite branch's General Problems Committee. In the 1930 *Gospel*

Herald numerous "General Problems" articles appeared, and later an eleven-page report the committee presented in 1931. Likely Kauffman himself wrote most of that material. The 1931 report won the approval the "old" Mennonites' general conference, which met near Archbold, Ohio.[31] The "problems" had to do with control, loyalty, and unity rather than with outward mission and witness. Small wonder that "liberals" were critical.

A conservative mood dominated also at the 1929 GC general conference at Hutchinson, Kansas. Most divisive was the issue of secret societies. Like some other American denominations, GC Mennonites had long wrestled with the question of lodge membership. Since the 1880s they had passed numerous resolutions against it. But the GC general conference did not speak with legislative authority. And apparently the resolutions had little effect upon local congregations, especially in the Eastern District. Quite a few eastern GC Mennonites were acculturated business and professional persons who were attracted to lodges. Eastern District representatives warned that if the general conference took strong action, then some of their congregations—perhaps even the entire district—might withdraw. Nonetheless, in 1929 the conference resolved to reduce by 50 percent the votes held by congregations who had members in lodges. It would rescind the action only if the congregations took remedial steps before the next meeting.[32] The conference allowed its executive committee five hundred dollars to use to oversee enforcement.

No previous resolution of the conference had departed so far from the GC ideal of congregational autonomy. And in fact, the decision was not enforced. Apparently conference leaders did not agree with it. In 1930 conference president Peter P. Wedel from Kansas smoothed things over with a reconciling tour in the Eastern District, speaking at the district conference and in a number of churches. Without mentioning the lodge question he then reported in *The Mennonite* that the East had a high level of spirituality.[33] At the 1933 conference, delayed one year because of the Great Depression, the executive committee reported lamely that one reason it had not carried out the resolution was that the treasurer never received the five hundred dollars.[34] Conference resolutions continued to be only advisory.

The 1929 conference at Hutchinson also wrestled inconclusively with conservative demands that the body officially adopt fourteen "Articles of Faith" drafted by a committee created in 1920. The proposed articles constituted a very conservative evangelical position, although not as strongly Fundamentalistic as the statement of the "old" Mennonites in 1921. Someone made a motion to table the articles and instead adopt an ancient Mennonite statement, the 1766 Ris Confession of Faith.[35] The motion failed. Then the conference instructed its executive committee to submit the articles to the congregations for approval or rejection, and report two years hence.[36] Later conferences kept deferring the issue, and the GC body never did adopt an official statement of faith. But between 1920 and 1930 the pressure to do so was quite strong.

Especially among "old" Mennonites another measure of conservative shift in the late 1920s was the disappearance of the progressive *Christian Exponent* in 1928 and the birth in 1929 of a conservative quarterly publication in Virginia, *The Sword and Trumpet*. Already before World War I, George R. Brunk had proposed to Daniel Kauffman that a separate organization be created to promote the cause of conservatism.[37] A "Fundamental Book Depot" published and distributed books from Scottdale, Pennsylvania, among them John Horsch's *Modern Religious Liberalism* in 1921. The *Sword and Trumpet* title was strange for nonresistant, quiet-in-the-land Mennonites, but appropriate for a paper with a shrill and cutting style.

Brunk, the editor, set about to combat a perceived drift toward liberalism, worldliness, and Calvinism.[38] His anti-Calvinism, including rejection of the doctrine of eternal security, was a newer theme which he emphasized increasingly as the paper developed. The Virginia bishop believed that the Reformation doctrine of salvation by faith *alone*—an outside import from such sources as the *Sunday School Times*, Moody Bible Institute, and the "Darbyite error"—undermined the church's ability to sustain a separated, nonresistant, unworldly community. His view was that humans contributed toward their own salvation, and loyalty to dress codes and conservative theology was part of the contribution. Brunk criticized Mennonite Fundamentalists for accepting the Scofield Bible's Darby-style, dispensationalist teaching. Such teaching held that Jesus' Sermon on the Mount was not applicable for the present "church age."[39]

While rejecting the *Sunday School Times* influence at one

level, *The Sword and Trumpet* borrowed at another. It became the first Mennonite periodical to make effective use of cartoons. Ernest G. Gehman, teacher of German at Eastern Mennonite School, was adept at drawing and took inspiration from a *Times* cartoonist, E. J. Pace.[40] Gehman's caricatures had Modernists ripping pages from the Bible, particularly the first chapter of Genesis (creation) and the first chapter of Matthew (virgin birth).[41] They showed loyalist Mennonites anchored to Scripture while liberals headed toward a precipice. Between were "laxitarians"—middle-of-the roaders—equivocating.[42] One cartoon showed Mennonite preachers atop the "Mennonite Stronghold" shooting bullets at outside enemies (Mormons, Russellites, Infidels, etc.) while ignoring the "World-lovers, Laxitarians, and Liberals" close at hand. The enemies at hand were dynamiting the Mennonite pillars of "regulation of dress," "regulation of conduct," "regulation of doctrine," and "all church authority."[43]

The sequence of vulnerability from "dress" to "all church authority" represented a kind of conservative "old" Mennonite domino theory. In the 1920s the first domino teetered dangerously. "*Dress is the test*," wrote Brunk; "if that is lost we drop to *Individual regulation* which certainly will mean World regulation."[44] Noah H. Mack, once the superintendent of Lancaster conference's Welsh Mountain Mission and now bishop in its Weaverland district, was a former progressive of the late nineteenth century "old" Mennonite "awakening" or "quickening." By the 1920s he had come to an embarrassingly hysterical view of the dress issue. "There is now a doom and an overthrow threatening the Mennonite Church in America," he wrote in a 1930 *Sword and Trumpet* article which was reprinted in the *Gospel Herald*.[45] Women who exposed their arms, necks, and knees were following "Queen Fashion," whose "overlord and dictator is Satan himself." "Mothers, daughters, sisters . . . YOU ARE OVERTHROWING THE CHURCH!" For men such as Mack, scriptural teachings on dress were clear. Changes in prescribed attire seemed to threaten the foundations of faith as well as a way of living.

BUILDING THE DENOMINATION: IRONIES AND ACHIEVEMENTS

An overview of American Mennonitism in about 1930 confirms the theme of rising denominational organization, activity, and mentality. Although descended from Reformation radicals and European sectarians, the enlarging mainstream of Mennonites increasingly flowed into the prevailing forms of Protestant denominational life in America. Denominational organizations—conferences, boards, committees, colleges, agencies for mutual aid—all these empowered Mennonites to mobilize resources for a host of activities. The activities both fostered a renewed Mennonite identity and fulfilled the need to live as God's people in mission to the world. Mennonites organized to become a people of mission as well as a people of preservation.

Ironies. As Edward Yoder's diary suggested, the survival of Mennonite peoplehood was overlaid with rich ironies, ironies which varied among different groups on the Mennonite spectrum. For Yoder's "old" Mennonites, the central irony grew from an attempt to be old and new at the same time. They tried to remain a separated people, not conformed to the world, even as they founded colleges and missions agencies that opened members to worldly insights and influences. They intentionally designed denominational structures to fend off the forces of change, but in fact their methods of organization were quite typically American.[46] For instance, the "old" Mennonites brought their women's mission society to heel in a similar way, for similar reasons, and at about the same time as the Presbyterians. Determined to be different, Mennonites thought and acted more than they knew like American Protestants rather than like their Anabaptist forebears.

For the Dutch-Russians, whose parents had arrived on the American plains in the 1870s and '80s, the ironies were different. The central irony was a disparity between the reasons for leaving the Russian Empire and the course of development in America. The parents had come for freedom, as did so many immigrants to the new world. But they had understood freedom in terms of communal autonomy rather than of American individualism and self-fulfillment. Their hope had been to make secure in America something which the Russian Empire had offered for a century and then begun to take away. That something was the opportunity to be in charge of their own communities, their community institutions, and their religious life and institutions. Until World War I the Dutch-Russians in America were quite successful in establishing the alternative institutions of a separate German-speaking congregation Christendom—schools, colleges, teachers' associations, hospi-

Ernest G. Gehman and George R. Brunk collaborated on cartoons upholding a conservative position. Informed readers know that representatives of the three positions were George R. Brunk, loyalist; Daniel Kauffman, laxitarian; and John E. Hartzler, liberal.

tals, deaconess societies. But American "freedom" severely eroded this separate Christendom. Not only did America make war upon *Deutschtum* in 1917-1918; American toleration and affluence were always enticing. Children of the immigrants began to think of freedom as individualism rather than as autonomy for their communities. Migrants in quest of autonomy, the Dutch-Russians accepted outside influences even more rapidly than did the "old" and Amish Mennonites.

The Old Order Mennonites and Old Order Amish represented a genuinely sectarian alternative and sustained their separate communities of radical separation and humility. But their situation was also ironic. Their irony was that they were committed to be a people of stability through being steadfastly loyal to charter documents created earlier by people of upheaval. Both the New Testament and the Anabaptist writings so prized by old order folk were created at moments of world-changing disorder. The original impacts had been dynamic and challenging. Old order people earnestly followed Jesus and the apostle Paul, but not into missionary witness or zealous religious change. They claimed to be children of the Anabaptists but they offered none of the direct and overt challenge or threat to the established order that had brought their forebears to martyrs' deaths. In America the old order groups were comfortably at home, although sure that they were separate and alien from the world.

Discipleship. However, as Edward Yoder's life and published writings suggest, there was more to Mennonite life than the irony born of the cultural ambiguity of experience in America. During World War II, Yoder wrote, "It is our conviction that the Scriptures teach the principle of nonresistance. . . . Loyalty to Christ as our Lord requires us as his followers to take up the cross and follow Him in the way of love and non-resistance as well as in other teachings He gave (Matthew 16:24)."[47] Mennonites believed that God's requirements were knowable, that discipleship could be costly, that obedience was possible. They acted with Bible-based intentions and managed at least partly to achieve some of their goals. They established thriving congregations and communities of work and worship. They founded churches overseas and nearer home. In the face of very great pressures they refused military service in World War I. They built up relief and service programs as a moral equivalent for war. They aided brothers and sisters in the faith from the USSR in times of famine and persecution. And they planned creatively to deal with another crisis of conscience and conscription when war would once again break out.

Mennonite denominational development was not smooth, nor was its progress uninterrupted. The years from 1890 to World War I were full of new experiments, aggressive organizing, and new institutions. The war itself sent shock waves through the entire subculture and forced new thought about membership both in American democracy and in Christ's kingdom. The postwar era was a troubled time of discord, reorientation, and reconsolidation. It was also a time for discovery of new ideas and energies for the future. Mennonite fragmentation into numerous subgroups remained an embarrassment, even as an atomistic structure embarrassed American Protestantism in general. But the variegated Mennonite structure also provided dynamism, as each group was free to work out its own balance

(*Sword and Trumpet*, April 1930, p. 19)

An E. G. Gehman cartoon portraying the fears of Mennonite parents whose children went to "modern educational institutions."

of separation from, and accommodation to, American society.[48] By 1930, despite the onset of the Great Depression, there were ample signs in congregations, in colleges, and in wider organizations such as the Mennonite Central Committee that American Mennonitism in all its variety had a future of great vitality—as well as of struggle with the seductions of modern American culture.

KEY TO ABBREVIATIONS

CB *Christlicher Bundesbote* (1882-1847). German-language organ of the General Conference Mennonite church.

GH *Gospel Herald* (1908-). Official periodical of the "old" or (MC) Mennonite church.

HT *Herald of Truth* (1864-1908). The journal (along with its German-language counterpart, *Herold der Wahrheit*) of pioneer "old" Mennonite publisher John F. Funk and his Mennonite Publishing Company at Elkhart, Indiana. In the last third of the nineteenth century the paper served as the semi-official organ of many "old" and Amish Mennonite district conferences.

ME *The Mennonite Encyclopedia*, Vols. I-IV. Ed. by Cornelius Krahn, *et al.* Published jointly by Mennonite Publishing House, Scottdale, Pa.; Mennonite Publication Office, Newton, Kans.; and Mennonite Brethren Publishing House, Hillsboro, Kans.; 1955-1959.

ML *Mennonite Life* (1946-). An illustrated journal of Mennonite history and heritage.

MQR *The Mennonite Quarterly Review* (1927-). Major scholarly journal of Anabaptist-Mennonite studies.

TM *The Mennonite* (1885-). English-language organ of the General Conference Mennonite church.

NOTES

CHAPTER 1

1. John S. Coffman diary, May 1, 1893, AMC.

2. Ind.-Mich. Menn. Conf., *Minutes*, Oct 12-14, 1893, p. 53.

3. *HT*, 30 (June 15, 1893), 193.

4. Coffman diary (note 1), Jul 7, 1893.

5. Christian Arbitration and Peace Society to John F. Funk, Aug 2, 1893, Funk papers, AMC.

6. Coffman diary (note 1), Jul 25, Aug 15-17, 1893.

7. On the meaning of the 1893 Columbian Exposition see Reid Badger, *The Great American Fair* (Chicago, 1979); David F. Burg, *Chicago's White City of 1893* (Lexington, 1976); Alan Trachtenberg, *The Incorporation of America* (New York, 1982), 208-34; and Jeanne Madeline Weimann, *The Fair Women* (Chicago, 1981).

8. "Ada Landes to Fannie Landes," Aug 26, 1893, printed with comment by Wilmer Reinford in *Mennonite Historical Bulletin*, 37 (Apr 1976), 6-8. "Fortune Awaits Zimmerman," *The Weekly Echo*, May 29, 1902, in MHL.

9. "First Annual Report of the Missionary Society, 'Light and Hope'" (Chicago, 1894), in MHL. See also "Light and Hope" entries in *ME*, IV, 1102.

10. *CB*, 12 (Dec 7, 1893), 2.

11. *CB*, 12 (Sep 28, 1893), p. 4.

12. "Conference Report," *TM*, 6 (Dec 1890), 36.

13. *CB*, 12 (Dec 7, 1893), 2.

14. Coffman diary (note 1), Jul 25, 1893.

15. On the history of this Chicago mission, see Theron Schlabach, *Gospel Versus Gospel: Mission and the Mennonite Church, 1863-1944* (Scottdale, Pa., and Kitchener, Ont., 1980), 54-68.

16. See Fred Eggan, "H. R. Voth: Ethnologist," *ML*, 37 (Jun 1982), 14-9. On Voth's early career see John F. Schmidt, ed., "Autobiography of H. R. Voth," *MQR*, 40 (Jul 1966), 217-26. Roland Jones of Fort Lewis College has translated Voth's diaries and plans to publish them soon.

17. See *Der Warheit*, No. 8 (Apr 15, 1893), 117; No. 20 (Oct 15, 1893), 306; *HT*, 30 (Oct 15, 1893), 314.

18. See, e.g., articles on the Fair in *CB*, in issues of Jan 26, May 25, Sep 21, and Aug 3, 1893; and in *Herold der Wahrheit*, Dec 15, 1893.

19. Amos B. Hoover, "Bishop Jonas H. Martin and His Impressions upon the

Mennonite Church," pp. 23-37, in *The Jonas Martin Era . . .* (Denver, Pa.: The author, 1982). See pp. 796-97 for letter (n.d.) from John H. Hess referring to the ten-minute ultimatum.

20. "The Outlook," *TM*, 8 (Jul 1893), 75.

21. "Aesthetics in Religion," *TM*, 7 (Jan 1892), 25.

22. Allen M. Fretz, "Proposition II," *TM*, 2 (May 1887), 120-21.

23. Franklin Littell, *From State Church to Pluralism: A Protestant Interpretation of Religion in American History* (Garden City, N.Y., 1962), pp. 139, 141-44.

24. For an introduction to the literature of American denominationalism, including selections from the writings of H. Richard Niebuhr, Timothy L. Smith, Sidney E. Mead, and Martin E. Marty, see Russell E. Richey, ed., *Denominationalism* (Nashville, 1977). There are wide disagreements among scholars on definitions and evaluations of denominationalism. My own perspective has benefited especially from Andrew M. Greeley, *The Denominational Society, a Sociological Approach to Religion in America* (Glenview, 1972).

25. Articles by Christian Herr, John Herr, and Shem Zook in I. D. Rupp, *An Original History of the Religious Denominations at Present Existing in the United States* (Philadelphia, 1844), 486-501, 502-10, 560-61.

26. One analysis and critique of dominant American social theory, especially relevant for understanding the Mennonite reality is Thomas Bender, *Community and Social Change in America* (New Brunswick, 1978), 31-32. Bender argues against a model of social change which focuses solely upon the loss of community, or upon a presumed shift from *Gemeinschaft* to *Gesellschaft*.

27. Among the many efforts to define a common Anabaptist-Mennonite heritage the most famous is the often reprinted essay by Harold S. Bender, "The Anabaptist Vision," first published in *Church History* 13 (Mar 1944), 3-24. In 1910 three Mennonite leaders addressed the question of doctrinal commonality: I. A. Sommer, "An Important Question for Mennonites," *TM*, 25 (5 May 1910), 4; John Horsch, "In What Fundamentals Do Mennonites Agree?" *GH*, 3 (May 26, 1910), 114-15; Daniel Kauffman, "In What Fundamentals Do Mennonites Agree?" *GH*, 3 (Jul 21, 1910), 251, and (Jul 28, 1910), 283.

28. Bender, review of J. E. Hartzler, *Education Among the Mennonites of America*, in *The Goshen College Record—Review Supplement*, 27 (May-June 1926) (often bound as early issue of *MQR*), 35-44. Two one-volume general histories of Anabaptist Mennonitism are C. Henry Smith, *The Story of the Mennonites* (3d ed.—Newton, KS, 1983), and C. J. Dyck, ed., *An Introduction to Mennonite History* (2d ed.—Scottdale, Pa., and Kitchener, Ont., 1983). There is surprisingly little Mennonite literature reflecting upon the cultural and theological differences between these two streams of Mennonite heritage. See Leo Driedger and J. Howard Kauffman, "Urbanization of Mennonites: Canadian and American Comparisons," *MQR*, 56 (Jul 1982), 269-90, and James C. Juhnke, "Mennonite History and Self-Understanding, North American Mennonitism as a Bipolar Mosaic," in *Mennonite Identity, Historical and Contemporary Perspectives* (Lanham, Md., 1988), 83-99.

29. A recent effort to define the common "charter" values of Swiss-background American Mennonite communities, which focuses on the Schleitheim Confession and Franconia-conference Mennonites, is ch. 2 (pp. 80-143) in Beulah Hostetler, *American Mennonites and Protestant Movements* (Scottdale, Pa., and Kitchener, Ont., 1987).

30. On musical instruments in worship see Orlando Schmidt, *Church Music and Worship Among Mennonites* (Newton, Kans., 1981), 18-19.

31. See Richard K. MacMaster, *Land, Piety, Peoplehood, The Establishment of Mennonite Communities in America 1683-1790* (Scottdale, Pa. and Kitchener, Ont., 1985), 249-80.

32. The standard work on Dutch Anabaptism is Cornelius Krahn, *Dutch Ana-baptism, Origin, Spread, Life and Thought (1450-1600)* (The Hague: Martinus Nij-hoff, 1968; 2d ed.—Scottdale, Pa., and Kitchener, Ont., 1981).

33. Exceptions included a few individual Dutch Mennonites in New Amster-dam; the failed communitarian colony of Cornelisz Pieter Plockhoy on the Delaware River in 1663; the Dutch-background Mennonites from Krefeld to Germantown in 1683; and individual emigrants in the 19th century.

34. Two excellent introductions to the Mennonite settlements in Russia are David G. Rempel, "The Mennonite Colonies in New Russia: A Study of Their Settle-ment and Economic Development from 1789 to 1914" (Ph.D. diss., Stanford Uni-versity, 1933); and John B. Toews, *Czars, Soviets and Mennonites* (Newton, Kans., 1982).

35. Heinrich Funck, *Ein Spiegel der Tauffe* (Germantown, Pa.); (Christoph Saur, 1744); Christian Burkholder, *Nützliche und erbauliche Anrede an die Jugend* (Allentown, Pa., 1829 [first published in 1804; in English, published be-ginning in 1857 as *Useful and Edifying Address to the Young*]); John M. Bren-neman, *Pride and Humility* (Elkhart, Ind., 1873). On origin and evolution of the "Gospel of Humility," see: Theron F. Schlabach, "Mennonites, Revivalism, Modern-ity," *Church History*, 48 (Dec 1979), 411-12; Schlabach's Vol. II of this MEA series, *Peace, Faith, Nation*, esp. ch. 4; MacMaster, *Land, Piety, Peoplehood* (note 31), 180-82; and esp. Joseph C. Liechty, "Humility: The Foundation of Mennonite Reli-gious Outlook in the 1860s," *MQR*, 54 (Jan 1980), 5-31.

36. See Wedel's four-volume history of the Mennonites, *Abriss der Ges-chichte der Mennoniten* (Newton, Kans.: Bethel College, 1900-1904).

37. Samuel Burkhard to J. E. Hartzler, Dec 14, 1919, box 4, Hartzler papers, AMC.

38. This theme is especially emphasized by Schlabach in: "The Humble Be-come Aggressive Workers: Mennonites Organize for Mission, 1880-1910," *MQR*, 52 (Apr 1978), 113-26; and *Gospel Versus Gospel* (note 15), ch. 1 and throughout.

39. James O. Lehman, *Creative Congregationalism: A History of the Oak Grove Mennonite Church in Wayne County, Ohio* (Smithville, Ohio: Oak Grove Mennonite Church, 1978), 21-26.

40. "Im östlichen Pennsylvanien," *Herold der Wahrheit*, Oct 15, 1893, 309-10.

41. Frederick Jackson Turner, "The Significance of the Frontier in American History," *Report of the American Historical Association for 1893*, 199-227.

42. The standard history of this branch is J. C. Wenger, *The Mennonite Church in America, Sometimes Called Old Mennonites* (Scottdale, Pa., 1966).

43. Wenger, *The Mennonite Church*, 123. The published histories of these conferences are as follows: Sanford G. Shetler, *Two Centuries of Struggle and Growth, 1763-1963: A History of the Allegheny Mennonite Conference* (Scottdale, Pa., 1963); Harry Anthony Brunk, *History of Mennonites in Virginia*, Vol. I, 1727-1900, (Harrisonburg, Va., 1959); Vol. II, 1900-1960 (Harrisonburg, Va., 1972); Grant M. Stoltzfus, *Mennonites of the Ohio and Eastern Conference from the Colonial Period in Pennsylvania to 1968* (Scottdale, Pa., 1969); J. C. Wenger, *The Menno-nites in Indiana and Michigan* (Scottdale, Pa., 1961); Paul Erb, *South Central Frontiers: A History of the South Central Mennonite Conference* (Scottdale, Pa., 1974); John Ruth, *Maintaining the Right Fellowship* (Scottdale, Pa., and Kitchener, Ont., 1984); Willard Smith, *Mennonites in Illinois* (Scottdale, Pa., and Kitchener, Ont., 1983); Melvin Gingerich, *The Mennonites in Iowa* (Iowa City, 1939).

44. "New Year's Greeting," *HT*, 27 (January 1, 1890), 1.

45. Tilman Smith, "Church-Wide Meetings," *Mennonite Historical Bulletin*, 46 (July 1983), 1. On the "old" Mennonites and the Illinois Conference, see ch. 9 of Smith, *Mennonites in Illinois*, 188-221.

46. Wilmer J. Eshleman, *A History of the Reformed Mennonite Church* (new rev. ed.—Lancaster, Pa.: n.p., 1969); *ME*, IV, 267-69.

47. Jasper Abraham Huffman, ed., *History of the Mennonite Brethren in Christ Church* (New Carlisle, Ohio, 1920); Eileen Lageer, *Merging Streams: Story of the Missionary Church* (Elkhart, Ind., 1979).

48. Hoover, *Jonas Martin Era* (note 19); J. C. Wenger, "Jacob Wisler and the Old Order Mennonite Schism of 1872 in Elkhart County, Indiana," *MQR*, 33 (Apr 1959), 108-13, and (Jul 1959), 215-40; and Frank Epp, *Mennonites in Canada 1786-1920* (Toronto: Macmillan of Canada, 1974), 259-81.

49. John A. Hostetler, *Amish Society* (3d ed.—Baltimore, 1980).

50. The three Amish-Mennonite conferences do not have separately published histories, although the Eastern Amish Mennonite Conference is covered in Stoltzfus, *Mennonites of the Ohio and Eastern Mennonite Conference* (note 43). *ME*: I, 93-98; III, 29; IV, 932-33; II, 130-32.

51. Samuel Floyd Pannabecker, *Faith in Ferment: A History of the Central District Conference* (Newton, Kans., 1968).

52. Stan Nussbaum, *You Must Be Born Again: A History of the Evangelical Mennonite Church* (n.p.: Evangelical Mennonite Church, 1980).

53. The 1890 U.S. Census lists this group as "The Apostolic Mennonite Church," and gives only two congregations, both in Ohio. Herman Ruegger, *Apostolic Christian Church History*, I (Chicago, 1949), trans. of 1948 German-language edition published in Zurich.

54. John A. Toews, *A History of the Mennonite Brethren Church: Pilgrims and Pioneers* (Fresno, 1975).

55. Toews, *History of the Mennonite Brethren Church*, 176-93. C. F. Plett, *The Story of the Krimmer Mennonite Brethren Church* (Hillsboro, Kans., 1985).

56. Kevin Rempel, "The Evangelical Mennonite Brethren: In Search of a Religious Identity," Research paper, Fresno Pacific College, 1982.

57. Epp, *Mennonites in Canada* (note 48); Epp, *Mennonites in Canada, 1920-1940* (Scottdale, Pa., and Kitchener, Ont.: Herald Press, 1982).

58. Leland Harder, *General Conference Mennonite Church Fact Book of Congregational Membership* (n.p.: Leland Harder, 1971). Henry Peter Krehbiel, *The History of the General Conference of the Mennonites of North America* (Vol. I—n.p.: The author, 1898; Vol. II—Newton, Kans.: The author, 1938). Samuel Floyd Pannabecker, *Open Doors: The History of the General Conference Mennonite Church* (Newton, Kans., 1975).

59. J. H. Langenwalter, "A Biography of a Conviction" (typed biography prepared by Harley J. Stucky, N. Newton, Kans., 1959), 67-68.

60. Ruth, *Maintaining the Right Fellowship* (note 43).

61. David Haury, *Prairie People: A History of the Western District Conference* (Newton, Kans., 1981), 25-59.

62. Clarence Hiebert, *The Holdeman People, The Church of God in Christ, Mennonite, 1859-1969* (South Pasadena Calif., 1973). See also Linda Louis Boynton, *The Plain People: An Ethnography of the Holdeman Mennonites* (Salem Wis., 1986).

63. John Hostetler and Gertrude Enders Huntington, *The Hutterites in North America* (New York, 1967).

64. Gary B. Nachtigall, "Mennonite Migration and Settlements of California" (M.A. thesis, California State University at Fresno, 1972), 27-33.

65. *The Brethren Encyclopedia*, I, 607-10.

66. Carlton O. Wittlinger, *Quest for Piety and Obedience: The Story of the Brethren in Christ* (Nappanee, Ind., 1978). E. Morris Sider, *Nine Portraits: Brethren in Christ Biographical Sketches* (Nappanee, Ind., 1978).

67. Harry F. Weber, *Centennial History of the Mennonites in Illinois 1829-1929* (Scottdale, Pa., 1931), pref.

68. Henry K. Carroll, "Statistics of Churches," *Census Bulletin*, No. 131, (Washington, Oct 29, 1891), 14.

69. U.S. Bureau of the Census, *Historical Statistics of the United States, Colonial Times to 1957* (Washington, 1960), 7.

70. Charles Stelzle, ed., *The New Handbook of the Churches* (New York, 1930), 261.

71. A. D. Wenger, "The Mennonites a Prey of Others," *The Sword and Trumpet*, 2 (Apr 1930), 15-23.

CHAPTER 2

1. The documents relating to the Lichty pulpit incident have been published in Amos Hoover, *The Jonas Martin Era . . .* (Denver, Pa.: The author, 1982). See esp. annotated docs. 141, 196, 531, 673, 727, 738, 757, and 762. Doc. 727 is a news article from the Lancaster *Examiner*, Oct 1, 1889. Doc. 757 is an article by J. C. Wenger, "A Tragic Error in Discipline," from *Mennonite Reporter*, May 15, 1978. The accounts vary on some details, such as for example, whether the Zimmerman daughter, Martha, was along on the expedition. See also George G. Sauder, *History of Lichty's Church and Cemetery* (East Earl, Pa.: George G. Sauder), 21-24. C. Z. Mast and Robert E. Simpson, *Annals of the Conestoga Valley* (Elverson, Pa., 1942), 64-69.

2. Convers. with Amos B. Hoover, Denver, Pa., Jun 5, 1980.

3. Quoted in Hoover, *Jonas Martin Era* (note 1), 622.

4. On the history of the Wisler Old Order Mennonites see J. C. Wenger, "Jacob Wisler and the Old Order Mennonite Schism of 1872 in Elkhart County, Indiana," *MQR*, 33: (Apr 1959), 108-31; (Jul 1959), 215-40.

5. Paul Martin to Jonas Martin, Sep 22, 1909, in Hoover, *Jonas Martin Era* (note 1), 385-86.

6. Weaverland Conference Resolution, Apr 5, 1907, in Hoover, *Jonas Martin Era* (note 1), 689. Minister Jacob Weaver, a strong opponent of telephones, broke with the conference on this point.

7. Robert Bates Graber, "The Sociocultural Differentiation of a Religious Sect: Schisms Among the Pennsylvania German Mennonites" (Ph.D. diss., University of Wisconsin, 1979), 196, 208 and 266. Graber included fifteen schisms involving Pennsylvania-German Mennonites rather than just schisms involving the Old Orders. In some schisms, notably the 1847 Franconia conference (Oberholzer) division, the progressives were younger and more affluent.

8. The standard interpretation of how the stern colonial Puritans turned into pragmatic Yankees, for example, supports this expection. For an analysis of the Quaker experience on this point, see Frederick B. Tolles, *Meeting House and Counting House* (Chapel Hill, 1948).

9. Graber, "Sociocultural Differentiation," 202.

10. Harold R. Kurtz, "Mennonite History and Life of John S. Kurtz," *Home Messenger*, 16 (May 1979), 9-14; Hoover, *Jonas Martin Era* (note 1), 287-88.

11. For evidence of Kurtz's commitment to old order ways, see letters to Jacob Mensch cited in Sandra Lee Cronk, "*Gelassenheit*: The Rites of the Redemptive Process in Old Order Amish and Old Order Mennonite Communities" (Ph.D. diss., University of Chicago, 1977), 306-08

12. The most complete interpretation of Old Order Mennonite and Old Order Amish life is Cronk (note 11), "*Gelassenheit*." This chapter is heavily indebted to Cronk's perspective and information.

13. Hoover, *Jonas Martin Era* (note 1), 767-68.

14. Cronk, "*Gelassenheit*" (note 11), 77-78.

15. Quoted in Hoover, *Jonas Martin Era* (note 1), 509.

16. John A. Hostetler, "Silence as a Coping Strategy of Old Order Types," in Calvin Redekop and Leo Driedger, eds., *The Mennonites: Studies in Ethnic Theory* (Vancouver, 1986).

17. John S. Kurtz and Maria Kurtz. Letter to John Dan Wenger, September 14, 1920, printed in *Mennonite Historical Bulletin,* 37 (Oct 1976), 5-6.

18. For example, Herr, *Der Wahre und Selige Weg* (Lancaster, Pa., 1815), 333 pp.; Stauffer, *Eine Chronik oder Geschicht-Büchlein on der sogenannten Mennonisten Gemeinde* (Lancaster, Pa., 1855), 439 pp.; and Holdeman, *Der Alte Grund und Fundament* (Lancaster, Pa., 1862), 146 pp.

19. See bibliographical notes in Hoover, *Jonas Martin Era* (note 1), 1035, 1092-93. Two Ontario Old Order Mennonites who were not leaders but who published material in behalf of their group were Moses G. Reist and Menno Sauder. Between 1922 and 1970, Sauder, who for a time was under church discipline for owning an automobile, published seventy books and tracts, many of which were excerpts from earlier Anabaptist and Mennonite writings. Hoover, *Jonas Martin Era,* 1054, 1061-70.

20. Baptism ritual instructions in Hoover, *Jonas Martin Era* (note 1), 712-13.

21. See Hoover, *Jonas Martin Era* (note 1), 992, 994, and 1001.

22. Hoover, *Jonas Martin Era* (note 1), 29.

23. Cronk, "*Gelassenheit*" (note 11), 215.

24. Menno Weaver, "On That Farm Near Martindale," Mar 1927, printed in *Home Messenger,* 14 (May 1, 1977), 9-14, and in Hoover, *Jonas Martin Era* (note 1), 831-42.

25. Weaver, "On That Farm" (note 24).

26. Letters from Gagetown, Michigan, 1905-06, in Hoover, *Jonas Martin Era* (note 1), 127-130.

27. Martin to Mensch, Dec 25, 1896, in Hoover, *Jonas Martin Era* (note 1), 666-67.

28. On this theme see Cronk, "*Gelassenheit*" (note 11), 201-217.

29. The corrosive effects of Pietism upon traditional Anabaptist understandings is a central thesis of Robert Friedmann, *Mennonite Piety Through the Centuries* (Goshen, Ind., 1949). For an insightful critique of Friedmann's thesis see Theron F. Schlabach, "Mennonites and Pietism in America, 1740-1880: Some Thoughts on the Friedmann Thesis," *MQR,* 57 (Jul 1983), 222-40.

30. Cronk, "*Gelassenheit*" (note 11), 217.

31. Samuel Wenger, *The Wenger Book,* 1979, quoted in Hoover, *Jonas Martin Era* (note 1), 36.

32. John A. Hostetler, *Amish Society* (3d ed. rev.—Baltimore, 1980), 98-100.

33. Ivan J. Miller, *History of the Conservative Mennonite Conference 1910-1985* (Grantsville, Md.: Ivan J. and Della Miller, 1985).

34. On the Amish in Iowa see Melvin Gingerich, *The Mennonites in Iowa* (Iowa City, 1939), and Elmer Schwieder and Dorothy Schwieder, *A Peculiar People: Iowa's Old Order Amish* (Ames, 1975).

35. Elmer S. Yoder, *The Beachy Amish Mennonite Fellowship Churches* (Sugar Creek, Ohio: Schlabach Printers, 1987), ch. 6.

36. See Alvin Beachy (Moses M. Beachy's son), "The Amish of Somerset County, Pennsylvania" (M.S.T. thesis, Hartford Seminary, 1952). Chs. 3, 4 appear in *MQR,* 28 (Oct 1954), 263-92.

37. Beachy, "The Amish" (note 36), 124-27.

38. J. D. Wenger, "A Confession of Faith," in Hoover, *The Jonas Martin Era* (note 1), 815.

39. Hoover, *Jonas Martin Era* (note 1), 813.

40. Emma Hurst, "Moses G. Horning and the Old Order Divisions in Pennsylvania," *Mennonite Historical Bulletin,* 21 (Apr 1960), 1-2, 4.

41. Hoover, *The Jonas Martin Era* (note 1), 243.

42. For an excellent analysis of this theme, see ch. 13, "Change and Fragmentation," in Hostetler, *Amish Society* (note 32), 270-91.

CHAPTER 3

1. *CB*, 9 (September 4, 1890), 5.

2. David C. Wedel, *The Story of Alexanderwohl* (Goessel, Kans., 1974), 21-40.

3. *ME*, IV, 652-53.

4. Fred Belk, *The Great Trek of the Russian Mennonites to Central Asia, 1880-1880* (Scottdale, Pa., and Kitchener, Ont., 1976).

5. Christian Krehbiel, "Autobiography," 1960, trans. from 1909 ed., MLA.

6. Peter J. Wedel, *The Story of Bethel College* (North Newton, Kans., 1954), 28-44.

7. *CB*, 9 (Sep 4, 1890), 5.

8. John H. Lohrenz, *The Mennonite Brethren Church* (Hillsboro, Kans., 1950), 328-29.

9. Among the best published writings on Russian Mennonites are John B. Toews, *Czars, Soviets and Mennonites* (Newton, Kans., 1982); David G. Rempel, "The Mennonite Commonwealth in Russia: A Sketch of Its Founding and Endurance, 1789-1919," *MQR*, 47 (Oct 1973), 259-308, and 48 (Jan 1974), 5-54; Peter M. Friesen, *The Mennonite Brotherhood in Russia (1789-1910)* (Fresno, 1978), trans. from the 1911 German edition. For a theological-sociological critique of the Russian Mennonite commonwealth, based upon ideal types, see Robert Kreider, "The Anabaptist Conception of the Church in the Russian Mennonite Environment 1789-1870," *MQR*, 25 (Jan 1951), 17-33.

10. C. H. Wedel, "Correspondence From Bethel College," *CB*, 13 (Mar 8, 1894), 5. See also Wedel's comparisons of Mennonites with Lutherans from Russia in "Correspondence From Bethel College," *CB*, 13 (Mar 29, 1894), 5.

11. Friesen, *Mennonite Brotherhood* (note 9), 231.

12. Friesen, *Mennonite Brotherhood* (note 9), 410-15, 540-44.

13. Abraham E. Janzen, ed., *Resolutions of the Mennonite Brethren Church, 1878-1863* (Hillsboro, Kans., 1964), 70, 156.

14. James C. Juhnke, *A People of Two Kingdoms: The Political Acculturation of the Kansas Mennonites* (Newton, Kans., 1975), 35-55.

15. On the changes in congregatonal life in Kansas see Dennis D. Engbrecht, "The Americanization of a Rural Immigrant Church: The General Conference Mennonites in Central Kansas 1874-1939" (Ph.D. diss., U. of Nebraska, 1985).

16. The most complete collection of these newspapers has been at the Kansas State Historical Society in Topeka. See William E. Connelley, *History of Kansas Newspapers* (Topeka, 1916), 203-05, 231-05. Eleanor L. Turk, "The German Newspapers of Kansas," *Kansas History*, (Spr 1983), 46-64. The Mennonite Brethren from 1905 to 1912 also published a monthly religious periodical in the Russian language, printed in Hillsboro and ed. by Hermann Fast in Saskatchewan.

17. *Marion County Anzeiger* (Jun 1, 1888).

18. *Zionsbote* (Sep 24, 1890), 4.

19. *The Review*, 3 (Nov 15, 1901).

20. W. J. Krehbiel, *History of One Branch of the Krehbiel Family* (McPherson, Kans., 1950), 80-81.

21. *CB*, 15 (May 21, 1896), 4-5.

22. Carl Wittke, *The German-Language Press in America* (Lexington, 1957). An excellent brief survey of German-America from 1870 to 1914 is in Frederick C. Luebke, *Bonds of Loyalty, German Americans and World War I* (DeKalb, 1974), 27-81.

23. "Pflegt und bewahrt die deutsche Sprache," *Zionsbote* (Aug 18, 1897), 4.

24. *Kasas Volksblatt und Anzeiger* (Mar 30, 1898), 2.

25. H. P. Peters, *History and Development of Education Among the Mennonites in Kansas* (Hillsboro, Kans., 1925), 78-99.

26. Report of the 24th Conference, Ebenfeld, *Kansas Volksblatt und Anzeiger*, 11 (Jan 7, 1898), 5.

27. Report of the 25th Conference, Grace Hill, *Kansas Volksblatt und Anzeiger Supplement,* 11 (Jun 2, 1898), 1.

28. Report of the 24th Conference (note 26), 5.

29. J. W. Kliewer, "The German Parochial Schools of the Mennonites in Central Kansas," *The Review,* 2 (Mar 1900), 1.

30. Cornelius Cicero Janzen, "A Social Study of the Mennonite Settlement in the Counties of Marion, McPherson, Harvey, Reno, and Butler, Kansas" (Ph.D. diss., U. of Chicago, 1926), 99-103.

31. Based on Menno S. Harder, "History of Mennonite Education" (Ph.D. diss., U. of Southern California, 1949), Tables 8 and 9, pp. 243, 247.

32. H. W. Lohrenz, "Der Wert der deutschen Bildung" (presentation to the German Verein at McPherson College, Sep 18, 1901), H. W. Lohrenz papers, MLA.

33. Christian Neff, "Unser Amerikareise," *Der Herold,* 27 (Dec 11, 1913), 1.

34. Joseph A. Wipf, "The Comparative Decline of the Three German Dialects Used by the Mennonites in the Freeman, South Dakota, Area" (Bethel College Social Science Seminar paper), 1961; John D. Unruh, *A Century of Mennonites in Dakota* (Freeman, SD, 1972), 60-61, 66-69, 80.

35. Dirks, "Rückerinnerungen, IX," *CB,* 15 (Jun 25, 1896), 1.

36. David A. Haury, *Prairie People, A History of the Western District Conference* (Newton, Kans., 1981).

37. Samuel Floyd Pannabecker, *Open Doors: A History of the General Conference Mennonite Church* (Newton, Kans., 1975), 118.

38. "English or German—Which?" *TM,* 15 (Nov 1899), 12. See also A. S. Shelly, "Zur Sprachenfrage," *CB,* 19 (Feb 1, 1900), 5-6.

39. Goerz, *Schul- und College-Journal,* 5 (Jan 1900), 5-6; 5 (Feb 1900), 13-14.

40. Christian Krehbiel, *Schul- und College-Journal* 5 (Feb. 1900), 12-13.

41. Silas M. Grubb, "Germans or Mennonites, Which?" *TM,* 15 (Feb 1900), 37.

42. See *Zionsbote* articles in the issues of May 22, Aug 28, Nov 27, and Dec 18, 1898.

43. Note from Hillsboro in *Kansas Volksblatt und Anzeiger,* 11 (Jun 30, 1898), 3. On MB-Baptist connections see: Abram J. Klassen, "The Roots and Development of Mennonite Brethren Theology to 1914" (M.A. thesis, Wheaton College, 1960); and Albert J. Wardin, Jr., "Baptist Influences on Mennonite Brethren with an Emphasis on the Practice of Immersion," *Direction,* VIII (Oct 1979), 33-38.

44. Jacob P. Bekker, *Origin of the Mennonite Brethren Church* (Hillsboro, Kans., 1973), 175-78. The Baptist pastor was probably the "Rev. Sievers," whose reports on the mission in Kansas City appeared in the *Zionsbote.* See *Zionsbote* (Nov 12, 1890), 2.

45. F. W. Hintz, "Das Verhältnis der Vereine zu der Gemeinde," *Zionsbote* (Apr 10, 1895), 3.

46. Janzen (note 30), "A Social Study," 108. John A. Toews, *A History of the Mennonite Brethren Church: Pilgrims and Pioneers* (Fresno, 1975), 268-70.

47. Harms, "Die Konferenz bei Gridley, Ills [sic]," *Zionsbote* (Feb 26, 1896), 22.

48. Dick Eitzen, *History of the Mennonite Brethren Church* (n.p., 1951).

49. Vernon R. Wiebe, *Come Let Us Stand United: A History of Corn Bible Academy 1902-1977* (Hillsboro, Kans.: The author, 1977), 42.

50. Toews, *A History of the Mennonite Brethren Church* (note 46), 200. John F. Harms, *Geschichte der Mennoniten Brüdergemeinde* (Hillsboro, Kans., n.d.), 115-18.

51. Wedel, *Randzeichnungen zu den Geschichten des Alten Testaments* (1899), 73 pp.; *Randzeichnungen zu den Geschichten des Neuen Testaments* (1900), 97 pp.; *Abriss der Geschichte der Mennoniten,: Die Geschichte ihrer Vorfahren bis zum Beginn des Täufertums im 16. Jahrhundert,* I (1900), 154 pp.; *Die Geschichte des Täufertums im 16. Jahrhundert,* II (1902), 180 pp.; *Die Geschichte der Täufer und Mennoniten in der Schweiz, in Mähren, in Süddeutschland, am Niederrhein und in Nordamerika,* III (1904), 211 pp. All were published by the School Press of Bethel College, North Newton, Kans.

52. *Randzeichnungen . . . des Alten Testaments* (note 52), 4.
53. *Abriss* (note 51), II, 148-49.
54. James C. Juhnke, "*Gemeindechristentum* and Bible Doctrine: Two Mennonite Visions of the Early Twentieth Century," *MQR*, 57 (Jul 1983), 208-10. See also Juhnke, *Dialogue With a Heritage* (North Newton, Kan., 1987).
55. H. Richard Niebuhr, *Christ and Culture* (New York, 1951).
56. Editorial in *HT* (Sep 24, 1903).
57. One example of use of "Gemeindechristentum" is David Goerz, *Zur Diakonissensache* (Newton, Kans., 1904), 36-38.
58. For an example of how the "Gemeinde" concept is individualized in translation, compare C. H. Wedel's original *Abriss* (note 51), Vol. IV, pt. 46, with the trans. in *ML*, 36 (Dec 1981), 27.

CHAPTER 4

1. Death notice, *HT*, 33 (Oct 15, 1896), 319.
2. Reports from congregations in *HT*, 33: (Nov 1, 1896), 329; (Nov 1, 1896), 345-46.
3. A. D. Wenger, "Requested Biography," ca. 1932; typed copy in A. D. Wenger papers, Virginia Conference Archives, Eastern Mennonite College; Sara Stambaugh, *I Hear the Reaper's Song* (Intercourse, Pa., 1984); Mark R. Wenger, "Ripe Harvest: A. D. Wenger and the Birth of the Revival Movement in Lancaster Conference," *Pennsylvania Mennonite Heritage*, 4 (Apr 1981), 2-14.
4. A. D. Wenger letter to L. J. Heatwole, Apr 20, 1897. File "A. D. Wenger," L. J. Heatwole papers, VCA (note 3).
5. Richard K. MacMaster, *Land, Piety, Peoplehood: The Establishment of Mennonite Communities in America, 1683-1790* (Scottdale, Pa., and Kitchener, Ont., 1985).
6. See Beulah Hostetler, *American Mennonites and Protestant Movements: A Community Paradigm* (Scottdale, Pa., and Kitchener, Ont., 1987), esp. ch.4, "The Encounter with Revivalism," pp. 150-75.
7. For brief narrative description of American revivalism, see the essay by Nathan Hatch, "The Swelling Tide of Revivalism," *Eerdmans' Handbook to Christianity in America* (Grand Rapids, 1983), 172-87.
8. Joseph N. Driver of Ladd, Va., to John S. Coffman of Elkhart, Ind., April 22, 1887. Driver Family papers, VCA (note 3).
9. Barbara F. Coffman, *His Name Was John* (Scottdale, Pa., 1964).
10. James O. Lehman, *Creative Congregationalism: A History of the Oak Grove Mennonite Church in Wayne County, Ohio* (Smithville, Ohio: Oak Grove Mennonite Church, 1978), 104-27.
11. Ibid.
12. See L. J. Burkholder, *A Brief History of the Mennonites in Ontario* (Mennonite Conference of Ontario, 1935), 197-216, 162-3. Burkholder described the division and the revival, but did not draw the connection between the two.
13. Amos Hoover, *The Jonas Martin Era. . .* (Denver, Pa.: The author, 1982).
14. Sanford G. Shetler, *Preacher of the People: A Biography of S. G. Shetler* (Scottdale, Pa., and Kitchener, Ont., 1982), 96.
15. Elaine Sommers Rich, *Mennonite Women: A Story of God's Faithfulness, 1683-1983* (Scottdale, Pa., and Kitchener, Ont., 1983), 164.
16. N. E. Byers, "The Times in Which I Lived," *ML*, 7 (Jan 1952), 44-47.
17. Alice K. Gingerich, *Life and Times of Daniel Kauffman* (Scottdale, Pa., 1954).
18. J. E. Hartzler, "Autobiographical Notes," *Mennonite Historical Bulletin*, 42 (Apr 1981), 4.
19. This discussion of doctrinal reorientation is indebted to Theron Schlabach, *Gospel Versus Gospel: Mission and the Mennonite Church, 1863-1944* (Scottdale, Pa., and Kitchener, Ont., 1980), 110-117.

20. For a description of the Bible-conference movement, see Shetler, *Preacher* (note 14), 100-110.

21. John S. Coffman, *Outlines and Notes Used at the Bible Conference Held at Johnstown, Pennsylvania* (Elkhart, Ind., 1898), 38.

22. Shetler, *Preacher* (note 14), 104.

23. Oscar Burkholder, "Ontario Mennonite Bible School and Institute," *ME*, IV, 66; Urie A. Bender, *Four Earthen Vessels* (Kitchener, Ont., 1982), 34-44.

24. *ME*, III, 118.

25. C. Y. Fretz, "A History of Winter Bible Schools in the Mennonite Church," *MQR*, 16 (1942), 51-81, 178-96.

26. Kauffman, *Manual of Bible Doctrines*, (Elkhart, Ind., 1898), 51-52.

27. Melvin Gingerich, *Mennonite Attire Through Four Centuries* (Breinigsville, Pa., 1970), 130-31.

28. Kauffman, *Manual* (note 26), 154.

29. Kauffman, *Manual* (note 26), 40.

30. *HT*, 32 (Mar 1, 1895), 67-68. Quoted in Schlabach, *Gospel Versus Gospel* (note 19), 52.

31. For a thorough study of millennialism, see Timothy Weber, *Living in the Shadow of the Second Coming* (New York, 1979).

32. Coffman, *Outlines* (note 21), 4.

33. On the relationship of Mennonites and the holiness movement, see chapter five, "The Second Work of Grace," in Joseph S. Miller, *Beyond the Mystic Border: A 100 Year History of the Whitestone Mennonite Church* (Hesston, Kans.: Whitestone Mennonite Church, 1985), 51-74.

34. Ibid. Other sources, in addition to Miller, on D. D. Zook and the Pennsylvania Church include Gladys Zook, "Stories from the Life and Christian Experience of D. D. Zook" (unpublished paper, 1947); Gideon Yoder, "The Oldest Living American Mennonite Congregations of Central Kansas" (M.A. thesis, Phillips University, 1948), 113-15; and Paul Erb, *South Central Frontiers: A History of the South Central Mennonite Conference* (Scottdale, Pa., 1974), 242-45.

35. Ibid., entire note.

36. J. G. Hartzler to J. E. Hartzler, Mar 18, 1913, f. 2, box 2, J. E. Hartzler papers, AMC.

37. *ME*, III, 29-31.

38. See Theron F. Schlabach, "Paradoxes of Mennonite Separatism," *Pennsylvania Mennonite Heritage*, 2 (Jan 1979), 12-17.

39. "A Sober Second Thought," *GH*, 2 (Mar 10, 1910), 789-90.

40. Kauffman, *Manual* (note 26), 137.

41. Samuel Floyd Pannabecker, *Faith in Ferment: A History of the Central District Conference* (Newton, Kans., 1968).

42. Stan Nussbaum, *You Must Be Born Again: A History of the Evangelical Mennonite Church* (Fort Wayne, Ind.: Evangelical Mennonite Church, 1980), 37-9.

43. Kevin Rempel, "The Evangelical Mennonite Brethren: In Search of a Religious Identity" (research paper, Fresno Pacific College, 1982), 25-28.

44. Kauffman, *Mennonite Cyclopedic Dictionary* (Scottdale, Pa., 1937), 262.

45. Delbert L. Gratz, *Bernese Anabaptists and Their American Descendants* (Scottdale, Pa., 1953).

46. James O. Lehman, *Sonnenberg: A Haven and a Heritage* (Kidron, Ohio, 1969).

47. Naomi Lehman, *Pilgrimage of a Congregation, First Mennonite Church, Berne, Indiana* (Berne, Ind., 1982).

48. P. B. Amstutz, *Geschichtliche Ereignisse der Mennoniten-Ansiedlung in Allen und Putnam County, Ohio* (Bluffton, Ohio, 1925), 36. (Abridged English ed., Anne Konrad Dyck, trans.—Bluffton, Ohio, 1978).

49. See "Report of Preliminary Conference Meeting," *HT*, 34 (Dec 15, 1897), 371-72.

50. D. J. Johns, Daniel Kauffman, and D. H. Bender, "Our Church Institutions," *HT*, 36 (Jan 1, 1899), 3.

51. *Proceedings of the Mennonite General Conference Including Discussions Leading to Its Origination* (n. place: n. publ., 1921), 46.

52. See M. S. Steiner, 1897-1905, *passim,* AMC.

53. N. O. Blosser, "General Conference," *HT,* 37 (Sep 15, 1900). Reprinted in *Proceedings* (note 51), 63.

54. For details on Funk's troubled years, see Aaron C. Kolb, "John Fretz Funk, An Appreciation," *MQR,* 6 (Jul, Oct 1932), 144-55, 250-63. See also correspondence among his antagonists, especially in the M. S. Steiner and J. S. Coffman papers, AMC.

55. Paul E. Whitmer, "The Autobiography of Paul E. Whitmer" (typed copy, Bluffton, Ohio, 1952), 92 (in MHL, etc.).

56. John A. Hostetler, *God Uses Ink: The Heritage and Mission of the Mennonite Publishing House After Fifty Years* (Scottdale, Pa., 1958).

57. Helen Kolb Gates and others, *Bless the Lord, O My Soul: A Biography of Bishop John Fretz Funk, 1835-1930* (Scottdale, Pa., 1964). Gingerich, *Daniel Kauffman* (note 17).

58. *Proceedings* (note 51), 110.

59. Daniel Kauffman to J. B. Smith, Mar 16, 1918. F. DK, box A2, J. B. Smith papers, Menno Simons Historical Library and Archives, Eastern Mennonite College, Harrisonburg, Va.

60. Bender to Kauffman, March 18, 1912, box 1, Daniel Kauffman papers, AMC.

61. Daniel Kauffman, ed., *Bible Doctrine: A Treatise on the Great Doctrines of the Bible* (Scottdale, Pa., 1914); Kauffman, *Doctrines of the Bible: A Brief Discussion of the Teachings of God's Word* (Scottdale, Pa., 1928), 639 pp.

62. Kauffman, *Manual* (note 26), 35.

63. Melvin Gingerich, *Mennonite Attire Through Four Centuries,* 28.

64. *Proceedings* (note 51), 149.

65. Ibid., 196.

66. Ibid., 163-64.

67. Gingerich, *Mennonite Attire* (note 27), 130.

68. Paul Erb, taped interview by Leonard Gross, Nov 10, 1980, transcript, p. 25, AMC.

69. Ibid., Nov 9, 1980, transcript, p. 7.

70. *Minutes of the Virginia Mennonite Conference (1835-1938)* (1939), report for 1918, p. 125.

71. Carbon copy of Virginia conference notes in f. "J. Earl Suter," VCA (note 3).

72. J. B. Smith to George R. Brunk, Apr 9, 1918, Brunk papers, VCA (note 3).

73. Franconia conference record book, at Oct 5, 1911, p. 5.

74. D. H. Bender, "The Mennonite Church," *Report of the Sixth All-Mennonite Convention, Hillsboro, Kansas, August 28-30, 1927* (n.p.: n.p., n.d), 84.

75. Funk editorial in *HT,* 35 (Jul 15, 1898), reprinted in *Proceedings* (note 50), 43.

76. For an example of competing claims of "old" and "new" Mennonites see A. B. Shelly, "A Sad Representation," *TM,* 5 (Dec 1890), 40-41. The "A" and "B" designation was used by P. M. Friesen in *Alt-Evangelische Mennonitische Brüderschaft in Russland* (Halbstadt, Taurin [the Ukraine], 1911), Pt. II, 83-4. See also I. A. Sommer to J. E. Hartzler, May 11, 1911, f. 6, box 1, Hartzler papers, AMC.

77. Quoted in Allan Teichroew, draft of first chapter for a history of Mennonites in World War I, p. 25.

78. Arthur S. Rosenburger, "N. B. Grubb—Editor and Minister," *ML,* 6 (Jan 1951), 42-45.

79. Naomi Lehman, *Pilgrimage of a Congregation: First Mennonite Church, Berne, Indiana* (Berne, Ind., 1982), 35-60; Eva F. Sprunger, *The First Hundred Years: A History of the Mennonite Church in Adams County, Indiana 1838-1938* (Berne, Ind., 1938).

80. Fred Rohrer, *Saloon Fight at Berne, Ind.* (Berne, Ind., 1913).

81. Samuel Floyd Pannabecker, *Open Doors: The History of the General Conference Mennonite Church* (Newton, Kans., 1975), 387. Howard J. Loewen, "One Lord, One Church, One Hope: Mennonite Confessions of Faith in America—An Introduction", *MQR*, 57 (Jul 1983), 270-71.

82. Two essays which compare the Dutch-Russian and Swiss-American Mennonite clusters in America are James C. Juhnke, "Gemeindechristentum and Bible Doctrine: Two Mennonite Visions of the Early Twentieth Century," *MQR*, (July 1983), 206-21; and Juhnke, "Mennonite History and Self-Understanding, North American Mennonitism as a Bipolar Mosaic" in *Mennonite Identity* (Lanham, MD, 1988), 83-99.

CHAPTER 5

1. Lois Barrett, "Sitting Bull and H. R. Voth," *TM*, 98 (Oct 11, 1983), 482-84. James C. Juhnke, "General Conference Mennonite Missions to the American Indians in the Late Nineteenth Century," *MQR*, 54 (Apr 1980), 117-34. For general information on these Plains Indians and the Ghost Dance, see Donald J. Berthrong, *The Cheyenne and Arapaho Ordeal: Reservation and Agency Life in the Indian Territory, 1875-1907* (Norman, Okla., 1976); Virginia Cole Trenholm, *The Arapahoes, Our People* (Norman Okla., 1970); and James Mooney, *The Ghost-Dance Religion and the Sioux Outbreak of 1890* (Chicago, 1965), originally published in 1896. Lois Barrett critiqued this section on H. R. Voth and the Ghost Dance and offered revisions.

2. Russell Thornton, "Demographic Antecedents of a Revitalization Movement: Population Change, Population Size, and the 1890 Ghost Dance," *American Sociological Review*, 46 (Feb 1981), 94.

3. H. R. Voth to A. M. Fretz, May 21, 1887, in *TM*, 2 (Jul 1887), 154.

4. Voth quarterly report, *TM*, 7 (Jul 1891), 154-55.

5. H. R. Voth, "From Our Mission Field," *TM*, 1 (Oct 1885), 11.

6. Quoted in Mrs. H. T. Esau, *First Sixty Years of M. B. Missions* (Hillsboro, Kans., 1954), 28-29.

7. Rodolphe Petter, "Some Reminiscences of Past Years in My Mission Service Among the Cheyenne," *TM*, 51 (Nov 10, 1936), 9, 13-14.

8. Kaufman, *The Development of the Missionary and Philanthropic Interest Among the Mennonites of North America*, (Berne, Ind., 1931), 33-35, 45-56.

9. See Theron Schlabach, *Gospel Versus Gospel: Mission and the Mennonite Church, 1863-1944* (Scottdale, Pa., and Kitchener, Ont., 1980), 155-56.

10. Samuel S. Haury, *Letters Concerning the Spread of the Gospel in the Heathen World Presented to All Mennonites in North America*, trans. by Marie Regier Janzen and Hilda Voth (Scottdale, Pa., and Kitchener, Ont., 1981), 52, 55. The original German edition was published at Halstead, Kansas, in 1877.

11. *The Holy Bible New International Version* (Grand Rapids, Mich.: Zondervan, 1978).

12. Schlabach, *Gospel Versus Gospel* (note 9), 42.

13. Margaret Dietzel Hillegass, "Rodolphe Petter: A 'Called' Linguist," *ML*, 37 (June 1982), 4-13; John D. Thiesen, "God's Chosen People: Rodolphe Petter and the Cheyennes," *The Prairie Scout*, 5 (1985), 119-35.

14. John H. Yoder, "Reformation and Missions: A Literature Review," *Occasional Bulletin from the Missionary Research Library* 22 (Jun 1971), 1-9; Cornelius J. Dyck, "Early Anabaptist *Sendungsbewusstsein*," 1957, MLA; Schlabach, *Gospel Versus Gospel* (note 9), 26-7; G. W. Peters, *Foundations of Mennonite Brethren Missions* (Hillsboro, Kans., 1984), 12-16.

15. Josiah Strong, *Unser Land*, trans. by W. Horn (Berne, Ind., 1892). See, e.g., *CB*, 12 (Jan 5, 1893), 7.

16. M. S. Steiner, *Pitfalls and Safeguards* (Elkhart, Ind., 1899), 26, 46.

17. "McKinley weiss, was sich schickt," *Zionsbote*, 12 (Feb 3, 1897), 4.

18. A. S. Shelly, *TM*, 13 (May 1898), 60-61; "Poor Cuba," *HT*, 35 (Apr 1, 1898), 9, *Kansas Volksblatt und Anzeiger* (May 5, 1898).

19. John Umble, *Goshen College 1894-1954* (Goshen, Ind., 1955), 212.

20. M. S. Steiner, "The Christian's Duty in Times of War and to Spain," *HT*, 35 (Aug 15, 1898), 242-43.

21. "Report of Sunday School Conference," *HT*, 35 (Sep 15, 1898), 277-78.

22. "Aid for Starving Cubans," *HT*, 35 (Mar 2, 1898). See also the Western District Conference resolution of May 17, 1898, endorsing aid through the Red Cross. James C. Juhnke, *A People of Two Kingdoms* (Newton, Kans., 1975), 58.

23. Lambert, *Around the Globe and Through Bible Lands* (Elkhart, Ind., 1896); and *India, the Horror Stricken Empire* (Elkhart, Ind., 1898).

24. Schlabach, *Gospel Versus Gospel* (note 9), 30-31. Harry Anthony Brunk, *History of the Mennonites in Virginia 1727-1900*, Vol. I (Harrisonburg, Va., 1959), 274ff., 360ff., 425ff.

25. On missions developments in the Lancaster conference, see A. Grace Wenger, "Home Missions 1894-1933," ch. 1 of a ms. history of the Eastern Mennonite Board of Missions and Charities; Schlabach, *Gospel Versus Gospel* (note 9), 73.

26. See, e.g., Steiner, *Pitfalls* (note 16), 15-33, 121-25; J. E. Hartzler, *Paths to Perdition* (Scottdale, Pa., 1910), 138-42, 211-15.

27. Robert Pierce Beaver, *American Protestant Women in World Mission* (Grand Rapids, 1968; rev. ed., 1980).

28. On the denominational function of Bible institute centers, see Ernest Sandeen, *Roots of Fundamentalism* (Chicago, 1970), 240-43, and Timothy P. Weber, *Living in the Shadow of the Second Coming* (New York, 1979), 173-74.

29. For the theme of Mennonite missions as Americanization or acculturation, particularly for the "old" Mennonites, see Schlabach, *Gospel Versus Gospel* (note 9), 47 and *passim*.

30. Everek Richard Storms, *What God Hath Wrought* (Springfield, Ohio, 1948), 93.

31. Margaret Epp, *This Mountain Is Mine* (Chicago, 1969).

32. Henry J. Brown, *Chips of Experience* (n.p.: n.p., 1929). James C. Juhnke, *A People of Mission* (Newton, Kans., 1979), 45-64. Edmund George Kaufman, *The Development of the Missionary and Philanthropic Interest Among the Mennonites of North America* (Berne, Ind., 1931), 323-78.

33. Epp, *This Mountain Is Mine* (note 31), 83

34. On the departure of the "old" Mennonite mission from western China see Dorothy S. McCammon, *We Tried to Stay* (Scottdale, Pa., 1953).

35. F. J. Wiens, *Fifteen Years Among the Hakkas of South China* (n.p.: n.p., n.d.), 14.

36. John H. Lohrenz, *The Mennonite Brethren Church* (Hillsboro, Kans., 1950), 250-57. Esau, *First Sixty Years* (note 6), 254-88.

37. On the history of Congo Inland Mission see Melvin Loewen, *Three Score: The Story of an Emerging Church in Central Africa* (Elkhart, Ind., 1972); William B. Weaver, *Thirty-Five Years in the Congo* (Chicago, 1945; and Juhnke, *A People of Mission* (note 32), 67-87.

38. J. B. Toews, *The Mennonite Brethren Church in Zaire* (Hillsboro, Kans., 1978), 71.

39. Lois Barrett, *The Vision and the Reality* (Newton, Kans., 1983), 1-16; Juhnke, *A People of Mission* (note 32), 2-14; Rodolphe Petter, "Mennonitische Mission in Indien," *CB*, 17 (Apr 14, 1898), 5.

40. See Schlabach, *Gospel Versus Gospel* (note 9), *passim*. Schlabach emphasizes the contrast between the traditional "old" Mennonite gospel of humility and peace with a Protestantized gospel.

41. Esau, *First Sixty Years* (note 6).

42. Franconia conference record book, 1907-1961, at May 2, 1918, p. 16. Schlabach, *Gospel Versus Gospel* (note 9), 133.

43. See ch. 5 in Schlabach, *Gospel Versus Gospel* (note 9), 148-66.

44. Congo Field Minutes, 1940, AIMM archives, Bluffton, Ohio.

45. See Juhnke, *A People of Mission* (note 32), 55-6.

46. Minnie Swartzendruber (Mrs. J. D.) Graber, "Preparation for the Mission Field" (draft of oral interview with Dwight Roth, n.d., 1981).

47. For an excellent study of women in mission, see Jane Hunter, *The Gospel of Gentility: American Women Missionaries in Turn-of-Century China* (New Haven, 1984).

48. Esther Jost, "Free to Serve: Katharina Schellenberg (1870-1945)," in Katie Funk Wiebe, ed., *Women Among the Brethren: Stories of Fifteen Mennonite Brethren and Krimmer Mennonite Brethren Women* (Hillsboro, Kans., 1979), 82-94.

49. Gladys Goering, *Women in Search of Mission: A History of the General Conference Mennonite Women's Organization* (Newton, Kans., 1980).

50. Sharon Klingelsmith, "Women in the Mennonite Church, 1890-1930," *MQR,* 54 (Jul 1980), 163-207.

51. Elaine Sommers Rich, *Mennonite Women: A Story of God's Faithfulness, 1683-1983* (Scottdale, Pa., and Kitchener, Ont., 1983), 201-06.

52. Gustav Harder, "Welchen Antheil nimmt die Mission an der Civilisation?" *CB,* 13 (Mar 1, 1894), 1.

53. Printed in *TM,* 20 (Aug 31, 1905), 4.

54. J. W. Kliewer, "Rückblick über die Missionsthätigkeit des letzten Jahrhunderts und Ausblick in das 20. Jahrhundert," *CB,* (Jul 18, 1901), 1. The article was continued in the Jul 25 and the Aug issues.

55. Schlabach, *Gospel Versus Gospel* (note 9), 95; John A. Lapp, *The Mennonite Church in India 1897-1962* (Scottdale, Pa., 1972).

56. *Twenty-five Years with God in India* (Berne, Ind., 1929), 246-47.

57. E. G. Kaufman, "The War and K'ai Chow," *Mennonite Weekly Review,* 3 (Jan 27, 1925), 1.

58. Melvin Loewen, "The Congo Inland Mission, 1911-1961," (Ph.D. diss., Free University of Brussels, 1961), 399.

59. Juhnke, *A People of Mission* (note 32), 80-81.

60. Schlabach *Gospel Versus Gospel* (note 9), 167. For the development of this thesis, see esp. ch. 6, pp. 167-94.

61. P. A. Penner to A. B. Shelly, Apr 26, 1906, f. 54, Foreign Mission Board Corresp., MLA.

62. Schlabach, *Gospel Versus Gospel* (note 9), 92.

CHAPTER 6

1. Lena Mae Smith, "Sister Frieda Kaufman 1883-1944," *General Conference Mennonite Pioneers,* ed. by Edmund G. Kaufman, (North Newton, Kans., 1973), 412-19. Marilyn Bartel, "Sister Frieda Kaufman: Builder of Institutions and Lives" (student paper, Bethel College, 1966).

2. Ibid., entire note.

3. The only published comprehensive history of Mennonite educational development in America is the inadequate and outdated book by John Ellsworth Hartzler, *Education Among the Mennonites of America* (Danvers, Ill., 1925). The published histories of the individual colleges include the following: Peter J. Wedel, *The Story of Bethel College* (North Newton, Kans., 1954); John Umble, *Goshen College 1894-1954* (Goshen, Ind., 1955); C. H. Smith and E. J. Hirschler, *The Story of Bluffton College* (Bluffton, Ohio, 1925); *Bluffton College: An Adventure in Faith 1900-1950* (Bluffton, Ohio, 1950); Von Hardesty, *A Narrative of Bluffton College* (Bluffton, Ohio, 1975); Mary Miller, *A Pillar of Cloud: The Story of Hesston College 1909-1959* (Hesston, Kans., 1959); Hubert R. Pellman, *Eastern Mennonite College, 1917-1967: A History* (Harrisonburg, Va., 1967). Marie Waldner, *For Half a Century: The Story of Freeman Junior College 1900-1950,* (Freeman, S. Dak., 1951); and Wesley J. Prieb and Don Ratzlaff, *To a Higher Plane of Vision* (Hillsboro, Kans., 1983).

4. C. Henry Smith, "Bondage," *Institute Monthly,* 1 (Apr 1899), 51.

5. Daniel Kauffman, "The Denominational School—Its Mission," *Institute Monthly*, 4 (Feb 15, 1902), 85.

6. C. H. Wedel to H. R. Voth, Jan 3, 1889, trans. by Hilda Voth, f. 69, box 10, H. R. Voth papers, MLA.

7. "Address of Rev. N. C. Hirschy," *The Review*, 2 (Aug 1900), pp. 1-2.

8. John S. Coffman, "The Spirit of Progress," *Young People's Paper*, 3 (Feb-Mar 1896), 3, 42-43, 51; M. S. Steiner, *John S. Coffman: Mennonite Evangelist* (Spring Grove, Pa., 1903).

9. Coffman, "Spirit of Progress" (note 8).

10. Coffman to L. J. Heatwole, Dec 21, 1893, f. 11, box 4, Coffman papers, AMC.

11. A. J. Bendle to J. B. Smith, 2 Jan 1918, box A1, J. B. Smith papers, Menno Simons Historical Library and Archives, Eastern Mennonite College, Harrisonburg, Va.

12. John H. Mosemann to George R. Brunk, Aug 8, 1916, George R. Brunk papers, Virginia Conference Archives, Eastern Mennonite College, Harrisonburg, Va.

13. Waldner, *For Half a Century* (note 3), 1-2.

14. C. H. Wedel, "Correspondence from Bethel College," *CB*, 13 (Mar 8, 1894), 5.

15. Paul Toews, "Henry Lohrenz and Tabor College," *ML*, 38 (Sep 1983), 14-15; James C. Juhnke, "*Gemeindechristentum* and Bible Doctrine: Two Mennonite Visions of the Early Twentieth Century," *MQR*, 57 (Jul 1983), 209-10.

16. See Richard A. Schmidt, "Bibliography of C. H. Wedel" (1945), MLA.

17. Wedel, *Story of Bethel College* (note 3), 92, 237.

18. Umble, *Goshen College* (note 3), 212-15; Miller, *A Pillar of Cloud*, 37, 50, 81; Wedel, *Story of Bethel College* (note 3), 93, 129-30, 309; Pellman, *Eastern Mennonite College* (note 3), 60-61; Waldner, *For Half a Century*, (note 3), 57-58.

19. Volume I of the *Tabor College Herold* began in the 1911-12 school year. See the editorial of (Dec 1912), no. 10, for Harder quotation.

20. *Tabor College Herold*, 5 (Mar 1916), 16.

21. *Tabor College Herold*, 1 (Dec 1912), 11-14.

22. *Tabor College Herold*, 5 (Oct 1916), 28-30.

23. A. Warkentin and Melvin Gingerich, *Who's Who Among the Mennonites* (North Newton, Kans., 1943). Compilation by D. J. Greaser of Goshen College.

24. Burton J. Bledstein, *The Culture of Professionalism: The Middle Class and the Development of Higher Education in America* (New York, 1976).

25. Wedel, *Story of Bethel College* (note 3), 592-93.

26. Umble, *Goshen College* (note 3), 59-62.

27. Pellman, *Eastern Mennonite College* (note 3), 44.

28. N. C. Hirschy, ed., *Sunday School Bible Lesson Quarterly*, 8 vols. (Berne, Ind., 1900-1905); D.H. Bender, ed., *Mennonite Advanced Lesson Quarterly*, Vol. I (Scottdale, Pa., 1907); Noah E. Byers, *Christian Worker's Manual: The Sunday School*, Vol. II (Scottdale, Pa., n.d.); H. F. Toews, *Handbuch für Sonntagschularbeiter* (Hillsboro, Kans., n.d.).

29. J. D. Charles, *Fallacies of Evolution* (Scottdale, Pa., 1917), 48 pp.; P. J. Wedel, *Evolution, Die Neue Religion der Wissenschaft* (n.p.: n.p., 1923), 28 pp.; Chester K. Lehman, *The Inadequacy of Evolution as a World View* (Scottdale, Pa., 1925), 28 pp.

30. See: Bethel College's *School and College Journal* (1896-1902); *Monatsblätter aus Bethel College* (1903-1920); *Bethel College Monthly* (1903-1935); *Tabor College Herold* (1912-1931); *Elkhart Institute Monthly* (1898-1903); and *Goshen College Record* (1903-present). Two monthly publications which for a time carried Education Sections edited by college faculty members were the *Christian Evangel* (1910-1956), publication of the Central Illinois Mennonite Conference, and the *Christian Monitor* (1909-1953), "old" Mennonite publication at Scottdale.

31. See ch. 3, note 51.

32. Smith, *The Mennonites of America* (Scottdale, PA, 1909); *The Mennonites: A Brief History of Their Origin and Later Development in both Europe and America* (Berne, Ind., 1920; rev. 1941, 1950, 1957, 1983 under the title *The Story of the Mennonites*); *The Coming of the Russian Mennonites: An Episode in the Settling of the Last Frontier 1847-1884* (Berne, Ind., 1927); *The Mennonite Immigration to Pennsylvania in the Eighteenth Century* (Norristown, Pa., 1929).

33. For a complete bibliography of Smith's writings, see Nelson P. Springer, "The Writings of C. Henry Smith," pp. 249-58 in C. Henry Smith, *Mennonite Country Boy* (Newton, Kans., 1962).

34. Rodney Sawatsky, "History and Ideology: American Mennonite Identity Definition Through History" (Ph.D. diss., Princeton U., 1977). Ch. IV, pp. 89-121, discusses Wedel and Smith as historians in greater detail than is possible here. Although Sawatsky's study is insightful, I do not agree that Smith stood "squarely in the tradition of C. H. Wedel's understanding of Mennonite identity" (pp. 105-06). Smith's individualism and nationalism were quite incompatible with Wedel's normative concept of *"Gemeinde."*

35. Smith, *Mennonites of America* (note 32), 33 pp.

36. Smith, *Mennonites in History* (Scottdale, Pa., 1907), 32-33.

37. Sawatsky, "History and Ideology" (note 34), 103.

38. Smith, "The Hand of God in American History," *The Christian Evangel,* 4 (Apr 1914), 186-87. See also Smith, "Some of the Providences of American History," *Christian Monitor* 3 (Jan, Feb 1911), 17, 51, 52.

39. Smith, "The Hand of God," *The Christian Evangel,* 4 (Jun 1914), 226, 227.

40. C. H. Wedel, *Geleitworten an junge Christen* (Newton, Kans., 1912), 33-4; Wedel, *Meditationen zu den Fragen und Antworten unseres Katechismus* (Newton, Kans., 1910), 177.

41. On Schellenberg, Ewert, and Krehbiel as progressives, see James C. Juhnke, *A People of Two Kingdoms* (Newton, Kans., 1975), 65-82.

42. C. Henry Smith, "All-Mennonite Convention," *ME,* I, 62.

43. Theron F. Schlabach, "Paradoxes of Mennonite Separatism," *Pennsylvania Mennonite Heritage,* 2 (Jan 1979), 12-17.

44. On Horsch, see *MQR,* 21 (Jul 1947), entire.

45. Sawatsky, "History and Ideology" (note 34), 103-11.

46. John Horsch, "The Anabaptist View of Toleration," *The Christian Evangel,* 1 (May 1911), 221-23.

47. Quotation from H. S. Bender, "Notes and Comments on the J. J. Hildebrand Article on the History of Goshen College," n.d., MHL. See also John Horsch, *The Mennonite Church and Modernism* (Scottdale, Pa., 1924), 114.

48. Hartzler spent three years at Bethel College (1918-21) before moving to Bluffton to become president of the new Witmarsum Seminary. See Umble, *Goshen College* (note 3), 57-87; Smith and Hirschler, eds., *The Story of Bluffton College* (note 3), 143-52. See also: C. Henry Smith, *Mennonite Country Boy* (note 33), 210-11; and Paul Whitmer, "The Autobiography of Paul E. Whitmer" (typed copy dated Bluffton, Ohio, Feb 15, 1952), 98-99. Also see fs. 2, 3, 6, 11 of box 3; fs. 1, 2, of box 4; J. E. Hartzler papers, AMC.

49. S. F. Coffman to J. E. Hartzler, Mar 16, 1918, f. 3, box 3, Hartzler papers, AMC.

50. C. Goldner, *Die Geschichte der weiblichen Diakonie* (Cincinnati, 1901), vii. For a survey of Anabaptist-Mennonitism and health care see Walter Klaassen, "The Anabaptist Tradition," in Ronald L. Numbers and Darrel W. Amundsen, eds. *Caring and Curing* (New York, 1986), 271-87.

51. Paul Starr, *The Social Transformation of American Medicine* (New York, 1982).

52. For examples of pre-scientific medicine and of Mennonite susceptibility to quack doctors, see John A. Hostetler, "Healing Arts and Cures," *Christian Living,* 1 (Aug 1954), 7-9, 38.

53. *Institute Monthly,* 2 (May 1900), 134-37; (Oct 1900).

54. Warkentin, *Who's Who Among the Mennonites* (note 23), 317-19.

55. From a typed list of Virginia conference deaconesses compiled by Grace Showalter, n.d. See also Lewis J. Heatwole, et al., *A History of the Mennonite Conference of Virginia and Its Work* (Scottdale, Pa., 1910), 7.

56. The first comprehensive book on the deaconess movement including developments in America, Goldner's *Die Geschichte der weiblichen Diakonie*, mentions (p. 180) that the founder of the modern deaconess movement in Germany, Theodore Fliedner, received inspiration from Mennonite congregational deaconesses in Amsterdam.

57. The congregation vs. association (*Gemeinde* vs. *Vereine*) issue was addressed by David Goerz in articles originally published in *Monatsblätter aus Bethel College* but compiled in *Zur Diakonissensache* (Newton, Kans., 1904), 36-38. Goerz's account, which emphasizes his own role and point of view, has influenced all subsequent writings on the Mennonite deaconess movement.

58. On the history of the deaconess movement see H. D. Penner, "Deaconess Work Among the Mennonites," *TM*, 40 (Aug 27, 1925), 3, and (Sep 3, 1925), 4, 6; Lois Barrett, *The Vision and the Reality* (Newton, Kans., 1983), 173-78; and Katie Funk Wiebe, *Our Lamps Were Lit* (Newton, Kans., 1978). There is no comprehensive history of Mennonite deaconess or health care development.

59. Rose Lambert interview with Melvin Gingerich, Dec 9, 1969, transcript in Lambert papers owned by Robert Kreider of Bethel College, N. Newton, Kans.

60. John A. Sprunger, et al., *Licht und Hoffnung "Ruf zu Jesu"* (Chicago, 1893). For information on Sprunger see Margaret Epp, *This Mountain Is Mine*, 23, 35; Naomi Lehman, *Pilgrimage of a Congregation* (Berne, Ind., 1982), 339-47; Steven R. Estes, *Christian Concern for Health: The Sixtieth Anniversary History of the Mennonite Hospital Association* (Bloomington, Ill., 1979); Barrett, *The Vision and the Reality* (note 58), 174-75. Goldner, *Geschichte* (note 50), 352-53.

61. David Goerz in *Zur Diakonissensache* (note 57) did not even mention Sprunger in his review of Mennonite deaconess history.

62. Sister Frieda Kaufman, "Der gegenwärtige Stand der Diakonissensache unter den Mennoniten" (16-page pamphlet—ca. 1930), 6-8.

63. Sister Magdalene Wiebe to Sister Frieda Kaufman, Aug 10, 1929, f. 28, box 3, "Deaconess Work and Deaconesses" papers, MLA.

64. Goerz, *Zur Diakonissensache* (note 58), 20-21, 32-35.

65. P. Richert, "Bethany Hospital, Gotebo, Oklahoma," *Der Bethesda Herold*, 5 (May 15, 1906), 18. Edward Richert, "Dr. Peter Richert" (research paper, Tabor College, 1973).

66. Aaron J. Epp, *Bethany Lives On!* (American Falls, Idaho: n.p., 1975), 1-5. See the dual-language monthly religious paper *Salems Stern* and *Salem Star*, ed. by Franz B. Wedel, Salem, Oregon, 1919-1930.

67. Goerz, *Zur Diakonissensache* (note 57), 36-38. The quotation was from Vol. IV of Wedel's *Abriss der Geschichte der Mennoniten* (1904), 114.

68. Goerz, *Zur Diakonissensache* (note 57), 36-38.

69. David Haury, *Prairie People: A History of the Western District Conference* (Newton, Kans., 1984), 156-60.

70. Theron Schlabach, *Gospel Versus Gospel: Mission and the Mennonite Church, 1863-1944* (Scottdale, Pa., and Kitchener, Ont., 1980), 97-99.

71. Allen Erb, "The Mennonite Church and Hospital Work," *MQR*, 1 (Jan 1927), 30-31.

72. Edna Hunsperger, "The Deaconess Movement in the Mennonite Church" (unpublished paper, 1948-49), in MHL.

73. Kaufman, "Der gegenwärtige Stand" (note 62), 2-3, 11-16.

74. Ibid.

75. Marvin H. Ewert, "Envisioning a Wider Service Through Our Deaconess Committee" (speech for the Western District Conference Council of Committees, Apr 12, 1956), f. 28, box 3, "Deaconess Work and Deaconesses" papers, MLA.

76. Edmund G. Kaufman, *The Development of the Missionary and Philanthropic Interest Among the Mennonites of North America* (Berne, Ind., 1931), 33-35, 45-56.

CHAPTER 7

1. C. H. Wedel, *Abriss der Geschichte der Mennoniten*, Vol. IV (Newton, Kans., 1904), 203-04.

2. Ibid., 190-91.

3. Merle Curti, *The Making of an American Community* (Stanford, 1959). Curti used federal census records.

4. The reverse of "turnover rate" is "rate of persistence," meaning the percentage of those who remained in a given area from one census to the next. A study which compares the rate of persistence in the Mennonite-dominated West Branch Township with the findings of Merle Curti in the non-Mennonite Trempealeau County is Rachel Waltner, "West Branch Township Census Project" (Mennonite Experience in America research paper, July 1982), in MLA. One problem of this comparative approach is that Curti's time frame, 1860-1880, barely overlaps the coming of the Mennonites to Kansas in the mid-1870s. The tendency of Mennonites to be less mobile than neighboring Americans is noted in an earlier study by James C. Malin, "Turnover of Farm Population in Kansas," *Kansas Historical Quarterly*, 4 (Nov 1935), 347, 361.

5. John A. Hostetler, *Amish Society* (3d ed. rev.—Baltimore, 1980), 106.

6. John A. Hostetler, *Hutterite Society* (Baltimore, 1972), 122.

7. Hostetler, *Hutterite Society* (note 6), 186-87.

8. *ME*, I, 491-93.

9. *ME*, IV, 74-75. See also a forthcoming volume by Hope K. Lind, tentatively titled "Mennonites in Oregon and Related Groups in Neighboring States (1876-1976)."

10. Sanford C. Yoder, *The Days of My Years* (Scottdale, Pa., 1959), 72-74. *ME*, IV, 460. *GH*, 7 (Jan 8, 1914), 655.

11. Yoder, *The Days of My Years* (note 10), 74.

12. Lois Barrett, *The Vision and the Reality* (Newton, Kans., 1983), 15-27. James C. Juhnke, "General Conference Mennonite Missions to the American Indians in the Late Nineteenth Century," *MQR*, 54 (Apr 1980), 117-34.

13. H. R. Voth, "From Our Mission Field," *TM*, 4 (Nov 1889), 26.

14. Marvin E. Kroeker, "Mennonites in the Oklahoma Land Rushes" (ms. for illustrated lecture in Hillsboro, Kansas, April 1985), in MLA. Kroeker's updated number of forty-four congregations is a revision of an earlier account in his article, "Mennonites in the Oklahoma 'Runs,'" *ML*, 10 (July 1955), 120, as well as in subsequent accounts on Mennonites in Oklahoma. See *ME*, IV, 33-36.

15. See the appendix of alumni and their vocations in Vernon R. Wiebe, *Come Let us Stand United: A History of Corn Bible Academy, 1902-1977* (Hillsboro, Kans.: The author, 1977), 135-62.

16. Orlando Harms, *Pioneer Publisher: The Life and Times of J. F. Harms* (Winnipeg, 1984), 41-47.

17. Peter Richert, "Bethany Hospital, Gotebo, Oklahoma," *Der Bethesda Herold*, 5 (May 15, 1906), 18.

18. Gordon R. Dyck, "The United States General Conference Extinct Churches (1847-1959)" (research paper, Mennonite Biblical Seminary, 1959), 9.

19. On the Warwick Settlement see Harry Anthony Brunk, *History of Mennonites in Virginia 1900-1960* Vol. II (Harrisonburg, Va., 1972), 278-302; and J. Harvey Yoder, ed., *Fifty Years Building on the Warwick* (Denbigh, Va., 1947).

20. Myra Miller Hahn, "The Christian K. and Abbie Yoder Miller Family," in Yoder, *Fifty Years* (note 19), 17-19.

21. J. Harvey Yoder, *Neighborhood Profiles and Vistas* (New York, 1971), 76-77.

22. J. C. Wenger, *Faithfully, Geo. R.: The Life and Thought of George R. Brunk I* (Harrisonburg, Va., 1978).

23. John Umble, "Factors Explaining the Disintegration of Mennonite Communities," *Proceedings of the Seventh Annual Conference on Mennonite Cultural Problems* (Hillsboro, Kans., 1949), 113, 128.

24. David Luthy, *The Amish in America: Settlements That Failed, 1840-1960* (Aylmer, Ont.: Pathway Publishers, 1986).

25. Dyck, "The United States General Conference Extinct Churches" (note 18), 8.

26. Ernest E. Leisy, "On a Kansas Farm," *ML*, 1 (Jan 1946), 18.

27. For a provocative essay on the meaning of Mennonite social-cultural transition to town life and beyond, see Delbert Wiens, "From the Village to the City, A Grammar for the Languages We Are," *Direction* (Oct 1973-Jan 1974).

28. *Fourteenth Census of the United States, 1920*, Vol. I, "Population, Numbers and Distribution of Inhabitants," (Washington, D.C., 1921).

29. Martin G. Weaver, *Mennonites of Lancaster Conference* (Scottdale, Pa., 1931), 116-19, 474.

30. See notes from bishop Benjamin W. Weaver's diary in Eli D. Wenger, *The Weaverland Mennonites* (Manheim, Pa., 1968), 130.

31. Weaver, *Mennonites of Lancaster Conference* (note 29), 116-17.

32. *Goshen, Sesquicentennial Edition, 1831-1981* (Goshen, Ind.: The News Printing Co., 1981), 136.

33. Interview with Elwood Landes and Ruth Lehman Landes, Goshen, Ind., Jun 1981. Notes in possession of the author. Elwood Landes was born in 1889.

34. *Vorwärts*, 10 (Nov 29, 1912), 4.

35. For information on Hillsboro see Sondra Van Meter, *Marion County Kansas Past and Present* (Hillsboro, Kans., 1972), 177-207.

36. *Vorwärts*, 12 (Feb 20, 1914) 4.

37. See the two articles in *Vorwärts*, 15 (Sep 21, 1917): James A. Ray, "An Explanation," 4, and J. G. Ewert, "Ein Angriff auf die deutschen Schulen in Marion County," 6.

38. See corresp. in the H. W. Lohrenz papers, MLA: Homer Hoch to Lohrenz, Apr 21, 1917; Lohrenz to M. M. Just, May 1, 1917; Lohrenz to Walter Burr, May 1, 1917; Lohrenz to C. P. Regier, Apr 3, 1918.

39. *Vorwärts*, 15 (Jul 13, 1917), 6. Marion *Record*, (Jun 7, 1917), 4.

40. Undated newspaper clipping, "Science Is God's Servant, Literary Society Is Told," in L. J. Heatwole papers, Virginia Conference Archives, Eastern Mennonite College, Harrisonburg, Va.

41. *Memoirs of Peter Jansen: A Record of a Busy Life* (Beatrice Nebr., 1921), 11. See also Cornelius J. Claassen, "Peter Jansen—Pioneer, Leader and Philanthropist," *ML*, 2 (Oct 1947), 41-43, 45.

42. John Ruth, *Maintaining the Right Fellowship* (Scottdale, Pa., and Kitchener, Ont., 1984), 449.

43. A. Warkentin and Melvin Gingerich, eds., *Who's Who Among the Mennonites* (North Newton, Kans., 1937), 86.

44. Bruce R. Leisy, *A History of the Leisy Brewing Companies* (Wichita, Kans.: The author, 1975).

45. Leisy, *History of the Leisy Brewing Companies* (note 44), 34.

46. Rebecca F. Krehbiel, "Albert Henry Krehbiel, 1873-1945: Early American Impressionist," *ML*, 40 (Mar 1985), 4-8.

47. *ME*, I, 626-27.

48. Allan Teichroew, "Gordon Friesen: Writer, Radical and Ex-Mennonite," *ML*, 38 (Jun 1983), 4-17.

49. Friesen, *The Flamethrowers* (Caldwell, Idaho, 1936).

50. *Who's Who* (note 43), 47; (1943), 74-75.

51. Letter to Allan Teichroew, Apr 7, 1983, quoted in Teichroew, "Gordon Friesen" (note 48), 11.

52. John S. Coffman diary, at Jul 28, 1893, Coffman papers, AMC.

53. Material in this section is drawn from Rachel Waltner, "Mennonite Conferences 1890-1930" (Mennonite Experience in America research paper, August 1984), in MLA.

54. Grubb, "Our Conference," *TM*, 32 (Sep 27, 1917), 1.

55. "A Week at Belleville," *GH*, 20 (Sep 1, 1927), 481-83.

56. Editorial in *TM*, 17 (Oct 16, 1907), 4.
57. Lester Hostetler, "General Impressions of the General Conference," *TM*, 44 (Oct 17, 1929), 4. See also Tilman Smith, "Church-Wide Meetings," *Mennonite Historical Bulletin*, 46 (Jul 1985), 1-4.

CHAPTER 8

1. Court-martial record of Private George S. Miller, #3953799, Co. 39, 163rd Depot Brigade, Microfilm #427B, MLA.
2. Sanford Yoder to J. S. Hartzler, Aug 30, 1918, f. 8, box 13, Sanford Yoder papers, AMC. The hazing incident is also described in a report by Major Percy Bordwell, Camp Inspector, to Commanding Officer, Camp Dodge, Sep 5, 1918, War Dept, U.S. Army Continental Commands, RG 39, box 2, World War I Collection #155, MLA.
3. Miller to S. C. Yoder, Mar 15, 1919, f. 5, box 13, Yoder papers, AMC.
4. Clemency Board Report, Apr 9, 1919, in Miller Court Martial Record (note 1).
5. Roger Golden interview with George S. Miller, Dec 28, 1968, Schowalter Oral History Collection, MLA.
6. *GH*, 7 (Aug 13, 1914), 313-14.
7. Smith, "The Great War," *The Christian Evangel*, 5 (Mar, May, Jun, Jul, Aug, Sep, Oct 1915), 104-06, 188-90, 226-28, 264-68, 305-07, 346-48, 392-94; *The Christian Monitor*, 7 (Feb, Mar, Apr, May, Jun, Jul, Aug, Sep 1915), 52, 53; 80, 81; 113, 114; 149, 150; 178, 179; 207, 208; 241, 242; 274, 275.
8. Smith, "The Great War," *The Christian Evangel*, 5 (Mar 1915), 104.
9. Gregory J. Stucky, "Fighting Against War: The Mennonite *Vorwärts* from 1914 to 1919," *Kansas Historical Quarterly*, 38 (Sum 1972), 169-86.
10. *Vorwärts*, 12 (Aug 7, 1914), 7.
11. *Vorwärts*, 12 (Sep 18, 1914).
12. *Vorwärts*, 12 (Oct 2, 1914), 4.
13. *Vorwärts*, 13 (May 21, 1915).
14. *Vorwärts*, 12 (Nov 27, Dec 18, 1914). H. P. Krehbiel's *Der Herold* of Newton also received gifts for the German Red Cross.
15. *Vorwärts*, 15 (Nov 9, 1917).
16. *Marion Record*, Jan 10, 1918. Clipping, f. PM-25, box 54, H. P. Krehbiel papers, MLA.
17. H. P. Krehbiel, *History of the General Conference of Mennonites of North America*, Vol. II (Newton, Kans., 1938), 324.
18. Krehbiel (note 17), 330.
19. For copies of these conference resolutions, see J. S. Hartzler, *Mennonites in the World War* (Scottdale, Pa., 1921), 56-65.
20. *GH*, 9 (May 31, 1917), 146, and 9 (Jun 14, 1917), 194.
21. Hartzler, *Mennonites in the World War* (note 19), 66-68. On the relationship of historic peace church groups to the government in setting conscription policies, see Albert N. Keim and Grant M. Stoltzfus, "Conscientious Objection and the Historic Peace Churches" (book ms. in preparation).
22. John A. Toews, *A History of the Mennonite Brethren Church* (Fresno, 1975), 200.
23. J. M. Enss, Chinook, Montana, to N. N. Hiebert, Mountain Lake, Minnesota, Jun 5, 1917, copy in H. W. Lohrenz papers, MLA.
24. Undated survey of MB drafted men by H. W. Lohrenz, Lohrenz papers.
25. *Vorwärts*, 15 (Jul 13, 1917), 6; *Marion Record* (7 Jun 1917), 4.
26. The Yellow Creek statement, for example, referred to William Penn, the U.S. Constitution, the state constitutions, and Civil War exemption. See Hartzler, *Mennonites in the World War* (note 19), 63. "A Petition to Congress," signed by J. W. Kliewer, President of the Western District Conference, Apr 21, 1917, mentions President Grant's 1873 assurances regarding conscription; copy in f. PM18, H. P. Krehbiel papers, MLA.

27. On the clergy's support for the war see Ray H. Abrams, *Preachers Present Arms* (Scottdale, Pa., 1969).

28. On American society and the war, see David M. Kennedy, *Over Here* (New York, 1980). On the government's campaign against pacifists and dissenters, see H. C. Peterson and Gilbert C. Fite, *Opponents of War 1917-1918* (Seattle, 1968).

29. McAdoo, *Crowded Years* (Boston, 1931), 278-79, quoted in Kennedy, *Over Here* (note 28), 105, and in Margaret Entz, "War Bond Drives and the Kansas Mennonite Response," *ML*, 30 (Sep 1975), 4.

30. Frederick C. Luebke, *Bonds of Loyalty: German Americans and World War I* (DeKalb, 1974), xv.

31. Allan Teichroew, "Military Surveillance of Mennonites in World War I," *MQR*, 53 (Apr 1979), 95-127.

32. *Der Herold*, 28 (Nov 5, 1914).

33. *Der Herold*, 31 (Apr 19, 1917).

34. Stucky, "Fighting Against War: The Mennonite *Vorwaerts* from 1914 to 1919," *Kansas Historical Quarterly*, 38 (Sum 1972), 169-86.

35. Schellenberg, "Amerikaner," *Vorwärts*, 14 (Mar 10, 1916), 6.

36. Report of Inspector W. F. Allmon, Dec 6, 1917, "Post Office Dept, RG 28, Solicitors Office," box 2, World War I Collection #155, MLA.

37. *Conference Reports, 1896-1956, Church of God in Christ, Mennonite* (Lahoma Okla., 1956), 20; Margaret Entz, "War Bond Drives and the Kansas Mennonite Response," *ML*, 30 (Sep 1975), 6.

38. *TM*, 33 (Oct 10, 1918), 4.

39. Loucks to S. C. Yoder, Mar 30, Apr 22, 1918, f. 6, box 13, Yoder papers, AMC. *Vorwaerts*, 16 (May 3, 1918), 1.

40. See, for example, the giving to the Bethel College fund drive in 1918-1919. Peter J. Wedel, *The Story of Bethel College* (North Newton, Kans., 1954), 250.

41. John L. Schrock, "Edward B. Frey: His Life and Work" (research paper, Associated Mennonite Biblical Seminaries, 1980), 10.

42. Willard Smith, *Mennonites in Illinois* (Scottdale, Pa., and Kitchener, Ont., 1983), 357.

43. Capper to Schrag, Oct 15, 1918. Kansas State Historical Society alphabetical file, counties, 1917-1919, Hamilton-Jackson. Note from Allan Teichroew in the author's possession.

44. Lohrenz to J. J. Kliewer, Mar 27, 1918, Lohrenz papers, MLA.

45. See clippings and notes on the Gingerich case in f. 12, box 2, J. C. Meyer papers, AMC.

46. James C. Juhnke, "Mob Violence and Kansas Mennonites in 1918," *Kansas Historical Quarterly*, 43 (Aug 1977), 334-50.

47. Schowalter Oral History Interviews with Henry Cooprider, Oct 23, 1966, and Charles Diener, Apr 29, 1969.

48. LaVernae J. Dick, "A Noose for the Minister," *TM*, 79 (Apr 21, 1964), 262-65. Rufus M. Franz, "It Happened in Montana," *ML*, 7 (Oct 1952), 181-84. Schowalter Oral History Interview with Anthony Unruh, Jun 19, 1970.

49. Ibid., entire note.

50. *Newton Evening Kansan-Republican* (Dec 27, 1918).

51. James C. Juhnke, "John Schrag Espionage Case," *ML*, 22 (Jul 1967), 121-22.

52. Peterson and Fite, *Opponents of War* (note 28), 208-21.

53. *The* [Sugar Creek, OH] *Weekly Budget* (May 15, 1918), 3. The letter was dated April 24. Quoted in Ted Joseph, "The United States vs. H. Miller: The Strange Case of a Mennonite Editor Convicted of Violating the 1917 Espionage Act," *ML*, (Sep 1975), 14-15.

54. Joseph, "United States vs. Miller" (note 53), 14-18.

55. Lewis J. Heatwole, *Moral Training in the Public Schools* (Scottdale, Pa., 1908), 25.

56. For accounts of the Heatwole-Benner prosecution, see the L. J. Heatwole

papers, Menno Simons Historical Library, Eastern Mennonite College, Harrisonburg, Va.; Harry Anthony Brunk, *History of the Mennonites in Virginia, 1900-
1960* (Harrisonburg, Va., 1972), 196-99, 455-58; Hartzler, *Mennonites in the World
War* (note 19), 159-63; and Wayne Smith, "Rockingham County Nonresistance"
(thesis abstract, Madison College, 1967), 74-89.

57. The Crooks plan is explained in documents from the Department of Jus-
tice, RG 60, copies in box 4, World War I Collection #155, MLA. See also Aaron
Loucks to David Goertz, Jun 22, 1918, Loucks-Hartzler corresp., Peace Problems
Committee papers, AMC.

58. John Lord O'Brian to Edwin S. Wertz, Sep 19, 1918, Microfilm #208,
MLA. On Espionage Act prosecutions in general see Kennedy, *Over Here* (note 28),
83. The possibility of a mass trial was mentioned the *New York Times* (Aug 20,
1918), 6.

59. J. S. Hartzler to J. E. Hartzler, May 17, 1919, f. 6, box 4, J. E. Hartzler
papers, AMC.

60. For a thorough study of Mennonite English-language rhetorical responses to the war, see Susan Schultz Huxman, "Mennonite Rhetoric in World War I:
Reconciling Loyalties to God and Country" (M.A. thesis, U. of Kansas, 1986).

61. W. W. Griest to Newton D. Baker, Nov 9, 1917, and attached Lancaster
Conference resolution signed by Benjamin Weaver, Noah L. Landis, Peter R.
Nissley, I. B. Good, and J. C. Habecker; "Records of the Selective Service System,"
RG 163, box 1, World War I Collection #155, MLA.

62. Quoted in Allan Teichroew, "Accommodation and Escape: The Mennonite
Response to World War I" (research paper, Bethel College, 1969), 39. See also
"Mennonites at Hillsboro Offer Rooms in Hospital to Care for Wounded Men,"
Topeka Capital (Sep 20, 1918); "Mennonite Clippings," Kansas State Historical Li-
brary.

63. Guy F. Hershberger, *War, Peace and Nonresistance* (Scottdale, Pa., 1953),
119.

64. *GH*, 9 (Aug 10, 1916), 353.

65. Statement inserted in *Congressional Record* by Senator Charles Curtis
of Kansas (65th Congress, First Session, Vol. 55, Part 1), 510.

66. All-Mennonite Convention committee report, copy in Daniel Kauffman
papers, box 4, Hist. Mss 1-20, AMC.

67. *Congressional Record* (Vol. 55, Part 1, Apr 5, 1917), 261, 412-13.

68. For background information on Baker and the conscientious objectors,
see Daniel R. Beaver, *Newton D. Baker and the American War Effort 1917-1919*
(Lincoln, 1966), 231-39; and Donald Johnson, *The Challenge to American Freedoms: World War I and the Rise of the American Civil Liberties Union* (Lexington, 1963), 26-54.

69. Newton D. Baker, *Frontiers of Freedom* (New York, 1918), 37.

70. Baker to Wilson, Oct 1, 1917, box 4, Baker papers, Library of Congress.

71. J. W. Kliewer, *Memoirs of J. W. Kliewer* (North Newton, Kans., 1943), 91-
92.

72. Telegram from Benjamin Esch to Baker, Sep 8, 1917; attached memo
from Baker to General Crowder, n.d., Records of the Selective Service System, RG
163, box 1, World War I Collection #155, MLA. I am indebted to Allan Teichroew
for his excellent collection of copies of government documents relating to Mennonites during the war.

73. Undated petition to the Secretary of War, signed by Jacob Fast, John
Esau, Johan J. Friesen, Peter A. Wiebe, and K. D. Willems; Baker to Jacob Fast, Sep
11, 1917; copies in Records of the Selective Service System, RG 163, box 1, World
War I Collection #155, MLA.

74. Account by Edward Yoder in "Mennonite CO's in World War I," f. 24, V-7-
19, AMC. There were also several isolated cases of Mennonites who refused the
draft call or deserted the army for reasons apparently unrelated to denominational policy. See the case of P. W. Leppke, in the *Cordell Beacon* (Feb 28, 1918), copy
in box 2, World War I Collection #155, MLA.

75. *Der Wahrheitsfreund*, 3 (Oct 3, 1917), 11.
76. Allan Teichroew, "World War I and the Mennonite Migration to Canada to Avoid the Draft," *MQR*, 45 (Jul 1971), 219-49.
77. Frank H. Epp, *Mennonites in Canada, 1786-1920* (Toronto, 1974), 373, 385.
78. Information on the feelings and attitudes of the Mennonite draftees is available in the extensive Schowalter Oral History Collection in MLA. See the index to the collection: Keith L. Sprunger, James C. Juhnke, and John D. Waltner, eds., *Voices Against War* (North Newton, Kans., 1973). For selected published interviews see Mary Sprunger, ed., *Sourcebook: Oral History Interviews with World War One Conscientious Objectors* (Akron, Pa., 1986). Two of the most revealing published draftee diaries are by Noah H. Leatherman (a Holdeman Mennonite), *Diary Kept by Noah H. Leatherman While in Camp During World War I* (Linden, Alta., 1951); and Jakob Waldner (a Hutterite), *An Account*, ed. by Theron Schlabach, trans. by Ilse Reist and Elizabeth Bender, *MQR*, 48 (Jan 1974), 73-111.
79. U.S. War Department, *Statement Concerning the Treatment of Conscientious Objectors in the Army*, prepared by Colonel James S. Easby-Smith, Judge Advocate (Washington, 1919), 17, 37.
80. Leonard Wood diary at Oct 16, 1917, box 9, Wood papers, Library of Congress. See also Wood's October corresp. to the Adjutant General, in Funston Decimal File, RG 393, National Archives.
81. "Mennonite CO's in World War I" (Mennonite Research Foundation Survey of Mennonite World War I Draftees), V-7-19, AMC.
82. Clarence S. Yoakum and Robert M. Yerkes, *Army Mental Tests* (New York, 1920), 196. Report by General B. P. Glenn after a visit to Camp Sherman, Ohio, n.d.; copy in War Department, Adjutant General's files, RG 407, box 2, World War I Collection #155, MLA.
83. To P. H. Unruh, October 24, 1918, Unruh papers, MLA.
84. Cornelius Voth, Schowalter Oral History Interview, Jun 9, 1968, transcription p. 13.
85. See J. Stanley Yake, "Treatment of Mennonite Conscientious Objectors in World War I Army Camps" (research paper, Goshen College, 1957), and Willard Martin, "World War I Conscientious Objectors in Fort Leavenworth" (research paper, Goshen College, 1957).
86. Willis Shumacher, Schowalter Oral History Interview, Jun 21, 1969.
87. E. Z. Yoder to Sanford Yoder, Jun 26, 1918, f. 8, box 13, Sanford Yoder papers, AMC.
88. David A. Janzen, "My Experiences as a Young Man in World War I" (mimeographed, 1940, in MLA), 6, 16.
89. Enos Stutzman, Schowalter Oral History Interview, Aug 3, 1968; excerpt published in *ML*, 30 (Sep 1975), 19.
90. "Court Martial 1918, Pvt. Ura V. Aschliman (420382)," *ML*, 31 (Sep 1976), 18-21.
91. Court Martial 1166001, Camp Travis, Texas; microfilm #427, MLA; Albert Voth, Schowalter Oral History Interview, Feb 1, 1969.
92. Warren Gish to Aaron Loucks, Jun 29, 1918, Loucks-Hartzler Corresp., Peace Problems Committee papers, 1-3-5, AMC.
93. Easby-Smith, *Statement Concerning* (note 79), 25. "Conscientious Objectors, A Brief Summary of the War Department Regulations for the Handling of this Class . . ."; copy in "Record of Adjutant General RG 407," box 3, World War I Collection #155, MLA.
94. J. D. Mininger, "Religious C.O.s Imprisoned at the U.S. Disciplinary Barracks, Ft. Leavenworth Kansas City" (Kansas City, Kans.: n.p., Mar 10, 1919), in author's possession.
95. Griest to E. H. Crowder, Jan 17, 1918, copy in the I. B. Good papers, Lancaster Mennonite Historical Society Archives, Lancaster, Pa.
96. C. C. Janzen, "A Social Study of the Mennonite Settlement in the Counties of Marion, McPherson, Harvey, Reno, and Butler, Kansas" (Ph.D. diss., U.

of Chicago, 1926), 66; Arlyn J. Parish, *Kansas Mennonites During World War I* (Hays, Kans., 1968), 45; John E. Lapp, "Peace Testimony of Mennonites in the 20th Century: Franconia and Eastern District" (taped lecture for the Mennonite Associated Librarians and Archivists, May 7, 1980; *Mennonite Yearbook and Directory, 1918* (Scottdale, Pa., 1918), 36-37; Ruth E. Stover, "The Franconia Conference and the Conscientious Objectors of World War I," *Mennonite Research Journal* (Jan 1965), 1, 7. The Western District conference had 24 congregations with 5,145 members and furnished more than 200 draftees.

97. Not all scholars agree that the Farm Furlough Act was designed to address the problem of conscientious-objector classification. For a contrasting view see Sarah D. Shields, "The Treatment of Conscientious Objectors during World War I," *Kansas History*, 4 (Win 1981), 255-69. There is evidence, however, that as early as February, 1918, President Wilson anticipated that this legislation would be used for COs. I have been helped on this topic by research notes from Al Keim, Harrisonburg, Va.

98. Walter Guest Kellogg, *The Conscientious Objector* (New York, 1919), 38-41.

99. Ibid.

100. Copy of a 44-page set of investigative reports on Loucks in "War Dept, MID, RG 165, file 10902-18/24," box 2, World War I Collection #155, MLA.

101. F. P. Keppel to J. J. Kerrigan, Aug 22, 1918, in Teichrow, "Military Surveillance," *MQR*, 53 (Apr 1979), 116.

102. An account of this case by Theo. H. Lunde, dated February 1919, is quoted at length in C. Henry Smith, *The Coming of the Russian Mennonites* (Berne, Ind., 1927), 277-82.

103. The contrast between Ewert and Mininger can be observed in Ewert's wartime writings in *Vorwärts* and in Mininger's papers in the AMC. In that collection see Ewert to Mininger, Dec 21, 1918, noting that several hundred people in the Hillsboro area had signed a petition to government asking for release of the imprisoned men by Christmas. "Old" Mennonites were less inclined to such aggressive action.

104. Kansas House Concurrent Resolution No. 11, 1919; copy in RG 98, USDB 7 Fort Leavenworth, file 383.2, box 24, National Archives.

105. J. L. Napier, "Baker and the C.O.," *Newton Evening-Kansan Republican*, 35 (Jan 29, 1919).

106. Baker to Colonel Sedgwick Rice, Copy in MLA World War I Collection #155, box 2, "War Dept, U.S. Disciplinary Barracks, Fort Leavenworth, RG 393, file 383.2.

107. Petition to Governor of Iowa, copy in "War Department, MID, RG 165, 10902:20-60," box 4, World War I Collection #155, MLA. S. C. Yoder to Milton Brenneman, Sep 13, 1918, f. 3, Yoder papers, AMC.

108. Memo from Brigadier General E. D. Anderson, Nov 15, 1918; copy "War Dept, War College Div, RG 165, in box 4, World War I Collection #155, MLA.

109. Hostetter to I. B. Good, Jul 21, 1918, I. B. Good papers, LMHS (note 95).

110. Investigative report filed by Paul Hawkinson, Aug 19, 1918 "MID PF Files, RG165," box 2, World War I Collection #155, MLA.

111. Peter H. Richert, *A Brief Catechism on Difficult Scripture Passages and Involved Questions on the Use of the Sword* (Newton, Kans., 1942), 5.

112. Military Intelligence Division report quoted in Allan Teichroew, "Military Surveillance of Mennonites in World War I," *MQR*, 53 (Apr 1979), 122.

113. For an survey essay on Mennonites and the draft, see James C. Juhnke, "Mennonites and Military Conscription in the Twentieth Century," *Mennonites and Conscientious Objection in 1980* (Akron, Pa.: Mennonite Central Committee, 1980), 19-29.

CHAPTER 9

1. Joan Hoff Wilson, *Herbert Hoover, Forgotten Progressive* (Boston, 1975), 46-64.

2. P. C. Hiebert, *Feeding the Hungry* (Scottdale, Pa., 1929), inset between 434-35.

3. Robert Handy, "The American Religious Depression, 1925-1935," *Church History*, 29 (1960), 3-16.

4. C. Henry Smith, "Mennonites and War," *Report of the Fourth All-Mennonite Convention* (Goshen, Ind.: n.p., 1922), 83.

5. W. S. Gottschall to P. H. Richert, Aug 6, 1917, f. 19, P. H. Richert papers, MLA.

6. *Franconia Conference Record Book 1907-1961* (at Oct 4, 1917), 15.

7. Richard K. MacMaster, *Land, Piety, and Peoplehood: The Establishment of Mennonite Communities in America, 1683-1790* (Scottdale, Pa., and Kitchener, Ont., 1985), 280.

8. Editorial, "Opportunities and Responsibilities," *Christian Monitor,* 12 (Mar 1920), 455.

9. "Report of the Foreign Mission Board, Report B," *Reports and Resolutions of the Foreign Mission Board 1901-1924,* 40.

10. L. O. King to Members of the Kansas-Nebraska Mission Board, May 1, 1918; copy in "Correspondence May 1918," box 5, J. D. Mininger papers, AMC.

11. U. S. Bureau of the Census, *Historical Statistics of the United States, Colonial Times to 1957* (Washington, 1960), 289, 294-95, 297, 302.

12. Edwin Alderfer, "The Giving of the Mennonite Church" (research paper, Goshen College, 1945).

13. Kaufman, *Development of the Missionary and Philanthropic Interest Among the Mennonites of North America* (Berne, Ind., 1931), 176. These figures do not represent the total giving of these two groups. They suggest increased giving by both groups, not comparative amounts between the groups.

14. William Derstine to Aaron Loucks, Jul 4, 1918, "Loucks-Hartzler Correspondence July 1-8, 1918," Peace Problems Committee papers, AMC.

15. Application form for Mennonite Relief Commission for War Sufferers, "General Correspondence, August 1920," box 1, Russian Relief Collection, AMC.

16. G. L. Bender to J. D. Mininger, Oct 7, 1918, Mininger papers, AMC.

17. Ira J. Miller to J. D. Mininger, Jun 26, Jul 9, 1918, Mininger papers, AMC.

18. Peter J. Wedel, ed., *The Story of Bethel College* (North Newton, Kans., 1954), 250-51.

19. Paul Toews, "Henry W. Lohrenz and Tabor College," *Mennonite Life,* 38 (Sep 1983), 18.

20. "Home and Foreign Relief Commission," *ME,* II, 796-97.

21. From *Reports of the Minutes of the General Conference of the Mennonites of North America,* 1902, 1905, 1908, 1911, and 1914.

22. Orlando Harms, *Pioneer Publisher: The Life and Times of J. F. Harms* (Winnipeg, 1984), 83.

23. M. B. Fast, "Abschied Nehmen," *Mennonitische Rundschau,* 33 (Sep 28, 1910), Vor10.

24. *Vorwärts* (Dec 4, Dec 18, 1914), 5, 6.

25. Guy F. Hershberger, "Historical Background to the Formation of the Mennonite Central Committee," *MQR,* 44 (Jul 1970), 237.

26. William J. Regier, "The Arrival of Milch Cows in Bremen, Germany," transl. of memoirs of Peter Andres, Elbing, Kans., one of the eight Mennonite boys who accompanied the cattle to Germany; in MLA.

27. John D. Unruh, *In the Name of Christ: A History of the Mennonite Central Committee and Its Service 1920-1951* (Scottdale, Pa., 1952), 14-15. Frank H. Epp, *Mennonite Exodus: The Rescue and Resettlement of the Russian Mennonites Since the Communist Revolution* (Altona, Man., 1962), 56-57.

28. Minutes of the annual meeting of the Mennonite Relief Commission for War Sufferers [MRCWS], Jun 3, 1919, minute book, box 4, MCC papers, AMC.

29. Exec. Comm. minutes, Aug 8, 1919, MRCWS minute book (note 28).

30. Annual meeting minutes, May 16-17, 1921, MRCWS minute book (note 28).

31. Paul Erb, *Orie O. Miller: The Story of a Man and an Era* (Scottdale, Pa., 1969), 159.

32. *ME*, IV, 262-63. J. C. Meyer, in *Mennonite Historical Bulletin*: "The Origin of the Young People's Conference Movement of 1918," 28 (Apr 1967), 4-5; "The Young People's Conference Movement Held in Clermont, France," 29 (Jul 1968), 5-7.

33. Vinora Weaver Salzman, *Day by Day—Year by Year* (n.p.: the author, 1982), 26, 17-18.

34. The story of the relief effort is told most fully in Hiebert, *Feeding the Hungry* (note 2). See also the summary by Harold S. Bender, "Hilfswerk der amerikanischen Mennoniten in Russland," *Bericht über die Mennonitische Welt-Hilfs-Konferenz* (Karlsruhe, 1930), 59-64.

35. G. A. Peters, "Clayton Kratz," trans. by A. W. Slagel, in Hiebert, *Feeding the Hungry* (note 32), 343-53.

36. Wesley J. Prieb, "Peter (P. C.) Hiebert" in Cornelius J. Dyck, ed., *Something Meaningful for God* (Scottdale, Pa., and Kitchener, Ont., 1981), 124-25. Harms, *Pioneer Publisher* (note 22), 79-83.

37. Minutes of Dec 28, 1923, "Executive Committee Minutes 1923-24," MCC papers, AMC.

38. John B. Toews, *Lost Fatherland: The Story of the Mennonite Emigration from Soviet Russia, 1921-1927* (Scottdale, Pa., 1967), 202.

39. On the story of the Mennonite migrations, see Epp, *Mennonite Exodus* (note 25), and Toews, *Lost Fatherland* (note 38).

40. Cornelius J. Dyck and Robert Kreider, "Mennonite World Conference in Review," *ML*, 33 (Jun 1978), 5.

41. Bender, *Bericht* (note 34), 64.

42. Ibid., 65.

43. Robert H. Bremner, *American Philanthropy* (Chicago, 1960), 1.

44. 1918 stationery of American Committee for Armenian and Syrian Relief, "Near East Relief 1917-1922," box 21, MCC papers, AMC.

45. MRCWS minutes, Jan 6, 1918, MRCWS minute book (note 28).

46. Hiebert, *Feeding the Hungry* (note 2), 436-37, 29.

47. See the General Conference Mennonite statement of August 1941, in Urbane Peachey, ed., *Mennonite Statements on Peace and Social Concerns, 1900-1978* (Akron, Pa.: MCC, 1980), 141. See also the "old" Mennonite statement of August 1937 in the same volume, 168-70.

48. MRCWS minutes, MRCWS minute book (note 28).

49. Aaron Loucks, "Relief Work," *GH*, 12 (Nov 18, 1920), 666.

50. John Horsch, "Mennonites as Recipients of Relief in Past History," *Christian Monitor*, 12 (Feb 1920), 439, 446.

51. Orie O. Miller to "Dear Brother," Apr 8, 1919, Aaron Loucks folder, Mennonite Board of Missions and Charities papers, AMC.

52. Minutes of Dec 28, 1923, "Executive Committee Minutes 1923-24," MCC papers, AMC.

53. MRCWS annual meeting minutes, May 3, 1924,, MRCWS minute book (note 28). P. C. Hiebert reported on the plans for this new and permanent organization at the 1927 All-Mennonite Convention; see *Report of the Sixth All-Mennonite Convention* (Hillsboro, Kans., 1927).

54. Minutes of the Preliminary Meeting of the American Mennonite Relief Commission, Dec 30, 1924, "Executive Committee Minutes 1923-24," MCC papers, AMC.

55. Minutes of the American Mennonite Relief Commission, Dec 30, 1926, "Executive Committee Minutes 1925-29," MCC papers, AMC.

56. Melvin Gingerich, "A Perspective of North American Mennonite Overseas Outreach 1890-1963," *Proceedings of Consultation on Relief, Services, and Missions Relationships Overseas* (Chicago: n.p., 1964), 24.

57. Paul Snyder, Interview, Jun 24, 1969, Schowalter Oral History papers, MLA.

58. Hiebert, *Feeding the Hungry* (note 2), 416. The Scripture reference, with Mennonites in the place of Christ, is from John 4:6.

59. "Christianity's Greatest Foe," *GH*, (Mar 27, 1919), 921.

60. Ernerst R. Sandeen, *The Roots of Fundamentalism* (Chicago, 1970). Sandeen's approach informed the pioneering work on Mennonite fundamentalism by Rodney Sawatsky; see Sawatsky, "The Influence of Fundamentalism on Mennonite Nonresistance 1908-1944" (M.A. thesis, U. of Minnesota, 1973).

61. George Marsden, *Fundamentalism and American Culture* (New York, 1980), 4.

62. John Horsch, *The Mennonite Church and Modernism* (Scottdale, Pa., 1924), 14.

63. John L. Stauffer, "Meditations on the Report of the General Conference of Mennonites in France in Reconstruction Work," *GH*, 12 (Feb 19, 1920), 892.

64. Guy F. Hershberger, "Comments on Sawatsky's Thesis" (unpub. ms., 1979, copy in AMC), 94-98.

65. Rodney Sawatsky, "Fundamentalism, Liberalism and Anabaptism: Mennonite Choices in the 1920's and 1930's" (unpub. paper, May 1979, copy in AMC).

66. N. C. Hirschy, "Higher Criticism," *The Review*, 1 (Jun 1899), 1.

67. *Institute Monthly*, 2 (Apr 15, 1900), 121-22.

68. "Evolution and Revelation," *TM*, 17 (Oct 2, 1902), 4-5. "Facts Suggesting Evolution," *TM*, 17 (Oct 9, 1902), 4.

69. C. H. Wedel, "Über neutestamentliche Textkritik," *Monatsblätter aus Bethel College*, 9: (May 1904), 50-51; (Jun 1904), 110-11; (Jul 1904), 122-23; (Aug 1904), 134-35.

70. J. W. Kliewer to J. E. Amstutz, Oct 27, 1910, f. 79, Foreign Mission Board Corresp. File, MLA.

71. C. Norman Kraus, "American Mennonites and the Bible," *MQR*, 41 (Oct 1967), 319.

72. J. B. Smith to George R. Brunk, Dec 17, 1935, Brunk papers, Virginia Conference Archives, Eastern Mennonite College, Harrisonburg, Va.

73. J. B. Smith to George R. Brunk, Apr 25, 1916, Brunk papers (note 72).

74. *Conference Record of the Kansas-Nebraska Mennonite Conference 1876-1914*, 166, 168.

75. George R. Brunk to J. B. Smith, Sep 27, 1919, Smith papers, box A1, Menno Simons Historical Library and Archives, Eastern Mennonite College, Harrisonburg, Va. See also Loren Johns, "The 1921 Garden City Confession of Faith or 'The Christian Fundamentals,' " (unpublished paper, 1984), 10-11.

76. *Minutes of the Virginia Mennonite Conference* (Scottdale, Pa., 1939), 128-31.

77. George R. Brunk to J. B. Smith, A. D. Wenger, and Daniel Kauffman, Dec 18, 1918, box 2, I-20, Kauffman papers, AMC.

78. See James C. Juhnke, "Mennonite Church Theological and Social Boundaries, 1920-1930—Loyalists, Liberals and Laxitarians," *ML*, 38 (Jun 1983), 18-24.

79. Brunk letter (note 77).

80. Comments by D. H. Bender, George R. Brunk, and L. J. Heatwole, Mar 1910, on *Paths to Perdition* manuscript in response to a request from Daniel Kauffman; box 1, I-20, Kauffman papers, AMC.

81. See synopsis of the inaugural address in *Goshen College Record*, 16 (Nov 1913), 7-12.

82. In 1931 Brunk wrote a five-column review of the 1914 edition of Kauffman's *Doctrines of the Bible* even though that book had been superseded by a 1928 revised edition; see "Corrupting a Book," *Sword and Trumpet*, 3 (Apr 1931), 2-4.

83. J. B. Smith to J. E. Hartzler, Apr 27, 1918, f. 11, box 3, I-62, Hartzler papers, AMC. See Joseph S. Miller, *Beyond the Mystic Border* (Hesston, Kans.: Whitestone Mennonite Church, 1985), 84-86.

84. J. E. Hartzler papers, I-62, AMC: Hartzler to Wm. B. Weaver, Dec 23, 1918, box 4; Hartzler to Weaver, Jan 10, Feb 9, Jun 21, Jul 3, Oct 25, Nov 22, Nov 30, 1920, f. 5/9, box 5; Weaver to Hartzler, Oct 21, Oct 22, Nov 11, Nov 27, Dec 15, 1920, f. 5/9, box 5; Hartzler to T. M. Erb, Apr 14, Apr 17, Jul 5, 1920, f. 5/3, box 5; Erb to Hartzler, Apr 16 and esp. Nov 26, 1920, f. 5/3, box 5. Tilman M. Erb diaries, box 2, Erb papers, I-525, AMC: at Apr 22, Jun 20, 1920. Daniel H. Bender diary, at Jul 4, 1920, box 1, Bender papers, I-17, AMC. D. H. Bender to Daniel Kauffman, Apr 27, Jun 29, 1920, box 2, Kauffman papers, 1-20, AMC. Hartzler to P. E. Whitmer, Jun 29, 1920, box 5, Hartzler papers, I-62, AMC.

85. Grant Stoltzfus, *Mennonites of the Ohio and Eastern Conference* (Scottdale, Pa., 1969), 192.

86. Ervin Schlabach, *The Amish Mennonites at Walnut Creek* (Millersburg, Ohio: The author, 1981). Lester Hostetler, "My Spiritual Pilgrimage" (unedited first draft of autobiography; typed, edited version at AMC). Lester Hostetler interview with author, Goshen, Ind., Feb 24, 1981. Lester and Charity Steiner Hostetler diary, box 1, Hostetler papers, AMC.

87. D. H. Bender to J. B. Smith, May 25, 1920, f. "Bender, D. H.," box A2,, J. B. Smith papers, MSHLA (note 75).

88. John Graybill, "The Search for Truth: A Study of the *Christian Exponent* and Its Place Within the Conservative-Progressive Conflict in the Mennonite Church in the 1920's" (research paper, Goshen College, 1982). Sawatsky, "The Influence of Fundamentalism" (note 60), 98-111. Janeen Bertsche, "Views of Atonement in the *Christian Exponent*" (research paper, Bluffton College, 1984).

89. O. B. Gerig to H. S. Bender, Mar 2, 1920, f. 1, box 2, Bender papers, AMC.

90. Daniel Kauffman to H. S. Bender, Apr 28, 1924, box 3, Bender papers, AMC.

91. *Christian Exponent*, 1 (Jan 4, 18, 1924), 6-8, 23-25.

92. J. E. Hartzler, "The 'Faith of Our Fathers,'" *Christian Exponent*, 1 (Feb 1, 1924). J. C. Meyer, "Modernism in the Mennonite Church," *Christian Exponent*, 2 (Dec 4, 1925), 391-92.

93. Vernon Smucker, "Fundamentals of the Faith," *Christian Exponent*, 2 (Jan 16, 1925), 20.

94. Janeen Bertsche, "Views of Atonement in the *Christian Exponent*," *ML*, 41 (Jun 1986), 4-8.

95. See letters of appreciation for Horsch's anti-Modernist writings in boxes 2 and 3, Horsch papers, AMC.

96. Horsch, *The Mennonite Church* (note 60), 131.

97. John S. Umble, *Goshen College 1894-1954* (Goshen, Ind., 1955), 115-51. Sanford C. Yoder, *The Days of My Years* (Scottdale, Pa., 1959), 203-19.

98. Mary Miller, *A Pillar of Cloud: The Story of Hesston College 1909-1959* (Hesston, Kans., 1959), 70-72. John D. Charles, *Fallacies of Evolution* (Scottdale, Pa., 1917).

99. Hubert R. Pellman, *Eastern Mennonite College, 1917-1967* (Harrisonburg, Va., 1967), 76-78.

100. Paul Toews, "Fundamentalist Conflict in Mennonite Colleges: A Response to Cultural Transitions," *MQR*, 57 (Jul 1983), 253-54.

101. Wedel, *The Story of Bethel College* (note 18), 235-326, 343. Toews, "Fundamentalist Conflict," 249-51. Delores Reimer, "Jacob Frank Balzer and the Experience at Bethel College 1913-1918" (Bethel College seminar paper, 1974).

102. R. H. Torrey to H. W. Lohrenz, Dec 1, 1920, Lohrenz papers, MLA.

103. H. W. Lohrenz to P. E. Schellenberg, Jun 29, 1922, Lohrenz papers, MLA.

104. C. C. Goosen, "Gebetserhörung," *Tabor College Herold*, 10 (Feb 19, 1922), 3.

105. "Y.W.C.A. Report," *Tabor College Herold*, 10 (19 Feb 1922), 4.

106. Report in *Zionsbote* (Feb 1, 1922), 10.

107. Dick Eitzen, "History of the Ebenfeld Mennonite Brethren Church" (n.p., ca. 1951), 2.

108. C. J. J., writing in *Vorwärts*, 20 (Feb 10, 1922).

109. Goosen, "Gebetserhörung" (note 104), 3.

110. James C. Juhnke, *A People of Two Kingdoms* (Newton, Kans., 1975), 117.

111. Juhnke, *A People of Two Kingdoms* (note 110), 119-22, 150.

112. James C. Juhnke, "Gerald B. Winrod and the Kansas Mennonites," *MQR*, 43 (Oct 1969), 293-98. James Schrag, "Gerald Burton Winrod: The Defender" (Bethel College seminar paper, 1966).

113. Frank Epp, "An Analysis of National Socialism in the Immigrant Newspaper of a Canadian Minority Group, the Mennonites" (Ph.D. diss, U. of Minnesota, 1965).

CHAPTER 10

1. H. P. Krehbiel, "Frau Harding mennonitischer Abstammung," *Der Herold*, 34 (Dec 2, 1920), 4.

2. Ibid.

3. Eugene Trani and David L. Wilson, *The Presidency of Warren G. Harding* (Lawrence, Kans., 1977), 189-92.

4. Among the exceptions to this generalization was Henry A. Fast of Mountain Lake, Minnesota, who had leadership roles at Bethel College, in the General Conference, and in Mennonite Central Committee subsequent to his noncombatant military service in World War I.

5. J. C. Meyer letter to H. S. Bender, Aug 5, 1919, f. 9, box 1, 1-44, Meyer papers, AMC.

6. This is based upon extensive interviewing of Mennonite World War I draftees in the late 1960s and early 1970s for the Schowalter Oral History Collection, MLA. See *Voices Against War, A Guide to the Schowalter Oral History Collection on World War I Conscientious Objection* (North Newton, Kans.: Bethel College, 1973, rev. 1981).

7. See the biography by Paul Erb, *Orie O. Miller: The Story of a Man and an Era* (Scottdale, Pa., 1969). Erb calls the period from 1920 to 1965 the "Bender-Miller era" (p. 68). There is no biography of H. S. Bender, but see the memorial issue of *MQR*, 38 (Apr 1964).

8. See the issue of *MQR* dedicated to Elizabeth Bender, 60 (Apr 1986).

9. Erb, *Orie O. Miller* (note 7), 47-51.

10. Stauffer, "Meditations on the Report of the General Conference of Mennonites in France in Reconstruction Work," *GH*, 12 (Feb 19, 1920), 891-92. The Bender-Stauffer exchange is in f. 6, box 4, Bender papers, AMC: Bender to Stauffer, Mar 1, 1920; Stauffer to Bender, Mar 19, 1920; Bender draft on dress and separation, n.d.; Bender to Stauffer, May 18, 1920; Stauffer to Bender, May 31m 1920; Brunk to Bender, Jun 16, 1920.

11. Bender to Stauffer, May 18, 1920 (note 10).

12. Vernon Smucker letter to H. S. Bender, Jul 30, 1924, f. 4, box 4, Bender papers, AMC.

13. S. C. Yoder to H. S. Bender, Oct 2 and Dec 1, 1923, f. 13, box 4, Bender papers, AMC.

14. S. C. Yoder to H. S. Bender, May 17, 1924, f. 13, box 4, Bender papers, AMC.

15. "Conversations with Elizabeth Bender IV" (interview by Leonard Gross), *Mennonite Historical Bulletin*, 47 (Jul 1986), 8.

16. H. S. Bender (from Tübingen) to John Horsch, Apr 29, 1924, f. 1, box 8, Horsch papers, AMC.

17. S. C. Yoder, *The Days of My Years* (Scottdale, Pa., 1959), 199-200.

18. In 1959 Bender did publish a statement on the basis of scriptural au-

thority, but it identified the wrong ways of Bible study without directly addressing the methods of historical library criticism: "Biblical Revelation and Inspiration" (Scottdale, Pa., 1959), 19 pp. See James C. Juhnke, "Mennonite Church Theological and Social Boundaries, 1920-1930—Loyalists, Liberals and Laxitarians," *ML*, 38 (Jun 1983), 18-24.

19. Bender, "To the Youth of the Mennonite Church," *MQR*, 1 (Jan 1927), inside front cover.

20. See Lester Hostetler to H. S. Bender, Jul 5, 1926, Dec 16, 1926, Nov 7, 1927; f. 9, box 2, Bender papers, AMC.

21. Hartzler, *Education. . .* (Danvers, Ill., 1925).

22. Bender, *The Goshen College Record—Review Supplement* (often bound with early issues of the *MQR*), 27 (May-Jun 1926), 35-44.

23. John H. Mosemann to Harold Bender, Jul 5, 1927, f. 6, box 3, Bender papers, AMC. See also appreciative letter from conservative bishop Noah Mack to Bender, Aug 21, 1926, in f. 7 of same box; and the approving statement of J. L. Stauffer in letter to J. B. Smith, Jul 14, 1926, f. "John L. Stauffer," box A2, Smith papers, Menno Simons Historical Library and Archives, Eastern Mennonite College, Harrisonburg, Va.

24. H. S. Bender to John Horsch, Dec 12, 1926, f. "1926 A-B," box 3, Horsch papers, AMC.

25. H. S. Bender to "Mr. Smith," n. date, f. 16, box 3, Bender papers, AMC.

26. For discussion of the Kaufman book issue and Bender's frustration over the Scottdale veto, see H. S. Bender to John Horsch, Aug 8, 1929, f. "1929 A-H," box 4, Horsch papers, AMC. See also Bender to Kaufman, September 28, 1929, and Kaufman to Bender, Oct 5, 1929, f. 2, box 3, Bender papers, AMC.

27. See the concluding chapter, "The Anabaptist Vision as Mennonite Ideology," in Sawatsky, "History and Ideology: American Mennonite Identity Definition Through History" (Ph.D. diss., Princeton U., 1977), 261-97.

28. Erb, *Orie O. Miller* (note 7), 17-21.

29. Mosemann to Horsch, Oct 11, 1927, f. "1927 M," box 4, Horsch papers, AMC.

30. Mosemann to Miller, Aug 16, 1926. Quoted in Guy F. Hershberger, "Questions Raised Concerning the World of the Committee on Peace and Social Concerns (of the ["old"] Mennonite Church) and Its Predecessors" (unpub. ms. in MHL).

31. Mosemann to Horsch, Oct 11, 1927, f. "1927 M," box 4, Horsch papers, AMC.

32. Miller to Mosemann, Jan 30, 1928, copy in f. "1928 M-Z," box 4, Horsch papers, AMC.

33. See John Howard Yoder, "Anabaptist Vision and Mennonite Reality," in *Consultation on Anabaptist-Mennonite Theology*, ed. by A. J. Klassen (Fresno, 1970), 1-46; Yoder argued that the "old" Mennonite leaders from John F. Funk through H. S. Bender all began as marginal men who engaged in "a series of borrowings from the surrounding Protestantism in an effort to renew the Mennonite reality."

34. See John Higham, "The Forms of Ethnic Leadership," in John Higham, ed., *Ethnic Leadership in America* (Baltimore, 1978), 1-18.

35. Paul Erb interview with Leonard Gross, Nov 9, 1980, transcript pp. 3, 6-7; AMC.

36. For general studies of the roles of women in American society, see Carl N. Degler, *At Odds: Women and the Family in America from the Revolution to the Present* (New York, 1980); Page Smith, *Daughters of the Promised Land* (Boston, 1970); Peter Gabriel Filene, *Him/Her/Self: Sex Roles in Modern America* (New York, 1974). For an excellent feminist historical summary and conceptual framework see the essays by Rosemary R. Ruether in Ruether and Bianchi, *From Machismo to Mutuality: Essays on Sexism and Woman-Man Liberation* (New York, 1976).

37. Edmund George Kaufman, "Social Problems and Opportunities of the

Western District Conference Communities of the General Conference of Mennonites of North America" (M.A. thesis, Bluffton College and Mennonite Seminary, 1917), 99.

38. The impact of the Mennonite nonresistant ethos upon male-female roles has not been systematically studied. Gayle Gerber Koontz alluded to the issue in her 1985 Bethel College Bible Lectures, "Two Bodies, One Bible: Women, Men, and the Word of God," Schowalter Oral History Collection, MLA. David Augsburger has produced evidence against the notion that the repressed anger of the pacifist results in dysfunctional or aggressive behavior of other kinds, and for the notion that "cognitive redefinition" of enemies as potential friends itself drains anger and allows for productive and gentle responses; see his "The Control and Management of Hostility in a Nonviolent-Nonresistant Community" (Ph.D. diss., Claremont School of Theology, 1974), 148-50.

39. Theron Schlabach, "The Humble Become 'Aggressive Workers': Mennonites Organize for Mission, 1880-1910," *MQR*, 52 (Apr 1978), 113-26.

40. Kliewer, "Rückblick über die Missionsthätigkeit des letzten Jahrhunderts und Ausblick in das 20. Jahrhundert," *CB*, 20 (Jul 18, 1901), 1. The article was continued in the July 25 and August issues; quots. from August 1 issue, p. 1.

41. Sherk, "If God Is for Us, Who Can Be Against Us," *HT*, 31 (Apr 1, 1894), 98; quoted by Theron Schlabach in "The Humble Become 'Aggressive Workers'" (note 39), 114.

42. John Ruth, *Maintaining the Right Fellowship* (Scottdale, Pa., and Kitchener, Ont., 1984), 411-13, 445.

43. J. W. Kliewer, "Is the Ordination of Women to the Gospel Ministry Biblical. [*sic*]" (paper read at 19th Session of the General Conference, Bluffton, Ohio, Aug 31-Sep 6, 1911), in *Supplement to the Mennonite*, 27 (Apr 11, 1912), 41-51.

44. Christine Kaufmann and Priscilla Stuckey Kauffman, "Mennonite Women's Calendar" (Notre Dame: Womensage, 1983), date Apr. 20 *Seventy-fifth Anniversary of the First Mennonite Church of Philadelphia* (Philadelphia: First Mennonite Church, 1940), 24.

45. Sharon Klingelsmith, "Women in the Mennonite Church, 1900-1930," *MQR*, 54 (Jul 1980), 172-73.

46. Good, "Girls in Education," *Institute Monthly*, 3 (Jun 15, 1901), 150-51.

47. Hartzler, *Paths to Perdition* (Scottdale, Pa., 1910), 199.

48. Steiner, *Pitfalls and Safeguards* (Elkhart, Ind., 1899), 176-77, 147.

49. For another statement of these same values by a progressive Mennonite educator, see N. E. Byers, "Normal Life of Woman," *GH*, 2 (Apr 4, 1908), 14-15.

50. Heatwole, "Why I Wanted My Wife to Be My Wife," *Youth's Christian Companion*, 23 (Nov 29, 1942), 380-82.

51. Steiner, *Pitfalls* (note 48), 72-73.

52. Hartzler, *Paths* (note 47), 191, 235, 246.

53. C. H. Wedel, *Briefliche Blätter an einen Lernenden über Bildung, Gesellschafts- und Heiratsfragen* (Newton, Kans., 1906).

54. Ibid., 21.

55. Ibid., 102.

56. Ibid., 25.

57. Ibid., 103-4.

58. John F. Funk, *HT*, 29 (Oct 15, 1892), 312.

59. Klingelsmith, "Women" (note 45), 176-77.

60. On John M. Shank's mission work see Theron Schlabach, *Gospel Versus Gospel* (Scottdale, Pa., and Kitchener, Ont., 1980), 159; and Paul Erb, *South Central Frontiers* (Scottdale, Pa., 1974), 129-135, 416-420.

61. Priscilla Stuckey Kauffman, "A Woman's Ministry: Clara Brubaker Shank, 1869-1958," *MQR*, 60 (Jul 1986), 404-28.

62. Ruth, *Maintaining the Right Fellowship* (note 41), 435.

63. "Women of Farm Hold Meeting" (unidentified newspaper clipping, dated Dec 15, 1926, attached to letter, John B. Senger to J. C. Clemens, Dec 20, 1926,

Clemens papers, Eastern Pennsylvania Mennonite Historical Library, Christopher Dock High School, Lansdale, Pa.

64. Noah E. Byers to J. E. Hartzler, Nov 24, 1919, box 4, Hartzler papers, AMC.

65. Klingelsmith, "Women" (note 45), 175.

66. Klingelsmith, "Women" (note 45), 180.

67. Based upon a topical index of *Christian Exponent* articles, in author's possession.

68. Clara Rupp Welty, "Frauenstimmrecht," *Der Herold*, 25 (Mar 2, 1911), 3.

69. Krehbiel, in *Der Herold*: editorial, 26 (Oct 24, 1912), 4; "Frauenrecht anerkannt," 25 (Nov 9, 1911), 4; "Florence Nightingale," 26 (Dec 19, 1912), 4; "Women Demand Wars Shall End," 33 (Aug 28, 1919), 3.

70. *Der Herold*, 26 (Oct 31, 1912): J. E. Wiebe, "Das Stimmrecht für Frauen"; a woman correspondent, "Korr."

71. Kaufmann and Kauffman, "Mennonite Women's Calendar" (note 44), Sep 26.

72. Ibid., Mar 4.

73. Katie Funk Wiebe, *Our Lamps Were Lit* (Newton, Kans.: Bethel Deaconess Hospital School of Nursing Alumnae Association, 1978), 112.

74. Melvin Gingerich, "The Mennonite Woman's Missionary Society," *MQR*, 37 (Apr, Jul 1963), 113-25 and 214-33; Klingelsmith, "Women in the Mennonite Church," 195-201; Elaine Sommers Rich, *Mennonite Women* (Scottdale, Pa., and Kitchener, Ont., 1983), 201-06.

75. Elizabeth Howell Verdesi, *In But Still Out* (Philadelphia, 1973, 1976).

76. See the published reports of the All-Mennonite Convention for 1913 (Berne, Ind.); 1916 (Carlock, Ill.); 1919 (Bluffton, Ohio); 1922 (Goshen, Ind.); 1925 (Nappanee, Ind.); 1927 (Hillsboro, Kans.); and 1930 (Berne, Ind.).

77. Daniel Kauffman, "The General Mennonite Convention at Berne, Indiana," *GH* (Aug 28, 1913), 338.

78. *Report of the Third All-Mennonite Convention* (Bluffton, Ohio, 1919), 11; *Report of the Sixth All-Mennonite Convention* (Hillsboro, Kans., 1927), 11; *Report of the Fifth All-Mennonite Convention* (Nappanee, Ind., 1925), 5.

79. *Report of the Seventh All-Mennonite Convention* (Berne, Ind., 1930), 45.

80. Christian Arbitration and Peace Society to John F. Funk, Aug 2, 1893, Funk papers, AMC.

81. Edwin D. Mead, "Peace Teaching in American Schools and Colleges," *The Outlook*, (Jun 16, 1906), 378.

82. On the peace movement between the wars, see Charles Chatfield, *For Peace and Justice: Pacifism in America 1914-1941* (Knoxville, 1971).

83. "Tentative Report of the Commission on the Coordination of Efforts for Peace," Sep 1, 1923, copy in f. 170, box 28, H. P. Krehbiel papers, MLA.

84. The Conference of Pacifist Churches was originally known as the "National Conference of Religious Bodies." For copies of the 1922 Bluffton program, see f. 163, box 27, H. P. Krehbiel papers, MLA.

85. The relationship between Horsch, Mosemann, and the "old" Mennonite Peace Problems Committee is reviewed and documented in Guy F. Hershberger, "Questions Raised Concerning the Work of the Committee on Peace and Social Concerns (of the Mennonite Church) and its Predecessors" (note 30).

86. Horsch, Nov 13, 1926, quoted in Hershberger (note 85), 11.

87. The correspondence between Krehbiel and Neuenschwander, and other documents relating to the committee's work, is in f. 163, box 27, the H. P. Krehbiel papers, MLA.

88. Neuenschwander to Krehbiel, Dec 17, 1928, f. 163, box 27, Krehbiel papers, MLA.

89. ACLU materials in f. 163, box 27, Krehbiel papers, MLA.

90. John H. Mosemann to John Horsch, Dec 21, 1926, f. "1926 I-M," box 3, Horsch papers, AMC.

91. Horsch, *Die Biblische Lehre von der Wehrlosigkeit* (Scottdale, Pa., 1920).

92. H. J. Krehbiel, *A Trip Through Europe: A Plea for the Abolition of War and A Report of the 400th Anniversary of the Mennonite Denomination* (Newton, Kans., 1926).

93. In the 1920s Krehbiel was working on his peace book, *War, Peace, Amity*, which was not published until 1937.

94. H. P. Krehbiel undated note (probably 1928) regarding a world peace movement, f. 163, box 27, Krehbiel papers, MLA.

95. Krehbiel, "Overture to the Historic Peace Groups of the World," printed letter with space for individual messages sent to peace church leaders in N. Amer. and Europe; copies in f. 170, box 28, Krehbiel papers, MLA.

96. Robert Kreider, "The Historic Peace Churches Meeting in 1935," *ML*, 31 (Jun 1976), 21-24. See also Paul Toews, "The Long Weekend or the Short Week: Mennonite Peace Theology, 1925-1944," *MQR*, 60 (Jan 1986), 38-57.

CHAPTER 11

1. Tim Falb, "A Mennonite Scholar, Edward Yoder (1893-1945)," Goshen College seminar paper, 1980.

2. Melvin Gingerich, "Lower Deer Creek," *ME* III, p. 406.

3. Ida Yoder, ed., *Edward, Pilgrimage of a Mind: The Journal of Edward Yoder* (Wadsworth, Ohio: the editor, 1985).

4. Yoder, *Edward*, 7. Diary entry for January 26, 1931. For a later academic treatment of this same idea, see Theron Schlabach, *Gospel Versus Gospel* (Scottdale, Pa.: Herald Press, 1980), pp. 83-108.

5. *Report of the Sixteenth Mennonite General Conference held near Goshen, Indiana, August 28-29, 1929*, (1929), p. 29.

6. The quoted characterization is from Yoder (note 3), *Edward*, 6. Diary entry for January 26, 1931. The General Problems Committee reported extensively on its discussions and recommendations in the summer and fall 1930 issues of *Gospel Herald*.

7. Yoder (note 3), *Edward*, 11. Diary entry for February 28, 1931.

8. Yoder (note 3), *Edward*, 5. Diary entry for January 17, 1931.

9. Yoder (note 3), *Edward*, 6. Diary entry for January 17, 1931. Part of the section referring to Smith (though not mentioning him by name) is in the published diary but not in the handwritten copy in the Edward Yoder Collection, AMC.

10. Yoder (note 3), *Edward*, 12. Diary entry for March 8, 1931.

11. "Letter of Conrad Grebel to Zwingli," *Goshen College Record*, Ernst Correll and H. S. Bender, eds., 27 (September 1926), 33-37; "Letter of Conrad Grebel to Andreas Castelberger," *MQR*, 1 (July 1927), 41-53; "Nine Letters of Conrad Grebel," *MQR*, 2 (October 1928), 229-259.

12. Yoder (note 3), "Conrad Grebel as a Humanist," *MQR*, 3 (April 1929), 132-46. Falb, "A Mennonite Scholar," 12.

13. Irvin B. Horst, "Edward Yoder: A Tribute," in Yoder (note 3), *Edward*, 471. Originally published in *Gospel Herald*, 50 (November 26, 1957), 1017.

14. United States Department of Commerce Bureau of the Census, *Religious Bodies: 1936*, 2 vols. (Washington, D.C.: Government Printing office, 1941), II, 1005-1006.

15. Ibid.

16. U.S. Bureau of the Census, *Historical Statistics of the United States, Colonial Times to 1957* (Washington, D.C.: Government Printing Office, 1960), 14.

17. P. P. Wedel, "Notes on My Trip to Pennsylvania," *The Mennonite*, 45 (July 31, 1930), 3.

18. J. B. Cressman, "The Need of a Standard College," *Gospel Herald*, 23 (December 4, 1930), 766.

19. Mrs. G. A. Linscheid, "1880-1930, Geschichtliche Überblick über die Oklahoma Mission der Allg. Konferenz der Mennoniten von Nord Amerika." The man-

uscript was published serially in *Christlicher Bundesbote*, 49 (June 5 to September 9, 1930). A typescript English translation is in the MLA.

20. "Society Publishes Petter's Translations," *Mennonite Weekly Review*, 7 (August 27, 1930), 1.

21. (R. Petter), "Dankbarer Rückblick auf 50 Jahre," *Christlicher Bundesbote*, 48 (July 18, 1929), 2.

22. E. G. Kaufman, "Chinese at Bluffton College," *The Mennonite*, 45 (October 2, 1930), 4.

23. E. G. Kaufman, "The Future of Mennonite Missions," *The Mennonite*, 45 (July 17, 1930), 3. See also Kaufman's review of the General Conference mission in China in his book, *The Development of the Missionary and Philanthropic Interest Among the Mennonites of North America* (Berne, Ind.: The Mennonite Book Concern, 1931), 323-78.

24. A. Grace Wenger, *Eastern Mennonite Board of Missions and Charities*, unpublished manuscript, 1985(?), Chapter 1, pp. 206-07.

25. The concerns are summarized in Schlabach (note 4), *Gospel Versus Gospel*, 137-39.

26. Kaufman interview by Fred Zerger, October 1970, Schowalter Oral History Collection, Tape #2, Transcript pp. 76-78 and Tape #3, Transcript pp. 125-26, MLA.

27. Charles Harvey Fahs, (n.p.: Institute of Social and Religious Research, 1929). Quoted in E. G. Kaufman, "The Future of Mennonite Missions," *The Mennonite*, 45 (July 10, 1930), 6-7.

28. *Report of the Sixteenth Mennonite General Conference, Held Near Goshen, Indiana, August 28-30, 1929*, 4-5.

29. C. E. Krehbiel, "In the Interests of the General Conference," *The Mennonite*, 44 (June 20, 1929), 6.

30. *Gospel Herald* 22 (September 5, 1929), 465.

31. *Report of the Seventeenth Mennonite General Conference Held Near Archbold, Ohio, August 26-28, 1931*, 81-92.

32. *Official Minutes and Reports of the Twenty-Fifth Session of the General Conference*, 1929, 41. "Einiges von der Allgemeinen Konferenz abgehalten in Hutchinson, Kans.," *Christlicher Bundesbote* (September 19, 1929), 7.

33. P. P. Wedel, "Notes on My Trip to Pennsylvania," *The Mennonite*, 44 (July 31, 1930), 2-4.

34. *Official Minutes and Reports of the Twenty-Sixth Session of the General Conference*, 1933, 49.

35. *Official Minutes and Reports*, 1929, 40.

36. See "To Pastors and Church Leaders," *The Mennonite*, 44 (December 5, 1929), 3, 5-7.

37. Letter from Daniel Kauffman to George R. Brunk, March 9, 1914, Brunk Collection, VCA.

38. See Brunk's editorial introduction, "The Drift," in the opening issue of *The Sword and Trumpet*, 1 (January, 1929), 2-8.

39. See the review of Brunk's *Sword and Trumpet* concerns in J. C. Wenger, *Faithfully, Geo. R.: The Life and Thought of George R. Brunk I (1871-1938* (Harrisonburg, Va.: *The Sword and Trumpet*, 1978), 145-71.

40. Ernest G. Gehman, telephone interview with the author, Harrisonburg, Va., July 29, 1981.

41. 1 (April 1929), 13.

42. 4 (July 1932), 5.

43. 2 (October 1930), 7.

44. Brunk letter to Noah Mack, October 9, 1929, Mack Collection, Lancaster Conference Archives.

45. Noah H. Mack, "The Situation in American Mennonitism," *Sword and Trumpet*, 2 (October 1930), 7-12; and *Gospel Herald*, 23 (December 25, 1930), 818-20.

46. Theron Schlabach, "Paradoxes of Mennonite Separatism," *Pennsylvania Mennonite Heritage* 2 (January 1979), pp. 12-17.

47. Edward Yoder, *Must Christians Fight?* {Akron, Pa.: Mennonite Central Committee, 1943), 9-10.

48. The classic work on irony and American history is Reinhold Niebuhr, *The Irony of American History* (New York: Scribner, 1952).

SELECT BIBLIOGRAPHY

BOOKS, ARTICLES

Amstutz, P. B. *Geschichtliche Ereignisse der Mennoniten-Ansiedlung in Allen und Putnam County, Ohio.* Bluffton, Ohio: The author, 1925. Abridged English edition, Anne Konrad Dyck, trans.—Bluffton: Swiss Community Historical Society, 1978. A history and characterization of a Swiss Mennonite settlement in western Ohio.

Apostolic Christian Church History. Eureka, Ill.: Apostolic Christian Publishers, 1985. 196 pp., MHL.

Barrett, Lois. *The Vision and the Reality: the Story of Home Missions in the General Conference Mennonnite Church.* Newton, Kans.: Faith and Life Press, 1983. A study of GC home missions which emphasizes the tensions between ethnocentrism and the missionary impulse.

Beachy, Alvin. "The Amish of Somerset County, Pennsylvania." Master of Sacred Theology thesis, Hartford Seminary, 1952.

Becker, Jacob P. *Origin of the Mennonite Brethren Church.* Hillsboro, Kans.: Mennonite Brethren Historical Society of the Midwest, 1973.

Bender, Harold S. "The Anabaptist Vision." *Church History,* 13 (March 1944), 3-14. An often-reprinted seminal essay which defined Anabaptism as the culmination of the sixteenth-century Reformation.

——————————., et al., eds. *The Mennonite Encyclopedia,* Vols. I-IV, Scottdale, Pa.: Herald Press, 1955-1959. An essential tool for Anabaptist-Mennonite studies, somewhat outdated. A supplementary updated volume currently in preparation.

——————————. Review of *Education Among the Mennonites of America,* by J. E. Hartzler. *The Goshen College*

Record—Review Supplement (often bound with *MQR*), 27 (May-June 1926), 35-44.

Bender, Urie A. *Four Earthen Vessels: Biographical Profiles of Oscar Burkholder, Samuel F. Coffman, Clayton F. Derstine, and Jesse B. Martin.* Kitchener, Ont.: Herald Press, 1982. Biographies of leaders in the "old" Mennonite Conference of Ontario, including human-interest detail and much about connections between Mennonites in Canada and the United States.

Bertsche, Janeen. "Views of Atonement" in the *Christian Exponent. ML*, 41 (June 1986), 4-8.

Boynton, Linda Louise. *The Plain People: An Ethnography of the Holdeman Mennonites.* Salem, Wis.: Sheffield Publishing Co., 1986.

Brunk, Harry Anthony. *History of Mennonites in Virginia,* Vol. I, 1727-1900. Harrisonburg, Va.: The author, 1959; Vol. II, 1900-1960. Harrisonburg, Va.: The author, 1972. Two volumes with a wealth of information about Virginia Mennonites, written by a history teacher at Eastern Mennonite College.

Burkholder, L. J. *A Brief History of the Mennonites of Ontario.* Markham, Ont.: Mennonite Conference of Ontario, 1935.

Charles, J. D. *Fallacies of Evolution.* Scottdale, Pa.: Mennonite Publishing House, 1917. A conservative critique of the theory of evolution by a teacher at Hesston College.

Coffman, Barbara F. *His Name Was John.* Scottdale, Pa.: Herald Press, 1964. A biography of John S. Coffman.

Coffman, John S. *Outlines and Notes Used at the Bible Conference Held at Johnstown, Pennsylvania. . . .* Elkhart, Ind.: Mennonite Publishing Co., 1898. An important document for understanding the teachings of the early Bible Conference movement among "old" Mennonites.

Cronk, Sandra L. "*Gelassenheit*: The Rites of the Redemptive Process in Old Order Amish and Old Order Mennonites." Ph.D. dissertation, University of Chicago, 1977. Study by a Quaker scholar, with a very positive view of the normative value of "yieldedness" among Old Order folk.

Denlinger, Steven L. *Glimpses Past: Annotations of Selected Social and Cultural History Materials in the Mennonite Herald of Truth, Gospel Witness, and early Gospel Herald.* Lancaster, Pa.: Lancaster Mennonite Historical Society, 1985. An annotated selection of articles from "old" Mennonite periodicals between 1864 and 1922. Sixteen topical categories including arts, dress, education, migration, pacifism, race relations, temperance, women's role, etc. A valuable aid to research, 155 pp.

Dreidger, Leo, and J. Howard Kauffman, "Urbanization of Mennonites: Canadian and American Comparisons." *MQR*, 56 (July 1982), 269-90. An essay which sees differences among Mennonite groups as a product of different experiences in Europe as well as different times of migration.

Durnbaugh, Donald, ed. *The Brethren Encyclopedia*, Vols. I-III. Philadelphia: The Brethren Encyclopedia Inc., 1983. An authoritative work which includes much information on Brethren-Mennonite relationships.

Dyck, C. J., ed. *An Introduction to Mennonite History*. 2nd ed., Scottdale, Pa., and Kitchener, Ont.: Herald Press, 1983. An excellent one-volume survey of Mennonite history from Anabaptism to the present day.

_____, and Robert Kreider, "Mennonite World Conference in Review." *Mennonite Life*, 33 (June 1978), 5-20.

_____, ed. *Something Meaningful for God*. Scottdale, Pa., and Kitchener, Ont.: Herald Press, 1981. Fifteen short biographies of workers in Mennonite Central Committee.

Dyck, Gordon R. "The United States General Conference Extinct Churches (1847-1959)." Research paper, Mennonite Biblical Seminary, 1959.

Eggan, Fred. "H. R. Voth: Ethnologist." *ML*, 37 (June 1982), 14-19. Essay on the multiple roles of a GC missionary to American Indians.

Engbrecht, Dennis. "The Americanization of a Rural Immigrant Church: The General Conference Mennonites in Central Kansas 1874-1939." Ph.D. dissertation, University of Nebraska, 1985.

Epp, Frank. *Mennonite Exodus: The Rescue and Resettlement of the Russian Mennonites Since the Communist Revolution*. Altona, Man.: D. W. Friesen and Sons, 1962.

_____. *Mennonites in Canada 1786-1920: the History of a Separate People*. Vol. I. Toronto: Macmillan of Canada, 1974. The first volume of a comprehensive history of Canadian Mennonites; includes much material on European background and American connections.

_____. *Mennonites in Canada 1920-1940: A People's Struggle for Survival*. Vol. II. Toronto: Macmillan of Canada, 1982.

Epp, Margaret. *This Mountain Is Mine*. Chicago: Moody Press, 1969. History of the independent Mennonite "Bartel Mission" in China, with fascinating information on inter-Mennonite conflicts.

Erb, Allen. "The Mennonite Church and Hospital Work." *MQR*, 1 (Jan. 1927), 28-33. Background to the "old" Mennonite hospital work at La Junta, Colorado.

Erb, Paul. *Orie O. Miller: The Story of a Man and an Era.* Scottdale, Pa.: Herald Press, 1969. Biography of a founder and longtime leader of Mennonite Central Committee.

——————————. *South Central Frontiers: A History of the South Central Mennonite Conference.* Scottdale, Pa., and Kitchener, Ont.: Herald Press, 1974. History of the "old" Mennonite conference with congregations in Kansas, Nebraska, Missouri, Colorado, Louisiana, Texas, and Mississippi.

Esau, Mrs. H. T. *First Sixty Years of M. B. Missions.* Hillsboro, Kans.: Mennonite Brethren Publishing House, 1954.

Esch, Henry D. *The Mennonites in Arizona.* Phoenix: G & G Printers, 1985.

Eshleman, Wilmer J. *A History of the Reformed Mennonite Church*, new rev. ed. Lancaster, Pa.: n.p., 1969.

Estes, Steven R. *Christian Concern for Health: The Sixtieth Anniversary History of the Mennonite Hospital Association.* Bloomington, Ill.: Mennonite Hospital Assn., 1979. Includes information on the pioneering deaconess and home mission work of John A. Sprunger.

Fretz, C. Y. "A History of Winter Bible Schools in the Mennonite Church." *MQR*, 16 (Apr., July 1942), 51-81, 178-96.

Friedmann, *Mennonite Piety Through the Centuries: Its Genius and Its Literature.* Goshen, Ind.: Mennonite Historical Society, 1949. The most thorough survey of Mennonite devotional literature; assumes that Pietism and Mennonitism are in tension with each other.

Friesen, Gordon. *The Flamethrowers.* Caldwell, Idaho: Caxton Printers, 1936. First novel by a disaffected Mennonite with bitter images of his heritage.

Friesen, Peter M. *The Mennonite Brotherhood in Russia (1789-1910): Translated from the German.* Fresno: Board of Christian Literature, General Conference of Mennonite Brethren Churches, 1978. An English translation of a massive study of Mennonitism in the Russian Empire, first published in 1910. The original edition has a significant section of Russian Mennonite impressions of American Mennonitism, not included in the English translation.

Gates, Helen Kolb, *et al. Bless the Lord, O My Soul: A*

Biography of Bishop John Fretz Funk 1835-1930. Scottdale, Pa.: Herald Press, 1958.

Gingerich, Alice K. *Life and Times of Daniel Kauffman.* Scottdale, Pa., and Kitchener, Ont.: Herald Press, 1982. A laudatory biography of the "old" Mennonite church leader by his daughter.

Gingerich, Melvin. *Mennonite Attire Through Four Centuries.* Breinigsville, Pa.: The Pennsylvania German Society, 1970. The most thorough survey of Mennonite clothing regulations and styles, emphasizes the innovative aspects of "old" Mennonite changes in the late nineteenth and early twentieth century.

_____. "The Mennonite Woman's Missionary Society." *MQR*, 37 (Apr., July 1963), 113-25, 214-33.

_____. *The Mennonites in Iowa.* Iowa City: State Historical Society of Iowa, 1939. A thorough study of all the Mennonite groups in Iowa.

Goering, Gladys. *Women in Search of Mission: A History of the General Conference Mennonite Women's Organization.* Newton, Kans.: Faith and Life Press, 1980.

Goerz, David. *Zur Diakonissensache.* Newton, Kans.: n.p., 1904. Promotional essay on the deaconess movement by a GC founder in Kansas.

Graber, Robert Bates. "The Sociocultural Differentiation of a Religious Sect." Ph.D. dissertation, University of Wisconsin, 1979. A comparative study of Mennonite group separations, with evidence that Mennonite social patterns do not fit expected sociological categories.

Gratz, Delbert L. *Bernese Anabaptists and Their American Descendants.* Scottdale, Pa.: Herald Press, 1953.

Gross, Leonard. "The Doctrinal Era of the Mennonite Church." *MQR*, 60 (Jan. 1986), 83-103. A provocative essay which argues that the Daniel Kauffman era of "old" Mennonite development, with its concern for prescriptive doctrine, was a deviation from the historical consciousness of preceding and following eras.

Harder, Leland. *General Conference Mennonite Church Fact Book of Congregational Membership.* N.p.: Leland Harder, 1971. A statistical study by a Mennonite sociologist.

Harder, Menno S. "History of Mennonite Education." Ph.D. dissertation, University of Southern California, 1949. Focuses on education among the Mennonites of Dutch-Russian background.

Hardesty, Von. *A Narrative of Bluffton College.* Bluffton, Ohio:

Bluffton College, 1975. A brief sketch of Bluffton's history on the seventy-fifth annniversary of the college.

Harms, John F. *Geschichte der Mennoniten Brüdergemeinde.* Hillsboro, Kans.: Mennonite Brethren Publishing House, n.d.

Harms, Orlando. *Pioneer Publisher: The Life and Times of J. F. Harms.* Winnipeg, Man.: Kindred Press, 1984. An excellent biography of a Mennonite Brethren leader.

Hartzler, J. E. *Education Among the Mennonites of America.* Danvers, Ill.: Central Mennonite Publishing Board, 1925.

————————————. *Paths to Perdition.* Scottdale, Pa.: Mennonite Publishing House, 1910.

Hartzler, J. S. *Mennonites in the World War.* Scottdale, Pa.: Mennonite Publishing House, 1921. A summary of "old" Mennonite experiences, including primary accounts, written shortly after the war.

Haury, David. *Prairie People: A History of the Western District Conference.* Newton, Kans.: Faith and Life Press, 1984. The history of a GC district conference, centered in Kansas, with emphasis upon Mennonite diversity.

Haury, Samuel S. *Letters Concerning the Spread of the Gospel in the Heathen World Presented to All Mennonites in North America,* trans. Marie Regier Janzen and Hilda Voth. Scottdale, Pa., and Kitchener, Ont.: Herald Press, 1981. An appeal for Mennonite missions work written by the first missionary to be sent by a Mennonite agency, shortly before leaving for his work with the Arapahoe and Cheyenne in 1880.

Heatwole, Lewis J., et al. *A History of the Mennonite Conference of Virginia and Its Work.* Scottdale, Pa.: Mennonite Publication Board, 1910.

————————————. *Mennonite Handbook of Information.* Scottdale, Pa.: Mennonite Publishing House, 1925. An "old" Mennonite summary which reveals the self-understanding of this group in relation to other Mennonites.

————————————. *Moral Training in the Public Schools.* Scottdale, Pa.: Mennonite Book and Tract Society, 1908. A book of strong public consciousness by a Virginia "old" Mennonite bishop and public school teacher.

Hershberger, Guy F. "Comments on Sawatsky's Thesis." In AMC; 1979. An extended critique of Rodney Sawatsky's master's thesis on "old" Mennonite Fundamentalism, argues that the divisive issues were more cultural than theological.

————————————. "Historical Background to the Formation of

the Mennonite Central Committee." *MQR*, 44 (July 1970), 237.

Hess, Mary. *Anatomy of a Town: Hesston, Kansas.* New York: The author, 1976.

Hiebert, Clarence. *The Holdeman People: the Church of God in Christ, Mennonite, 1859-1969.* South Pasadena: William Carey Library, 1973.

Hiebert, P. C. *Feeding the Hungry: Russia Famine, 1919, 1925. American Mennonite Relief Operations Under the Auspices of Mennonite Central Committee.* Scottdale, Pa.: Mennonite Central Committee, 1929. The story of the origins of Mennonite Central Committee in relief work in the Ukraine, USSR, in the early 1920s.

Hoover, Amos B., trans., ed., and comp. *The Jonas Martin Era: Presented in a Collection of Essays, Letters, and Documents That Shed Light on the Mennonite Churches During the 50 Year Ministry (1875-1925) of Bishop Jonas H. Martin.* Denver, Pa.: the editor, 1982. An extensive (1128 pp.) collection of documents and essays relating to Old Order Mennonites; a veritable research archive in itself.

Horsch, John. *Die biblische Lehre von der Wehrlosigkeit.* Scottdale, Pa.: Mennonitische Verlagsanstalt, 1920.

_____. *The Mennonite Church and Modernism.* Scottdale, Pa.: Mennonite Publishing House, 1924.

Horst, Isaac R. *Close Ups of the Great Awakening.* Mt. Forest, Ont.: The author, 1985.

_____. *Up the Conestoga.* Mt. Forest, Ont.: The author, 1979.

Hostetler, Beulah Stauffer. *American Mennonites and Protestant Movements: A Community Paradigm.* Scottdale, Pa., and Kitchener, Ont.: Herald Press, 1987. A study of the Franconia Mennonite Conference in relationship to Pietism, Revivalism, Fundamentalism, and modern currents of Protestant life and organization.

_____. "Franconia Mennonite Conference and American Protestant Movements 1840-1940." Ph.D. dissertation, University of Pennsylvania, 1977.

Hostetler, John, and Gertrude Enders Huntington. *The Hutterites in North America.* New York: Holt, Rinehart and Winston, 1967.

Hostetler, John A. *Amish Society,* 3rd ed. Baltimore: Johns Hopkins, 1980. Definitive anthropological study of Amish life.

_____. *God Uses Ink: The Heritage and Mission of*

the Mennonite Publishing House After Fifty Years. Scottdale, Pa.: Herald Press, 1964.

_____. Hutterite Society. Baltimore: Johns Hopkins University Press, 1972.

Huffman, Jasper Abraham, ed. History of the Mennonite Brethren in Christ Church. New Carlisle, Ohio: Bethel Publishing Co., 1979.

Jansen, Peter. The Memoirs of Peter Jansen: A Record of a Busy Life. Beatrice, Nebr.: The author, 1921. Memoirs of a Dutch-Russian immigrant to Nebraska who was public-spirited, wealthy, and much involved in state politics.

Janzen, Cornelius Cicero. "A Social Study of the Mennonite Settlement in the Counties of Marion, McPherson, Harvey, Reno, and Butler, Kansas." Ph.D. dissertation, University of Chicago, 1926.

Juhnke, James C. Dialogue with a Heritage: Cornelius H. Wedel and the Beginnings of Bethel College. North Newton, Kans.: Bethel College, 1987. The Menno Simons Lectures for 1986, examining the origins and meaning of Wedel's concept of Gemeindechristentum.

_____. "Gemeindechristentum and Bible Doctrine: Two Mennonite Visions of the Early Twentieth Century." MQR, 57 (July 1983), 208-10. A comparison and contrast of Cornelius H. Wedel and Daniel Kauffman as Mennonite leaders.

_____. "Gustav H. Enss, Mennonite Alien (1885-1965)." ML, 36 (Dec. 1981), 9-15.

_____. "Mennonite Church Theological and Social Boundaries, 1920- 1930—Loyalists, Liberals and Laxitarians." ML, 38 (June 1983), 18-24.

_____. "Mennonite History and Self Understanding: North American Mennonitism as a Bipolar Mosaic," in Mennonite Identity: Historical and Contemporary Perspectives. Lanham, Md.: University Press of America, 1988, 83-99.

_____. "Mennonite Progressives and World War I." ML, 41 (Dec. 1986), 14-16.

_____. A People of Mission: A History of General Conference Mennonite Overseas Missions. Newton, Kans.: Faith and Life Press, 1979.

_____. A People of Two Kingdoms: The Political Acculturation of the Kansas Mennonites. Newton, Kans.: Faith and Life Press, 1975.

Kauffman, Daniel, ed. *Bible Doctrine*. Scottdale, Pa.: Mennonite Publishing House, 1914.

———. *Doctrines of the Bible, A Brief Discussion of the Teachings of God's Word*. Scottdale, Pa.: Mennonite Publishing House, 1928.

———. "In What Fundamentals Do Mennonites Agree?" *GH*, 3 (July 21, 28, 1910), 251, 283. A thorough "old" Mennonite explanation of points of inter-Mennonite commonality as well as the reasons why ecumenical cooperation with more progressive groups must be limited.

———. *Manual of Bible Doctrines*. Elkhart, Ind.: Mennonite Publishing Co., 1898. The first of Kauffman's three "Bible Doctrine" books which provided authoritative teaching for "old" Mennonites in the first half of the twentieth century.

———. *The Mennonite Church and Current Issues*. Scottdale, Pa.: Mennonite Publishing House, 1923.

———. *Mennonite Cyclopedic Dictionary*. Scottdale, Pa.: Mennonite Publishing House, 1937.

Kaufman, Edmund G. *The Development of the Missionary and Philanthropic Interest Among the Mennonites of North America*. Berne, Ind.: Mennonite Book Concern, 1931.

———. "Social Problems and Opportunities of the Western District Conference Communities of the General Conference of Mennonites of North America." M.A. thesis, Bluffton College and Mennonite Seminary, 1917.

Keim, Albert N., and Grant M. Stoltzfus. *The Politics of Conscience: The Historic Peace Churches and America at War, 1917-1955*. Scottdale, Pa., and Kitchener, Ont.: Herald Press, 1988.

Kellogg, Walter Guest. *The Conscientious Objector*. New York: Boni and Liveright, 1919. A account by a member of the government's Board of Inquiry which examined conscientious objectors in World War I; critical of COs.

Kliewer, J. W. *Memoirs of J. W. Kliewer*. North Newton, Kans.: Bethel College, 1943. Autobiography of a president of Bethel College (1911-1920, 1925-1932).

Klingelsmith, Sharon. "Women in the Mennonite Church, 1890-1930." *MQR*, 54 (July 1980). A study of the role of women among the "old" Mennonites.

Kraus, C. Norman. "American Mennonites and the Bible." *MQR*, 41 (Oct. 1967), 309-29. Background to the influence of Fundamentalism among the "old" Mennonites.

Krehbiel, H. J. *A Trip Through Europe: A Plea for the Abolition* of War and a Report of the 400th Anniversary of the Mennonite Denomination. Newton, Kans.: The Herald Publishing Co., 1926.

Krehbiel, Henry Peter. *The History of the General Conference of the Mennonites of North America*, Vol. I. N.p.: The author, 1898. Vol. II. Newton, Kans.: The author, 1938.

Krehbiel, W. J. *History of One Branch of the Krehbiel Family*. McPherson, Kans.: W. J. Krehbiel, 1950.

Kreider, Robert. "'Let a Hundred Flowers Bloom' and 'One Lord, One Faith, One Baptism'." *MQR*, 57 (July 1983), 181-93.

Kroeker, Marvin E. "Mennonites in the Oklahoma 'Runs.'" *ML*, 10 (July 1955), 120.

Kyle, Richard G. *From Sect to Denomination: Church Types and Their Implications for Mennonite Brethren History*. Hillsboro, Kans.: Center for Mennonite Brethren Studies, 1985.

Lageer, Eileen. *Merging Streams: Story of the Missionary Church*. Elkhart, Ind.: Bethel Publishing Co., 1979. A popular account of the church which before 1947 was known as Mennonite Brethren in Christ.

Lambert, George. *Around the Globe and Through Bible Lands*. Elkhart, Ind.: Mennonite Publishing Company, 1898. An influential travel account by a promoter of Mennonite relief and missionary efforts.

_____. *India, the Horror Stricken Empire*. Elkhart, Ind.: Mennonite Publishing Company, 1898.

Lapp, John A. *The Mennonite Church in India, 1897-1962*. Scottdale, Pa.: Herald Press, 1972. The story of the church founded in India by "old" Mennonite missionaries.

Lehman, Chester K. *The Inadequacy of Evolution as a World View*. Scottdale, Pa.: Mennonite Publishing House, 1925. A critique of the theory of evolution by a teacher at Eastern Mennonite College.

Lehman, James O. *Creative Congregationalism: A History of the Oak Grove Mennonite Church in Wayne County, Ohio*. Smithville, Ohio: Oak Grove Mennonite Church, 1978.

_____. *Sonnenberg, A Haven and a Heritage*. Kidron, Ohio: Kidron Community Council, 1969.

Lehman, Naomi. *Pilgrimage of a Congregation: First Mennonite Church, Berne, Indiana*. Berne, Ind.: First Mennonite Church, 1982.

Leisy, Bruce R. *A History of the Leisy Brewing Companies*. Wichita, Kans.: The author, 1975.

Lichty, Richard J. "Keeping House as the Lord Gives Grace: The Story of a Bishop and his Church." A biography of J. Paul Graybill (1900-1975), bishop of the Weaverland District of the Lancaster Mennonite Conference, Pennsylvania. Available at Lancaster Conference Historical Society, Lancaster, Pennsylvania, and from the author, a teacher at Christopher Dock High School near Lansdale, Pennsylvania.

Liechty, Joseph C. "Humility: The Foundation of Mennonite Religious Outlook in the 1860s." *MQR*, 54 (Jan. 1980), 5-31. An excellent article which defines the "old" Mennonite ethos and its development.

Lind, Hope K. "Mennonites in Oregon and Related Groups in Neighboring States (1876-1976)." Book manuscript on the history of Mennonites in the Northwest, planned for later publication.

Linscheid, Mrs. G. A. "1880-1930, geschichtliche Überblick über die Oklahoma Mission der Allg. Konferenz der Mennoniten von Nord Amerika." Published serially in *Christlicher Bundesbote*, 49 (June 5 to Sep. 9, 1930).

Loewen, Howard J. *One Lord, One Church, One Hope, and One God: Mennonite Confessions of Faith*. Elkhart, Ind.: Institute of Mennonite Studies, 1985. Loewen analyzed Mennonite confessions of faith and found great commonality of expression.

Loewen, Melvin. *Three Score: The Story of an Emerging Church in Central Africa*. Elkhart, Ind.: Congo Inland Mission, 1945.

Lohrentz, John H. *The Mennonite Brethren Church*. Hillsboro, Kans.: The Board of Foreign Missions of the Conference of the Mennonite Brethren Church of North America, 1950.

Luebke, Frederick C. *Bonds of Loyalty, German Americans and World War I*. DeKalb: Northern Illinois University Press, 1974.

Luthy, David. *The Amish in America: Settlements That Failed, 1840-1960*. Aylmer, Ont.: Pathway Publishers, 1986.

Mast, C. Z., and Robert E. Simpson. *Annals of the Conestoga Valley*. Elverson, Pa.: Mast and Simpson, 1942.

MacMaster, Richard K. *Land, Piety, and Peoplehood: The Establishment of Mennonite Communities in America, 1683-1790*. Scottdale, Pa., and Kitchener, Ont.: Herald Press, 1985. The first volume in this Mennonite Experience in America series.

Meyer, J. C. "The Origin of the Young People's Movement of 1918." *Mennonite Historical Bulletin*, 28 (Apr. 1967), 4-5.

The story of the progressive youth movement in the "old" Mennonite church as remembered by a participant a half century later.

_____. "The Young People's Conference Movement Held in Clermont, France." *Mennonite Historical Bulletin,* 29 (July 1968), 5-7.

Miller, Ivan J. *History of the Conservative Mennonite Conference 1910-1985.* Grantsville, Md.: Ivan J. and Della Miller, 1985.

Miller, Mary. *A Pillar of Cloud: The Story of Hesston College 1909-1959.* Hesston, Kans.: Mennonite Board of Education, 1959.

Nachtigall, Gary B. "Mennonite Migration and Settlements of California." M.A. thesis, California State University at Fresno, 1972.

Nussbaum, Stan. *You Must Be Born Again: A History of the Evangelical Mennonite Church.* N.p.: Evangelical Mennonite Church, 1980. History of the Mennonite body earlier known as the "Egly Amish" and as the Defenseless Mennonites.

Pannabeker, Samuel Floyd. *Faith in Ferment: A History of the Central District Conference.* Newton, Kans.: Faith and Life Press.

_____. *Open Doors: The History of the General Conference Mennonite Church.* Newton, Kans.: Faith and Life Press, 1975. A slightly revised version of the author's 1944 Ph.D. dissertation at Yale University.

Parish, Arlyn J. *Kansas Mennonites During World War I.* Hays, Kans.: Fort Hays Kansas State College, 1968.

Peachey, Urbane, ed. *Mennonite Statements on Peace and Social Concerns, 1900-1978.* Akron, Pa.: Mennonite Central Committee, 1980. A collection of official statements from a variety of Mennonite groups.

Pellman, Hubert R. *Eastern Mennonite College, 1917-1967: A History.* Harrisonburg, Va.: Eastern Mennonite College, 1967.

Peters, G. W. *Foundations of Mennonite Brethren Missions.* Hillsboro, Kans.: Kindred Press, 1984.

Peters, H. P. *History and Development of Education Among the Mennonites in Kansas.* Hillsboro, Kans.: H. P. Peters, 1925.

Plett, Delbert F. *Storm and Triumph: the Mennonite Kleine Gemeinde (1850-1875).* Steinbach, Man.: D.F.P. Publications, 1986. 337 pp.

Prieb, Wesley J. "Peter (P. C.) Hiebert." Essay in *Something Meaningful for God,* ed. by C. J. Dyck, 1981, pp. 99-130. A biography of the MB leader who served as first chairman of Mennonite Central Committee.

Prieb, Wesley J., and Don Ratzlaff. *To a Higher Plane of Vision.* Hillsboro, Kans.: Tabor College, 1983. A brief overview of the history of Tabor College.

Ramseyer, Robert, and Alice Pannabecker Ramseyer. *Mennonites in China.* Winnipeg, Man.: China Educational Exchange, 1988.

Redekop, Calvin. "The Emergence of Mennonite Leadership on the Frontier: A Case Study of H. W. Lohrenz." *ML,* 39 (Dec. 1984), 23-31. Study of a president of Tabor College and leader in the Mennonite Brethren Church.

Rempel, Kevin. "The Evangelical Mennonite Brethren: In Search of a Religious Identity." Research paper, Fresno Pacific College, 1982.

Rich, Elaine Sommers. *Mennonite Women: A Story of God's Faithfulness 1683-1983.* Scottdale, Pa., and Kitchener, Ont.: Herald Press, 1983. Brief biographies of "old" Mennonite women in various roles.

Rohrer, Fred. *Saloon Fight at Berne, Ind.* Berne: The Berne Witness Co., 1913. A spirited account of a small town and its struggle over the alcohol question.

Ruth, John L. *Maintaining the Right Fellowship: A Narrative Account of Life in the Oldest Mennonite Community in North America.* Scottdale, Pa., and Kitchener, Ont.: Herald Press, 1984. The history of the Franconia area Mennonite settlement in eastern Pennsylvania and development of the two groups after a division of 1847—the Franconia "old" Mennonite conference and the Eastern District of the General Conference Mennonite church.

_____. Manuscript history of Lancaster Mennonite Conference, planned for publication; parts made available for this study. Inquire at Lancaster Mennonite Historical Society, Lancaster, Pennsylvania.

Salzman, Vinora Weaver. *Day by Day—Year by Year.* N.p.: The author, 1982. Biography of an early woman Mennonite Central Committee volunteer worker.

Sauder, George G. *History of Lichty's Church and Cemetery.* East Earl, Pa.: George G. Sauder, n.d.

Sawatsky, Rodney, *Authority and Identity: The Dynamics of the General Conference Mennonite Church.* North Newton, Kans.: Bethel College, 1987. The Menno Simons Lectures of 1985.

_____. "Defining Mennonite Diversity and Unity." *MQR*, 57 (July 1983), 282-92.

_____. "History and Ideology: American Mennonite Identity Definition Through History." Ph.D. dissertation, Princeton University, 1977. An excellent study of ways Mennonites have defined themselves in historical terms.

_____. "The Influence of Fundamentalism on Mennonite Nonresistance 1908-1944." M.A. thesis, University of Minnesota, 1973. A pioneering study of Fundamentalism in the "old" Mennonite church.

Schlabach, Ervin. *The Amish Mennonites at Walnut Creek.* Millersburg, Ohio: The author, 1981.

Schlabach, Theron. *Gospel Versus Gospel: Mission and the Mennonite Church, 1863-1944.* Scottdale, Pa., and Kitchener, Ont.: Herald Press, 1980. An important study of the rise of missionary consciousness among "old" Mennonites which emphasizes the tension between the understandings of gospel in traditional Mennonitism and in American evangelical Protestantism.

_____. "The Humble Become 'Aggressive Workers': Mennonites Organize for Mission, 1880-1910." *MQR*, 52 (April 1978), 113-26.

_____. "Mennonites and Pietism in America, 1740-1880: Some Thoughts on the Friedmann Thesis." *MQR*, 57 (July 1983), 222-40.

_____. "Paradoxes of Mennonite Separatism." *Pennsylvania Mennonite Heritage*, 2 (Jan. 1979), 12-17. A provocative essay on the irony of "old" Mennonite borrowings from American culture in order to remain separate from the world.

_____. *Peace, Faith, Nation: Mennonites and Amish in Nineteenth-Century America.* Scottdale, Pa., and Kitchener, Ont.: Herald Press, 1988. The second volume in this Mennonite Experience in America series.

Schmidt, John F., ed. "Autobiography of H. R. Voth." *MQR*, 40 (July 1966), 217-26.

Schmidt, Orlando. *Church Music and Worship Among Mennonites.* Newton, Kans.: Faith and Life Press, 1981.

Shetler, Sanford G. *Preacher of the People: A Biography of S. G. Shetler.* Scottdale, Pa., and Kitchener, Ont.: Herald Press, 1982.

_____. *Two Centuries of Struggle and Growth, 1763-1963: A History of the Allegheny Mennonite Conference.* Scottdale, Pa.: Herald Press, 1963.

Smith, C. Henry. *The Coming of the Russian Mennonites.* Berne, Ind.: Mennonite Book Concern, 1927.

_____. *Mennonite Country Boy.* Newton, Kans.: Faith and Life Press, 1962.

_____. *The Mennonites: A Brief History of Their Origin and Later Development in Both Europe and America.* Berne, Ind.: Mennonite Book Concern, 1920. Revised 1941, 1950, 1957, 1983, under the title *The Story of the Mennonites.*

_____. *The Mennonites of America.* Goshen, Ind.: The author, 1909.

_____, and E. J. Hirschler. *The Story of Bluffton College.* Bluffton, Ohio: Bluffton College, 1925.

_____. *Bluffton College: An Adventure in Faith 1900-1950.* Bluffton, Ohio: Bluffton College, 1950.

Smith, Willard. *Mennonites in Illinois.* Scottdale, Pa., and Kitchener, Ont.: Herald Press, 1983.

Sprunger, Eva F. *The First Hundred Years: A History of the Mennonite Church in Adams County, Indiana 1838-1938.* Berne, Ind.: First Mennonite Church, 1938.

Sprunger, John A., et al. *Licht und Hoffnung "Ruf zu Jesu."* Chicago: Missionary Society Light and Hope, 1893.

Stambaugh, Sara. *I Hear the Reaper's Song.* Intercourse, Pa.: Good Books, 1984. A historical novel about the impact of revivalism on Mennonites of the Lancaster, Pennsylvania, region in the 1890s.

Steiner, Menno S. *John S. Coffman: Mennonite Evangelist.* Spring Grove, Pa.: Mennonite Book and Tract Society, 1903.

_____. *Pitfalls and Safeguards.* Elkhart, Ind.: Mennonite Publishing Company, 1899. A book of moral advice and exhortation by an "old" Mennonite leader of the turn of century "awakening" or "quickening."

Stoltzfus, Grant M. *Mennonites of the Ohio and Eastern Conference: the Colonial Period in Pennsylvania to 1968.* Scottdale, Pa.: Herald Press, 1969. The history of a Mennonite conference created in 1927 in a merger of "old" Mennonite and Amish Mennonite bodies.

Storms, Everek Richard. *What God Hath Wrought.* Springfield, Ohio: United Missionary Society, 1948. A history of the group formerly known as Mennonite Brethren in Christ.

Stucky, Gregory J. "Fighting Against War: The Mennonite *Vorwaerts* from 1914-1919." *Kansas Historical Quarterly*, 38

(Summer 1972), 169-86. Article on a Mennonite Brethren German-language newspaper in Hillsboro, Kansas, in World War I.

Stucky, Harley J. "J. H. Langenwalter: A Biography of a Conviction." North Newton, Kans., 1959.

Teichroew, Allan. "Gordon Friesen: Writer, Radical and Ex-Mennonite." *ML*, 38 (June 1983), 4-17.

――――――. "World War I and the Mennonite Migration to Canada to Avoid the Draft." *MQR*, 45 (July 1971), 219-49.

Toews, J. B. "The Influence of Fundamentalism on Mennonite Brethren Theology." *Direction* (July 1981), 20-29.

――――――. *The Mennonite Brethren Church in Zaire.* Hillsboro, Kans.: Mennonite Brethren Publishing House, 1978.

――――――. "Mennonite Brethren in the Larger Mennonite World." *MQR*, 57 (July 1983), 256-64.

Toews, John A. *A History of the Mennonite Brethren Church: Pilgrims and Pioneers.* Fresno, Calif.: Mennonite Brethren Board of Christian Literature, 1975.

Toews, John B. *Lost Fatherland, The Story of the Mennonite Emigration from Soviet Russia, 1921-1927.* Scottdale, Pa.: Herald Press, 1967.

Toews, Paul. "Dissolving the Boundaries and Strengthening the Nuclei." *Christian Leader* (July 27, 1982), 6-8. An important essay for conceptualizing the stages of denominational development in different Mennonite groups, by the author of Vol. IV in the Mennonite Experience in America series.

――――――. "Henry W. Lohrenz and Tabor College." *ML*, 38 (Sep. 1983), 14-15.

――――――. "Fundamentalist Conflict in Mennonite Colleges: A Response to Cultural Transitions?" *MQR*, 57 (July 1983), 241-56.

――――――. "The Long Weekend or the Short Week: Mennonite Peace Theology, 1925-1944." *MQR*, 60 (Jan. 1986), 38-57.

Umble, John. "Factors Explaining the Disintegration of Mennonite Communities." *Proceedings of the Seventh Annual Conference on Mennonite Cultural Problems.* Hillsboro, Kans.: Council of Mennonite Colleges, 1949.

――――――. *Goshen College, 1894-1954.* Goshen, Ind.: Goshen College, 1955.

Unruh, John D. *A Century of Mennonites in Dakota.* Freeman, S. Dak.: n.p., 1972.

_____. *In the Name of Christ: A History of the Mennonite Central Committee and Its Service 1920-1951.* Scottdale, Pa.: Herald Press, 1952.

Voices Against War, A Guide to the Schowalter Oral History Collection on World War I Conscientious Objection. North Newton, Kans.: Bethel College, 1973, rev. 1981.

Waldner, Marie. *For Half a Century: The Story of Freeman Junior College 1900-1950.* Freeman, S. Dak.: Freeman Junior College, 1951.

Warkentin, A., and Melvin Gingerich. *Who's Who Among the Mennonites.* North Newton, Kans.: A. Warkentin, 1943. Information on more than a thousand prominent Mennonites. Expansion of a 1937 edition.

Weaver, J. Denny. "The Quickening of Soteriology: Atonement from Christian Burkholder to Daniel Kauffman." *MQR,* 61 (Jan. 1987), 5-45.

Weaver, Martin G. *Mennonites of Lancaster Conference.* Scottdale, Pa.: Mennonite Publishing House, 1931.

Weaver, William B. *Thirty-Five Years in the Congo.* Chicago: Congo Inland Mission, 1945. A history of the inter-Mennonite mission work in Zaire.

Weber, Harry F. *Centennial History of the Mennonites in Illinois 1829-1929.* Scottdale, Pa.: Herald Press, 1931.

Wedel, Cornelius H. *Abriss der Geschichte der Mennoniten,* Vols. I-IV. Newton, Kans.: Bethel College, 1900-1904. An early survey of Anabaptist-Mennonite history from the time of Christ through the nineteenth century.

_____. *Briefliche Blätter an einen Lernenden über Bildung, Gesellschafts-und Heiratsfragen.* Newton, Kans.: Bethel College, 1906.

_____. *Randzeichnung zu den Geschichten des Alten Testaments,* 1899, 73 pp.

_____. *Randzeichnung zu den Geschichten des Alten Testaments,* 1900, 97 pp.

Wedel, David C. *The Story of Alexanderwohl.* Goessel, Kans.: Goessel Centennial Committee, 1974.

Wedel, Peter J. *Evolution: Die neue Religion der Wissenschaft.* N.p.: n.p., n.d. An essay evaluating and opposing the theory of evolution; by a science teacher at Bethel College.

_____. *The Story of Bethel College.* North Newton, Kans.: Bethel College, 1954.

Wenger, A. Grace. "Eastern Mennonite Board of Missions and Charities." Manuscript intended for publication; inquire at the board, Salunga, Pennsylvania.

Wenger, Eli D. *The Weaverland Mennonites*. Manheim, Pa.: The author, 1968.

Wenger, John C. *Faithfully, Geo. R.: The Life and Thought of George R. Brunk I*. Harrisonburg, Va.: Sword and Trumpet, 1978.

_____. *History of the Mennonites of the Franconia Conference*. Telford, Pa.: Franconia Mennonite Historical Society, 1937.

_____. "Jacob Wisler and the Old Order Mennonite Schism of 1872 in Elkhart County, Indiana." *MQR*, 33 (Apr. 1959), 108-13, and (July 1959), 215-40.

_____. *The Mennonite Church in America, Sometimes Called Old Mennonites*. Scottdale, Pa.: Herald Press, 1966.

_____. *The Mennonites in Indiana and Michigan*. Scottdale, Pa.: Herald Press, 1961.

Whitmer, Paul. "The Autobiography of Paul E. Whitmer." Typescript copy, Bluffton, Ohio, Feb. 15, 1952.

Wiebe, Katie Funk. *Our Lamps Were Lit*. Newton, Kans.: Bethel Deaconess Hospital School of Nursing Alumnae Association, 1978. The story of the deaconess movement and nursing education among Kansas Mennonites.

_____, ed. *Women Among the Brethren, Stories of Fifteen Mennonite Brethren and Krimmer Mennonite Brethren Women*. Hillsboro, Kans.: The Board of Christian Literature of the General Conference of Mennonite Brethren Churches, 1979.

Wiebe, Raymond F. *Hillsboro: the City on the Prairie*. Hillsboro, Kans.: the author, 1985.

Wiebe, Vernon R. *Come Let Us Stand United: A History of Corn Bible Academy 1902-1977*. Hillsboro, Kans.: The author, 1977.

Yoder, Edward. *Must Christians Fight?* Akron, Pa.: Mennonite Central Committee, 1943.

Yoder, Elmer S. *The Beachy Amish Mennonite Fellowship Churches*. Sugar Creek Ohio: Schlabach Printers, 1987).

Yoder, Gideon. The Oldest Living American Mennonite Congregations of Central Kansas." M.A. thesis, Phillips University, 1948.

Yoder, Ida, ed. *Edward, Pilgrimage of a Mind: The Journal of*

Edward Yoder. Wadsworth, Ohio: The editor, 1985. The revealing diary of an Amish-background Mennonite intellectual, including keen, private commentary on "old" Mennonite affairs from the 1920s to the 1940s.

Yoder, J. Harvey. *Fifty Years Building on the Warwick.* Denbigh, Va.: Warwick River Mennonite Church, 1947. The story of a Virginia tidewater Mennonite settlement.

Yoder, Sanford C. *The Days of My Years.* Scottdale, Pa.: Herald Press, 1959. Autobiography of "old" Mennonite denominational leader and president of Goshen College from 1923 to 1940.

ARCHIVAL COLLECTIONS

Historical materials on Anabaptist and Mennonite history are concentrated in a number of archival collections attached to Mennonite institutions. The largest of these collections is in the Archives of the Mennonite Church (AMC) at Goshen (Ind.) College. The AMC has official records of agencies of the "old" Mennonite church, Goshen College, Mennonite Central Committee, and Mennonite World Conference. Among its personal collections of special value for this study were those of Harold S. Bender, John S. Coffman, John F. Funk, John E. Hartzler, John Horsch, Daniel Kauffman, Jacob C. Meyer, Jonas D. Mininger, Menno S. Steiner, and Sanford Yoder. The collections at AMC of boards and institutions most useful for this study were those of the Mennonite Central Committee, the Mennonite Board of Missions and Charities, the Peace Problems Committee, and the Russian Relief Collection.

The Mennonite Library and Archives (MLA) at Bethel College, North Newton, Kansas, is the official depository for records of the General Conference Mennonite church and of Bethel College. Personal collections of special interest for this study have been those of Edmund George Kaufman, Henry Peter Krehbiel, Peter H. Richert, Henry R. Voth, and Peter C. Hiebert. The MLA has substantial materials on the Mennonite experience in World War I, including documents collected by Allan Teichroew in the National Archives, Washington, D.C., and the Showalter Oral History Collection with more than 250 interviews with Mennonite World War I draftees. For this study I examined the Bethel College archives as well as the records of the GC Commission on Overseas Mission.

The Menno Simons Historical Library and Archives (MSHLA) at Eastern Mennonite College, Harrisonburg, Virginia, has the records of the Virginia Mennonite Conference and Eastern Mennonite College. Personal collections I investigated at MSHLA included those of George R. Brunk, Lewis J. Heatwole,

Amos D. Wenger, Jacob B. Smith, John L. Stauffer, Ernest G. Gehman, J. Harvey Yoder, Chester K. Lehman, and Clayton F. Derstine.

The Eastern Pennsylvania Mennonite Historical Library (EPMHL) at Christopher Dock High School near Lansdale, Pennsylvania, has documents relating to the history of Franconia conference and of congregations and individuals of that area. Of exceptional interest are the collections of Jacob C. Clemens and Jacob Mensch, as well as the Franconia conference record book for 1907-1961. The EPMHL has generously supplied microfilm copies of key holdings.

The Mennonite Historical Library at Bluffton College, Bluffton, Ohio (MHLB), has the papers of C. Henry Smith, as well as the official records of Africa Inter-Mennonite Mission (formerly Congo Inland Mission).

The Centers for Mennonite Brethren Studies in Fresno, California (Pacific College), and in Hillsboro, Kansas (Tabor College), contain materials on the history of Mennonite Brethren leaders, congregations, and institutions. Of special interest for this study was the personal collection of Mennonite Brethren educator and denominational leader Henry W. Lohrenz. Lohrenz's daughter, Mariana Lohrenz Remple of Lawrence, Kansas, holds the original collection and has made arrangements for extensive copying of the documents.

The Lancaster Mennonite Historical Society (LMHS) collection at Lancaster, Pennsylvania, has holdings of Lancaster conference documents and other Mennonite materials from southeastern Pennsylvania. Of particular interest for this study were the papers of Israel B. Good.

The Muddy Creek Farm Library, at the home of Amos B. Hoover near Denver, Pennsylvania, is an extensive private collection of Anabaptist and Mennonite materials gathered by Hoover, with special emphasis on Old Order Mennonite history.

NEWSPAPERS, JOURNALS

Bethel College Monthly, 1896-1934. Publication of GC college in Kansas.

Christian Evangel, 1910-1957. Publication of the Central Conference of Mennonites, Illinois, an Amish-origin group which eventually merged with the General Conference Mennonite church.

Christian Exponent, 1924-1928. Voice of progressive insurgents, mostly of "old" Mennonite background. Handwritten annotated index of articles on selected topics available in MLA.

Christian Monitor, 1909-1953. "Old" Mennonite family and community journal, Scottdale, Pa. For selected annotated index see Denlinger, *Glimpses Past.*

Christlicher Bundesbote, 1882-1947. Official German organ of the General Conference Mennonite church. Annotated index of articles on selected topics for 1896 available in MLA.

Direction, 1975- . A quarterly published by Mennonite Brethren schools.

Elkhart Institute Monthly. Publication of the Elkhart Institute, precursor of Goshen College, in Indiana.

Goshen College Record, 1903- .

Gospel Herald, 1908- . Scottdale, Pa. Official organ of the "old" Mennonite church. For selected annotated index see Denlinger, *Glimpses Past.*

Herald of Truth, 1864-1908. The English-language edition of *Herold der Wahrheit*, progressive paper for "old" Mennonites, edited by John F. Funk, Elkhart, Ind.. For selected annotated index see Denlinger, *Glimpses Past*; the index is helpful but incomplete—see its introduction, by Theron F. Schlabach.

Der Herold, 1910-1941. German-language weekly newspaper primarily for GC constituency. Newton, Kans. Annotated index of articles on selected topics for 1910-13, 1919-20 and 1928, available in MLA.

Herold der Wahrheit, 1864-1901. German-language progressive paper for "old" Mennonites, edited by John F. Funk, Elkhart, Ind.

Home Messenger, 1963- . Old Order Mennonite publication, includes historical articles by Amos Hoover.

Kansas Volksblatt und Anzeiger, 1902-1909. Kansas Mennonite newspaper in Kansas. Merged with *Der Herold.*

The Mennonite, 1885- . Official organ of the General Conference Mennonite church. Annotated index of articles on selected topics for 1885-1929 available in MLA.

Mennonite Historical Bulletin, 1940- . Published by the Historical Committee of the "old" Mennonites' general conference.

Mennonite Life, 1946- . Illustrated quarterly published by Bethel College.

Mennonite Research Journal, 1966-1977. Quarterly publication of the Lancaster Mennonite Historical Society.

Mennonite Weekly Review, 1923- . Newton, Kans. Annotated index of articles on selected topics for 1923-1930 available in MLA.

The Review, 1899-1904. Progressive monthly edited by H. P. Krehbiel in Canton, Ohio. Annotated index of articles on selected topics available in MLA.

The Sword and Trumpet, 1929- . Conservative monthly, Denbigh, Va.

Tabor College Herold, 1912-31. German-English monthly published by Mennonite Brethren college in Hillsboro, Kans.

Vorwärts, 1910-1940. Progressive German-language weekly in Hillsboro, Kans., primarily for Mennonite Brethren constituency, edited by Abraham L. Schellenberg, 1913-1919, 1922-1930.

Der Wahrheitsfreund, 1915-1947. German organ of the Krimmer Mennonite Brethren.

Young People's Paper, 1894-1906. Illustrated youth paper edited by "old" Mennonite progressives and published by the Mennonite Publishing Company, Elkhart, Ind.

Zionsbote, 1884-1906. Official German organ of the Mennonite Brethren Church.

PROCEEDINGS (SELECTED)

Amish Mennonite Eastern District Conference Reports 1893-1926. Reports of annual meetings of conference which then merged with the "old" Mennonites' Ohio conference.

Conference Record of the Kansas-Nebraska Mennonite Conference 1876-1914. N.p., n.d. Record of one of the "old" Mennonnite district conferences.

Conference Reports, 1896-1956, Church of God in Christ, Mennonite. Lahoma, Okla.: Church of God in Christ Mennonite, 1956. Reports of the "Holdeman" Mennonites.

"First Annual Report of the Missionary Society, 'Light and Hope.' " Chicago, 1894. An account of the beginnings of John A. Sprunger's independent benevolent work in Berne, Ind., and Chicago.

"Franconia Conference Record Book, 1907-1961." An unofficial handwritten record of Franconia Conference proceedings kept by Jacob B. Mensch. Inquire at Eastern Pennsylvania Mennonite Historical Library, Christopher Dock High School, Lansdale, Pennsylvania; microfilm copies available in some other Mennonite historical libraries or archives.

Gesamtprotokolle der Kansas-und Westlichen Distrikt-Konfer-

enzen. N.p., n.d. Proceedings and reports of the largest GC district conference, in three volumes, 1877-1937.

Konferenzberichte der Mennoniten Brüdergemeinde von Nord Amerika 1883-1919. Hillsboro, Kans.: Mennonite Brethren Publishing House, 1920. MB North American general conference reports.

Mennonite General Conference: Report. 1893-1929. Proceedings of the "old" Mennonite biennial conference meetings.

Minutes of the Indiana-Michigan Mennonite Conference 1864-1929. Scottdale, Pa.: Mennonite Publishing House, n.d.

Minutes of the Virginia Mennonite Conference (1835-1938). Scottdale, Pa.: Virginia Mennonite Conference, 1939.

Proceedings of the Mennonite General Conference Including Discussions Leading to its Origination. N.p., 1921. Includes proceedings of the "old" Mennonite General Conference beginning with discussions in 1890 to the eleventh meeting in 1919.

Report of the Eastern Amish-Mennonite Conference, Constitution and Appendix 1912-1929. Sugarcreek, Ohio: Budget Publishing Co., 1920.

Reports of the All-Mennonite Convention, Vol. 1-17, 1913-30. Publisher varies.

Reports of the Minutes of the General Conference of the Mennonites of North America. N.p., n.d. Includes minutes of GC triennial sessions, 1902-1929.

Index

••••

acculturation, 30, 43
Adams County, Indiana, 47
Adams, Henry, 22
adaptation, 27
Africa, 150, 160, 308
agricultural, 172
agricultural exemptions, 237
Alcatraz, 240
Alexanderwohl, 80-81, 86, 95, 190, 237
Allebach, Ann Jemima, 286, 287-288, 291
Allebach, H. G., 261
Allegheny conference, 114
Allen county, Ohio, 124
Allgyer, J. Roy, 250
All Mennonite Convention, 229, 294-295
Altoona, Pennsylvania, 114
American Civil Liberties Union, 296
American Dairy Company, 248
American Falls, Idaho, 183
American Friends Service Committee, 295
Americanism, 171
Americanization, 24, 31, 39, 147, 173, 272, 314
American Legion, 235
American Mennonite Relief Commission, 256
American Protective League, 218
American Relief Administration, 243, 251
Amish, 33, 45, 195, 301
Amish Mennonites, 38, 46, 73, 74, 121, 304
Amstutz, Peter B., 124
Anabaptism, 33, 142, 159, 174, 302
Anabaptist-Mennonite history, 280, 281
Anabaptists, 102, 176
Anthony, Susan B., 22
Anti-modernism, 257ff., 301, 309
Apostolic Christian Church, 47
Arapahoes, 25, 136, 151

architecture, 33
Argentina, 153
Armenians, 143, 144
Army Camps, 229
Arndt, Johann, 67
Aschliman, Ura V., 236
assimilation, 186
athletics, 171
atonement, 268
attire, 112, 249, 278, 301
    Old Order Amish, 45
    "Old" Mennonite, 109, 115-116, 130-132
    and college education, 169
    and hospitals, 185
    see also, dress
Ausbund, 71
automobile, 68, 75, 76, 77, 207, 305

••••

Baehr, Herman C., 204
Baergen, J. J., 87
Baker, Newton D., 209, 230, 234, 236, 238, 240, 242
Bakewell, Mary E., 288
Balzer, Peter, 92
baptism, 32, 67, 72, 99, 115, 147, 150, 189, 190, 214
Baptist, 97, 153
Baptist Theological Seminary in Rochester, New York, 97
Barge, Enos, 106
Bartel, Henry C., 147
Bartel Mission, 147, 148
Bartel, Nellie Schmidt, 147
Beachy Amish, 74, 75
Beachy, Moses M., 74
beards, 46, 52, 74
Beatrice, Nebraska, 182
beer, 203
Bender, Daniel H., 118, 129, 132, 173, 266
Bender, George L., 116, 126, 161, 247, 277
Bender, Harold S., 33, 105, 253, 267, 276, 277-282, 302

Bendle, A. J., 168
benevolence, 246ff., 255
Benner, Rhine, 226
Berne, Indiana, 95, 133
Bethany Deaconess Hospital,
        Idaho, 179
Bethany Hospital, Oklahoma, 179,
        194
Bethel Academy, Kansas, 92
Bethel College, Kansas, 87, 93,
        101, 162, 164, 172, 177,
        203, 248
Bethel congregation, Missouri,
        107, 110
Bethel Deaconess Home and
        Hospital, Kansas, 162,
        179, 182
Bethel Deaconess Society, 293
Bethesda Hospital, Kansas, 179
Bible, 66, 129, 261, 301
        verbal inspiration, 263
Bible conference, 113
Bible conferences, 42, 113, 114
Bible Doctrine, 129
Bible institute, 113
Bible Institute of Los Angeles, 271
birth rate, 54
bishops, 41, 119
Bismarck, Otto von, 90, 94, 210
Bixler, Jacob K., 119, 265
Black bumpers, 61, 64
blacks, 48, 143, 146, 170
Bloomfield Seminary, 80, 165
Blosser, N. O., 125
Bluffton College, Ohio, 110, 152,
        164, 168, 176, 177, 265,
        269
Bluffton, Ohio, 24, 185
Board of Education, 120
Board of Inquiry, 238
Board of Missions and Charities,
        120, 247, 293
Board of Publication, 297
bond drives, 222, 227-228
Bontrager, Mannasses E., 225
borrowings, 28
Brandt, Christian, 38
Brenneman, Daniel, 44, 45
Brenneman, John M., 36, 67
Brethren in Christ, 53, 117
Brinkley, John R., 273

Brown, Henry J., 149, 309
Brown, Maria Miller, 149
Brubaker, Clara, 291
Bruderhofs, 52
Brunk, George R., 129, 131, 195,
        262, 263, 278, 312-313,
        315
Bryan, William Jennings, 258
Bucks County, Pennsylvania, 27,
        38
buggy tops, 68
Buhler Vereins Schule, Kansas, 92
Buller, Jacob, 80
bureaucracy, 160
Burgess, E. W., 186
Burkhard, Samuel, 37
Burkholder, Christian, 36, 67, 68
Burkholder, Daniel, 64
Burkholder, Peter, 68
Byers, Noah E., 110, 163, 165, 167,
        173, 176, 267, 292, 295

●●●●
California, 192
Cameroons, 153
Camp Dodge, Iowa, 239
Camp Funston, Kansas, 231, 234
Camp Lewis, Washington, 239
Camp Sheridan, Alabama, 236
Camp Sherman, Ohio, 235
Camp Travis, Texas, 236
Canada, 49, 52, 220, 233, 252,
        273, 305
Canadian Board of Colonization
        and Mennonite Land
        Settlement, 252
Canadian Pacific Railway, 252
Canton, Ohio, 114
Capper, Arthur, 222
Carnegie, Andrew, 210
catechism, 68
Catherine the Great, 34
Central Asia great trek, 82, 138
Central Conference of Menno-
        nites, 47, 150, 232, 265,
        304
Central Illinois conference, 121
Central Illinois Mennonite con-
        ference, 122
Central Mennonite College, 122,
        124, 164, 168

Charles, John D., 269
Cheyenne Indians, 151
Chiang Kai-shek, 159
Chicago, 21, 26
Chicago World's Fair, 21-27, 137
China, 147-150, 159
China Mennonite Mission Society,
	148
Christendom, 35, 36, 90, 93, 142
Christian and Missionary Alliance,
	146
Christian Arbitration and Peace
	Society, 21, 295
Christian Endeavor Society, 289
Christian Evangel, 175
Christian Exponent, 267-268,
	279, 312
Christian Monitor, 267
Christlicher Bundesbote, 88, 96,
	133, 211
church history, 101
Church of God in Christ, Menno-
	nite (Holdeman), 51-52,
	221, 304
Church of the Brethren, 70, 99,
	109, 214, 294, 296
church-world dualism, 33, 142
City Hospital, 180
Civilian Public Service, 276, 299
Civil Liberties Bureau, 240
Clemens, Jacob C., 292
Clinton Frame congregation, In-
	diana, 199
Coffman, John S., 21, 26, 108,
	110, 113, 114, 118, 131,
	165, 204, 268, 291, 300
Coffman, S. F., 132, 177
colleges, 163ff., 196
	see also, individual college
		names
Colorado, 192
Columbian Exposition, 21, 22
Committee on Education for
	Peace, 296
Committee on Fundamentals, 263
Committee on Public Information,
	217
communion, 115
Communist Party, 204
Communist Revolution, 34
Community Hospital, 180

Concordia Hospital, 179
Conestoga Valley, Pennsylvania,
	56
conference meetings, 205
Conference of Pacifist Churches,
	283, 296
Conference of United Mennonite
	Brethren in North
	America, 48, 100
Congo Inland Mission, 47, 122,
	150, 155, 160
congregational autonomy, 311
congregational polity, 51
Congregation Christendom, 86,
	101, 169, 183, 202, 271,
	314
Congregations, 86
	disintegration, 195
Conrad, George N., 226
conscientious objectors, 214, 232,
	233, 237, 238, 240
conscription, 217, 229
Conservative Amish Mennonites,
	74, 304
conversion, 112
Cooprider, George, 223
Cooprider, Walter, 223
Corn Bible School, Oklahoma, 92
Cornies, Johann, 34
Corn, Oklahoma, 86, 100, 194
Councils of Defense, 218, 222
court-martial, 237
Creel, George, 217
Cressman, Joseph B., 306
Crooks, W. L., 227
Crowder, Enoch, 232, 234
Cuba, 143
culture, 102-104, 155

●●●●
Dakota-Montana, 114
Dale Enterprise Literary Society,
	202
Darrow, Clarence, 258
Darwinism, 174
Das Echo, 88
*Das Kansas Volksblatt und An-
	zeiger*, 87
Dawes Severalty Act, 193
deaconess, 24, 147, 162, 177, 178,
	180, 289

deaconess homes, 95
Debs, Eugene, 225
Deep Run Mennonite church, 28
Defenseless Mennonite Brethren
      in Christ of North
      America, 123
Defenseless Mennonite church,
      47, 99, 121, 148, 150
de Gobineau, Arthur, 220
Denck, Hans, 166
Denlinger, Mary, 110
Denner, Jacob, 67
Dennis, James S., 158
denomination, 73, 139, 150, 186,
      187, 248, 300, 303, 309,
      313
denominationalism, 28, 37, 285
      and peoplehood, 187
denominational merger, 121
Department of Justice, 228
Der Freundschaftskreis, 87
Der Herold, 88
Dettwiler, Matilda, 69
Detwiler, Irvin R., 267
Deutsche Westen, 88
Deutschtum, 91, 93, 97
Dewey, John, 269
Die Mennonitische Rundschau,
      87, 88
Diener, Charles, 223
Diener, Daniel, 223
Dirks, Heinrich, 89, 94
discipleship, 72, 316
dispensationalism, 117
dispensationalist, 22, 258, 312
doctrine, 112, 114
Doctrines of the Bible, 129
Doering, Alma, 150, 157, 289
Dordrecht, 216
Dordrecht Confession of Faith, 32,
      71
Douglass, Janet, 44
draft resistance, 232
dress, 112, 130, 131, 169, 249,
      251, 266, 278, 313
Dress Committee, 130
dualism of church and world, 158
Duerksen, John F., 99
Dunkers, 109
Dunkers (Church of the Brethren),
      53, 275

Dutch Mennonites Indonesia, 141
Dutch-Russian Mennonites, 34,
      36, 37, 48, 83, 250
Dutch-Russian Mennonites,
      and benevolence, 256
      deaconess hospitals, 182
      fundamentalism, 270ff.
      higher education, 169
      ironies, 314

●●●●
East Emmet church, Kansas, 118
Eastern Amish conference, 46
Eastern Amish Mennonite con-
      ference, 73, 109, 121,
      265
Eastern District, 27, 230, 311
Eastern Mennonite Board of Mis-
      sions and Charities, 153,
      283
Eastern Mennonite School, Vir-
      ginia, 128, 164, 168, 262,
      269, 313
East Pennsylvania Mennonite con-
      ference, 40
Ebenezer, 124
Ebenfeld Mennonite Brethren
      congregation, Kansas, 86,
      100, 206, 272
Ebersole, Solomon D., 25
Eby, Benjamin, 68
Eby, H. W., 178
Eden congregation, 287
education
      and Mennonite identity, 173
      of teachers, 172
Egly Amish, 74, 121, 122
Egly, Henry, 47
Eighth Street Mennonite Church,
      Indiana, 198
Elbing, Kansas, 32
elder, 41
Elkhart, 114
Elkhart and Lagrange Counties,
      Indiana, 73
Elkhart board, 152
Elkhart/Goshen, Indiana, 198
Elkhart, Indiana, 25, 42
Elkhart Institute, 110, 125, 126,
      127, 144, 164, 165, 168,
      179, 198, 288, 291

Elk Park, North Carolina, 48, 143
Emergency Quota Act, 252
Emergency Relief Commission, 248, 249
emigration, 233
Engineer Corps, 238
Enns, Heinrich, 153
Enns, Maria, 153
Entz, J. J., 202
Epp. Ida, 178
Epp, Jacob B., 158
Erasmus, Desiderius, 302
Erb, Allen, 229
Erb, Allen H., 185
Erb, Paul, 285
Erb, Tilman (T. M.), 265
Espionage Act, 221, 225, 228, 239
Evangelical Alliance, 289
Evangelical Mennonite Brethren, 49, 100, 122, 148, 171, 304
Evangelical Mennonite Church, 47, 49, 171, 304
evangelism, 42
evolution, 173, 258
Ewert, Jacob G., 202, 212, 240, 252, 272
Exemption Committee, 212
Exponent, 292
extinct congregations, 195-196

●●●●

Fairview, Michigan, 218
"faith" missions, 146
farm, 246
Farmers Alliance, 89
Farmers Anzeiger, 87
Farm Furlough Bill, 234, 238
Farm Loan Bonds, 222
Fast, Martin B., 88, 233, 248
Federal Council of Churches, 134, 205, 296
Fellowship of Evangelical Bible Churches, 49
Feng Yu-hsiang, 159
Fire Baptized Holiness Association, 117
First Mennonite church, Bluffton, 124
First Mennonite Church of Berne, Indiana, 50, 133

First Mennonite Church of Philadelphia, 50, 287
Fisher, John J., 267
flag, 91
food draft plan, 252
foot-washing, 115
foot washing, 124, 129, 155
Forks congregation, 199, 277
Fort Dodge, 208
Fort Leavenworth, 236, 237
Franconia, 38, 40, 43, 132, 237
Franconia Mennonite conference, 41, 42, 70, 108, 154, 237, 245, 247, 252
Franklin and Marshall College, 196
Franklin County, Pennsylvania, 38
Frantz, Adolf, 269
Franz, Adolf I., 171
Franz, John M., 223
Freed, Barbara, 291
Freeman Academy, 94
Freeman College, 164
Freeman Preparatory School, South Dakota, 92
Free Methodists, 118
Fretz, Allen, 28
Frey, Elias, 266
Fricke, Frederick C., 52
Friends Reconstruction Service, 223
Friesen, Abraham, 153
Friesen, Gordon, 204
Friesen, Helena Hiebert, 123
Friesen, Maria, 153
Friesen, Peter A., 123
frontier, 39, 190
Fulton County, Ohio, 227
Funck, Heinrich, 36, 67
Fundamental Book Depot, 312
Fundamentalism, 122, 129, 130, 257, 258, 309
fundamentals conferences, 206
Funk, Annie, 154, 157
Funk, Ferdinand J., 86
Funk, John F., 21, 26, 42, 43, 46, 87, 97, 104, 108, 116, 125, 126, 132, 198, 248, 267
Funk, Joseph, 43

••••
Galle, Peter J., 86
Garrett Theological Seminary, 279
Gehman, Ernest G., 313, 315, 317
Gelassenheit, 71
Gemeindechristentum, 37, 104
General Conference, 132
General Conference (GC) Menno-
          nite Church (and its
          people), 24, 29, 49, 95,
          120, 122, 205, 247, 304
    benevolence, 247ff.
    conference meetings, 205ff.
    congregational autonomy,
          134
    Eastern District, 27-28, 50
    ethnic variety, 49-50
    and *Kirchliche* Mennonites,
          95
    membership growth, 305
    missions, 97, 134, 151
    peace, 296
    polity, 51
    relation to "Old" Mennonites,
          43, 120
    secret societies, 311
    statement of faith, 311
    Wadsworth School, 133
    Western District, 50
    on World's Fair, 24
General Conference of the "Old"
          Mennonite Church, 124-
          130, 214
    Yellow Creek Statement, 213,
          228
    see also "Old" Mennonite
          Church
General Problems Committee, 301,
          310-311
Gerber, Maria Anna, 147, 157,
          180-181
Gerig, Daniel S., 267
Gerig, Orie B., 250
German, 34
German-Americanization, 93
German culture, 90, 93, 290
Germanism, 212
German language, 90
German Teachers Association, 90,
          91, 92
Ghost Dance, 136, 138

Gingerich, Simon, 222
Gish, Warren, 237
Goertz, Peter S., 177, 269
Goerz, David, 86, 88, 96, 162, 183
Goessel Preparatory School,
          Kansas, 92
Good, DeWitt, 25
Good, Dewitt R., 178
Good, Israel B., 197
Good, Olivia W., 288
Goshen College, Indiana, 110, 122,
          127, 128, 164, 168, 169,
          172, 199, 264, 265, 269,
          279, 288, 308
Goshen, Indiana, 114
Goshen Milk Condensery, 198
Gospel Banner, 45
Gospel Herald, 127, 176, 267
Gospel Witness, 267
Gospel Witness Company, 127
Gotebo Bible School, Oklahoma,
          92
Gottshall, William S., 245, 309
Graber, Martha, 296
Graber, Minnie Swartzendruber,
          156
Grace congregation, Pandora,
          Ohio, 124
Grantsville, Maryland, 74
Grant, Ulysses S., 216
Great Awakenings, 28, 107
Grebel, Conrad, 280, 302
Griest, W. W., 197, 228, 237
Groffdale conference, 61, 76
Groffdale congregation, Pennsyl-
          vania, 106
Grubb, Nathaniel B., 50, 133, 213
Grubb, Silas M., 96, 133, 222, 230

••••
Habermann, Johann, 67
Hallman, Mary Ann, 44
Halstead, Kansas, 86
Halstead Preparatory School,
          Kansas, 82, 92, 164
Harder, David E., 88, 171, 177,
          233
Harder, David W., 165
Harder, Gustav, 158
Harding, Florence Kling, 275
Harding, Warren G., 275

Harms, Abraham J., 269
Harms, John F., 88, 97, 98, 99,
    144, 248, 272
Harrisonburg, 114
Hartzler, John E., 110, 126, 129,
    165, 176, 177, 199, 264,
    267, 281, 288, 289
Hartzler, Jonas S., 228
Haury, Gustav A., 91, 165
Haury, Richard S., 178
Haury, Samuel S., 141, 142, 151
Haury, Susannah Hirschler, 151
Heatwole, Cornelius J., 203
Heatwole, David A., 202
Heatwole, Lewis J., 226, 289
Heatwole, Mary A. Coffman, 289
Heatwole, Timothy O., 203
Heils-Bote, 47
Henderson Bible School,
    Nebraska, 92
Henderson, Nebraska, 100
Hepzibah Faith Mission, 146
Hepzibah Faith Missionary Associ-
    ation, 118
Herald of Truth, 21, 26, 42, 46,
    127, 267
Herbert Bible School, Sas-
    katchewan, 92
Herold der Wahrheit, 26, 42
Herr, John, 44, 58, 66
Hershey, Barbara, 106
Hershey, Eusebius, 45
Hesston College, Kansas, 128, 164,
    168, 262, 269, 300
Hesston, Kansas, 114
Hey-Friesen, Alice, 171
Hiebert, Nikolai N., 153
Hiebert, Peter C., 165, 214, 243,
    250, 255, 285
Hiebert, Susanna Wiebe, 153
higher criticism, 261, 280
Hillsboro Herald, 87
Hillsboro, Kansas, 101, 199ff.
Hillsboro Post, 88
Hillsboro Preparatory School,
    Kansas, 92
Hirschy, Noah C., 165, 173, 261
historical consciousness, 32, 33,
    173-175, 255, 280-281
historical literature, 42, 102-105
Historic Peace Churches, 297, 298

Hodel, Esther Elizabeth Smucker,
    179
Hofer, David, 239
Hofer, Joseph, 239
Hofer, Michael, 239
Hoffnungsau Bible School,
    Kansas, 92
Hoffnungsfeld congregation,
    Kansas, 87, 224
Holdeman, John, 51, 66
holiness, 117, 258
Holmes County, Ohio, 73
holy kiss, 115
Home and Foreign Relief Commis-
    sion, 145, 248
Hoover, Herbert, 243
Hopi, 25, 138, 151
Horning, Maria, 62
Horning, Moses G., 62, 64, 76
Horsch, Elizabeth, 277
Horsch, John, 26, 39, 176, 255,
    259, 268, 281, 283, 296,
    297, 312
hospitals, 24, 95, 177, 178, 194
Hostetler, Charity Steiner, 265
Hostetler, Charles K., 144
Hostetler, Lester, 265, 267, 295
Hostetter, D. Ralph, 241
Houlding, Horace, 147
Howe, Julia Ward, 22
Hubmaier, Balthasar, 166
Huffman, J. A., 229
Huguenots, 187
humility, 33, 36, 37, 62, 65, 83,
    108, 283, 286
Hurst, Frank, 64
Hutchinson, Kansas, 207, 311
Hutterian Brethren (Hutterites),
    52, 191, 233, 239, 304
    mobility, 192
Hutter, Jacob, 52
Hyderabad, India, 153
Hygema, Katie, 44
hymnals, 68
hymnody, 71
hymns, 72, 73, 156

●●●●

Idaho, 192
Illinois, 38
Illinois Conference of Mennonites,
    41, 44, 47

immigration, 54, 252
imperialism, 143
independent missions, 146
India, 143, 145, 151, 153, 159,
       308
Indiana, 38, 55
Indiana Amish Mennonite con-
       ference, 121
Indiana conference, 40, 41, 44
Indiana-Michigan Amish Menno-
       nite conference, 46
Indiana-Michigan Mennonite con-
       ference, 21, 73, 119, 121,
       126, 265, 279
Indian Territory, 193
individualism, 30, 71, 174
Inola, Oklahoma, 218
insurance, 266
Intercollegiate Peace Conference,
       295
Iowa, 38, 74
irony, 55, 85, 119, 209, 300, 302,
       313

••••
Jansen, Peter, 203
Janzen, Aaron F., 150
Janzen, Cornelius, 177
Janzen, David A., 236
Janzen, Ernestina Strauss, 150
Jehovah's Witnesses, 58
Jews, 69
Johns, Daniel J., 109, 199
Johnstown Bible conference, 117
Johnstown Bible School, 114
Jura Swiss, 49, 123
Justice Department, 239, 241

••••
Kansas, 55, 182
Kansas City Mission, 240
Kansas Conference Mennonites,
       50, 95
Kansas-Nebraska "Old" Mennonite
       conference, 40, 41, 118,
       263
Kauffman, Daniel, 43, 111, 114,
       118, 121, 123, 125, 126,
       127, 128, 130, 165, 176,
       210, 213, 250, 257, 264,
       267, 278, 285, 292, 295,
       301, 310

anti-modernism, 262ff.
conversion, 110
Bible doctrine, 114-116
Dress Committee, 130-132
World War, 210, 213
Kaufman, Edmund G., 139, 140,
       152, 156, 159, 186, 282,
       307, 309
Kaufman, Frieda, 162, 178, 180,
       182
Keller, Ludwig, 103, 174, 297
Kellogg-Briand Pact, 296
Kellogg, Walter Guest, 238
Keppel, Frederick P., 230, 239
Kirchliche Mennonites, 35, 48, 95
Kleine Gemeinde, 48, 51, 304
Kliewer, C. E., 98
Kliewer, John W., 212, 262, 269,
       285, 287
Kohfeld, Henry, 139
Kratz, Clayton, 247, 251
Kratz, Maxwell, 203
Krehbiel, Albert Henry, 204
Krehbiel, Anna Leisy, 204
Krehbiel, Christian, 24, 80, 86
Krehbiel, Christian E., 292, 310
Krehbiel, Henry J., 297
Krehbiel, Henry P., 89, 175, 212,
       229, 272, 275, 296-298
Krehbiel, J. J., 204
Krehbiel, Johann J., 203
Krehbiel, Susanna, 82
Krehbiel, William J., 89, 90
Kreider, Amos E., 267, 295
Kreider, Robert S., 112
Krimmer Mennonite Brethren, 48,
       53, 88, 99, 143, 148, 232,
       304
Kruse, Matilda, 298
Kuhlman, Ernst, 149
Kuhlman, Maria Dyck, 149
Ku Klux Klan, 257
Kurtz, John S., 61, 64
Kurtz, Maria, 66

••••
LaFollette, Robert, 273
La Junta, Colorado, 178, 185, 229
Lambert, George, 144
Lambert, Rose, 147
Lancaster, 38, 43, 237, 284

Lancaster conference, 41, 108, 119, 143, 145, 237, 283-284, 308
Lancaster County, Pennsylvania, 26, 35, 53, 56, 73, 106, 110, 191, 196, 283
Landes, Ada May, 23
land rush
  Oklahoma, 193
Langenwalter, Jacob H., 49
language, 94, 123, 221, 225, 232, 272
  Low German, 34, 37
  Pennsylvania Dutch, 34
  transition from German to English, 60
language tradition, 170
lawsuits, 116
Laxitarian, 263
leaders, 61, 276
leadership, 63, 172
Leavenworth, Kansas, 209, 240
Leavenworth prison, 240
Lehman, Chester K., 269
Lehman, Mahlon C., 154
Leibig, Martha, 98
Leisy, Christine, 203
Leisy, Elizabeth Geber, 203
Leisy, Ernest E., 196
Leisy, Isaac, 203
Leisy, Otto, 203
Libby, Frederick J., 295
liberalism, 176
Liberty Bonds, 224
Liberty Loan, 217, 223, 227
Light and Hope Deaconess Home, 179
Light and Hope Hospital, 179
Light and Hope Mission, 99
Light and Hope Society, 24, 143, 148, 181
Lima, Ohio, 114
Lincoln, Abraham, 175
Line Lexington congregation, 291
Linscheid, Anna Hirschler, 152, 307
literary societies, 170
Liu, James Chung-fu, 307
lodge, 311
Lohrenz, Henry W., 93, 165, 169, 177, 202, 214, 222, 271, 285

lot, 41, 63, 82, 282
Loucks, Aaron, 126, 213, 214, 227, 239, 254
Lower Deer Creek Amish congregation, Iowa, 300
Luebke, Frederick, 218
Lusitania, 211
Luthy, David, 195

••••

Machen, J. Gresham, 280
Mack, Noah H., 123, 131, 313
Manual of Bible Doctrine, 129
Marion County, 91
Marion County Anzeiger, 87, 88
Marion County Council of Defense, 202
Marion County, Kansas, 35
Marsden, George, 258
Martin, Abraham, 66
Martin, John W., 60
Martin, Jonas H., 26, 45, 57, 58, 59, 64, 65, 66, 70, 72, 76
martyrdom, 72
Martyrs Mirror, 34, 68, 71, 174
materialism, 30
Matthew 16:24, 316
McAdoo, William Gibbs, 217, 242
McKinley, William, 143
McLean County, Illinois, 47
McPherson Anzeiger, 87
McPherson College, 93, 99
Meck, A. J., 222
Medical Corps, 235, 236, 238
meetinghouse, 64
Mennonite Aid Plan, 125
Mennonite Bible Academy, Nebraska, 92
Mennonite Board of Charitable Homes, 152
Mennonite Board of Education, 176, 265
Mennonite Board of Missions and Charities, 152, 308
Mennonite Book and Tract Society, 126
Mennonite Book Concern, 143
Mennonite Brethren Church (and its people), 35, 48, 82, 84, 85, 95, 97, 99, 148, 206, 214, 271, 304

and Baptists, 97-99
centralization, 101
and Church of the Brethren, 99
fundamentalism, 271-272
location of members, 306
missions, 98, 153
Russian origins, 84-86
in World War, 214
Mennonite Brethren in Christ, 40, 44, 117, 144, 147, 148, 187, 229, 230, 304
Mennonite Central Committee, 203, 243, 249, 250, 251, 255, 282, 284, 294, 310
Mennonite Collegiate Institute, Manitoba, 92
Mennonite Deaconess Home and Hospital, 179, 185
Mennonite Evangelizing and Benevolent Board, 125
Mennonite Evangelizing Board of America, 25, 152
Mennonite Executive Committee for Colonization, 252
Mennonite Hospital of Mountain Lake, Minnesota, 179
Mennonite identity, 245
Mennonite mission in Chicago, 120
Mennonite Publishing Company, 126, 127
Mennonite Publishing House, 282
Mennonite Relief Commission, 256
Mennonite Sanitarium, 180
Mennonite Sunday School Mission, 145
Mennonite Teachers Association, 91
Mennonite Woman's Missionary Society, 158, 293
Mennonite World Conference, 253
Mennonitische Rundschau, 248
Meno Preparatory School, Oklahoma, 92
Mensch, Jacob, 70
merger of Mennonites and Amish, 122
Methodists, 117
Meyer, Jacob C., 250, 276

microphone, 207
Mifflin County, Pennsylvania, 38
militarism, 242, 294
militarization, 255
military, 145
military camps, 233
Military Committee, 213
military service, 32
millenarianism, 258
millennialism, 129
Miller, Christian K., 195
Miller, Daniel D., 199, 277
Miller, George S., 208, 225
Miller, Orie O., 255, 256, 276, 282-285
Miller, Samuel H., 225, 266
Millersville, 196
Mininger, J. D., 247
Mininger, Jonas, 291
Mininger, Jonas (J. D.), 240
Missionary Church Association, 122, 181, 187
missions, 136, 141-161, 287, 307-309
    and American expansionism, 143
    bureaucracy, 161-162
    and civilization, 158
    and culture, 155
    denominational, 146-151
    and denominational progress, 139-141
    European origins, 141-142
    and gospel, 160
    and Mennonite culture, 155-156
    nondenominational, 146, 151
    Protestant influences, 142-143
    and renewal, 156
Missouri, 38
Missouri-Iowa conference, 41
mobility, 30, 189, 190ff., 306
modernism, 176, 283, 308
Modernists, 129, 257, 309
Monatsblätter aus Bethel College, 88
Montana, 192
Montgomery County, Pennsylvania, 38
Moody Bible Institute, 24, 107, 150, 271, 312

Moody, Dwight L., 22, 42, 108, 300
Mosemann, John H., 197, 281, 283, 296, 297
Mosiman, Samuel K., 165, 176, 212, 285
Mott, John R., 158
Moundridge Bible School, Kansas, 92
Mountain Lake Bible School, Minnesota, 92
Mountain Lake, Minnesota, 100
Mumaw, Levi, 243, 244, 250, 256, 310
museums, 37
musical instruments, 33
mustaches, 75
mutual aid, 191, 246ff.
    Mennonite World Conference, 253

●●●●
Naftzger, Peter, 38
National Council for the Prevention of War, 295
nationalism, 23, 144, 174
National Origins Act, 252
Native Americans, 138
Nebraska-Minnesota Conference, 100, 123
neckties, 131
Neff, Christian, 253
Neuenschwander, Andrew J., 296
"new" Mennonites, 23, 43, 132
Newport News, 195
Newspapers, 87-89, 175, 272
Newton Anzeiger, 87
Newton Kansan, 240
Newton, Kansas, 298
nonconformity, 29, 109, 130
non conformity, 116
nonconformity, 291
nondenominationalism, 181
nonresistance, 36, 65, 215, 259, 286
nurses training institutions, 178, 180
nurses training school, 184

●●●●
Oak Grove congregation, Ohio, 39, 109, 121

oaths, 116
Oberlin College, 261
Ohio, 38, 55
Ohio Mennonite conference, 41, 44, 265
Ohio Northern University, 129
Oklahoma, 193
Oklahoma Bible Academy, 194
Old-Evangelical, 297
"Old" Mennonite Church (and its people), 21, 40-43, 60, 120, 247, 304
    anti-Modernism, 259, 262
    benevolence, 247ff.
    Bible Conference movement, 113
    conference meetings, 205ff.
    district conferences, 40-41
    doctrine, 112-119, 129-130
    and Evangelical Mennonite Brethren, 122-123
    Fundamentalism, 259ff.
    Funk, John F. leadership, 42-43
    General Problems Committee, 301
    generational transitions, 125-126, 267
    hospitals, 184
    leadership recruitment, 276-285
    MCC cooperation, 255-256, 284
    membership growth, 305
    Mennonite Women's Missionary Society, 293
    merger with Amish, 121-123
    Military Committee, 229, 233
    missions, 152-153
    organizational development, 119-120, 124-130, 293
    peace, 296
    polity, 41
    relation to General Conference (GC) Mennonite Church, 120, 132-134, 310
    relation to Jura Swiss, 123-124
    relation to Russian Mennonites, 122-123

response to World War, 213ff.
revivalism, 106-110
youth movement, 250-251
Old Order Amish, 30, 45, 72, 73,
    74, 120, 304, 315
    mobility, 191
Old Order Mennonites, 26, 30, 43,
    45, 60, 120, 304
    automobile division, 76-77
    and benevolence, 256
    humility, 63
    ironies, 315
    lot, 63
    ordination, 64
    polity, 284
    schism, 58-62, 76
    wartime position, 228, 233
old people's home at Rittman,
    Ohio, 125
Ontario, 60, 68, 110
Ontario conference, 40, 41, 44
Ontario Mennonite Bible School
    and Institute, 114
oratory, 170
ordinances, 115, 168
ordination, 64, 80, 107, 265, 287
Ordnung, 64, 66, 67, 68, 69, 75,
    77, 83, 113
Oregon, 192
organization, 29, 31, 40, 119, 120,
    124, 314
orphans' home at West Liberty,
    Ohio, 125
Orrville Milk Company, 198
Osceola County, Iowa, 45
Ostrogers, 51

● ● ● ●
Pace, E. J., 313
Pacific Coast conferences, 114
pacifists, 294
Page, William B., 25, 179, 198
Paradise congregation, Pennsyl-
    vania, 158
Paraguay, 253
Park, R. E., 186
parliamentary procedure, 91, 119,
    170
patriotism, 91
peace, 294-299
Peace Congress, 22

Peace Problems Committee, 283,
    284
Penn College, 107
Penner, Peter A., 161
Pennsylvania, 38, 55, 68
Pennsylvania Mennonite church,
    Kansas, 117
Penn, William, 216
peoplehood, 31, 78-79, 85, 104-
    105, 187, 257
Pequea District, 106
Pestalozzi, 91
Peters, Isaac, 100
Petter, Marie Gerber, 181
Petter, Rodolphe, 142, 181, 307
Philippines, 143
Philips, Dirk, 67
Pickett, Clarence E., 295
Pietism, 35, 36, 48, 71, 72, 84
plain coat, 116, 168, 195, 301
plan of salvation, 109, 113, 115
pluralism, 28, 29, 53, 55, 84
Poindexter, John B., 208
political, 85, 88, 143-144, 175,
    197, 203, 245, 273, 275,
    292, 294, 296, 297
population, 54, 303
Post und Volksblatt, 88
Prairie Street congregation, In-
    diana, 198, 277
prayer covering, 115, 129, 155
premillenialism, 258
premillennialism, 117, 122, 278,
    283
Presbyterian, 117, 268, 293
pride, 75, 108
Princeton Theological Seminary,
    279
Princeton theology, 258
professional, 63, 172, 185
progress, 166
Progressive Party, 175
Prohibitionist Party, 203
Protestant influences, 28
    deaconesses, 180
Protestantism, 28, 147, 245, 316
Protestant missionary movement,
    141
Protestant Reformation, 166
protracted meetings, 109
Prussia, 34

Publication Board, 120
Public speaking, 170
pulpit, 56, 63
Putnam county, Ohio, 124

••••
Quakers, 36, 53, 107, 197, 214,
    230, 275, 294, 296
Quartermaster Corps, 238

••••
racism, 174, 220
radio, 78
railroad, 206
Ramseyer, C. W., 229
Ramseyer, Joseph, 122
Randolph County, 226
Red Cross, 197, 202, 211, 223,
    224, 247, 248
Reformation, 32
Reformed Mennonites, 40, 44, 304
Regier, Mary J., 293
Regional variation, 17-19, 38, 60,
    68
Relief Commission for War Suf-
    ferers, 248, 249, 284
Relief work, 254
renewal, 27, 31, 171
Republican, 175
Restrictions, 115, 116, 168
revitalization, 27, 246
revival, 31, 100, 106, 110, 271,
    272
revivalism, 36, 71, 72, 106, 107,
    108, 110, 117, 130
    and schism, 110
Revolutionary War, 36
Rhodesia, 143
Richert, Heinrich, 80
Richert, Peter, 183, 194
Richert, Peter H., 212, 241
Richert, Susanna, 80
Ris Confession, 134, 312
rituals, 65
Roberts, Tom, 225
Rochester Theological Seminary,
    150
Rock Creek congregation, 47
Roman Catholicism, 143
Roosen, Gerhard, 67
Rundschau, 97

Rupp, Christian, 39
rural, 306
Russian, 34
Russian Mennonite com-
    monwealth, 84
Rutt, A. B., 175

••••
Salem Deaconess Home and
    Hospital, Oregon, 179
Salem Home and Hospital, Kansas,
    179, 229
Salem, Oregon, 183
salvation and discipleship, 108,
    114
salvation and ethics, 116
Sandeen, Ernest, 258
Sawatsky, Rodney, 260
Schabalje, Jan Philip, 34
Schantz, John Wenger, 287
Schellenberg, Abraham, 48, 86,
    101, 157, 175, 190, 211,
    220
Schellenberg, Abraham L., 101,
    201, 214, 248, 272
Schellenberg, Katharina, 101, 157,
    182, 289
Schellenberg, Peter E., 177
Schellenberg, Sarah Schroeder,
    101
Schellenberg, Suzanna Flaming,
    101
schism, 33, 58, 60, 305
schism and revivalism, 110
Schlabach, Theron, 160
Schlegel, Joseph, 192
Schlegel, Mary Miller, 192
Schleitheim Confession, 33
Schlichting, M. H., 269
Schmidt, J. E., 272
schools, 90-93
Schrag, John, 223, 224
Schrag, Jonathan, 149
Schrag, Joseph, 222
Schultz, George P., 272
Scofield Bible, 312
Scofield, Cyrus I., 22, 117, 262
Scopes trial, 258
Scottdale, Pennsylvania, 127, 198,
    250

Scripture
  1 Corinthians 11, 130, 131
  1 John 3:17, 254
  Acts 15:6-33; 16:14;, 131
  Amos 6:1-6, 76
  Gal. 1:8,9, 131
  Galatians 6:10, 254
  Heb. 13:17, 131
  I Tim. 3:15, 131
  Matt. 18:17, 131
  Matthew 5-7, 67
  Matthew 18, 67
  Matthew 22:21 Romans 12:2,
      216
  Matthew 25:35-36, 254
  Matthew 28:18-20 Mark
      16:15, 141
  Proverbs 16:33, 63
secret societies, 116
sectarians, 29, 55
sect cycle, 186-187
Sedition Act, 225
Seferian, Abraham, 147
Seibert, George C., 102
Selective Service, 214, 232
separation, 29, 34, 36, 70, 131,
          221, 244, 245, 278, 283
separatism, 90
sewing circles, 157
sewing machines, 69
Shank, John, 291
Shelly, Andrew B., 95
Shenk, Chrissie, 267
Sherk, Barbara, 287
Shetler, Samuel G., 110
Shoemaker, Joseph S., 112, 153
Showalter, William J., 203
Shumacher, Willis, 235
shunning, 74, 75
silence, 65
Simons, Menno, 32, 34
simplicity, 108, 130
Singers Glen, 43
Sister Frieda, 185
Sitting Bull, 136, 138
Smissen, Carl H. A. van der, 211,
      212
Smissen, Carl J. van der, 134, 142
Smith, C. Henry, 164, 165, 173,
          176, 187, 210, 245, 261,
          267, 281, 295

Smith, Jacob B., 118, 128, 129,
      132, 262, 266, 269, 302
Smith, Jasper, 226
Smucker, Jonathan P., 109
Smucker, Vernon, 267, 268
Snavely, Louisa Kunkleman
      Wohlford, 292
social gospel, 175
socialism, 175
Social Mobility, 202
sociological theory, 30, 186-187
Somerset County, Pennsylvania,
      38, 74
Sommer, Isaac A., 133, 175
Sonnenberg congregation, 123
South Dakota, 94
Southwestern Pennsylvania con-
      ference, 41
Soviet Union
  relief work, 251
Spanish-American War, 91, 143,
      204
sports, 154
Springfield Mennonite congrega-
      tion, Pennsylvania, 27
Spring Valley congregation,
      Kansas, 223
Sprunger, John A., 24, 99, 147,
      176, 181
Sprunger, Samuel F., 124, 133
Stalin, Josef, 253
statement of faith, 312
Stauffer, Jacob, 43, 58, 66
Stauffer, John L., 259, 260, 277
Stauffer Mennonite church, 45,
      304
Stauffer schism, 60
Staufffer, Jacob, 67
Steiner, Clara Eby, 158, 293
Steiner, Menno S., 25, 120, 123,
          124, 126, 143, 144, 152,
          158, 289
St. Johns, 124
Stoltzfus, John A., 75
Stone, Lucy, 22
Strong, Josiah, 143
Stuckey Amish, 46, 74, 121, 122
Stuckey, Joseph, 46
study commission, 249
Stutzman, Enos, 236
Suderman, Leonhard, 80

suffering, 36, 71
Sugar Creek Amish Mennonite church, Ohio, 222
Sumner, Charles, 144
Sunday school, 58, 142, 173, 302
Sunday School Conference, 25, 291
Sunday schools, 42, 119
Sunday School Times, 271, 312
Sun Yat-sen, 159
Swiss, 35
Swiss and south-German groups, 12-14, 33, 35, 40, 106
Swiss Mennonite Church, 309
Swiss South German and benevolence, 256
Switzerland, 50
Switzer, Susanna, 69
Sword and Trumpet, 270, 312, 315, 317

••••

Tabor College, 87, 93, 99, 164, 166, 177, 218, 248, 269, 272, 293
Tabor College Herald, 88
Tabor College Herold, 170
Tanganyika (Tanzania), 153
tax, 221, 246
Taylor, Hudson, 150
Taylor, Joseph S., 27, 30
team Mennonites, 61, 76
telephones, 60
television, 78
Texas, 192, 236
The Budget, 208, 225
The Mennonite, 27, 50, 133
The Mennonite Quarterly Review, 280
tobacco, 65, 246, 264, 291
Toews, Henry F., 173
Toews, Jacob, 80
Torrey, Reuben A., 24, 108, 271
traditionalism, 285
travel, 89
Turkey, 143, 147
Turner, Frederick Jackson, 22, 39

••••

Ukraine, 84, 249, 251
Ukrainian, 35

Umble, John, 195
Unevangelized Tribes Mission, 150
Union Biblical Seminary, 266
Union Missionary Training Institute, 158
Union Theological Seminary, 265, 289
United Deaconess Association, 179
United Mennonite Brethren, 122
United Missionary Church, 45
United Missionary Society, 147
United Orphanage and Mission Board, 147
University of Chicago, 186, 264
University of Tübingen, 279
Unser Besucher, 87
urbanized, 306
urban missions, 146

••••

van Braght, Thieleman Jansz, 34, 67
Virginia, 43, 68, 77, 145
Virginia conference, 41, 107, 119, 132, 145
deaconesses, 180
von Bernhardi, Friedrich, 220
Vorwärts, 88, 211
Voth, Albert, 236
Voth, Catherine, 178
Voth, Cornelius, 235
Voth, Heinrich R., 25, 136-139, 153
voting, 245

••••

Wadsworth Institute, 123, 133, 134
Wadsworth Institute, Ohio, 50
Wadsworth, Ohio, 50, 141, 142
Wahrheitsfreund, 88
Waldensians, 297
Walker, Stuart W., 226
Wall, Aaron, 100
Walnut Creek Amish Mennonite congregation, Ohio, 265-267
Wandering Soul, 34
Wang, Stephen Hsin-fu, 152, 307
War bonds, 221, 227, 247, 248

War Department, 218, 234, 239
Warkentin, Bernhard, 86, 184
Warkentin, Wilhelmina Eisen-
         mayer, 184, 293
Warwick River settlement, 194
Washington County, Maryland, 38
Washington-Franklin conference,
         41
Wayne County, Ohio, 38, 51
wealth, 61
Weaver, Benjamin, 58
Weaver, George, 60
Weaverland, 61
Weaverland conference, 77
Weaverland congregation,
         Pennsylvania, 110, 237
Weaverland district, 57
Weaver, Menno, 69
Weavertown, 75
Weaver, Vinora, 251
Wedel, Cornelius H., 36, 80, 84,
         101, 103, 165, 169, 187,
         189, 261, 290
    and German culture, 93
    historical vision, 102-105
    ordination, 80
    on Mennonite mobility, 189
Wedel, Cornelius P., 82
Wedel, Franz B., 183
Wedel, Marie, 183
Wedel, Martha, 183
Wedel, Peter, 98, 153
Wedel, Peter P., 306, 311
Welsh Mountain Mission, 143, 313
Welty, B. F., 229
Welty, Clara Rupp, 292
Wenger, Amos D, 54
Wenger, Amos D., 61, 106, 117,
         126, 269
Wenger, John Dan, 64, 66, 68, 76
Wenger, Joseph, 64
Wenger, Joseph O., 76
Wenger Mennonites, 76
Wertz, Edwin S., 225, 228
Westerdijk, Pieter Bernard, 253-
         254
Western Amish Mennonite con-
         ference, 46, 74, 121
Western District GC conference,
         50, 95, 247
West Virginia, 43, 145

wheat, 247
Whitewater Bible School, Kansas,
         92
White, William Allen, 273
Whitmer, Paul E., 176, 267
Wiebe, Alfred, 154
Wiebe, Jacob A., 48
Wiebe, Magdalene, 182
Wiens, Agnes Harder, 149
Wiens, Frank J., 100, 149, 272
Wiens, Jacob N., 233
Wilson, Woodrow, 217, 230, 238,
         269
Winrod, Gerald B., 273
Wipf, Joseph, 239
Wisler, Jacob, 44, 45, 58, 66, 77
Witmarsum Seminary, 265, 269
Wolf, Elta H., 277, 282
women, 113, 130-131, 156-158,
         251, 275, 285-294, 349
Women's Congress, 22
Women's Missionary Association,
         157
women's missionary societies, 157
women's suffrage, 292
Wood, Leonard, 234
work, 90
World Alliance for International
         Friendship Through the
         Churches, 296
World Missionary Conference, 153
World's Conference on Christian
         Fundamentals, 271
World's Fair, 300
World War I, 91, 177, 194, 208-
         242
worship, 73
Wovoka, 138

●●●●
Yellow Creek congregation, 44, 45,
         213
Yellow Creek statement, 213, 215,
         228
yieldedness, 62, 65
Yoder, Edward, 300-303, 314
Yoder, Harvey, 118
Yoder, Ira, 118
Yoder, J. Harvey, 195
Yoder, John M., 198
Yoder, Mahlon T., 300

Yoder, Mary C. (Yoder), 300
Yoder, Moses, 74
Yoder, Sanford C., 239, 269, 279,
    293
Young Men's Christian Associa-
    tion, 289
Young People's Conference, 259,
    277
Young People's Movement, 250,
    280-281

●●●●
Zimmerman, Anna Martin, 56, 58
Zimmerman, Franklin, 23
Zimmerman, John M., 57
Zimmerman, Martin, 58
Zimmerman, Martin W., 56
Zimmerman, Menno, 64
Zionsbote, 48, 88, 97
Zoar Bible School, Kansas, 92
Zook, David D., 117, 118
Zook, Vesta, 251
Zur Heimath, 87
Zwingli, Ulrich, 33

THE AUTHOR

James C. Juhnke is Professor of History at Bethel College, North Newton, Kansas. He is the author of three earlier books, four historical dramas, and numerous articles on themes of Anabaptist and Mennonite history. As part of the Schowalter Oral History project at Bethel College, he interviewed many people who had special experiences during World War I.

Juhnke served in church-related overseas assignments in West Germany (1958-1960), Botswana (1971-1973), and the People's Republic of China (1987-1899). For fifteen years he has served on the board of the Africa Inter-Mennonite Mission and the General Conference Commission on Overseas Mission.

He has been active in the peace movement and in civil affairs. In 1979 he won the nomination as a Democratic Party peace candidate in a Kansas congressional primary.

Juhnke was born and reared in a Swiss-Volhynian Mennonite community in Kansas. He is married to Anna Kreider Juhnke, also a college teacher active in denominational activities. The Juhnkes have two college-age children, Joanne and Karl.